Towards Understanding the Qur'ān

Vol. V

SŪRAHS 17–21

English version of

Tafhīm al-Qur'ān

SAYYID ABUL A'LĀ MAWDŪDĪ

Translated and edited by

Zafar Ishaq Ansari

assisted by

A.R. Kidwai

The Islamic Foundation

Translated and edited by Zafar Ishaq Ansari

Published by
THE ISLAMIC FOUNDATION,
Markfield Conference Centre,
Ratby Lane, Markfield,
Leicester LE67 9SY
United Kingdom
Tel: (01530) 244944/5, Fax: (01530) 244946
E-Mail: info@islamic-foundation.org.uk
Website: www.islamic-foundation.org.uk

Quran House,
PO Box 30611,
Nairobi,
Kenya

PMB 3193,
Kano,
Nigeria

British Library Cataloguing in Publication Data

Mawdūdī, Sayyid Abul A'lā
Towards Understanding the Qur'ān
Vol. 5, Surahs 17–21
1. Islam, Koran – Critical Studies,
I. Title II. Anṣārī, Ẓafar Isḥāq
III. Islamic Foundation IV. Tafhīm
al-Qur'ān. *English*
297'.1226

ISBN 0-86037-255-3
ISBN 0-86037-256-1 Pbk

Contents

MAPS

TRANSLITERATION TABLE

Consonants. Arabic

initial: unexpressed

medial and final: ء	ʾ	د	d	ض	ḍ	ك	k
ب	b	ذ	dh	ط	ṭ	ل	l
ت	t	ر	r	ظ	ẓ	م	m
ث	th	ز	z	ع	ʿ	ن	n
ج	j	س	s	غ	gh	ه	h
ح	ḥ	ش	sh	ف	f	و	w
خ	kh	ص	ṣ	ق	q	ي	y

Urdu and Persian the same except the following:

پ	p	ڈ	d̲	ژ	z̲
ٹ	t̲				
چ	ch	ڑ	r̲	گ	g

Vowels, diphthongs, etc.

short: ـَ a; ـِ i; ـُ u.

long: ـَا ā ـُو ū ـِي ī ـِيّ īy

diphthongs: ـَوْ aw

ـَيْ ay

Editor's Preface

The fifth volume of *Towards Understanding the Qur'ān,* comprising *Sūrahs* 17–21 (*Banī Isrā'īl, al-Kahf, Maryam, Ṭā Hā* and *al-Anbiyā'*), is at long last seeing the light of day. In certain ways it has been the most difficult volume so far because it abounds in allusions and references to Near Eastern history and geography and to Judaeo-Christian texts. This called for a great deal of painstaking and time-consuming research.

The present volume, as were volumes III and IV, has been prepared with the assistance of Dr. A.R. Kidwai, who originally translated the notes of *Tafhīm* into English. That draft served as the base out of which the notes of the present volume have developed after a long, tedious and thoroughgoing process of editing and re-editing. While we gratefully acknowledge the assistance provided by Dr. Kidwai, the responsibility for the present draft, with whatever inadequacies, rests with the present writer. The English rendering of the text of the *sūrahs* has, however, been done by this writer alone.

It may be noted that in the notes of *Sūrah al-Kahf* in the original *Tafhīm,* the author has two appendices: the first, an appendix to n. 9 and the second, an appendix to n. 71. These two Appendices appear on pages 305 and 309 of the volume.

In this volume, as in previous ones, we have attempted to provide adequate documentation. In documenting the *Ḥadīth* we have followed the system of A.J. Wensinck in his *Concordance.* However, instead of referring to the number of the *'Bāb'* of a tradition we have referred to the title of the *'Bāb'*. It may also be noted that while referring to explanatory notes in the works of *Tafsīr,* we have generally referred to the relevant verses and *sūrahs* of the explanatory notes in question rather than to the volume and page numbers of the *Tafsīr* works cited. As for the Bible, all quotations are from its *Revised Standard Edition.* Furthermore, we have retained in this volume the features that we have followed in the previous volumes of this work, namely maps, Glossary of Terms, Biographical Notes, and Bibliography.

In finalizing the manuscript, I have greatly benefited from the editorial suggestions of Mrs. Susanne Thackray. Dr. A.R. Kidwai also kindly looked at the draft and favoured me with useful comments. I received much valuable assistance from my colleague, Dr. A.R. Ashraf Baloch of the Islamic Research Institute in documentation and referencing as well as in preparing the Biographical Notes and Glossary of Terms. Dr. Baloch also favoured me with similar assistance in volumes III and IV. In the present volume, he further assisted me by casting a last look at the whole manuscript, and offering his critical comments. Dr. Idrees Zubayr, Assistant Professor, International Islamic University, Islamabad also painstakingly checked many references. Mr. Amjad Mahmood of the Islamic Research Institute, International Islamic University, assiduously typed the manuscript many times. Mr. Alam Zeb Khan of the Sharī'ah Academy, International Islamic University, also extended a helping hand in typing a part of the manuscript. Mr. E.R. Fox rendered valuable assistance in technical editing and proofreading and Mr. Naiem Qaddoura in setting the Arabic material. Dr. M. Manazir Ahsan, by his constant reminders, did not permit this writer to remain indolent for long. Whenever I was confronted with any academic difficulty, I consulted my friend and colleague, Dr. Mahmood Ahmad Ghazi, presently Vice-President, International Islamic University, Islamabad, and found him as ready to help as ever before.

Last, but not least, I must gratefully mention my wife and my children – Asma, Yasir, Sarah, and Anas – who provide much of the warmth and sunshine that makes life enjoyable. To this list one more name was added in the summer of 1993, that of Sumairi, my daughter-in-law. All of them encouraged me and made my life pleasant in ways too numerous to mention. What is new, and quite welcome, is that my wife has begun to assist me directly in my work. Occasionally after completing the daily chores of a responsible and active housewife, she sat with me in the long hours of the night, and read out the portions of *Tafhīm* on which I was working, thus helping me to carefully compare the English version with the original. This proved a great help in finalizing the draft. Valuable as this assistance was, her very presence in my life is a source of strength, happiness and peace of mind.

My mother remains, as always, a major inspiration; a saintly figure I always look up to. She is a good example of how the Qur'ānic Message raises mortals of flesh and blood to great heights of spirituality. May she have a long and healthy life and remain a source of strength and inspiration for the whole family.

To all those mentioned above, and to many others who assisted and encouraged me and inspired me in various ways, I record my profound sense of gratitude. May Allah bless them all.

Islamabad **Zafar Ishaq Ansari**
Ramaḍān 1415 A.H.
February 1995 C.E.

N.B. ▶ *refers to the continuation of the paragraph adopted by Mawdūdī in the Urdu translation.*

Sūrah 17

Banī Isrā'īl

(Children of Israel)

(Makkan Period)

Title

The title of this *sūrah* is derived from verse 4 where the expression 'Children of Israel' occurs: 'Then We clearly declared to the Children of Israel in the Book.' This does not mean, however, that the *sūrah* focuses on the Israelites. The title of the present *sūrah,* like the titles of most *sūrahs* of the Qur'ān, simply serves the purpose of marking it out from others. It is also known as *Sūrah al-Isrā'*.

Period of Revelation

The very first verse indicates that this *sūrah* was revealed at the time of the Ascension *(mi'rāj)*. Now we know from a large number of reports in the works of *Ḥadīth* and *Sīrah* that the Ascension of the Prophet (peace be on him) took place about one year before *Hijrah*. The present *sūrah,* therefore, belongs to the group of *sūrahs* which were revealed during the last part of the Makkan period of the Prophet's life.

Historical Background

By the time this *sūrah* was revealed, the Prophet (peace be on him) had already spent some twelve years calling people to monotheism. During this time his opponents too did not remain idle; in fact, they left no stone unturned in their efforts to obstruct the way of the Prophet (peace be on him). Despite this, however, the Prophet's message spread across the length and breadth of Arabia. Every tribe had at least some members who were influenced by the teachings of Islam. In Makka, the centre of the Prophet's mission, a band of sincere and devoted believers had come together and were ready to stake everything for the success of their cause. A sizeable number of the Aws and Khazraj – the two most powerful tribes of Madina – had become the Prophet's supporters. The time had drawn close when the Prophet (peace be on him) would move out from Makka to Madina, and avail himself of the opportunity to bring together the scattered body of Muslims and strive to establish a state based on the principles of Islam.

These were the circumstances in which the Prophet's Ascension took place. The present *sūrah* was revealed following that great event, expounding the message which the Prophet (peace be on him) gave to the whole world.

Subject Matter

The elements of warning, exhortation and instruction are all judiciously blended in the *sūrah,* each in their right proportion.

The note of warning is directed at the Makkan unbelievers. They are asked to learn a lesson from the tragic end of the Israelites and other nations and to mend their ways, and to do so before the respite granted them by God expired. For it indeed was about to expire. They are asked to embrace the message expounded by the Prophet (peace be on him) as embodied in the Qur'ān, failing which they would be destroyed and would be replaced by some other people. Moreover, the Israelites – who would be among the main addressees of the Qur'ān during the Madinan period of the Prophet's life – are being asked to take heed and bear in mind the chastisement which they had suffered in the past for their misdeeds. They are also asked to avail themselves of the opportunity they had been granted as a result of the Prophet's advent. Were they to allow this opportunity to slip away and were they to persist in their evil ways, they were bound to court disaster.

As for the element of exhortation, it consists of explaining, in highly persuasive terms, what leads to true happiness and what leads to perdition; what leads to well-being and what leads to utter loss. Arguments and evidence are marshalled to confirm the soundness of the fundamental truths propounded by Islam – God's unity, the Next Life, and the position of the Qur'ān as the dependable source of guidance. Additionally, the misgivings which were created by the unbelievers of Makka concerning these fundamental truths are dispelled. These arguments are interlaced with laconic remarks reproaching the deniers of the truth for their follies.

As for the element of instruction, it consists of enunciating certain broad principles of morality and collective behaviour. These principles were to serve as the foundation for the right way of life, the establishment of which was envisaged in the Prophet's message. In other words, the *sūrah* spells out to the Arabs the manifesto of Islam at a very significant moment – just one year before the Islamic state was established. Thus, this *sūrah* provides the guidelines according to which the Prophet (peace be on him) wanted to initially fashion the lives of his compatriots and subsequently of all human beings.

In addition to all this, the Prophet (peace be on him) is directed to remain undaunted in the face of the adversities which confronted him, and not even to consider the idea of striking a compromise with paganism. At the same time the Muslims who were occasionally irritated by the persecution to which they were exposed by the slanderous propaganda campaign unleashed against them by the unbelievers, and by the petty and crooked arguments of their opponents, are urged to face the situation with calm nerves and patience. They are also directed to act with restraint in preaching their message and striving for reform. The Muslims are also required to vigorously engage in their own reform, in the purification of their own lives. In this regard they are directed to depend mainly on Prayer which will equip them with the qualities that are becoming of those who strive in the cause of truth.

According to traditions, this was the first occasion when the five daily Prayers were declared obligatory and when their timing was laid down. (Al-Bukhārī, *Kitāb al-Ṣalāh, 'Bāb Kayfa Furiḍat al-Ṣalāh fī al-Isrā'* ' – Ed.)

In the name of Allah, the Merciful, the Compassionate.

(1) Holy is He Who carried His servant by night from the Holy Mosque (in Makka) to the farther Mosque (in Jerusalem) – whose surroundings We have blessed – that We might show him some of Our signs.[1] Indeed He alone is All-Hearing, All-Seeing.

سُبْحَٰنَ ٱلَّذِىٓ أَسْرَىٰ بِعَبْدِهِۦ لَيْلًا مِّنَ
ٱلْمَسْجِدِ ٱلْحَرَامِ إِلَى ٱلْمَسْجِدِ ٱلْأَقْصَا
ٱلَّذِى بَٰرَكْنَا حَوْلَهُۥ لِنُرِيَهُۥ مِنْ ءَايَٰتِنَآ إِنَّهُۥ
هُوَ ٱلسَّمِيعُ ٱلْبَصِيرُ ١

---

1. This is an allusion to the event known as *Mi'rāj* (Ascension) and *Isrā'* (Night Journey). According to most traditions – and especially the authentic ones – this event took place one year before *Hijrah*. Detailed reports about it are found in the works of *Ḥadīth* and *Sīrah* and have been narrated from as many as twenty-five Companions. The most exhaustive reports are those from Anas ibn Mālik, Mālik ibn Ṣa'ṣa'ah, Abū Dharr al-Ghifārī and Abū Hurayrah. Some other details have been narrated by 'Umar, 'Alī, 'Abd Allāh ibn Mas'ūd, 'Abd Allāh ibn 'Abbās, Abū Sa'īd al-Khudrī, Ḥudhayfah ibn al-Yamān, and 'Ā'ishah among other Companions of the Prophet (peace be on him).

The Qur'ān here only mentions that the Prophet (peace be on him) was taken from the Ka'bah to the mosque in Jerusalem, and specifies that the purpose of the journey was such that God might 'show him some of His signs'. Beyond this, the Qur'ān does not concern itself with any detail. However, according to *Ḥadīth* reports, Gabriel took the Prophet (peace be on him) at night from the Ka'bah to the mosque in Jerusalem on a *burāq*.* On reaching Jerusalem the Prophet (peace be on him), along with other Prophets offered Prayers. (Al-Nasā'ī, *Sunan, K. al-Ṣalāh, 'Bāb Farḍ al-Ṣalāh wa Dhikr Ikhtilāf al-Nāqilīn . . . .'* – Ed.) Gabriel then took him to the heavens and the Prophet (peace be on him) met several great Prophets in different heavenly spheres. (See al-Nasā'ī, *Sunan, K. al-Ṣalāh, 'Bāb Farḍ al-Ṣalāh'* – Ed.) Finally, he reached the highest point in the heavens and was graced with an experience of the Divine Presence. On that occasion the Prophet (peace be on him) received a number of directives including that Prayers were obligatory five times a day. (Al-Bukhārī, *K. Manāqib al-Anṣār, 'Bāb al-Mi'rāj'; K. al-Tawḥīd, 'Bāb Kallama Mūsá Taklīmā'* – Ed.) Thereafter, the Prophet (peace be on him) returned from the heavens to Jerusalem, and from there to the Holy Mosque in Makka. Numerous reports on the subject reveal that the Prophet (peace be on

---

*For *burāq,* see the Glossary of Terms – Ed.

him) was also enabled on this occasion to observe Heaven and Hell. (Al-Bukhārī, *K. al-Ṣalāh, 'Bāb Kayfa Furiḍat al-Ṣalāh fī al-Isrā'* ' and Ibn Hishām, *Sīrah,* vol. I, p. 404 – Ed.)

It may be recalled that according to authentic reports when the Prophet (peace be on him) narrated the incidents of this extraordinary journey the following day to the people in Makka, the unbelievers found the whole narration utterly amusing. (Muslim, *K. al-Īmān, 'Bāb Dhikr al-Masīḥ ibn Maryam'* – Ed.) In fact, even the faith of some Muslims was shaken because of the highly extraordinary nature of the account. (See Ibn Hishām, *Sīrah,* vol. I, p. 398 and al-Qurṭubī, comments on verse 1 of the *sūrah* – Ed.)

The details of the event provided by the *Ḥadīth* supplement the Qur'ānic account. There is no reason, however, to reject all this supplementary information on the grounds that it is opposed to the Qur'ān. Nevertheless, if someone is not quite convinced and hence does not accept some of the details concerning the Ascension mentioned in the *Ḥadīth* as true, he should not be considered an unbeliever. On the contrary, if someone were to clearly deny any part of the account categorically mentioned in the Qur'ān, he would be deemed to have gone beyond the fold of Islam.

What was the nature of this journey? Did it take place when the Prophet (peace be on him) was asleep or when he was awake? Did he actually undertake a journey in the physical sense or did he have a spiritual vision while remaining in his own place? These questions, in our view, have been resolved by the text of the Qur'ān itself. The opening statement: 'Holy is He Who carried His servant by night from the Holy Mosque to the farther Mosque . . .' (verse 1) itself indicates that it was an extraordinary event which took place by dint of the infinite power of God. For quite obviously, to be able to perceive the kind of things mentioned in connection with the event, either in a dream or by means of intuition, is not so wondrous that it should be prefaced by the statement: 'Holy is He Who carried His servant by night . . .'; a statement which amounts to proclaiming that God was free from every imperfection and flaw. Such a statement would make absolutely no sense if the purpose of it was merely to affirm that God had the power to enable man to have either visions in the course of a dream, or to receive information intuitively. In our view, the words of the verse clearly indicate that the event, far from being merely a spiritual experience or a dream vision, was an actual journey, and the observation in question was a visual observation. All was contingent upon God's will that truths be revealed to the Prophet (peace be on him) in this fashion.

Now, let us consider the matter carefully. The Qur'ān tells us, in clear terms, that the Prophet (peace be on him), went from Makka to Jerusalem and then returned to Makka during the night (obviously, without the use of anything resembling an aircraft), owing to God's power. Now, if we believe this to be possible, what justification can there be to reject as inherently impossible the additional details of the event mentioned in the traditional sources? Statements declaring certain acts to be possible and others to be beyond the range of possibility are understandable if these acts are deemed to have been performed by creatures in exercise of the natural powers with which they are endowed.

However, when it is clearly stated that it is God Who did something out of His power, any doubts about the possibility of these acts can be entertained only by those who do not believe God to be all-powerful.

Those who reject the *Ḥadīth* as such raise several objections against the traditions concerning this incident. It seems that only two of these objections are worth any consideration.

First, it is claimed that the contents of the traditions relating to the Ascension imply that God is confined to a particular place. For had that not been the case, it is argued there would have been no need to transport the Prophet (peace be on him) in order for him to experience the presence of God. Second, it is questionable whether the Prophet (peace be on him) was enabled to observe Heaven and Hell and to see people being chastised for their sins even though they had not yet even been judged by God. How is it that people were subjected to punishment even before the coming of that Day when all will be judged?

Both these objections, however, carry little substance. The first objection is to be rejected on the grounds that although the Creator is infinite and transcends both time and place, yet in dealing with His creatures He has to have recourse to the means which are finite and are circumscribed by time-space limitations. This is because of the inherent limitations of man. Hence when God speaks to His creatures, He employs, of necessity, the same means of communication which can be comprehensible to the latter even though His Own speech transcends the means employed in the speech. In like fashion, when God wants to show someone the signs of His vast kingdom, He takes him to certain places and enables him to observe whatever he is required to observe. For it is beyond the power of man to view the universe in the manner God can. While God does not stand in need of visiting a certain place in order to observe something that exists there, man does need to do so. The same holds true of having a direct encounter with the Creator. Although God is not confined to a particular place, man needs to experience His presence at a defined place where the effulgence of His Being might be focused. For it is beyond man's power to encounter God in His limitlessness.

Let us now consider the second objection. That too is fallacious for the simple reason that the objects shown to the Prophet (peace be on him) represented, in symbolic form, certain truths. For instance, a mischievous statement has allegorically been represented by a fat ox that could not return via the small hole through which it had come. (See Ibn Kathīr, *Tafsīr,* comments on *Banī Isrā'īl* 17: 1 – Ed.) Or the other allegory relating to those who indulge in fornication – that they prefer to eat rotten meat when fresh, clean meat is available to them. (*Loc. cit.*; see also Ibn Hishām, vol. 1, p. 406 – Ed.) The same holds true for the punishments to which sinners will be subjected in the Next Life – they are anticipatory representations of the sufferings to which they will be subjected in the Life to Come.

The main point which needs to be appreciated regarding the Ascension is that it belongs to a genre of experience through which each Prophet is enabled to observe – consonant with his standing and mission – aspects of God's dominion of the heavens and the earth. Once the material barriers to the normal

(2) We gave Moses the Book, and made it a source of guidance[2] for the Children of Israel, commanding: 'Take no other guardian beside Me.'[3] (3) You are the descendants of those whom We carried (in the Ark) with Noah.[4] He was truly a thankful servant.' (4) Then We clearly declared to the Children of Israel in the Book:[5] 'Twice you will work corruption in the earth and will act with great arrogance.'[6] ▶

وَءَاتَيْنَا مُوسَى ٱلْكِتَٰبَ وَجَعَلْنَٰهُ هُدًى
لِّبَنِىٓ إِسْرَٰٓءِيلَ أَلَّا تَتَّخِذُوا۟ مِن دُونِى
وَكِيلًا ﴿٢﴾ ذُرِّيَّةَ مَنْ حَمَلْنَا مَعَ
نُوحٍ إِنَّهُۥ كَانَ عَبْدًا شَكُورًا ﴿٣﴾
وَقَضَيْنَآ إِلَىٰ بَنِىٓ إِسْرَٰٓءِيلَ فِى ٱلْكِتَٰبِ
لَتُفْسِدُنَّ فِى ٱلْأَرْضِ مَرَّتَيْنِ وَلَتَعْلُنَّ
عُلُوًّا كَبِيرًا ﴿٤﴾

vision of human beings are removed, it becomes possible to view, physically, the realities which the Prophets are required to summon others to believe in as part of faith in the Unseen. This is done in order to distinguish the Prophets from mere speculative philosophers. For a philosopher's contentions are based on speculative reason and hence are essentially conjectural. Were a philosopher to recognize his true position – the position of a philosopher – he would shrink from testifying to the truth of his contentions. In contrast, what the Prophets say is based on their direct knowledge and observation. They can testify before others with full conviction that whatever they expound are realities which they themselves have directly perceived.

2. This transition from a narration of the Ascension to observations about the history of the Israelites may appear, at first glance, somewhat abrupt, rendering the passages in question disjointed. However, if one bears in mind the main purpose of this *sūrah,* the link between the two subjects becomes readily clear. Now, as we are aware, the main purpose of this *sūrah* is to warn the Makkan unbelievers. Therefore, the *sūrah* begins by referring to the Ascension so as to bring home to its addressees the fact that the Prophet (peace be on him) who was expounding God's Message, had himself observed, shortly before, immense signs of God. Thereafter, the attention of the Makkan unbelievers is drawn to the history of the Israelites, pointing out that when those bestowed with the Scripture rise in revolt against God, they are subjected to terrible punishments.

3. The word *wakīl* signifies one upon whom a person totally relies; one in whom full trust is reposed; to whose care one entrusts one's affairs, to whom one looks to for guidance and support.

4. The Israelites were descendants of the Prophet Noah (peace be on him) and his Companions. Hence it behoves them to place their trust in and leave their affairs to the One True God. For they are well aware that their ancestors survived the Flood because they had placed their full confidence in God and had entrusted their affairs to Him.

5. The word 'Book' here does not specifically signify the Torah. Rather, it stands for the heavenly Scripture as such. On several occasions the Qur'ān uses the term *al-Kitāb* in the sense of heavenly Scripture as such rather than in the sense of just one specific revealed book. (See *al-A'rāf* 7: 37 and 52; *Yūnus* 10: 61; *Hūd* 11: 6; *al-Ra'd* 13: 39; *Banī Isrā'īl* 17: 4 and 58; and often elsewhere in the Qur'ān – Ed.)

6. These warnings occur at several places in the Bible. The Israelites were warned in the *Psalms, Jeremiah* and *Ezekiel* of the consequences that would ensue from the first great corruption they might work. As to their second corruption, Jesus (peace be on him) forewarned them of its severe consequences, and these are recorded in the Gospels of *Matthew* and *Luke*. The following Biblical passages bear out fully the veracity of the above Qur'ānic statement.

David was the first to have warned against the first corruption in the following words:

> They did not destroy the peoples, as the Lord commanded them, but they mingled with the nations and learned to do as they did. They served their idols, which became a snare to them. They sacrificed their sons and their daughters to the demons; they poured out innocent blood, the blood of their sons and daughters. Then the anger of the Lord was kindled against his people, and he abhorred his heritage; he gave them into the hand of the nations, so that those who hated them ruled over them (*Psalms* 106: 34–8 and 40–1).

In the above passage, the events of the future are mentioned in the past tense which emphasizes that the occurrence of those events was beyond all doubt. This is a peculiar mode of expression which is employed in the Scriptures.

Once this corruption had actually taken place, its dire consequences were foretold by Isaiah:

> Ah, sinful nation, a people laden with iniquity, offspring of evildoers, sons who deal corruptly! They have forsaken the Lord, they have despised the Holy One of Israel, they are utterly estranged. Why will you still be smitten, that you continue to rebel? (*Isaiah* 1: 4–5).

> How the faithful city has become a harlot, she that was full of justice! Righteousness lodged in her. Your princes are rebels and companions of thieves. Every one loves a bribe and runs after gifts. They do not defend the fatherless, and the widow's cause does not come to them. Therefore the Lord says, the Lord of hosts, the Mighty One of Israel: 'Ah, I will vent my wrath on my enemies' (*Isaiah* 1: 21–4).

They are full of diviners from the east and of soothsayers like the Philistines, and they strike hands with foreigners. Their land is filled with idols; they bow down to the work of their hands, to what their own fingers have made (*Isaiah* 2: 6 and 8).

The Lord said: Because the daughters of Zion are haughty and walk with outstretched necks, glancing wantonly with their eyes, mincing along as they go, tinkling with their feet; the Lord will smite with a scab the heads of the daughters of Zion, and the Lord will lay bare their secret parts. Your men shall fall by the sword and your mighty men in battle. And her gates shall lament and mourn; ravaged, she shall sit upon the ground (*Isaiah* 3: 16–17 and 25–6).

Behold, the Lord is bringing up against them the waters of the River, mighty and many, the king of Assyria and all his glory; and it will rise over all its channels and go over all its banks (*Isaiah* 8: 7).

For they are a rebellious people, lying sons, sons who will not hear the instruction of the Lord; who say to the seers, 'See not'; and to the prophets, 'Prophesy not to us what is right; speak to us smooth things'. Therefore thus says the Holy One of Israel, 'Because you despise this word, and trust in oppression and perverseness, and rely on them; therefore this iniquity shall be to you like a break in a high wall, bulging out, and about to collapse, and its breaking is like that of a potter's vessel which is smashed so ruthlessly that among its fragments not a sherd is found with which to take fire from the hearth, or to dip up water out of the cistern (*Isaiah* 30: 9–10, 12–13 and 14).

Thus says the Lord, 'What wrong did your fathers find in me that they went far from me, and went after worthlessness, and became worthless? And I brought you into a plentiful land, to enjoy its fruits and its good things. But when you came in you defiled my land, and made my heritage an abomination. For long ago you broke your yoke and burst your bonds; and you said, 'I will not serve'. Yea, upon every high hill and under every green tree you bowed down as a harlot. As a thief is shamed when caught, so the house of Israel shall be shamed; they, their kings, their princes, their priests, and their prophets, who say to a tree, 'You are my father', and to a stone, 'You gave me birth'. For they have turned their back to me, and not their face. But in the time of their trouble they say, 'Arise and save us!' But where are your gods that you made for yourself? Let them arise, if they can save you, in your time of trouble; for as many as your cities are your gods, O Judah (*Jeremiah* 2: 5, 7, 20 and 26–8).

The Lord said to me in the days of King Josiah: 'Have you seen what she did, that faithless one, Israel, how she went up on every high hill and under every green tree, and there played the harlot?' And her false sister Judah saw it. She saw that for all the adulteries of that faithless one, Israel, I had sent her away with a decree of divorce; yet her false sister Judah did not fear, but she too went and played the harlot. Because harlotry was so light to her, she polluted the land, committing adultery with stone and tree (*Jeremiah* 3: 6 and 8–9).

Run to and fro through the streets of Jerusalem, look and take note! Search her squares to see if you can find a man, one who does justice and seeks truth; 'How can I pardon you? Your children have forsaken me, and have sworn by those who are no gods. When I fed them to the full, they committed adultery and trooped to the houses of harlots. They were well-fed lusty stallions, each neighing for his neighbour's wife. Shall I not punish them for these things? says the Lord; and shall I not avenge myself on a nation such as this? (*Jeremiah* 5: 1, 7–9).

Behold, I am bringing upon you a nation from afar, O house of Israel, says the Lord. It is an enduring nation, it is an ancient nation, a nation whose language you do not know, nor can you understand what they say. Their quiver is like an open tomb, they are all mighty men. They shall eat up your harvest and your food; they shall eat up your sons and your daughters; they shall eat up your flocks and your herds; they shall eat up your vines and your fig trees; your fortified cities in which you trust they shall destroy with the sword (*Jeremiah* 5: 15–17).

And the dead bodies of this people will be food for the birds of the air, and for the beasts of the earth; and none will frighten them away. And I will make to cease from the cities of Judah and from the streets of Jerusalem the voice of mirth and the voice of gladness, the voice of the bridegroom and the voice of the bride; for the land shall become a waste (*Jeremiah* 7: 33–4).

Send them out of my sight, and let them go! And when they ask you, 'Where shall we go?' you shall say to them, 'Thus says the Lord: Those who are for pestilence, to pestilence, and those who are for the sword, to the sword; those who are for famine, to famine, and those who are for captivity, to captivity (*Jeremiah* 15: 1–2).

A city that sheds blood in the midst of her, that her time may come, and that makes idols to defile herself! Behold, the princes of Israel in you, every one according to his power, have been bent on shedding blood. Father and mother are treated with contempt in you; the sojourner suffers extortion in your midst; the fatherless and the widow are wronged in you. You have despised my holy things, and profaned my sabbaths. There are men in you who slander to shed blood, and men in you who eat upon the mountains; men commit lewdness in your midst. In you men uncover their fathers' nakedness; in you they humble women who are unclean in their impurity. One commits abomination with his neighbour's wife; another lewdly defiles his daughter-in-law; another in you defiles his sister, his father's daughter. In you men take bribes to shed blood; you take interest and increase and make gain of your neighbours by extortion; and you have forgotten me, says the Lord God.

(5) So, when the time for the fulfilment of the first prophecy drew near, We raised against you some of Our creatures who were full of might, and they ran over the whole of your land. This was a prophecy that had to be fulfilled.[7] ▶

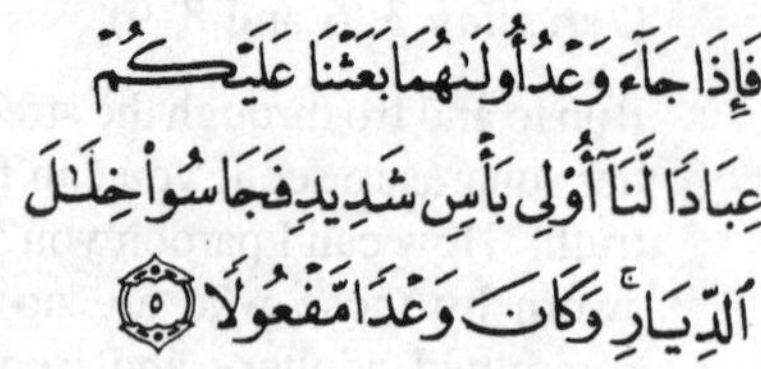

> Can your courage endure, or can your hands be strong, in the days that I shall deal with you?
>
> I will scatter you among the nations and disperse you through the countries, and I will consume your filthiness out of you. And I shall be profaned through you in the sight of the nations; and you shall know that I am the Lord (*Ezekiel* 22: 3, 6–12, 14–16).

These warnings were served on the Israelites at the time of the first corruption. Later on, Jesus (peace be on him) warned them against the dire consequences of the second corruption that they would cause. In a lengthy sermon recorded in *Matthew,* Jesus (peace be on him) denounced the moral degeneration of his people:

> O Jerusalem, Jerusalem, killing the prophets and stoning those who are sent to you! How often would I have gathered your children together as a hen gathers her brood under her wings, and you would not (*Matthew* 23: 37).
>
> Truly, I say to you, there will not be left here one stone upon another, that will not be thrown down (*Matthew* 24: 2).

As Jesus (peace be on him) was being carried by the Roman guards for crucifixion, a crowd of people, which also included wailing women, followed him. Addressing them in what was his last address, Jesus said:

> Daughters of Jerusalem, do not weep for me, but weep for yourselves and for your children. For behold, the days are coming when they will say, 'Blessed are the barren, and the wombs that never bore and the breasts that never gave suck!' Then they will begin to say to the mountains, 'Fall on us'; and the hills, 'Cover us' (*Luke* 23: 28–30).

7. This alludes to the terrible destruction suffered by the Israelites at the hands of the Assyrians and the Babylonians. In order to grasp the historical

background of this incident, it is not sufficient to just bear in mind the Biblical material we have cited earlier (see n. 6, above). In addition, it is also necessary to have a bird's-eye view of Israeli history. This will help us clearly grasp the reasons why God removed this nation, which had been entrusted with the Scripture, from the pedestal of universal leadership and reduced it to an utterly defeated, enslaved and backward nation.

In order to understand things clearly, we must look at the period immediately following the death of the Prophet Moses (peace be on him), when the Israelites entered Palestine. This land was then inhabited by several nations such as the Hittites, Amorites, Canaanites, Perizzittels, Hivites, Jebusites and the Philistines. All had been affected by the worst forms of idolatry. Their supreme deity, Ayl, they regarded as the father of gods, and was usually represented by bull images. His consort was Asherah from whom there had descended a whole pantheon of gods and goddesses, numbering around seventy. Of the supreme deity's offspring the most powerful was Baal, the god of rain and fertility, and the lord of the heavens and the earth. In the northern regions his consort was known as Anathoth and in Palestine as Ashtaroth. They were respectively considered goddesses of love and procreation. Also, there was a god of death, and another of epidemic and famine, and there was a goddess of health; and so on and so forth.

Thus, godhead was split over a number of deities. To crown it all, the acts ascribed to these deities were so despicable and ignoble that even men of exceptionally low character would feel ashamed of being ascribed to them. Naturally, it was impossible for those people who had accepted and worshipped beings of such degraded character to be saved from sliding into the abyss of crass immorality and rank corruption. Archaeological excavations have brought to light their lurid state of morality, confirming that they were steeped in moral degeneration. To mention just a few examples, child sacrifices at the altars of these deities were quite common. Their temples had become virtual dens of adultery. Women consecrated themselves to the service of the temples and on that pretext lived in them. Illicit sexual relations with these women were rampant and were even considered an integral part of acts of devotion. These and a host of other vices corrupted their lives.

According to the Torah, Moses had commanded the Israelites to destroy these iniquitous people, wrest Palestine from them, and to stay away from them lest they were affected by their moral and religious degeneration.

However, when the Israelites entered Palestine, they paid no heed to this directive. They failed to set up a unified state. Driven by tribalism, each tribe preferred to own a part of the conquered land. Owing to dissensions in their ranks, no tribe could gain enough power to fully rid themselves of the polytheists and drive them from their land. Eventually, the Israelites had to bear the polytheists in their midst. Even in the conquered land some of the city states of these polytheistic communities, which the Israelites were unable to overpower, survived. This point is eloquently made in a passage from the *Psalms* quoted earlier (see n. 6 above).

The first catastrophic consequence which the Israelites faced as a result of these errors was that polytheistic practices crept into their lives. By and by other moral vices also made inroads into their society. The Bible vehemently denounces these vices in the following terms:

> And the people of Israel did what was evil in the sight of the Lord and served the Baals; and they forsook the Lord, the God of their fathers, who had brought them out of the land of Egypt; they went after other gods, from among the gods of the peoples who were round about them, and bowed down to them; and they provoked the Lord to anger. They forsook the Lord, and served the Baals and the Ashtaroth. So the anger of the Lord was kindled against Israel . . . (*Judges* 2: 11–14).

The second catastrophic consequence which the Israelites faced was that the nations whose city states they had failed to annex formed a united front against them in collaboration with the Philistines, whose territory had also not been seized by the Israelites. The axis of these nations launched a series of attacks and drove out the Israelites from a large part of Palestine. They even managed to seize the Holy Ark of their Lord from them. All this drove the Israelites to establish a unified state under one of their rulers. It was at the request of the Israelites that the Prophet Samuel appointed Saul as their King in 1020 B.C. (For further details, see *Towards Understanding the Qur'ān,* vol. I, *al-Baqarah* 2, verses 246–8, and nn. 268–70, pp. 188–91.)

Three rulers governed the kingdom that was so established – Saul (1020 B.C.–1004 B.C.), the Prophet David (1004 B.C.–965 B.C.) and the Prophet Solomon (965–926 B.C.). These rulers were able to complete the task of bringing under control those neighbouring powers, a task which the Israelites had failed to carry out after the time of Moses (peace be on him). It was only the states of the Phoenicians on the northern coast and of the Philistines on the southern coast that they were unable to subdue. Nevertheless, even these states were made tributaries.

After the Prophet Solomon (peace be on him), the Israelites again succumbed to worldliness. Dissension and feuding broke out in their ranks, causing their state to be split into two independent and separate kingdoms. One of these comprised the northern part of Palestine and Transjordan and was called the kingdom of Israel with Samaria as its capital. The second – the kingdom of Judah – comprised the southern part of Palestine and Edom with Jerusalem as its capital. The relations between the two kingdoms were marked by bitter rivalry and strife from the very beginning, a feature which was to endure.

The rulers and inhabitants of the kingdom of Israel were the first to be affected by polytheistic beliefs and the moral corruption of neighbouring communities. Their degeneration reached its zenith when Ahab, the King of Israel, married the idolatrous princess Jezebel of Sidon.

At this point, under state patronage, virtually a flood of polytheistic ideas, practices and moral vices was let loose upon the Israelites. The Prophets Elias and Elisha spared no effort to stem the tide. However, the Israelites continued

PALESTINE AFTER PROPHET MOSES

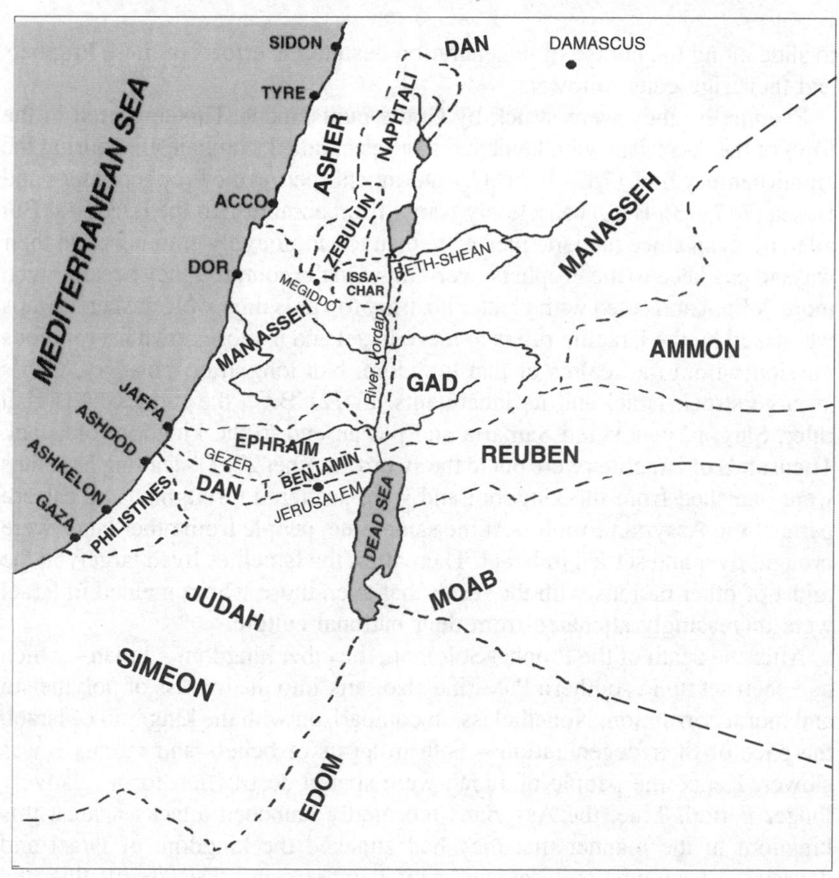

Explanation:

After the death of Prophet Moses, the Children of Israel conquered the whole of Palestine under Joshua, but instead of establishing a united kingdom they divided the land among themselves as inheritance.

This map shows how Palestine was divided into lots and taken over by the 12 tribes of the Israelites, who were the children of Judah, Simeon, Dan, Benjamin, Ephraim, Reuben, Gad, Manasseh, Issachar, Zebulun, Naphtali and Asher.

Being weak and divided, they could not fulfil the mission of the Torah, which was to drive out the idolatrous Canaanites from Palestine. The Canaanites still dwelt among them and retained strongholds in the shape of city states. According to the Bible, up to the time of Saul, the cities of Sidon, Tyre, Dor, Megiddo, Beth-Shaan, Gezer, Jerusalem, etc. were still in the hands of the Canaanites and their idolatrous culture was influencing the Israelites.

Furthermore, on the borders of the Israelite territories, there still existed powerful states of the Philistines, the Edomites, the Moabites, and the Ammonites, who later subjected them to incessant attacks and annexed large areas of their lands. The Israelites might even have been driven out of Palestine had they not been shown grace by God and in time united under Saul.

to slide along the course of degeneration despite the efforts of these Prophets and their righteous followers.

Eventually, they were struck by God's punishment. This appeared in the form of the Assyrians who launched a series of attacks on Palestine during the eighth century B.C. (787–747 B.C.). During this period the Prophets Amos and Hosea (747–735 B.C.) ceaselessly warned and admonished the Israelites. But all to no avail since the Israelites were then too thoroughly entrenched in their ways to pay heed to the Prophets' warnings. On the contrary, they became even more defiant and acted with greater hostility towards their well-wishers. Amos was asked by the Israelite rulers to leave Israel and to close down his religious mission within the realms of that kingdom. Not long after, however, God's scourge struck Israel and its inhabitants. In 721 B.C., the ruthless Assyrian ruler, Sargon, conquered Samaria and put an end to the kingdom of Israel. Thousands of Israelites were put to the sword; another 27,000 leading Israelites were banished from the kingdom and were scattered throughout the eastern parts of the Assyrian Empire. At the same time, people from other lands were brought over and settled in Israel. Thereafter, the Israelites lived largely in the midst of other nations with the result that even those who remained in Israel were increasingly alienated from their national culture.

After the death of the Prophet Solomon, the other kingdom – Judah – which had been set up in southern Palestine also sank into the morass of polytheism and moral corruption. Nonetheless, in comparison with the kingdom of Israel, the pace of their degeneration – both in terms of beliefs and morals – was slower. Hence the people of Judah were spared destruction for a relatively longer period. True, the Assyrians repeatedly launched attacks against this kingdom in the manner that they had attacked the kingdom of Israel and devastated its towns and held its capital under siege. Despite all this, the kingdom of Judah did not disintegrate, but was reduced to the position of an Assyrian tributary. At a later stage when, despite the efforts of Isaiah and Jeremiah, the Israelites did not give up idolatry, nor purged themselves of moral corruption, the Babylonian King, Nebuchadnezzar, carried out a devastating attack on the kingdom in 586 B.C. and razed all the towns of the kingdom – large and small – to the ground. Jerusalem and Solomon's temple were totally destroyed. A large number of Jews were driven out of their land and scattered in different areas. As for those who stayed behind, they were ravaged and subjected to a life of ignominy and humiliation by their neighbouring nations. This was the first corruption of the Israelites and this was the price they were made to pay for it.

(6) Then We granted you an upper hand against them, and strengthened you with wealth and children, and multiplied your numbers.[8] ▶	ثُمَّ رَدَدْنَا لَكُمُ الْكَرَّةَ عَلَيْهِمْ وَأَمْدَدْنَاكُم بِأَمْوَالٍ وَبَنِينَ وَجَعَلْنَاكُمْ أَكْثَرَ نَفِيرًا ﴿٦﴾

8. This refers to the respite granted the Jews of Judah after their captivity at the hands of the Babylonians. As for the inhabitants of Samaria and of the kingdom of Israel, they were unable to pull themselves out of their morass of doctrinal error and moral corruption. However, there was a section of people in Judah who continually adhered to righteousness and did not cease to call others to it. They continued their efforts to reform the Jews who lived in Judah and also urged the Jews who had been banished to Babylonia and other lands to mend their ways and turn to God in penitence.

Eventually, out of compassion and mercy, God came to their rescue and the Babylonian Empire collapsed. In 539 B.C. the Persian Emperor Cyrus conquered Babylonia and the following year he issued a decree allowing the Israelites to return and to settle once again in their homeland. As a result, large numbers of Jews set out towards Judah – a movement which continued for a very long time. Cyrus also allowed the Israelites to rebuild the Temple of Solomon. However, neighbouring nations which had also settled in the region put up stiff resistance to the same. At last, in 522 B.C., Darius I appointed Zerubbabel, grandson of the last king of Judah, as governor of Judah. He arranged for the Temple of Solomon to be rebuilt under the direction of the Prophets Haggai and Zechariah and the Chief Rabbi Joshua. Later, in 458 B.C., Ezra, along with a group of exiles, was entrusted with considerable authority by the Persian Emperor Artaxerxes:

> And you, Ezra, according to the wisdom of your God which is in your hand, appoint magistrates and judges who may judge all the people in the province Beyond the River, all such as know the laws of your God; and those who do not know them, you shall teach. Whoever will not obey the law of your God and the law of the king let judgement be strictly executed upon him, whether for death or for banishment or for confiscation of his goods or for imprisonment (*Ezra* 7: 25–6).

Taking advantage of this proclamation, Ezra brought about the revival of the religion of Moses. He brought together the righteous people of the Jewish community and established an effective organization which assisted him in carrying out his task. He compiled and published the five books of the Old Testament, including the Torah. He made arrangements for the religious instruction of the Jews. He enforced God's laws as a result of which the Jews

THE KINGDOM OF PROPHETS DAVID AND SOLOMON (1000-930 B.C.)

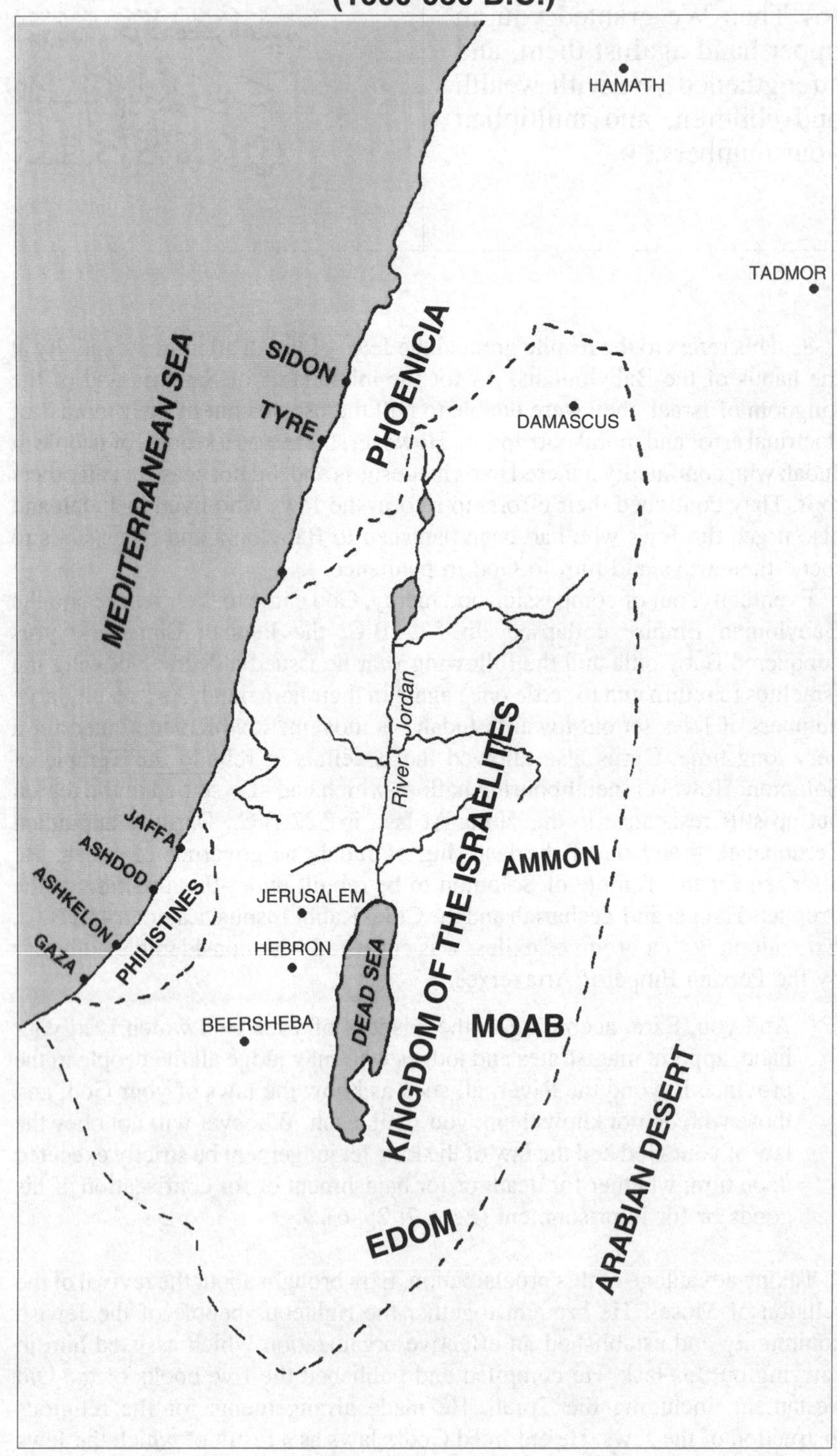

began to purge themselves from the doctrinal errors and moral corruption which had crept into their lives. He made them divorce all idolatrous women whom they had married. And above all, he had them renew their covenant with God – that they shall worship only the One True God and follow His Law.

Under the leadership of Nehemiah, another group of exiles returned to Judah in 445 B.C. The Persian King appointed Nehemiah as the Governor of Jerusalem and allowed him to build a protective wall around the city. Thus, after a lapse of 150 years, Jerusalem was restored and became, once again, the focal point of Judaic religion and culture. However, the Israelites of northern Palestine and Samaria derived no benefit from Ezra's reform efforts. Rather, they set up a rival sanctuary at Mount Gerizim and tried to make it the centre for all Jews. This led to further estrangement between the Jews of the two kingdoms – Judah and Samaria.

The Jews suffered serious setbacks by a succession of events – the decline of the Persian Empire, the conquests of Alexander the Great and the rise of the Greeks. After Alexander's death, his Empire was split up into three kingdoms. Out of Alexander's possessions, Syria was wrested by the Seleucid Empire with Antioch as its capital. The Seleucid ruler, Antiochus III, annexed Palestine in 198 B.C. The Greek conquerors held polytheistic beliefs and their lives were permeated with permissiveness and licentiousness. Naturally, they felt uncomfortable with Jewish religion and culture. Out of hostility to Judaism, they resorted to political and economic pressures so as to promote Greek culture, and a sizeable number of Jews themselves did not hesitate to act as their agents. This caused divisions among the Jews. A section of them enthusiastically adopted Greek dress, the Greek language, the Greek lifestyle and Greek sports whereas another section staunchly clung to the Jewish culture.

In 175 B.C., Antiochus IV, also known as Epiphanies (i.e. the manifestation of God), ascended the throne; his efforts to root out the Judaic religion and culture were ruthless. He had idols installed in the Temple of Solomon in Jerusalem and he forced the Jews to prostrate themselves before those idols. Likewise, he prohibited the offering of sacrifices at the altar in the Temple. Instead, he ordered the Jews to make sacrificial offerings at idolatrous altars. He laid down capital punishment for those who kept a copy of the Torah in their homes, or followed the laws of the Sabbath, or who circumcized their children.

The Israelites were not, however, daunted by these oppressive measures. Instead, their suffering led to the rise of the great resistance movement known in history as the Maccabean Revolt. In this conflict between Greek and Judaic cultures, the sympathies of the Hellenized Jews lay with the Greeks and they collaborated with the oppressive rulers of Antioch in their bid to suppress the Revolt. However, the generality of Jews were deeply imbibed with the religious spirit inspired by Ezra so that eventually they were able to drive out the Greeks and set up their own independent, religious state which lasted till 67 B.C. The frontiers of their state gradually expanded so that in the course of time

ISRAELITE KINGDOM OF JUDAH AND ISRAEL
(860 B.C.)

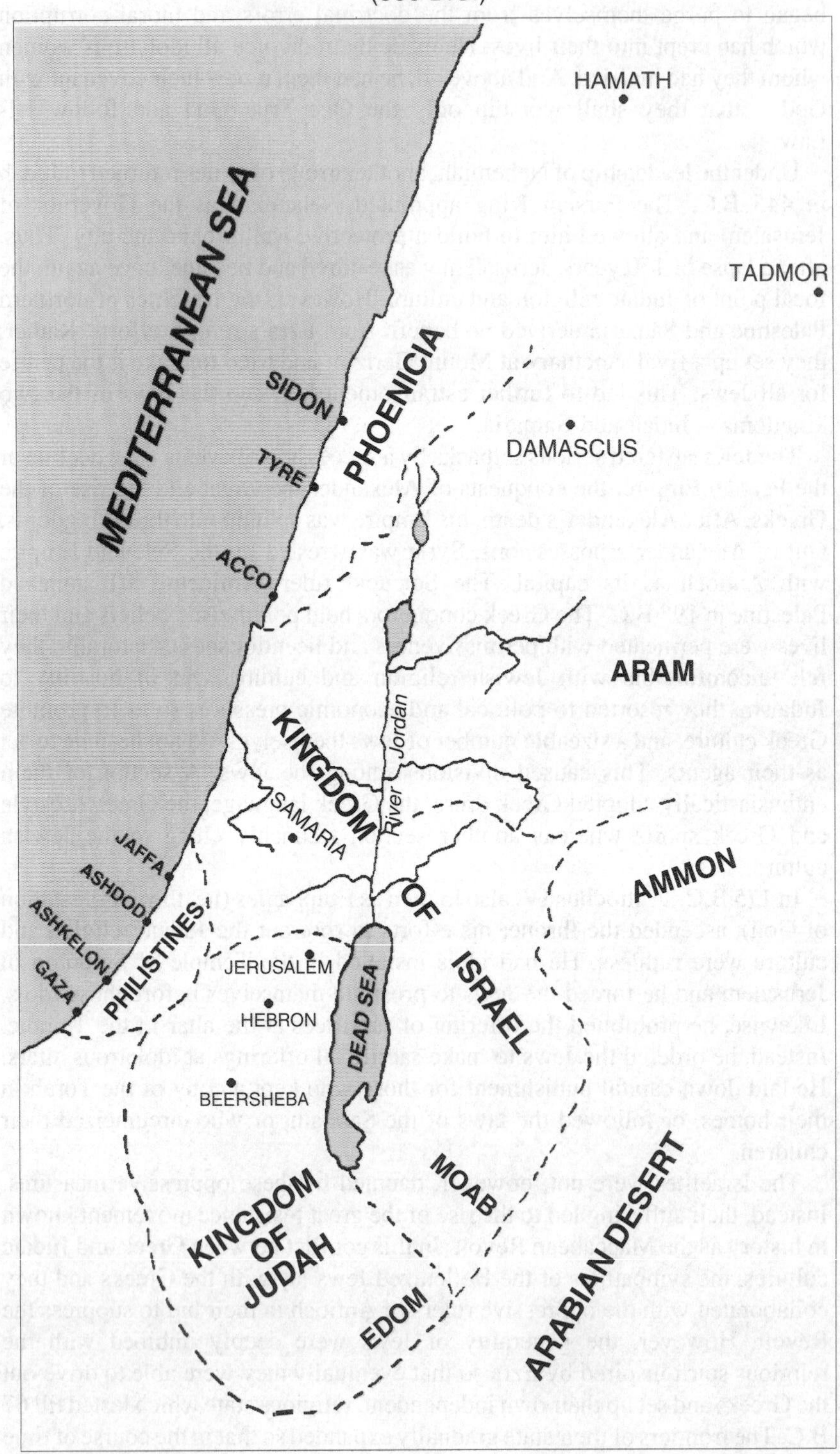

(7) Whenever you did good, it was to your own advantage; and whenever you committed evil, it was to your own disadvantage. So, when the time of the fulfilment of the second prophecy drew near, (We raised other enemies that would) disfigure your faces and enter the Temple (of Jerusalem) as they had done the first time, and destroy whatever they would lay their hands on.[9] ▶

إِنْ أَحْسَنتُمْ أَحْسَنتُمْ لِأَنفُسِكُمْ وَإِنْ أَسَأْتُمْ فَلَهَا فَإِذَا جَآءَ وَعْدُ ٱلْآخِرَةِ لِيَسُـۥٓـُٔوا۟ وُجُوهَكُمْ وَلِيَدْخُلُوا۟ ٱلْمَسْجِدَ كَمَا دَخَلُوهُ أَوَّلَ مَرَّةٍ وَلِيُتَبِّرُوا۟ مَا عَلَوْا۟ تَتْبِيرًا ۝٧

it embraced the entire territory that had once been under the control of the two Jewish kingdoms of Judah and Israel. A sizeable part of the land under the control of the Philistines and over which the Jews had been unable to gain control even in the times of the Prophets David and Solomon was also seized. The above verse alludes to these historical events.

9. Now we proceed to discuss the second corruption of the Israelites and the punishment which ensued from it. These can be better appreciated if the following facts which provide the necessary historical background are borne in mind.

The Maccabean Revolt, as we have seen, was marked by moral and religious fervour. In the course of time, however, this fervour declined and was replaced by rank worldliness and a mechanical adherence to the externals of religious rites. Eventually, serious divisions appeared among the Jews. So much so that some of them invited the Roman General, Pompey, to attack Palestine. Pompey returned to Palestine in 63 B.C., annexed Jerusalem and put an end to the independence of the Israelites. However, instead of establishing their direct rule, the Roman emperors preferred to enforce their policies through local rulers, who worked as their agents. In pursuance of this policy, they established a seemingly native regime in Palestine, but one which was to remain under their thumb.

In 40 B.C. the control of this state passed to a shrewd Jew named Herod. Known as Herod the Great, he held sway over the whole of Palestine and Transjordan from 40 B.C. to 4 B.C. He tried to win over the hearts of the Jews by patronizing the rabbis. At the same time, he also tried to curry favour with the Caesar of the time by enthusiastically promoting Roman civilization and

PALESTINE UNDER THE MACCABEES
(168-63 B.C.)

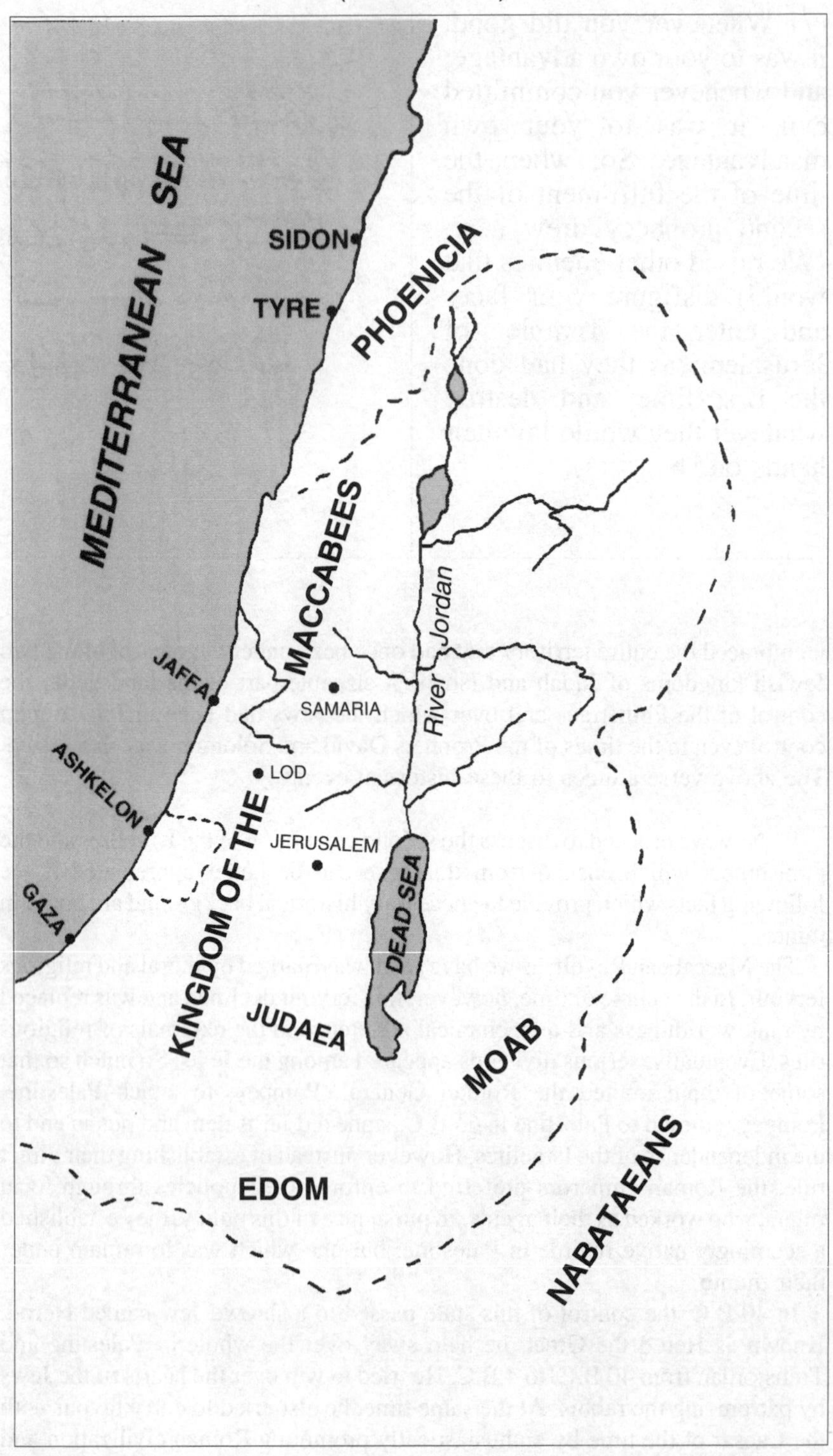

KINGDOM OF HEROD THE GREAT

(40-4 B.C.)

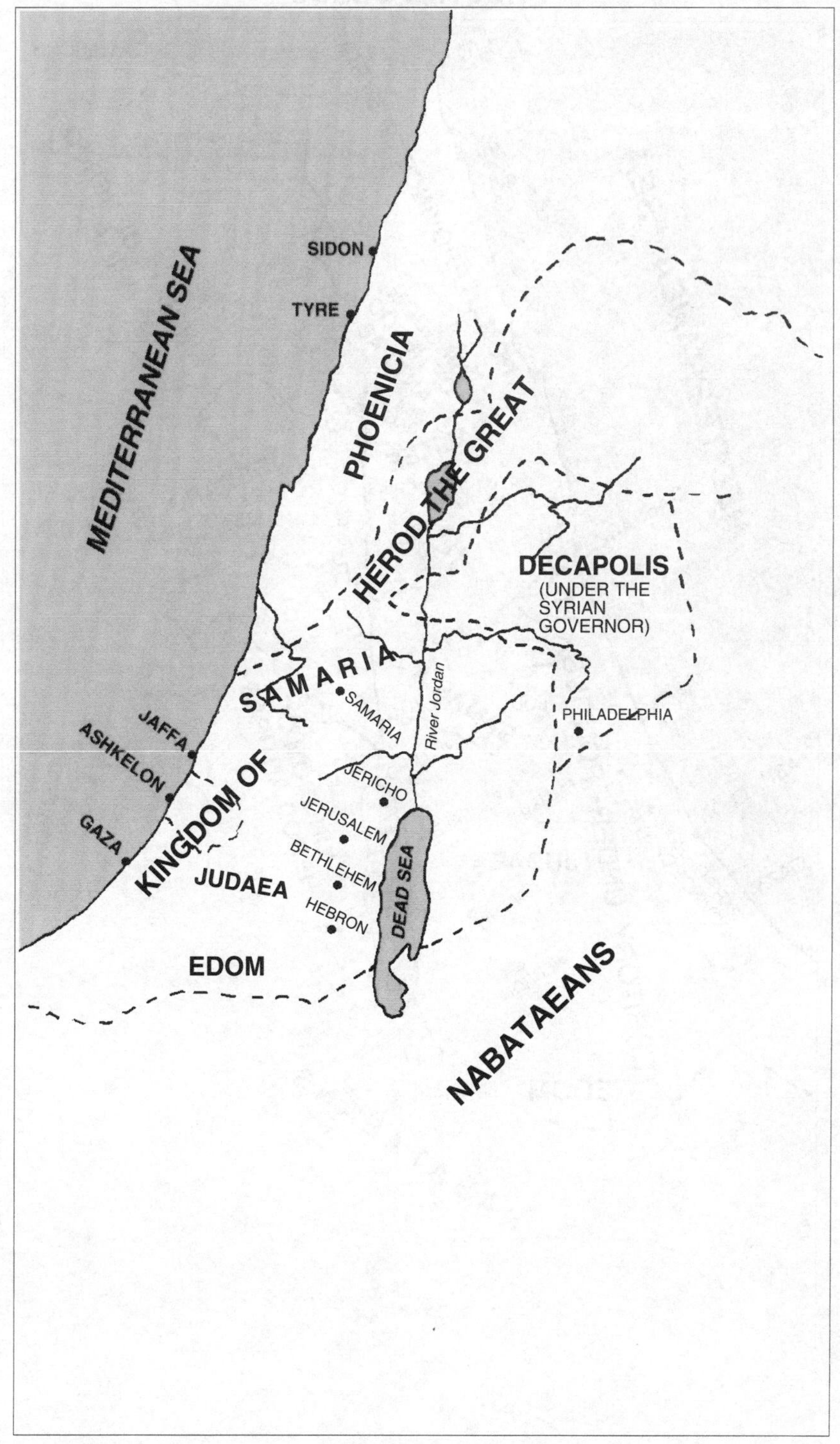

PALESTINE IN THE TIME OF PROPHET JESUS

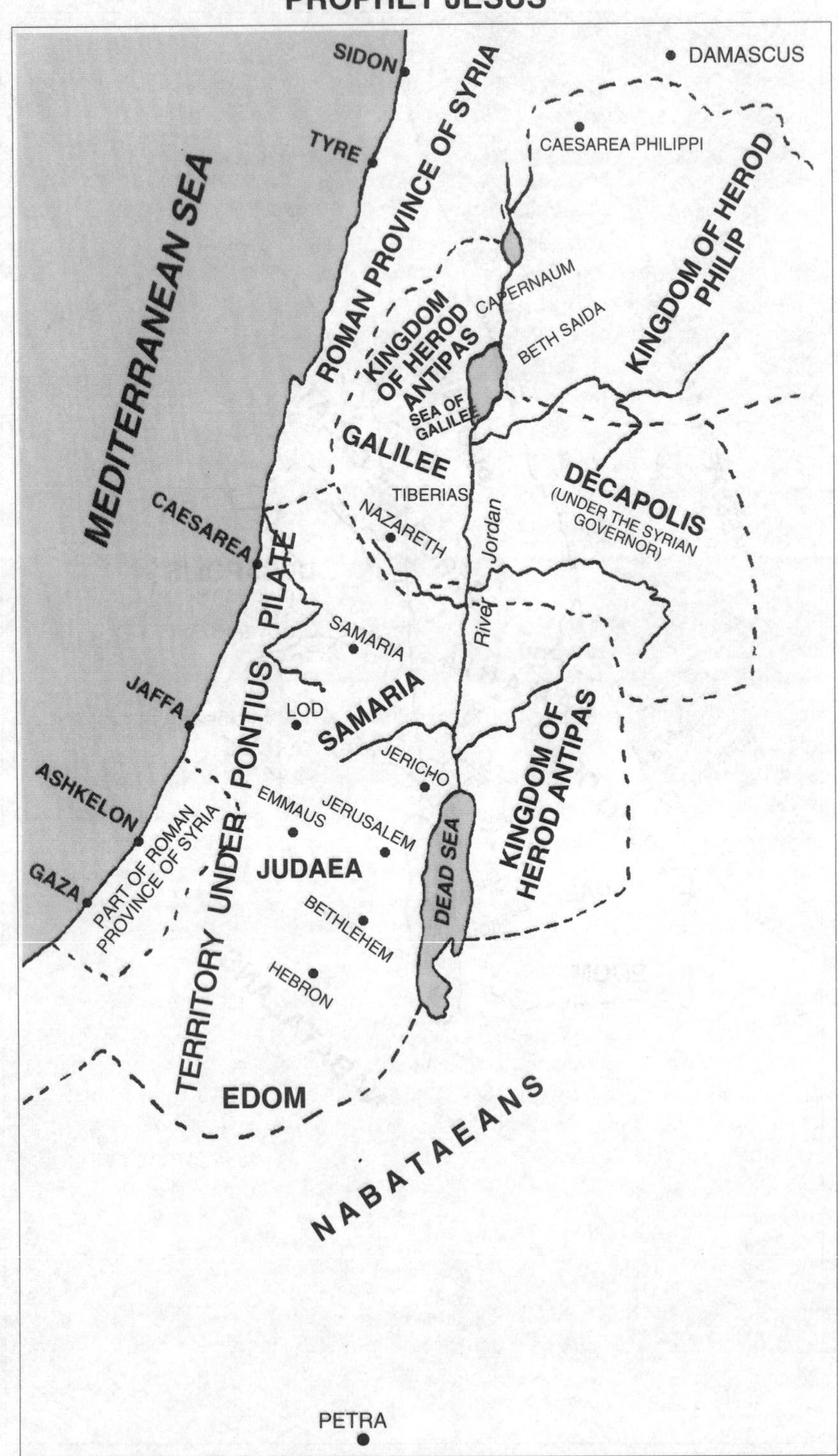

culture. This period witnessed the lowest water-mark of Jewish degeneration.

After Herod, the realm was divided into three parts. One of Herod's sons, Archelaus, assumed the reins of Samaria, Judah and Northern Edom. He was, however, dethroned by the Caesar Augustus in 6 C.E. and who placed the state under the control of a governor appointed by him. This situation lasted until 41 C.E. This was the time when the Prophet Jesus (peace be on him) appeared on the scene and began his movement to reform the Israelites. The religious leadership of the Jews fiercely opposed Jesus (peace be on him) and persuaded the Roman Governor, Pontius Pilate, to have him put to death.

Herod Antipas, another of Herod's sons, gained control over northern Palestine, Galilee and Transjordan. It may be recalled that it was he who had the Prophet John (peace be on him) decapitated and then had his head placed at the feet of a dancing maiden at whose behest this heinous crime had been committed.

Philip, Herod's third son, succeeded to the territories lying between Mount Hermon and the River Yarmuk. He was even more enamoured of the Graeco-Roman culture than his father and brothers. No wonder then that it was even more difficult for the word of truth to prosper in his realm than in any other part of Palestine.

In 41 C.E., the Romans placed Herod the Great's grandson, Herod Agrippa, at the helm of all the territories which had once been governed by his grandfather. After assuming power, Agrippa persecuted Jesus' followers and spared no effort in stamping out the movement which, under the leadership of Jesus' apostles, sought to promote piety and righteousness.

In order to fully appreciate the condition of the Jews, including their rabbis, during this period one should cast a glance at the sharp criticism and reproach directed at them in the sermons of the Prophet Jesus (peace be on him). These sermons are to be found in the four Gospels. The moral degeneration of the Jews can be appreciated if we recall the barbarous execution of the Prophet John (peace be on him). He was both righteous and innocent, but was beheaded before the Jews' very eyes without the least justification. The entire Jewish population remained mute, uttering not even a single word in support or defence of the Prophet. Furthermore, the depth of Jewish moral insensitivity is blatantly evident from their attitude towards the Prophet Jesus (peace be on him). The entire leadership of the Jews demanded, as one man, that Jesus (peace be on him) be put to death; no more than a handful of people lamented their depravity. On the occasion of the Passover, Pilate informed them that under the law he could release only one of those sentenced to death. So saying, he asked them whose release they preferred – that of Jesus or Barabbas the robber? The whole audience, with one voice, asked for Barabbas' release. This was the lowest level of depravity to which the Jews could have sunk and this particular incident provided incontrovertible evidence of their guilt, guilt which called for punishment from God.

Not long after a fierce conflict ensued between the Israelites and the Romans, culminating in an open rebellion by the Jews in 64 C.E. Both Herod Agrippa II and the Roman procurator Floris failed to crush the rebellion and

(8) Your Lord may well show mercy to you, but if you revert to your evil behaviour, We shall revert to chastising you. We have made Hell a prison for those who are thankless of Allah's bounties.[10]

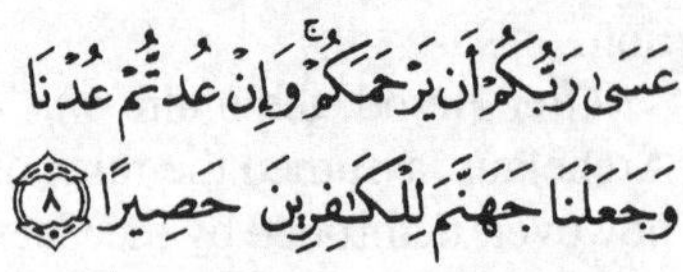

eventually a large-scale military operation was carried out by the Roman Empire. The rebellion was suppressed and in 70 C.E. Titus forcibly seized Jerusalem. A massacre followed in which 133,000 people lost their lives and a further 67,000 were made captive and subsequently enslaved. Additionally, thousands were conscripted to work in the mines in Egypt and thousands of others were dispatched to amphitheatres and coliseums in different parts of the Roman Empire to face either gladiators or wild beasts who tore their bodies to pieces. All tall and attractive girls were picked out as potential candidates for pandering to the lusts of the conquerors. The city of Jerusalem, along with Solomon's Temple, was razed to the ground. All this put an end to Jewish power in Palestine for about 2,000 years. As for the Temple of Solomon, it was never restored. In the course of time the Roman Emperor Hadrian was able to rebuild Jerusalem. However, he renamed it Aelia, and for centuries Jews were forbidden to enter it. This was the punishment which the Israelites had to suffer for their second major corruption. (For the prophecy that the Israelites would twice work corruption in the earth, see verses 4–5 – Ed.)

10. This should not give rise to the misconception that this discourse is addressed to the Israelites. For it is in fact addressed to the unbelievers of Makka. These significant incidents from the history of the Israelites were mentioned so that the unbelievers might take heed. It is in this connection that an observation has been addressed in parenthesis to the Israelites. This was to serve as a preface to a discourse on moral reform, the occasion for which would arise only one year after the establishment of an Islamic community in Madina.

(9) Verily this Qur'ān guides to the way that is the straight-most. To those who believe in it, and to righteous works, it gives the good news that a great reward awaits them; (10) and warns those who do not believe in the Hereafter that We have prepared for them a grievous chastisement.[11]

(11) Man prays for evil in the manner he ought to pray for good. Man is ever hasty.[12]

إِنَّ هَٰذَا ٱلۡقُرۡءَانَ يَهۡدِي لِلَّتِي هِيَ
أَقۡوَمُ وَيُبَشِّرُ ٱلۡمُؤۡمِنِينَ ٱلَّذِينَ يَعۡمَلُونَ
ٱلصَّٰلِحَٰتِ أَنَّ لَهُمۡ أَجۡرٗا كَبِيرٗا ﴿٩﴾
وَأَنَّ ٱلَّذِينَ لَا يُؤۡمِنُونَ بِٱلۡأٓخِرَةِ أَعۡتَدۡنَا
لَهُمۡ عَذَابًا أَلِيمٗا ﴿١٠﴾ وَيَدۡعُ ٱلۡإِنسَٰنُ
بِٱلشَّرِّ دُعَآءَهُۥ بِٱلۡخَيۡرِۖ وَكَانَ ٱلۡإِنسَٰنُ
عَجُولٗا ﴿١١﴾

11. The purpose of the statement is to impress upon those who fail to heed the warning and the admonition embodied in the Qur'ān that they should get ready to receive the punishment which had once afflicted the Israelites.

12. This is in response to the foolish demands that the unbelievers of Makka occasionally made upon the Prophet (peace be on him). Again and again they asked the Prophet (peace be on him) to bring upon them the punishment of which he had so often warned them. This particular statement follows the preceding verse which promises a large reward for those who believe and do good and a painful chastisement for those who do not believe in the After-Life, and is intended to jolt the persons concerned into recognizing their folly. For, instead of asking for good, they are asking for God's punishment. Do they have no idea at all of the havoc that God's punishment wreaks upon those who are smitten by it?

Implicit in this statement is a subtle warning to the Muslims as well. Irked by constant persecution at the hands of the unbelievers the Muslims sometimes prayed that God's scourge might seize the unbelievers. They did so without realizing that there were many among the unbelievers who were to embrace Islam and uphold its cause all across the world at one time or another during the future. Hence, it was deemed necessary to point out that man is impatient; that he is prone to ask for whatever he is immediately in need of and which he wants to have forthwith. However, after the passage of time, it becomes evident to him that had his prayer been answered instantly, it would have been no good for him.

(12) We have made night and day as two signs. We made the sign of the night devoid of light, and made the sign of the day radiant that you may seek the bounty of your Lord and know the computation of years and numbers. Thus We have explained everything in detail, to keep everything distinct from the other.[13]

(13) We have fastened every man's omen to his neck.[14] On the Day of Resurrection We shall produce for him his scroll in the shape of a wide open book, [saying:] (14) 'Read your scroll; this Day you are sufficient to take account of yourself.'

وَجَعَلْنَا ٱلَّيْلَ وَٱلنَّهَارَ ءَايَتَيْنِ فَمَحَوْنَآ
ءَايَةَ ٱلَّيْلِ وَجَعَلْنَآ ءَايَةَ ٱلنَّهَارِ مُبْصِرَةً
لِّتَبْتَغُوا۟ فَضْلًا مِّن رَّبِّكُمْ وَلِتَعْلَمُوا۟
عَدَدَ ٱلسِّنِينَ وَٱلْحِسَابَ وَكُلَّ شَىْءٍ
فَصَّلْنَٰهُ تَفْصِيلًا ﴿١٢﴾ وَكُلَّ إِنسَٰنٍ
أَلْزَمْنَٰهُ طَٰٓئِرَهُۥ فِى عُنُقِهِۦ وَنُخْرِجُ لَهُۥ يَوْمَ
ٱلْقِيَٰمَةِ كِتَٰبًا يَلْقَىٰهُ مَنشُورًا ﴿١٣﴾
ٱقْرَأْ كِتَٰبَكَ كَفَىٰ بِنَفْسِكَ ٱلْيَوْمَ عَلَيْكَ
حَسِيبًا ﴿١٤﴾

13. Man should not feel exasperated by the differences that he observes, nor clamour for total uniformity. For diversity and variety are a basic operative principle of the universe. The alternation of day and night is an obvious example of this diversity and something which everyone can observe. Just a little reflection will show that this arrangement is immensely beneficial. Without diversity and variety life would lose much of its charm, and a great deal of its colour. Corresponding to the diversities of the physical universe, there are also diversities of temperament, view and inclination among human beings and these too are highly beneficial. It would not be at all wholesome to remove these differences and, either compel human beings – all of them – to believe and act righteously, or annihilate unbelievers and transgressors, allowing only those who believe and act righteously to survive. To wish for such a thing to happen is no different from wishing that the world should have only the day but not the night. What is indeed desirable is that those who have been blessed with the light of true guidance should ceaselessly strive to dispel the darkness of error and misguidance. In the pursuit of this goal they should act like the sun. Whenever the darkness of night covers the world, they should,

(15) He who follows the right way shall do so to his own advantage; and he who strays shall incur his own loss.[15] No one shall carry another's burden.[16] And never shall We punish any until We send a Messenger (to make the truth distinct to them from falsehood).[17]

مَّنِ اهْتَدَىٰ فَإِنَّمَا يَهْتَدِي لِنَفْسِهِ ۖ وَمَن ضَلَّ فَإِنَّمَا يَضِلُّ عَلَيْهَا ۚ وَلَا تَزِرُ وَازِرَةٌ وِزْرَ أُخْرَىٰ ۗ وَمَا كُنَّا مُعَذِّبِينَ حَتَّىٰ نَبْعَثَ رَسُولًا ﴿١٥﴾

as the sun does, chase darkness away and persevere in their efforts until the rise of a bright, new day.

14. The causes that lead a man to his ultimate salvation or perdition, to his perpetual happiness or unending misery, lie within himself. It is the proper use of his natural endowments, his power of discernment and decision, his volition and choice which makes man merit either happiness or misery. People who do not understand things properly hold external factors to be responsible for their fortune. The fact, however, is that a man's good or bad fortune rests with himself. If people were to critically examine themselves, they would appreciate that the factors which had put them on the road to their destruction and ultimately led to their undoing lay within themselves – their own bad character traits and bad decisions. Their destruction was not thrust upon them by outside factors.

15. It is obvious that if a man follows the right way, he does no favour to God, or His Prophet (peace be on him) or to those who seek to bring about reform. For his righteousness will be to his own advantage. Likewise, when he adopts a wrong course, or stubbornly clings to it, he harms no one but himself. When God's Messengers call people to follow the right way or when well-meaning reformers strive to direct people to righteousness and dissuade them from evil ways, they do so in order to be genuinely helpful to people. Once the truth is convincingly placed before a wise person, and falsehood is shown to be untrue, he should not allow his biases or excessive concern for material interests to deter him from following the truth and instead should adopt a straightforward attitude to it. For if he clings to his biases and remains enmeshed in worldly interests at the cost of truth, he will only hurt himself.

16. This is a significant truth, brought home to man at several places in the Qur'ān. For without fully appreciating it one cannot follow the right course of conduct. The statement made here emphasizes that every man has been encumbered with moral responsibility, that each person is accountable to God in his personal capacity, that no man has a co-sharer in this accountability. Regardless of the number of people, groups or generations who participate in a particular act, or follow a certain policy, ultimately when a man is judged by God, his performance will be considered in isolation, divorced from the performance of those who had previously acted together. Thus, the responsibility of each person will be precisely determined. A person will be called to account for and will be rewarded or punished for deeds which are truly his deeds. Such is the Balance by which man's deeds will be weighed; no one else's misdeeds will adversely affect him, nor will his own misdeeds harm anyone else. Hence, a wise person should not be overly concerned with the actions of others. He should rather be concerned with what he himself does for if a man has a clear sense of his responsibility, he will be able to follow a course of action that will bring him success and credit on the Day of Judgement, and all this regardless of what others do.

17. This is another fundamental truth which the Qur'ān repeatedly expounds and in many diverse ways. In the scheme of things relating to God's Judgement of man, the Messengers occupy a central position. The Messengers who carry God's Message also constitute God's evidence which, at the end of the day, also establishes man's responsibility. For had no Messengers been sent and no Message conveyed, there would be little justification to hold men to account and to punish them. Men would have been able to come forth with the excuse that since they had not even been told what they were required to do they ought not to be held to account for what they did not know. But once a Messenger has been sent with God's Message, it stands to reason and justice that those who turned away or deviated from the Message that was communicated to them ought to be punished.

Some people, as a result of their unclear thinking, are apt to raise questions with regard to verses such as the above. They ask: What will happen to those who do not receive the Message of any of God's Prophets? If they were wise, they should rather be concerned with themselves alone for they had already received the Message.

Man's responsibility is so grave that he ought to remain wholly absorbed with the question: 'What will happen to me? How will God treat me?' So far as others are concerned, God knows best as to how, when and to what extent His Message reached each of them, and how each of them responded to it, and why. All these are far too complex matters to be known to anyone other than the One, Omniscient God. No one knows about others: no one knows who received God's Message and in such a manner as to leave no justification for them that owing to their ignorance of His Message it is not fair to hold them responsible.

(16) When We decide to destroy a town We command the affluent among them, whereupon they commit sins in it, then the decree [of chastisement] becomes due against them and then We destroy that town utterly.[18] (17) Many a generation has been destroyed by Our command since Noah's time. Your Lord is well aware and fully observant of the sins of His servants.

وَإِذَآ أَرَدۡنَآ أَن نُّهۡلِكَ قَرۡيَةً أَمَرۡنَا
مُتۡرَفِيهَا فَفَسَقُواْ فِيهَا فَحَقَّ عَلَيۡهَا
ٱلۡقَوۡلُ فَدَمَّرۡنَٰهَا تَدۡمِيرٗا ١٦
وَكَمۡ أَهۡلَكۡنَا مِنَ ٱلۡقُرُونِ
مِنۢ بَعۡدِ نُوحٖۗ وَكَفَىٰ بِرَبِّكَ بِذُنُوبِ
عِبَادِهِۦ خَبِيرَۢا بَصِيرٗا ١٧

18. The word *amr* (command) used in this verse refers to the laws operating in the physical realm, the laws of nature in the sense of signifying causal relationships. Taken in this sense, God's 'command' mentioned here simply means that those nations whose affluent members act wickedly always meet with a tragic end.

The statement that 'When We decide to destroy a town . . .', does not mean that God decides to punish a people without just cause. Rather it means that when a people immerse themselves in evil, God decides – and He does so precisely because of their immersion in evil – to destroy them, and that decision manifests itself in the manner referred to here.

The pith of the matter, as embodied in the present verse, is that it is the corruption of the affluent sections of the upper classes of a society which truly brings about that society's destruction. When a nation is close to its doom, its wealthy and influential sections blatantly resort to all kinds of evil practices, to injustice and oppression, to wickedness and mischief, and this is what leads to its destruction. Hence, if a people truly care about their collective well-being, they should ensure that its political power and riches do not pass on to those that are unworthy of them, to those that are conspicuously iniquitous, to those that are altogether incapable of judiciously using political and economic power.

(18) Whosoever desires immediate benefits in this fleeting life,[19] We hasten to grant the benefits in the present life that We please to whomsoever We like but thereafter We decree for him Hell wherein he shall burn, condemned and rejected.[20] (19) But he who desires the Hereafter and strives for it as he should, and is a true believer, his striving will come to fruition.[21] (20) To all of these as well as those, We shall provide the wherewithal of this life in the present world by dint of your Lord's bounty; and from none shall be withheld the bounty of your Lord.[22] (21) See, how We have exalted some above others in this world, and in the Life to Come they will have higher ranks and greater degrees of excellence over others.[23]

مَّن كَانَ يُرِيدُ ٱلْعَاجِلَةَ عَجَّلْنَا
لَهُۥ فِيهَا مَا نَشَآءُ لِمَن نُّرِيدُ ثُمَّ
جَعَلْنَا لَهُۥ جَهَنَّمَ يَصْلَىٰهَا
مَذْمُومًا مَّدْحُورًا ﴿١٨﴾ وَمَنْ
أَرَادَ ٱلْـَٔاخِرَةَ وَسَعَىٰ لَهَا
سَعْيَهَا وَهُوَ مُؤْمِنٌ فَأُو۟لَـٰٓئِكَ
كَانَ سَعْيُهُم مَّشْكُورًا
﴿١٩﴾ كُلًّا نُّمِدُّ هَـٰٓؤُلَآءِ وَهَـٰٓؤُلَآءِ
مِنْ عَطَآءِ رَبِّكَ ۚ وَمَا كَانَ عَطَآءُ
رَبِّكَ مَحْظُورًا ﴿٢٠﴾ ٱنظُرْ كَيْفَ
فَضَّلْنَا بَعْضَهُمْ عَلَىٰ بَعْضٍ ۚ
وَلَلْـَٔاخِرَةُ أَكْبَرُ دَرَجَـٰتٍ
وَأَكْبَرُ تَفْضِيلًا ﴿٢١﴾

19. The Qur'ān employs this term to signify the present world. By contrast, the term *ākhirah* is used in the Qur'ān to denote one whose benefits and gains will be available later, after the present world. The success and prosperity that such a person achieves will be at the cost of success and prosperity in the Hereafter. Not only that, the excessive worldliness and lack of concern about his accountability in the Hereafter will have given such an essentially wrong twist to the lives of such people that they will end up suffering the torments of Hell.

20. This simply means one who does not believe in the Hereafter or is not willing to wait patiently to receive his reward there, one who keeps his

attention focused on the present world. The success and prosperity in it, will be totally excluded from success and prosperity of such a person in the Hereafter. Not only that, but excessive worldliness and lack of concern of such a person about his accountability in the Hereafter will have given such an essentially wrong twist to his life that he will end up suffering the torments of Hell.

21. In contrast to the above, he who seeks success in the Hereafter will receive full reward for his efforts towards that end – a reward that will fully correspond to that effort, both qualitatively and quantitatively.

22. So far as this worldly life is concerned, God is still the Giver of all the provisions and sustenance needed in it to everyone, regardless of whether they merely seek the good of this life, or seek success in the Hereafter. Both kinds of people receive this as a gift from Him, and Him alone. Hence, it ought to be clear that neither of the two groups can deprive the other of the provisions required for this worldly life.

23. It is quite evident even during the course of this worldly life that seekers of the Hereafter are perceptibly better than those who seek the good of this worldly life alone. Quite obviously, the superiority of the former does not consist in the fact that they eat tastier food, or clothe themselves in more attractive garments, or dwell in more splendid houses, or go about in impressive vehicles, or enjoy any other trapping of material progress and prosperity. The true cause of their superiority is essentially their morality. Regardless of whether the worldly possessions of people of the former category are abundant or meagre, it is certain that they would have earned them by honest and fair means.

This is in sharp contrast to the predicament of those who exclusively seek the good of this world. For scarcely anything prevents them from employing dishonest means and resorting to all kinds of wrong and injustice to achieve their worldly objectives. Similarly, the people who essentially seek the success of the Hereafter, can also be distinguished by the manner in which they spend their earnings: they spend them with moderation. They allocate a part of their earnings in discharging their obligations to their kith and kin. They also devote a part of their earnings to assisting the needy and the indigent, as well as to other charitable purposes with a view to pleasing God. In sharp contrast to this, the people who seek nothing but worldly prosperity, are intent upon self-indulgence, upon satisfying their lusts in every conceivable way, legitimate or illegitimate. In sum, the lives of the former group of people are characterized by piety and righteousness, and this lends them a rare lustre. As a result, the lives of such people do not fail to glitter even though they may be dressed in tatters or dwell in the most humble abodes. All those who have eyes to see are not slow to note that, as compared with such people, the lives of the seekers of this world appear dark, dismal and barren. It is for this reason that even mighty rulers and men possessed of vast riches have never evoked the true respect, love or admiration of other human beings. On the contrary, the

(22) Do not set up any other god beside Allah lest you are rendered humiliated and helpless.[24]

(23) Your Lord has decreed:[25]

(i) Do not worship any but Him;[26]

(ii) Be good to your parents; and should both or any one of them attain old age with you, do not say to them even 'fie' neither chide them, but speak to them with honour, (24) and be humble and tender to them and say: 'Lord! Show mercy to them as they nurtured me when I was small.'

لَا تَجْعَلْ مَعَ ٱللَّهِ إِلَٰهًا ءَاخَرَ فَتَقْعُدَ
مَذْمُومًا مَّخْذُولًا ﴿٢٢﴾ ۞ وَقَضَىٰ
رَبُّكَ أَلَّا تَعْبُدُوٓا۟ إِلَّآ إِيَّاهُ وَبِٱلْوَٰلِدَيْنِ
إِحْسَٰنًا ۚ إِمَّا يَبْلُغَنَّ عِندَكَ
ٱلْكِبَرَ أَحَدُهُمَآ أَوْ كِلَاهُمَا
فَلَا تَقُل لَّهُمَآ أُفٍّ وَلَا تَنْهَرْهُمَا
وَقُل لَّهُمَا قَوْلًا كَرِيمًا
﴿٢٣﴾ وَٱخْفِضْ لَهُمَا جَنَاحَ
ٱلذُّلِّ مِنَ ٱلرَّحْمَةِ وَقُل رَّبِّ
ٱرْحَمْهُمَا كَمَا رَبَّيَانِى صَغِيرًا ﴿٢٤﴾

---

worth of God-fearing men – even those that are ill-fed or dressed in tatters – has been generously recognized by all, including the seekers of this world.

These obvious indicators show the intrinsic difference between the people of the two groups. These indicators also make it obvious as to which of the two groups deserves the enduring success of the Hereafter.

24. This part of the verse may also be translated as follows: 'Do not invent (or declare) any other than Allah as your God.'

25. From here on, the basic principles which according to Islam ought to serve as the foundations of man's life are expounded. Put differently, these principles constitute the manifesto of the Prophet's mission. It is noteworthy that this manifesto was proclaimed at a highly appropriate moment – at a time when the Makkan period of the Prophet's life was coming to an end, and when the Madinan period was about to begin. This meant making the intellectual, moral, cultural, economic and legal bases of the Islamic society and state of the future known to the world. (For a fuller appreciation of this see *Towards Understanding the Qur'ān,* vol. II, *al-An'ām* 6, nn. 127–35, pp. 284–94.)

(25) Your Lord is best aware of what is in your hearts. If you are righteous, He will indeed forgive those who repent and revert (to serving Allah).[27]

رَّبُّكُمْ أَعْلَمُ بِمَا فِي نُفُوسِكُمْ إِن تَكُونُوا۟ صَٰلِحِينَ فَإِنَّهُۥ كَانَ لِلْأَوَّٰبِينَ غَفُورًا ﴿٢٥﴾

26. The verse does not merely have a negative message – that we may not worship aught other than the One True God. It also has a positive message – that we should serve, worship and obey Him, and Him alone, and do so unreservedly. We should consider only His command as the command and only His law as the law that ought to be obeyed. We should recognize and submit to His sovereignty to the exclusion of any other sovereignty. This is at once a religious belief, a guidance for individual conduct, as well as the cornerstone of man's entire life system encompassing moral conduct, political behaviour and social relationships, a system that was to be established by the Prophet (peace be on him) in Madina. The foundational concept of the new body-politic was nothing other than the principle that God alone is the Sovereign and Lord of the world, and that His law is the true law that ought to prevail.

27. This verse enjoins duty to one's parents; and significantly enough, it is mentioned immediately after duty to God. Children are required to be obedient and respectful to their parents and to do all they can to be of assistance to them. Rather than encourage an attitude of indifference and unconcern, society should nurture feelings of gratitude and an attitude of respect for parents. Children should be taught to be mindful of their parents especially when the latter are age-stricken, to take good care of them and to provide them with every comfort, and while so doing they ought to remember the love and compassion which their parents lavished upon them when they were small.

The present verse is not simply a moral exhortation. Rather, it lays down a fundamental principle on the basis of which the legal rights of parents have been elaborated in *Ḥadīth* and *Fiqh*. Not only that, to obey, to respect and to serve one's parents is an essential element in the intellectual and moral upbringing of people in an Islamic society, and is also an inalienable aspect of Islamic behaviour. This attitude towards parents also demands that the legal enactments, administrative fiats, and educational policies of the Islamic state should be geared towards strengthening and safeguarding the family institution, and to discouraging those trends which are likely to weaken it.

(26) (iii) Give to the near of kin his due, and also to the needy and the wayfarers.
(iv) Do not squander your wealth wastefully;
(27) for those who squander wastefully are Satan's brothers, and Satan is ever ungrateful to his Lord.
(28) (v) And when you must turn away from them – from the destitute, the near of kin, the needy, and the wayfarers – in pursuit of God's mercy which you expect to receive, then speak to them kindly.[28]

وَءَاتِ ذَا ٱلْقُرْبَىٰ حَقَّهُۥ وَٱلْمِسْكِينَ
وَٱبْنَ ٱلسَّبِيلِ وَلَا تُبَذِّرْ تَبْذِيرًا ﴿٢٦﴾
إِنَّ ٱلْمُبَذِّرِينَ كَانُوٓا۟ إِخْوَٰنَ ٱلشَّيَـٰطِينِ ۖ
وَكَانَ ٱلشَّيْطَـٰنُ لِرَبِّهِۦ كَفُورًا ﴿٢٧﴾
وَإِمَّا تُعْرِضَنَّ عَنْهُمُ ٱبْتِغَآءَ رَحْمَةٍ مِّن رَّبِّكَ
تَرْجُوهَا فَقُل لَّهُمْ قَوْلًا مَّيْسُورًا ﴿٢٨﴾

28. The contents of (iii), (iv) and (v) above require that man should not consider his wealth to be exclusively meant for himself. Instead, after moderately meeting his own needs he should spend it on his relatives, neighbours, and other human beings who are in need of it. Man's social life should also be permeated with a spirit of sympathy and recognition of the rights of others and a spirit of mutual co-operation. Relatives should be specially helpful towards each other. The 'haves' should extend to the 'have-nots' whatever aid they may be in a position to provide. If a traveller arrives in a city, town or village, he should find himself in the midst of hospitable people who are ready to act as his host and entertain him. The concept of the rights of others should be so pervasive that a person should consider those among whom he lives to have claims against him and his resources.

If a person helps others, he should do so with a feeling that he is merely discharging the obligations he owes them rather than burdening them with a debt of gratitude. And whenever a person is unable to be of any service to someone who is in need of it, he should seek the latter's indulgence at his inability to do so, and should pray to God to bless him with the means that will enable him to serve others.

(29) (vi) Do not keep your hand fastened to your neck nor outspread it, altogether widespread, for you will be left sitting rebuked, destitute.[29] ▶	وَلَا تَجْعَلْ يَدَكَ مَغْلُولَةً إِلَىٰ عُنُقِكَ وَلَا تَبْسُطْهَا كُلَّ ٱلْبَسْطِ فَتَقْعُدَ مَلُومًا مَّحْسُورًا ﴿٢٩﴾

The above provisions of the Islamic manifesto are not merely meant to teach people the norms of good conduct for their individual lives; they are also intended to serve as the basis on which the rules of obligatory and supererogatory alms are laid down for the Islamic society and especially for the state of Madina. It is on the same basis that detailed rules of will, inheritance and *waqf* (trust) were promulgated, that prescriptions for protecting the rights of orphans were laid down, and that a minimum of three days' hospitality for the traveller was made obligatory on the inhabitants of any hamlet he may happen to visit. Above all, the moral values propounded by Islam created an atmosphere in which the spirit of magnanimity, sympathy and cooperation came to prevail in society. The result was that people did not merely render to others what they owed them by way of legal obligations, but rather that they went beyond that and treated them with benevolence and generosity – a mode of behaviour to which men can never be prompted merely by the force of law.

29. 'To keep one's hand fastened to one's neck' is an Arabic idiom that denotes miserliness, and 'to outspread it, altogether widespread', denotes extravagance. When the content of the present provision, i.e. (vi), is read in conjunction with (iv), the purpose becomes very obvious. Human beings are required to act with moderation in financial matters. They should neither prevent the flow of wealth out of miserliness, nor should they waste financial resources by irresponsible extravagance. Instead, they should have such an instinctive sense of balance and moderation that they should not shrink from spending when that is genuinely needed, and should abstain from spending when it is not truly needed or is not justified. Expenses incurred for show, or out of vanity or on sheer luxury, and for sinful purposes. In fact, every misdirected expense which is made at the expense of genuine needs and beneficial purposes amounts to ingratitude to God for His bounty. It is for such reasons that those who indulge in extravagance have been dubbed 'brothers of Satan'. (See *Banī Isrā'īl* 17: 27 – Ed.)

Again, the provisions that have been laid down here are not simply moral exhortations or merely guidelines for individual conduct. They rather suggest that through moral instruction, social pressure and legal measures people should be prevented from indulging in unjustified expenditure. Hence, when the state of Madina came into existence, it adopted various practical measures

(30) Certainly your Lord makes plentiful the provision of whomsoever He wills and straitens it for whomsoever He wills. He is well-aware and is fully observant of all that relates to His servants.[30]	إِنَّ رَبَّكَ يَبْسُطُ ٱلرِّزْقَ لِمَن يَشَآءُ وَيَقْدِرُ ۚ إِنَّهُۥ كَانَ بِعِبَادِهِۦ خَبِيرًا بَصِيرًا ﴿٣٠﴾

to implement the purposes underlying these provisions. On the one hand, several forms of extravagance and luxurious modes of living were legally prohibited. Indirect legal measures were also employed to prevent wasteful expenditure. Moreover, several customs involving extravagance were ended. Furthermore, the state was empowered to adopt administrative measures to prevent blatant forms of extravagance. Likewise, through *zakāh* and *ṣadaqāt,* a blow was struck at miserliness and steps were taken to prevent the kind of acquisitiveness which prevents the free flow of wealth. In addition, a carefully engineered public awareness enabled people to distinguish between generosity and wasteful expenditure on the one hand, and between miserliness and judicious moderation in expenditure on the other.

Thanks to such healthy public awareness, misers have always been looked down upon in Islamic society and those who are moderate in their expenditure are always respected. In like manner, the extravagant are censured and the generous admired. Owing to the guidance provided by the Qur'ān, Muslim society continues to look down upon the miserly and the overly acquisitive and holds the generous in high esteem.

30. Man fails to grasp the wisdom and benevolent consideration underlying the disparity in God's scheme of distributing financial resources among human beings. This being the case, man should not interfere, by introducing artificial measures, in this natural scheme of distribution of worldly provisions. Neither should natural inequality be replaced by artificial equality; nor should natural inequality be carried to the extent of perpetrating injustice. Both are equally wrong. An economic system that is sound and healthy ought to remain close to the scheme of wealth distribution devised by God.

In view of the natural law enshrined in the present verse, the scheme of reform implemented in the state of Madina was not at all premised on the principle that economic disparity is an intrinsic evil; or that the creation of a totally classless society is a desirable objective. On the contrary, the Madinan endeavour to establish a healthy society was guided by the idea that differences among human beings ought to be maintained, but only to the extent that this

(31) (vii) Do not kill your children for fear of want. We will provide for them and for you. Surely killing them is a great sin.[31]

(32) (viii) Do not even approach fornication for it is a monstrous act, and an evil way.[32]

وَلَا تَقْتُلُوٓا أَوْلَٰدَكُمْ خَشْيَةَ إِمْلَٰقٍ نَّحْنُ
نَرْزُقُهُمْ وَإِيَّاكُمْ إِنَّ قَتْلَهُمْ كَانَ
خِطْـًٔا كَبِيرًا ﴿٣١﴾ وَلَا تَقْرَبُوا الزِّنَىٰٓ
إِنَّهُۥ كَانَ فَٰحِشَةً وَسَآءَ سَبِيلًا ﴿٣٢﴾

was natural. At the same time, both the moral conduct and legal enactments of society should be so restructured that economic disparity is prevented from promoting injustice; instead, it should become instrumental in fostering the innumerable moral, spiritual and social benefits for the sake of which God had presumably allowed such economic disparity among human beings.

31. This verse totally demolishes the economic basis on which birth control movements have arisen in different periods of human history, starting from ancient times until the present. In the past, fear of poverty drove people to infanticide and abortion. Today it drives people towards a third alternative – prevention of conception. However, according to this provision of the Islamic manifesto, man is required not to waste his energies on the destructive task of reducing the number of mouths that have to be fed. Instead, man should devote his energies to constructive tasks which, under God's Law, leads to increases in the production of wealth.

It is evident from the above verse that one of man's major blunders is that he often decides to put a brake on procreation for fear of paucity in economic resources. The verse warns man that in no way does he control the process of providing sustenance for God's creatures. That control rests with God alone Who has created and placed mankind on earth. Now, in the same manner that God has provided men with their sustenance in the past, He will also do so in the future. Human history also bears witness to the fact that economic resources in different parts of the world have increased in proportion to the growth of human population; and at times, these resources have increased at an even higher pace than growth in population. Hence, man's amateurish interference in the providential arrangements of God amounts to nothing short of folly.

This explains the fact that since the time the Qur'ān was revealed and until the present Muslims have, on the whole, never cherished ideas that might indeed be considered genocidal.

(33) (ix) Do not kill any person whom Allah has forbidden to kill,[33] except with right.[34] We have granted the heir of him who has been wrongfully killed the authority to (claim retribution);[35] so let him not exceed in slaying.[36] He shall be helped.[37]

وَلَا تَقْتُلُوا۟ ٱلنَّفْسَ ٱلَّتِى حَرَّمَ ٱللَّهُ إِلَّا بِٱلْحَقِّ ۗ وَمَن قُتِلَ مَظْلُومًا فَقَدْ جَعَلْنَا لِوَلِيِّهِۦ سُلْطَٰنًا فَلَا يُسْرِف فِّى ٱلْقَتْلِ ۖ إِنَّهُۥ كَانَ مَنصُورًا ﴿٣٣﴾

32. The command: 'Do not even approach fornication' is directed both at individuals and at society. Individuals are required not only to shun fornication, but also to strictly stay away from all that leads to it. As for human society, it is incumbent upon it to root out fornication as well as the causes and factors which lead to it. To this end, all possible measures – legislation, education, reform of public life, and a healthy restructuring of society – all should be effectively employed.

The present provision ultimately served as the basis of a substantial part of the Islamic way of life. In accordance with the above verse, both fornication and false allegations of fornication were declared cognizable offences; rules designed to prevent promiscuity and to ensure the observance of grace and modesty in the public appearance of women, and to minimize the chances for inducing sexual excitement were laid down; intoxicants, music, and the spread of every kind of lewdness and obscenity were forbidden; dances and pictures – which are closely linked with, and impel people towards illicit sex – were prohibited, and a set of rules for conjugal relationships encouraging people towards formal marriage and eradicating the causes of illicit sex were promulgated.

33. The command: 'Do not kill any person' does not merely signify killing someone else, but also includes oneself. God has declared human life to be sacrosanct, and thus not only slaying others, but killing oneself is also a heinous crime. One of man's major follies is that he considers himself his own master, and hence believes that he is entitled to destroy himself if he so wishes. The fact, however, is that our lives belong to God. In fact, we are not even entitled to misuse, let alone destroy human life. God has placed us in this world in order to test us. He has the right to test us as He wishes. As for us, we are duty-bound to face the test and persist in it until the very end regardless of the

(34) (x) And do not even go near the property of the orphan, except that it be in the best manner, till he attains his maturity.[38]	وَلَا تَقْرَبُوا مَالَ الْيَتِيمِ إِلَّا بِالَّتِي هِيَ أَحْسَنُ حَتَّىٰ يَبْلُغَ أَشُدَّهُ

conditions imposed. To flee from the test is bad enough, but to do so by recourse to suicide is not only monstrous but has been categorically forbidden. Such a flight simply means that the man concerned runs from the trivial discomforts, slights and affronts which he encounters in the present world, only to end up facing the greater and unending torment and humiliation which awaits those who commit suicide.

34. Later on, Islamic law declared taking life as legitimate in only five specific cases: retribution against one guilty of deliberate murder; fighting and killing those who wage [militant] resistance against the true faith; capital punishment for those engaged in any uprising against the Islamic system of government; capital punishment for those men or women convicted of unlawful sexual intercourse; capital punishment for those who committed apostasy. It is only in these five cases that human life forfeits its sanctity, and the taking of human life becomes lawful.

35. That 'We have granted the heir of him who has been wrongfully killed the authority to demand *qiṣāṣ* (retribution)' means that the heir of someone who has been murdered is entitled to claim retribution for that crime, i.e. the murderer's life be taken in retribution. This verse accounts for the principle of Islamic law which stipulates that in the case of homicide it is the heirs of the person slain rather than the state who are the plaintiffs. As a consequence, the heirs have the right both to full retribution or gratuitously forgive the culprit or to altogether forego the right of retribution in lieu of blood-money.

36. There are many ways in which one can overstep the legitimate bounds of 'slaying'; all of which are prohibited. For instance, swayed by vengefulness, a wronged person may kill others than the actual culprit, or subject the culprit to torture, mutilate his corpse, or even kill him after he has taken blood-money from him.

37. As the Islamic state had not been established when this verse was revealed, who will 'help' the heir is not specified. However, after the Islamic state was established, it was made clear that 'helping' the legal heir was neither the responsibility of the slain person's tribe nor of that tribe's allies. Instead,

(xi) And fulfil the covenant, for you will be called to account regarding the covenant.[39]
(35) (xii) Give full measure when you measure, and weigh with even scales.[40] That is fair, and better in consequence.[41]

وَأَوْفُوا۟ بِٱلْعَهْدِ ۖ إِنَّ ٱلْعَهْدَ كَانَ
مَسْـُٔولًا ﴿٣٤﴾ وَأَوْفُوا۟ ٱلْكَيْلَ إِذَا كِلْتُمْ
وَزِنُوا۟ بِٱلْقِسْطَاسِ ٱلْمُسْتَقِيمِ ۚ ذَٰلِكَ
خَيْرٌ وَأَحْسَنُ تَأْوِيلًا ﴿٣٥﴾

---

the responsibility fell upon the Islamic state and its judicial system. Individuals or groups were not entitled to seek retribution for murder on their own; rather, they were required to approach the Islamic state for the redress of such grievances.

38. This was not merely a moral precept. After the establishment of the Islamic state, it ensured protection for the rights of orphans by a variety of administrative and legal measures embodied in the works of *Ḥadīth* and *Fiqh*. Another broad principle derived from this verse is that the Islamic state is required to protect the interests of all its citizens who are unable to protect their own rights. (See Ibn Mājah, *al-Sunan, K. al-Ṣadaqāt, 'Bāb li Ṣāḥib al-Ḥaqq Sulṭān'* – Ed.) The Prophet's saying: 'I am the guardian of he who has no guardian' (Aḥmad ibn Ḥanbal, *Musnad,* vol. 4, p. 133 – Ed.) points to the same premise and constitutes a basic principle underlying several provisions of Islamic law.

39. Once again, this was not merely a moral directive to embellish the conduct of individuals; it also served as the basis of both the internal and external policies of the Islamic state.

40. This directive too was not meant to be of relevance only to inter-personal affairs. After the establishment of the Islamic state, it became the basis for supervizing the use of correct weights and measures in market places, and prevented all forms of cheating and wrong-doing to others on this count. This verse also accounts for the general principle that the state is obligated to prevent all forms of malpractice and wrong-doing in business and financial dealings.

41. That is, such conduct will lead to felicitous results in both worlds – the present and the Next. In so far as the present life is concerned, such conduct

(36) (xiii) Do not follow that of which you have no knowledge. Surely, the hearing, the sight, the heart – each of these shall be called to account.[42]

(37) (xiv) Do not strut about the land in arrogance. Surely, you cannot cleave the earth, nor reach the heights of the mountains in stature.[43]

وَلَا تَقْفُ مَا لَيْسَ لَكَ بِهِۦ عِلْمٌ ۚ إِنَّ
ٱلسَّمْعَ وَٱلْبَصَرَ وَٱلْفُؤَادَ كُلُّ أُو۟لَٰٓئِكَ
كَانَ عَنْهُ مَسْـُٔولًا ﴿٣٦﴾ وَلَا تَمْشِ فِى
ٱلْأَرْضِ مَرَحًا ۖ إِنَّكَ لَن تَخْرِقَ ٱلْأَرْضَ
وَلَن تَبْلُغَ ٱلْجِبَالَ طُولًا ﴿٣٧﴾

will be advantageous since it is likely to promote mutual confidence and helps to build genuine trust between buyers and sellers which, in turn, leads to success in business and to prosperity as such. As for a felicitous end in the Next Life, it is quite obvious that this depends entirely on faith and pious conduct in this world.

42. The purpose of this Qur'ānic verse is that people should be guided by knowledge rather than conjecture both in their individual and collective lives. In an Islamic society, this directive found its reflection in ethics and law, in politics and administration, and in arts, sciences and education; in short, in all spheres of human life. This perspective ensured that human thought and action were made safe from the many evil consequences which ensue from relying on guesswork and conjecture instead of knowledge. In matters of conduct and behaviour, people are asked to abstain from entertaining misgivings about others and to avoid levelling unfounded charges against both individuals and groups. Similarly, Islamic law prohibited both the consigning of people to prison or their manhandling merely on the grounds of suspicion. Additionally, in their relations with other nations, Muslims were prevented, by law, from taking steps against them merely on the grounds of unsubstantiated misgivings. Rumour-mongering based on unsubstantiated suspicions were also proscribed. In the field of education, disciplines based on sheer speculation and conjecture were discouraged. Above all, a blow was struck against all superstitions in matters of religious belief since believers were asked to accept only that which had any basis in the knowledge vouchsafed by God or His Messenger (peace be on him).

(38) The wickedness of each of that is hateful to your Lord.[44] (39) That is part of the wisdom your Lord has revealed to you. So do not set up any deity beside Allah lest you are cast into Hell rebuked and deprived of every good.[45] (40) What! Your Lord has favoured you with sons and has taken for Himself daughters from among the angels. You are indeed uttering a monstrous lie.[46]

(41) We have expounded (the truth) in diverse ways in this Qur'ān, that they might take it to heart but all this only aggravates their aversion. ▶

كُلُّ ذَٰلِكَ كَانَ سَيِّئُهُۥ عِندَ رَبِّكَ مَكْرُوهًا
٣٨ ذَٰلِكَ مِمَّآ أَوْحَىٰٓ إِلَيْكَ رَبُّكَ مِنَ
ٱلْحِكْمَةِ ۗ وَلَا تَجْعَلْ مَعَ ٱللَّهِ إِلَٰهًا ءَاخَرَ
فَتُلْقَىٰ فِى جَهَنَّمَ مَلُومًا مَّدْحُورًا ٣٩
أَفَأَصْفَىٰكُمْ رَبُّكُم بِٱلْبَنِينَ وَٱتَّخَذَ مِنَ
ٱلْمَلَٰٓئِكَةِ إِنَٰثًا ۚ إِنَّكُمْ لَتَقُولُونَ قَوْلًا عَظِيمًا
٤٠ وَلَقَدْ صَرَّفْنَا فِى هَٰذَا ٱلْقُرْءَانِ
لِيَذَّكَّرُوا۟ وَمَا يَزِيدُهُمْ إِلَّا نُفُورًا ٤١

---

43. This verse teaches men to eschew the ways of the arrogant and the vainglorious. As we have noted in earlier instances, this directive embraces both individual and collective behaviour. Guided by this, the rulers, governors and military commanders of the Islamic state of Madina bore no trace of pride and arrogance. Even on the battlefield they scarcely uttered anything that smacked of vanity. Their demeanour, their dress, their homes, their means of transport, and their general mode of conduct with others were all distinguished by humility, self-negation and a detached attitude towards this worldly life. When as victors they entered their conquered territories, they did not strike terror into the hearts of the conquered by ostentatious display of pomp and power.

44. After enumerating upon evil traits of conduct, it is emphasized how each of these traits are hateful in the sight of God. To put it differently, infraction of any of the commands mentioned above is disapproved of by God.

45. Although here the discourse is ostensibly addressed to the Prophet (peace be on him), the purpose of the discourse on such occasions is to provide directives to all human beings.

(42) Say (O Muḥammad!): 'Had there been other gods with Him, as they claim, they would surely have attempted to find a way to the Lord of the Throne.[47] ▶

قُل لَّوْ كَانَ مَعَهُۥٓ ءَالِهَةٌ كَمَا يَقُولُونَ إِذًا لَّٱبْتَغَوْا۟ إِلَىٰ ذِى ٱلْعَرْشِ سَبِيلًا ﴿٤٢﴾

46. For further elucidation see *Towards Understanding the Qur'ān*, vol. IV, *al-Naḥl* 16: 57–9, nn. 50–2, pp. 336–8.

47. Had there been any other who shared with God His godhead, he would have certainly tried to place himself on God's Throne. For, if several deities exist, then only two alternatives are possible. First, that each of them is God and that they are independent of the others. Second, one of the gods is the True God, the rest are subordinate to Him but have had some of His powers delegated to them. In the former situation, it is simply inconceivable that several deities, who are independent and sovereign, would always concur on all matters; and this concurrence, as we all know, is necessary for the perfect harmony, uniformity, coherence and balance which characterize the workings of this vast universe. Had there been a multiplicity of gods, it is likely that there would have been clashes and discordance at every step. And when a god became aware that things were not going his way, he would have struggled to become the sole master of the entire universe.

However, if that were not the case, let us consider the alternative – that there were gods other than the One True God to whom some of God's powers had been delegated. Now such is the mettle of creatures, that were any invested with some of God's powers, even had the faintest suspicion of divinity, it would suffice to turn their heads, making it impossible for them to be satisfied with anything other than becoming Lord of the universe.

It is quite evident that in this universe in which we have been placed, there grows neither a blade of grass nor a grain of wheat unless the immense forces of the heavens and the earth collaborate to bring this about. This being the case, only an ignoramus or an utter fool believes that such a universe is governed by a variety of independent or semi-independent gods. Anyone who has made any serious effort to reflect on the universe can never escape the conclusion that it is under the firm control of One God alone, and that it is simply out of the question that anyone could share any of His powers with Him.

(43) Holy is He and far above all that they say. (44) The seven heavens, the earth, and all within them give glory to Him.[48] There is nothing but gives glory to Him with His praise,[49] but you do not understand their hymns of praise. He is much forbearing, exceedingly forgiving.'[50]

(45) When you recite the Qur'ān, We place a hidden barrier between you and those who do not believe in the Hereafter; ▶

سُبْحَٰنَهُۥ وَتَعَٰلَىٰ عَمَّا يَقُولُونَ عُلُوًّا كَبِيرًا
﴿٤٣﴾ تُسَبِّحُ لَهُ ٱلسَّمَٰوَٰتُ ٱلسَّبْعُ وَٱلْأَرْضُ
وَمَن فِيهِنَّ وَإِن مِّن شَىْءٍ إِلَّا يُسَبِّحُ بِحَمْدِهِۦ
وَلَٰكِن لَّا تَفْقَهُونَ تَسْبِيحَهُمْ إِنَّهُۥ كَانَ
حَلِيمًا غَفُورًا ﴿٤٤﴾ وَإِذَا قَرَأْتَ ٱلْقُرْءَانَ
جَعَلْنَا بَيْنَكَ وَبَيْنَ ٱلَّذِينَ لَا يُؤْمِنُونَ
بِٱلْءَاخِرَةِ حِجَابًا مَّسْتُورًا ﴿٤٥﴾

---

48. The universe and all that there is in it bears ample testimony to the fact that its Creator, Master and Lord is free from every blemish, weakness and fault; He is far too exalted to have anyone as an associate or partner in His godhead.

49. 'There is nothing but gives glory to Him with His praise' means that everything in the universe eloquently testifies that its Creator and Lord is free from every weakness, defect and fault. Not only that, it also affirms that God's attributes are characterized by perfection, and that He alone is worthy of all praise.

50. It is only because of God's forbearance and forgiveness that even when man shows temerity and insolence and even when he foists lies on God, He may let him go unpunished. God neither withholds from such people their sustenance nor unnecessarily deprives them of other mundane bounties. Even when man utters a blasphemy, he is not necessarily struck down by a thunderbolt. Thanks to God's forbearance and forgiveness, both individuals and communities are granted ample respite to mend their ways, and Prophets, Messengers, reformers and preachers are continually raised to guide and admonish them. In this way, all those who show any propensity to be good and repent and put themselves on the right way are instantly forgiven all their past misdeeds.

(46) and We place a covering on their hearts that they do not comprehend it, and We cause a heaviness in their ears;[51] and when you mention the One and Only Lord in the Qur'ān, they turn their backs in aversion.[52] ▶

وَجَعَلْنَا عَلَىٰ قُلُوبِهِمْ أَكِنَّةً أَن يَفْقَهُوهُ
وَفِيٓ ءَاذَانِهِمْ وَقْرًا ۚ وَإِذَا ذَكَرْتَ رَبَّكَ فِي
ٱلْقُرْءَانِ وَحْدَهُۥ وَلَّوْا۟ عَلَىٰٓ أَدْبَٰرِهِمْ
نُفُورًا ﴿٤٦﴾

51. When a man denies the Hereafter, it naturally leads to his heart being sealed, and his ears becoming incapable of heeding the message of the Qur'ān. For, the very cornerstone of the Qur'ānic message to man is that he should not be deceived by the external manifestations of this worldly life. For, even if we do not observe anyone calling people to account, this should not mislead us into believing that man is not accountable to anyone. Likewise, we also observe that people freely choose to become polytheists, atheists and monotheists, and the consequences of such a choice seemingly remain much the same as far as the present world is concerned.

This should not, however, give rise to the misconception that there are no ultimate consequences of making right or wrong choices. People have been granted the freedom to act in the world as they wish. As a result of this freedom, some immerse themselves in sin and evil while others live in righteousness and piety. Now so far as this worldly life is concerned, righteousness does not always lead to felicitous results, nor does evil always lead to misery and suffering.

This should not, however, lead us to the false notion that no moral law exists, or that actions will not have their natural results. The fundamental truth is that accountability will certainly take place and that man will bear the consequence of his actions. All this, however, will happen in the Next Life. It is true that man has been given the freedom to choose whichever doctrine he likes, be it monotheism or polytheism or atheism. This freedom should not give rise to the misunderstanding that all doctrines – monotheism, polytheism and atheism – are of equal value, and that they will ultimately lead to much the same results. It should be clearly understood that monotheism is the only sound and correct doctrine and that all other doctrines are false. Likewise, the worldly consequences of righteous and evil behaviour might not be very conspicuously different. But all this is illusory since the true consequences of the attitudes man adopts will surface in the Hereafter. There the truth, which is bound to remain hidden in the present world, will be fully unveiled. For there does certainly exist a moral law according to which sin and evil are harmful whereas

(47) We are well aware what they wish to hear when they listen to you, and what they say when they confer in whispers, when the wrong-doers say: 'You are only following one who is be-witched.'[53] (48) How strange are the things they invent about you. They have altogether strayed, and are unable to find the right way.[54]

نَّحْنُ أَعْلَمُ بِمَا يَسْتَمِعُونَ بِهِۦٓ إِذْ يَسْتَمِعُونَ
إِلَيْكَ وَإِذْ هُمْ نَجْوَىٰٓ إِذْ يَقُولُ ٱلظَّٰلِمُونَ
إِن تَتَّبِعُونَ إِلَّا رَجُلًا مَّسْحُورًا ﴿٤٧﴾
ٱنظُرْ كَيْفَ ضَرَبُوا۟ لَكَ ٱلْأَمْثَالَ
فَضَلُّوا۟ فَلَا يَسْتَطِيعُونَ سَبِيلًا ﴿٤٨﴾

---

obedience to God is beneficial. However, the judgements according to this law will only be passed in the Life to Come.

Thus, there is no reason for man to be overly enamoured of the life of this world. Nor should man rely on the deceptive consequences that come to the surface in the course of this transient phase of his existence. Instead, he should keep his eyes focused on his ultimate accountability before God and should adopt the beliefs and practices that will see him through the test of the Hereafter and thereby to success.

This is what the Qur'ān invites man to. It is quite obvious that those who altogether reject the Hereafter and place their reliance solely on the phenomenal world, and who rely on nothing else but sense perception and experience, will never be inclined to see the point of the Qur'ānic message. The Qur'ānic message will reach their ears, but will not penetrate their hearts. This is the truth which is stated here. Furthermore, it is the enunciation of a natural law which operates in the manner stated above and in respect of a certain type of person.

It should also be noted that the present verse recounts a statement that the Makkan unbelievers proudly and frequently made. 'They say: "Our hearts are under veils, (concealed) from that to which you invite us, and in our ears is a deafness, and between us and you is a screen: so do (what you will); as for us, we shall do (what we will!)" ' (*Fuṣṣilat* 41: 5). This contention is taken over by the Qur'ān and turned against them. Repeating their utterance, the Qur'ān advises the Makkan unbelievers that what they proudly extol as their virtue is indeed a curse which has been inflicted upon them – in accordance with natural law and as a result of their denial of the Hereafter.

52. The unbelievers of Makka found that the Prophet (peace be on him) regarded God as the only true Lord, to the exclusion of all other deities. It was

(49) They say: 'When we are turned to bones and particles (of dust), shall we truly be raised up as a new creation?' (50) Tell them: '(You will be raised afresh even if) you turn to stone or iron; ▸

وَقَالُوٓاْ أَءِذَا كُنَّا عِظَٰمًا وَرُفَٰتًا أَءِنَّا
لَمَبْعُوثُونَ خَلْقًا جَدِيدًا ﴿٤٩﴾ ۞
قُلْ كُونُواْ حِجَارَةً أَوْ حَدِيدًا ﴿٥٠﴾

---

intolerable for them that the Prophet (peace be on him) should talk only about God without waxing lyrical about the supernatural powers of saints and holy men and without paying tribute to those who, in the popular view, had been granted a part of God's power and authority by God Himself. They were astonished that a person should believe that God – and He alone – possessed virtually everything – full knowledge of the realm beyond the ken of sense-perception, absolute power to do as He pleased, and total control over everything. It was inconceivable to them that someone should pay no heed to the saints by dint of whose grace people were granted offspring, the sick were healed, sagging businesses began to flourish, and all wishes were fulfilled. (For further elaboration see *al-Zumar* 39: 45, n. 64.)

53. This is an allusion to conversations between the leaders of the Makkan unbelievers. They were wont, surreptitiously, to listen to the Qur'ān and then consult with one another as to how they could effectively refute it. At times they suspected that some among their ranks were gradually succumbing to the spell of the Qur'ān. Whenever they became aware of this they approached the persons concerned and tried to dissuade them from taking the Prophet (peace be on him) seriously, arguing that he was under a magic spell and thus was given to saying crazy things.

54. It is pointed out here that the Prophet's Makkan opponents were not of one opinion. From time to time they made statements that were not only different but even mutually contradictory. At times they alleged that the Prophet (peace be on him) was himself a magician. On other occasions, they claimed that he was under the spell of someone else's magic. They also variously labelled him a poet and a lunatic.

These discrepant statements made it quite evident that whatever they said was not based on knowledge of fact. For had it been so they would have expressed one definite opinion and stuck to it. Their mutually contradictory statements proved that they were unsure of what they said. Hence they expressed one hostile opinion after another about the Prophet (peace be on

(51) or any other form of creation you deem hardest of all (to recreate from).' They will certainly ask: 'Who will bring us back (to life)?' Say: 'He Who created you in the first instance.' They will shake their heads at you[55] and inquire: 'When will that be?' Say: 'Perhaps that time might have drawn near; (52) on the Day when He will call you and you will rise praising Him in response to His call, and you will believe that you had lain in this state only for a while.'[56]

أَوْ خَلْقًا مِّمَّا يَكْبُرُ فِي صُدُورِكُمْ
فَسَيَقُولُونَ مَن يُعِيدُنَا قُلِ الَّذِي فَطَرَكُمْ
أَوَّلَ مَرَّةٍ فَسَيُنْغِضُونَ إِلَيْكَ رُءُوسَهُمْ
وَيَقُولُونَ مَتَىٰ هُوَ قُلْ عَسَىٰ أَن
يَكُونَ قَرِيبًا ﴿٥١﴾ يَوْمَ يَدْعُوكُمْ
فَتَسْتَجِيبُونَ بِحَمْدِهِ
وَتَظُنُّونَ إِن لَّبِثْتُمْ إِلَّا قَلِيلًا ﴿٥٢﴾

---

him) only to realize that none were applicable to him. They would continuously come forward with some fresh slander about the Prophet (peace be on him). All this demonstrated the utter falsity of their statements and was indicative of their inveterate hostility towards the Prophet (peace be on him).

55. The gesture referred to here consists of shaking one's head up and down; something one resorts to either to express amazement or derision.

56. The period between a person's death and resurrection on the Last Day will appear as if no longer than, say, a few hours. One will assume that one has just had a brief sleep and been woken by the din and noise of the Day of Reckoning.

As regards the Qur'ānic statement that man will rise, praising God, this points to a significant reality. For on the Day of Resurrection everyone, both believers and unbelievers, will have God's praise on their lips. A believer's praise of God will be in keeping with his practice in the worldly phase of his life – a praise emanating from his faith and conviction. As for the unbeliever, he will praise God in the Hereafter since to do so is innate in human nature and despite the fact that his inherent conviction about God had remained suppressed and hidden in the present world because of his own folly. Naturally, with the commencement of a fresh phase of existence, when all artificial barriers have been removed, the unbeliever will be forced to give vent to what had always been embedded in his nature; in the Hereafter he too will praise God.

(53) Tell My servants[57] (O Muḥammad), to always say that which is best.[58] Verily it is Satan who sows discord among men. Satan indeed is an open enemy to man.[59] (54) Your Lord knows you best. He will have mercy on you if He wills and chastise you if He wills.[60] We have not charged you, (O Muḥammad), to be an overseer over them.[61]

وَقُل لِّعِبَادِي يَقُولُوا الَّتِي هِيَ أَحْسَنُ
إِنَّ الشَّيْطَانَ يَنزَغُ بَيْنَهُمْ إِنَّ الشَّيْطَانَ
كَانَ لِلْإِنسَانِ عَدُوًّا مُّبِينًا ﴿٥٣﴾ رَّبُّكُمْ
أَعْلَمُ بِكُمْ إِن يَشَأْ يَرْحَمْكُمْ أَوْ إِن يَشَأْ
يُعَذِّبْكُمْ وَمَا أَرْسَلْنَاكَ عَلَيْهِمْ
وَكِيلًا ﴿٥٤﴾

57. That is, the believers.

58. In their discussions with the unbelievers and polytheists, in fact with all opponents of their faith, Muslims should refrain from losing their temper. Additionally, they should not resort to exaggerated and extremist statements. Even in the face of provocation from their opponents, Muslims should not utter even a word that is contrary to the truth; nor should they lose their temper at the vulgarities which are flung at them by their opponents, nor should they be provoked to the point of paying back their opponents in the latters' own coins. Instead, they should keep their composure and say only that which is balanced and true, and is in keeping with the grace and dignity of the faith which they seek to uphold.

59. The Qur'ān tells believers that whenever in the course of their discussions on contentious issues with unbelievers, they feel overly provoked and overwhelmed with rage, they should immediately realize that such reactions are instigated by Satan who is keen to hurt the cause of their faith. Satan will certainly try to prompt the believers to give up, as their opponents had done, all efforts of reform, and to become entangled in futile wranglings and strife. For it is Satan's aim that all mankind remain perpetually enmeshed in such controversies.

60. The believers should never go about bragging that they are going to enter Paradise, or cockily name other persons or groups as the ones destined to enter Hell. For it is God alone Who has the authority to decide such matters. It is He alone Who fully knows about all human beings, about all things both

(55) Your Lord knows all who dwell in the heavens and the earth. We have exalted some Prophets over others,[62] and We gave the Psalms to David.[63]

وَرَبُّكَ أَعْلَمُ بِمَن فِي ٱلسَّمَٰوَٰتِ وَٱلْأَرْضِ ۗ وَلَقَدْ فَضَّلْنَا بَعْضَ ٱلنَّبِيِّـۧنَ عَلَىٰ بَعْضٍ ۖ وَءَاتَيْنَا دَاوُۥدَ زَبُورًا ﴿٥٥﴾

apparent and hidden, which took place before or which will take place in the future. It is He alone Who will judge, He alone Who will decide to whom He should show mercy and whom He should punish. All that a human being can say, enunciating the teachings of the Qur'ān, is what kind of people deserve mercy, and what kind deserve punishment. No one has the right to categorically say that a particular person will be either chastised or pardoned by God.

Presumably this directive was occasioned by the constant oppression to which the Muslims were subjected by the unbelievers. For some of the former may have been tempted to say of their more cruel opponents that they would be consigned to Hell or that God would chastise them for their behaviour.

61. A Messenger's mission is simply to invite people to the right way. The destinies of people have not been placed in his hands, nor has he been empowered to sit in judgement over them, deciding who should be cast into Hell and who should be shown mercy.

The observation made here does not imply that the Prophet (peace be on him) had committed such a lapse and that this needed to be pointed out to him. The purpose of the statement is rather to warn the generality of Muslims against adopting such an attitude. For if even the Prophet (peace be on him) does not have the authority to judge who deserves Hell and who deserves Heaven, then how can ordinary Muslims be justified in making these decisions.

62. Although the above statement is apparently addressed to the Prophet (peace be on him), it is in fact meant for the unbelievers. The Prophet's contemporaries – in keeping with the wont of contemporaries – could not recognize his true worth nor appreciate his intrinsic greatness. They looked upon him as someone not much different from the common run of people who lived in their town. Greatness was conceived to have been the exclusive prerogative of those who had lived in some bygone age, several centuries previously. Hence when the Prophet (peace be on him) claimed that he had been designated by God, they decried the claim as sheer boastfulness. They simply could not believe how he could be a peer of those great Prophets of yore whose holiness was universally recognized.

(56) Tell them: 'Call upon those whom you fancy to be [your helpers] beside Him! They have no power to remove any affliction from you, nor can they shift it.'[64] (57) Those whom they call upon are themselves seeking the means of access to their Lord, each trying to be nearer to Him. They crave for His mercy and dread His chastisement.[65] Surely your Lord's punishment is to be feared.

قُلِ ٱدْعُوا۟ ٱلَّذِينَ زَعَمْتُم مِّن دُونِهِۦ فَلَا
يَمْلِكُونَ كَشْفَ ٱلضُّرِّ عَنكُمْ وَلَا
تَحْوِيلًا ﴿٥٦﴾ أُو۟لَٰٓئِكَ ٱلَّذِينَ يَدْعُونَ
يَبْتَغُونَ إِلَىٰ رَبِّهِمُ ٱلْوَسِيلَةَ أَيُّهُمْ
أَقْرَبُ وَيَرْجُونَ رَحْمَتَهُۥ وَيَخَافُونَ
عَذَابَهُۥٓ ۚ إِنَّ عَذَابَ رَبِّكَ كَانَ مَحْذُورًا ﴿٥٧﴾

In response, God succinctly points out that He fully knows all His creatures wherever they may be whereas men are in no position to know accurately about others, nor can they know the true merit of others. God alone selected those creatures on whom to bestow His special grace – prophethood. It was for this reason that He had as a result raised a whole series of great Prophets in the past.

63. The reference to bestowing the Psalms on David is probably prompted by the fact that David was a king and, generally speaking, kings are disposed towards some remoteness from God.

Contemporaries of the Prophet Muḥammad (peace be on him) did not accept his claim to be God's Messenger basically because he lived a normal conjugal life, like others he married and had children, ate and drank as they did and went to the market-place as any other mortal would do. For the Makkan unbelievers, if someone lived a normal worldly life, this rendered him incapable of reaching the high level of spirituality required of a Prophet. They believed that only those who renounced this worldly life, who spent their time in a monastery devoting themselves wholly to God's remembrance, and who had no worldly concerns, could be truly close to God. The Qur'ān counters this suggestion by citing the example of the Prophet David (peace be on him) who combined the roles of Messenger and king. A king is obviously a worldly person and yet David (peace be on him) was endowed with prophethood and was granted Scripture.

64. This clearly shows that not only prostrating oneself before someone other than God, but also that praying to and invoking anyone other than God

(58) There is not a town but that We shall destroy it or upon which We shall inflict severe chastisement before the Day of Resurrection.[66] This is written down in the Eternal Book (of Allah).

(59) Nothing hindered Us from sending Our signs[67] except that the people of olden times rejected them as lies. We publicly sent the she-camel to the Thamūd to open their eyes but they wronged her.[68] We never send Our signs except to cause men to fear.[69] ▶

وَإِن مِّن قَرْيَةٍ إِلَّا نَحْنُ مُهْلِكُوهَا
قَبْلَ يَوْمِ ٱلْقِيَـٰمَةِ أَوْ مُعَذِّبُوهَا عَذَابًا
شَدِيدًا ۚ كَانَ ذَٰلِكَ فِى ٱلْكِتَـٰبِ مَسْطُورًا
﴿٥٨﴾ وَمَا مَنَعَنَآ أَن نُّرْسِلَ بِٱلْـَٔايَـٰتِ
إِلَّآ أَن كَذَّبَ بِهَا ٱلْأَوَّلُونَ ۚ
وَءَاتَيْنَا ثَمُودَ ٱلنَّاقَةَ مُبْصِرَةً فَظَلَمُوا۟
بِهَا ۚ وَمَا نُرْسِلُ بِٱلْـَٔايَـٰتِ إِلَّا
تَخْوِيفًا ﴿٥٩﴾

---

amounts to associating others in His Divinity, i.e. to polytheism. Prayer and invocation are modes of worship and anyone who invokes someone other than God is as guilty of polytheism as an idol-worshipper. Nor can anyone other than God avert a calamity or alter anyone's plight. If someone entertains such beliefs about anyone other than God, then such beliefs are false and betray the fact that he associates others with God in His Divinity.

65. The actual words used in the verse make it clear that the polytheists' deities and objects of prayer were angels and saints of the past rather than idols made of stone. The Qur'ān candidly states that no one – whether Messenger, saint or angel – has the power to hear and answer man's prayers or to come to his help. How ironic that those whom the polytheists invoked and whom they sought to intercede with God on their behalf were themselves in need of God's mercy, dreaded His punishment, and were constantly on the look-out for the means which would bring them close to Him.

66. No one is immortal. Every habitation will either perish in the course of time by the natural death of its inhabitants, or will be destroyed by God's scourge. There is no basis whatsoever for the misconception that the towns and so on where people live will remain for ever.

67. This refers to those tangible miracles which provided evidence in support of the Prophet's claim to be designated by God. It may be recalled that

(60) And recall when We said to you, (O Muḥammad), that your Lord encompasses these people;[70] and that We have made the vision which We have shown you,[71] and the tree accursed in the Qur'ān,[72] to be only a trial for men.[73] We go about warning them, but each warning leads to greater transgression.

وَإِذْ قُلْنَا لَكَ إِنَّ رَبَّكَ أَحَاطَ بِالنَّاسِ
وَمَا جَعَلْنَا الرُّءْيَا الَّتِي أَرَيْنَٰكَ إِلَّا
فِتْنَةً لِّلنَّاسِ وَالشَّجَرَةَ الْمَلْعُونَةَ فِي
الْقُرْءَانِ وَنُخَوِّفُهُمْ فَمَا يَزِيدُهُمْ
إِلَّا طُغْيَٰنًا كَبِيرًا ٦٠

the Quraysh unbelievers had repeatedly asked the Prophet (peace be on him) to produce such signs.

68. Once people witness such a miracle and still refuse to believe it, they inevitably invite God's chastisement upon themselves. Such people are not spared from destruction. This is borne out by mankind's past record; for several nations witnessed clear miracles in the past and yet did not shrink from decrying them as false. As a result, they were destroyed. If, in certain periods of history, God has not confronted a people with miracles, this was by dint of His mercy; it meant that He provided them with a respite such that they might mend their ways. Was it not then sheer folly for people to continuously ask God for miracles? For if they did not care to accept the truth even after witnessing miracles, then they were bound to meet the calamitous end of nations like the Thamūd.

69. Miracles are never performed to entertain people. Their underlying purpose has always been to make people realize that the Prophets enjoyed the support of God's infinite power. Additionally, they served to warn people of the dire consequences of disobeying Him.

70. Even in the early phase of Muḥammad's prophethood, when the Makkan unbelievers had set out on a course of opposition to him, God had declared, unequivocally, that He encompassed the unbelievers. Regardless of the extent of the unbelievers' resistance, it would simply be impossible for them to prevent the Prophet's call from spreading. The task assigned to the Prophet Muḥammad (peace be on him) was bound to be accomplished, and in the teeth of their opposition. If the unbelievers truly needed a miracle in order to mend their ways, they should reflect upon what they had already witnessed, i.e. that which had been foretold in the very early days of Islam had already

come to pass and that their opposition and hostility towards the Prophet (peace be on him) had proved to be of no avail in preventing the spread of Islam. Nor had they been able to bring about any harm upon the Prophet (peace be on him). So for all those who had eyes to see, it was quite obvious that the Prophet's mission enjoyed God's support.

The statement that Allah encompassed the Prophet's enemies and that his mission enjoyed God's support is a recurrent theme in the Qur'ān and occurs many times in the early Makkan *sūrahs*. For example, consider the following verse: 'And yet the unbelievers persist in rejecting the truth. But Allah does encompass them from behind' (*al-Burūj* 85: 19–20).

71. This is an allusion to the Ascension. The word *ru'yā* is not used here as a synonym of a dream, rather it signifies seeing something with one's own eyes. Obviously, if the Ascension had been merely a dream and the Prophet (peace be on him) had narrated it to the unbelievers as such, then they would not have had any difficulty in believing in it. People experience all kinds of strange dreams and narrate them to others. There is nothing particularly unusual about dreams that would prompt people to deride the person narrating a strange experience, or lead them to accuse the person of making false claims, or to brand him as mad.

72. According to the Qur'ān, *zaqqūm* is the name of the tree that will grow in the depths of Hell and the inmates of Hell will be obliged to eat of it. To describe *zaqqūm* as an accursed tree suggests its remoteness from God's mercy. To put it differently, this tree does in no way manifest God's mercy for it is not meant to provide sustenance for people. On the contrary, it is a sign of God's wrath for the inmates of Hell. We are told (see *al-Dukhān* 44: 43–6) that whoever eats of this tree will experience an intense burning in their bellies as if they were boiling away.

73. God enabled the Prophet (peace be on him) to witness a number of things in the course of the Ascension. This was in order that people might learn certain truths for sure through no less truthful and trustworthy a person than the Prophet (peace be on him) who could report to them the truths that he had witnessed at first hand. This was done in order to help people follow the right way as a result of their having fully dependable knowledge of the truth. However, far from taking any heed of all this, the unbelievers launched a campaign of ridicule against the Prophet (peace be on him). For example, they had been told by the Prophet (peace be on him) that their wilful disregard of the distinction between legitimate and illegitimate earning would lead them to live upon *zaqqūm*. Rather than this producing a healthy response from them, instead the unbelievers made fun of the Prophet, saying, in effect: 'Look at this man! In one breath he says that Hell is a pit of blazing fire, and in the next, that trees grow in it.'

(61) And recall when We asked the angels to prostrate themselves before Adam, all prostrated themselves except Iblīs,[74] who said: 'Shall I prostrate myself before him whom You created of clay?' (62) He then continued: 'Look! This is he whom You have honoured above me! If You will grant me respite till the Day of Resurrection, I shall uproot the whole of his progeny barring only a few.'[75]

(63) Thereupon He retorted: 'Be gone! Hell shall be the recompense – and a most ample one – of whosoever of them follows you. ▶

وَإِذْ قُلْنَا لِلْمَلَٰٓئِكَةِ ٱسْجُدُوا۟ لِءَادَمَ
فَسَجَدُوٓا۟ إِلَّآ إِبْلِيسَ قَالَ ءَأَسْجُدُ لِمَنْ
خَلَقْتَ طِينًا ﴿٦١﴾ قَالَ أَرَءَيْتَكَ هَٰذَا
ٱلَّذِى كَرَّمْتَ عَلَىَّ لَئِنْ أَخَّرْتَنِ إِلَىٰ
يَوْمِ ٱلْقِيَٰمَةِ لَأَحْتَنِكَنَّ ذُرِّيَّتَهُۥٓ
إِلَّا قَلِيلًا ﴿٦٢﴾ قَالَ ٱذْهَبْ فَمَن تَبِعَكَ
مِنْهُمْ فَإِنَّ جَهَنَّمَ جَزَآؤُكُمْ جَزَآءً
مَّوْفُورًا ﴿٦٣﴾

74. Cf. *Towards Understanding the Qur'ān,* vol. I, *al-Baqarah* 2: 30–9, pp. 59-67; vol. II, *al-Nisā'* 4: 117–21, pp. 85–7; vol. III, *al-A'rāf* 7: 11–25, pp. 7–14; and vol. IV, *al-Ḥijr* 15: 26–42 and *Ibrāhīm* 14: 22, pp. 288–91 and 265 respectively.

Satan's story is narrated here so as to bring home to the unbelievers the fact that their defiance, imperviousness to warnings, and their persistent pursuit of evil was tantamount to following in Satan's footsteps, the one who has always been man's mortal enemy. By following in Satan's footsteps, man falls into a trap which Satan had laid for him from the very beginning. It would be pertinent to remember that Satan had threatened at the very commencement of human life on earth that he would never cease in his efforts to mislead mankind. (See *al-A'rāf* 7: 16–17 – Ed.)

75. The words of the verse, viz. that 'I shall uproot the whole of his progeny' means that he will cause man's feet to swerve from the path that leads to his well-being, and instead put him on a road which leads to his destruction. The root *ḥ n k* denotes uprooting, extirpation. Since man has been invested with the vicegerency of God, he is required to be constant in his obedience to Him. Any deviation from this is similar to uprooting a tree by its very roots.

(64) Tempt with your call all whom you wish.[76] Muster against them all your forces – your cavalry and your foot soldiers;[77] share with them riches and offspring,[78] and seduce them with rosy promises[79] – and Satan's promise is nothing but a deception – (65) but know well that you will have no power against My servants.[80] Your Lord is sufficient for them to place their trust in.'[81]

وَٱسْتَفْزِزْ مَنِ ٱسْتَطَعْتَ مِنْهُم بِصَوْتِكَ
وَأَجْلِبْ عَلَيْهِم بِخَيْلِكَ وَرَجِلِكَ
وَشَارِكْهُمْ فِى ٱلْأَمْوَٰلِ وَٱلْأَوْلَٰدِ
وَعِدْهُمْ ۚ وَمَا يَعِدُهُمُ ٱلشَّيْطَٰنُ إِلَّا
غُرُورًا ﴿٦٤﴾ إِنَّ عِبَادِى لَيْسَ لَكَ
عَلَيْهِمْ سُلْطَٰنٌ ۚ وَكَفَىٰ بِرَبِّكَ
وَكِيلًا ﴿٦٥﴾

76. The word *istifzāz* [in its imperative form] used in the present verse conveys the idea of sweeping someone away or causing his feet to swerve because he is weak.

77. Satan's assault, with his cavalry and infantry, conjures up an image of a robber who wreaks havoc upon a town. Satan's infantry and cavalry are men and *jinn* who are engaged in promoting Satan's mission by a variety of ways and means.

78. This statement is especially significant and full of meaning, for it accurately portrays the relationship between Satan and his followers. Anyone who follows Satan in matters relating to the earning and spending of their wealth in fact follow Satan's complete dictates and thus make Satan their partner. This is true even though Satan neither contributes to man's effort by sharing in his labour nor shares in the tragic consequences which ensue from the sins that are committed. And yet man faithfully follows Satan's directives as if the latter had an equal or even the lion's share in his enterprise. Likewise, a man's children are his own and it is he who toils in bringing them up. However, people who lack a correct perspective lead their children towards wrong beliefs and practices almost as if Satan had a share in their parenthood.

79. Satan misleads man by making him cherish false expectations, by holding out rosy promises which have no relation to reality.

80. This statement has two alternative meanings, each of which is correct. In one sense, it means that Satan has no authority over God's servants in so far

(66) Your Lord is He Who
drives your vessels across the
seas[82] that you may seek of
His bounty.[83] He is ever
merciful towards you. (67)
When a calamity befalls you
on the sea, all those whom you
invoke forsake you except
Him.[84] But when He delivers
you safely to the shore you
turn away from Him, for man
is indeed most thankless. ▶

رَبُّكُمُ ٱلَّذِى يُزْجِى لَكُمُ ٱلْفُلْكَ
فِى ٱلْبَحْرِ لِتَبْتَغُوا۟ مِن فَضْلِهِۦٓ ۚ إِنَّهُۥ
كَانَ بِكُمْ رَحِيمًا ﴿٦٦﴾ وَإِذَا
مَسَّكُمُ ٱلضُّرُّ فِى ٱلْبَحْرِ ضَلَّ مَن
تَدْعُونَ إِلَّآ إِيَّاهُ ۖ فَلَمَّا نَجَّىٰكُمْ إِلَى
ٱلْبَرِّ أَعْرَضْتُمْ ۚ وَكَانَ ٱلْإِنسَٰنُ
كَفُورًا ﴿٦٧﴾

---

as he is not able to compulsively drive them along his way – for this is beyond his power. Satan only has the power to try to mislead man, to coax him towards evil, to furnish him with false advice, and to hold out false promises. The decision, however, as to listening to Satan's suggestions or to turning them down, is man's alone. Satan is not in a position to make man follow his ways whether he wants to do so or not.

The verse can also be interpreted as meaning that Satan has no power in respect of God's chosen men – the righteous. It is only men of weak resolve who may be deceived by the false promises held out by Satan. As for men who are firm in their devotion to God, Satan cannot possibly sway them.

81. Those who place their trust in God and who look to His guidance and help will never be disappointed. God will provide them with adequate guidance and ample help. Conversely, those who rely on their own resources and repose their trust in anyone other than God will certainly fail this test.

82. In order to appreciate the connection between the present discourse and the previous one, the reader should recall the contents of the foregoing verses (verse 61 ff.). These verses emphasize Satan's erstwhile desire to mislead Adam's offspring by enmeshing them in false hopes and expectations. Satan misleads man so as to prove that the latter does not deserve the exalted status which God has conferred upon him. The only way for man to defeat Satan's design is to remain firm in obedience to God, to turn only to Him for guidance and help, and to place reliance on Him alone. Any other course means that man will end up falling into Satan's trap.

From all this it is quite obvious that those who reject Islam's message and persist in their polytheistic beliefs and practices are in fact only harming

(68) Do you, then, feel secure against His causing you to be swallowed up by a tract of the earth, or letting loose a deadly whirlwind charged with stones towards you, and then you will find none to protect you? (69) Or do you feel secure that He will not cause you to go back to the sea, and let a tempest loose upon you and then drown you for your ingratitude whereupon you will find none even to inquire of Us what happened to you? (70) Indeed, We honoured the progeny of Adam, and bore them across land and sea and provided them with good things for their sustenance, and exalted them above many of Our creatures.[85] ▶

أَفَأَمِنتُمْ أَن يَخْسِفَ بِكُمْ جَانِبَ ٱلْبَرِّ
أَوْ يُرْسِلَ عَلَيْكُمْ حَاصِبًا ثُمَّ لَا
تَجِدُوا۟ لَكُمْ وَكِيلًا ﴿٦٨﴾ أَمْ أَمِنتُمْ
أَن يُعِيدَكُمْ فِيهِ تَارَةً أُخْرَىٰ فَيُرْسِلَ
عَلَيْكُمْ قَاصِفًا مِّنَ ٱلرِّيحِ فَيُغْرِقَكُم
بِمَا كَفَرْتُمْ ثُمَّ لَا تَجِدُوا۟ لَكُمْ عَلَيْنَا
بِهِۦ تَبِيعًا ﴿٦٩﴾ ۞ وَلَقَدْ كَرَّمْنَا بَنِىٓ
ءَادَمَ وَحَمَلْنَٰهُمْ فِى ٱلْبَرِّ وَٱلْبَحْرِ
وَرَزَقْنَٰهُم مِّنَ ٱلطَّيِّبَٰتِ
وَفَضَّلْنَٰهُمْ عَلَىٰ كَثِيرٍ مِّمَّنْ
خَلَقْنَا تَفْضِيلًا ﴿٧٠﴾

---

themselves. It is in this context that the doctrine of monotheism is here reinforced and that of polytheism repudiated.

83. God has enabled man to make sea-going vessels such that he can obtain the economic, cultural, scientific and intellectual benefits which accrue from such voyages.

84. This proves that man's true nature has an inherent consciousness of the only One True God. In the very depths of his heart, man is well aware that God has the power to cause benefit or harm. This is why man turns to the One True God alone whenever he is in serious crisis and when he desperately needs effective support. (For further details see *Towards Understanding the Qur'ān*, vol. IV, *Yūnus* 10, n. 31, p. 28.)

85. It is well known that the power enjoyed by the human race on earth has not been granted by any *jinn* or angel, nor by any heavenly body, saint or

(71) Then think of the Day We shall summon every community with its leader. Those who are given their records in their right hands shall read the record of their doings[86] and shall not be wronged a whit. (72) Those who lived in this world as blind shall live as blind in the Life to Come; rather, he will be even farther astray than if he were blind.

(73) (O Muḥammad!) They had all but tempted you away from what We have revealed to you that you may invent something else in Our Name.[87] Had you done so, they would have taken you as their trusted friend. ▶

يَوْمَ نَدْعُوا۟ كُلَّ أُنَاسٍۭ بِإِمَـٰمِهِمْ ۖ فَمَنْ
أُوتِىَ كِتَـٰبَهُۥ بِيَمِينِهِۦ فَأُو۟لَـٰٓئِكَ
يَقْرَءُونَ كِتَـٰبَهُمْ وَلَا يُظْلَمُونَ
فَتِيلًا ﴿٧١﴾ وَمَن كَانَ فِى هَـٰذِهِۦٓ
أَعْمَىٰ فَهُوَ فِى ٱلْـَٔاخِرَةِ أَعْمَىٰ وَأَضَلُّ
سَبِيلًا ﴿٧٢﴾ وَإِن كَادُوا۟ لَيَفْتِنُونَكَ
عَنِ ٱلَّذِىٓ أَوْحَيْنَآ إِلَيْكَ لِتَفْتَرِىَ
عَلَيْنَا غَيْرَهُۥ ۖ وَإِذًا لَّٱتَّخَذُوكَ
خَلِيلًا ﴿٧٣﴾

Prophet. Beyond doubt, all the power that has been granted to man is from God and is by way of a special favour. There can be no greater act of ignorance and folly for man than to prostrate himself before any one other than God, God Who has granted him, to the exclusion of all other species, a uniquely exalted position in His scheme of things.

86. The Qur'ān repeatedly mentions that the righteous will be handed the scroll of their deeds in their right hand, and that they will rejoice looking at it and will even show the scroll to others. As for the evil-doers, they will be handed this scroll in their left hand, and instead of rejoicing they will try to hide it behind their backs. For details see *al-Ḥāqqah* 69: 19–28 and *al-Inshiqāq* 84: 13.

87. This alludes to the circumstances confronting the Prophet (peace be on him) during the last ten to twelve years in Makka. The Makkan unbelievers spared no effort in trying to dissuade the Prophet (peace be on him) from propagating his message of God's unity, and in forcing him to strike some kind of a compromise with them in respect of their polytheistic doctrines and

(74) Indeed, had We not strengthened you, you might have inclined to them a little, (75) whereupon We would have made you taste double [the chastisement] in the world and double [the chastisement] after death, and then you would have found none to help you against Us.[88]

(76) They were bent upon uprooting you from this land and driving you away from it. But were they to succeed, they would not be able to remain after you more than a little while.[89]

وَلَوْلَآ أَن ثَبَّتْنَـٰكَ لَقَدْ كِدتَّ
تَرْكَنُ إِلَيْهِمْ شَيْـًٔا قَلِيلًا
﴿٧٤﴾ إِذًا لَّأَذَقْنَـٰكَ ضِعْفَ
ٱلْحَيَوٰةِ وَضِعْفَ ٱلْمَمَاتِ ثُمَّ
لَا تَجِدُ لَكَ عَلَيْنَا نَصِيرًا ﴿٧٥﴾
وَإِن كَادُوا۟ لَيَسْتَفِزُّونَكَ
مِنَ ٱلْأَرْضِ لِيُخْرِجُوكَ مِنْهَا ۖ
وَإِذًا لَّا يَلْبَثُونَ خِلَـٰفَكَ
إِلَّا قَلِيلًا ﴿٧٦﴾

practices. In pursuance of this aim, they subjected him to a variety of tests. These ranged from trying to trick him, to seducing him with various temptations, carrying out false propaganda against him, subjecting him to persecution, and by putting pressure on him through economic sanctions and social boycotts.

88. Here, the situation obtaining at the time is reviewed. In this context, it is emphasized that if the Prophet (peace be on him) had struck a compromise with the forces of falsehood despite his full knowledge of the truth, he might have pleased his degenerate people, but would have incurred God's wrath and punishment both in the present life and the Next. The Prophet (peace be on him) is also informed that left entirely to oneself no one, not even a Prophet, has the power to successfully withstand the onslaught of falsehood. One can only do so with God's help and succour. In the face of fierce opposition, the Prophet's patience and steadfastness enabled him to stand firm in his adherence to the truth, but this had been granted by none other than God Himself.

89. Although this was an unequivocal prediction, at the time it may have seemed little more than a mere threat. It became reality, however, within a period of ten to eleven years. Barely more than one year after the revelation of this *sūrah*, the Makkan unbelievers forced the Prophet Muḥammad (peace be

(77) This has been Our way with the Messengers whom We sent before you.[90] You will find no change in Our way.

(78) Establish Prayer[91] from the declining of the sun[92] to the darkness of the night;[93] and hold fast to the recitation of the Qur'ān at dawn,[94] for the recitation of the Qur'ān at dawn is witnessed.[95] ▶

سُنَّةَ مَن قَدْ أَرْسَلْنَا قَبْلَكَ مِن رُّسُلِنَا وَلَا تَجِدُ لِسُنَّتِنَا تَحْوِيلًا ﴿٧٧﴾ أَقِمِ الصَّلَوٰةَ لِدُلُوكِ الشَّمْسِ إِلَىٰ غَسَقِ الَّيْلِ وَقُرْءَانَ الْفَجْرِ إِنَّ قُرْءَانَ الْفَجْرِ كَانَ مَشْهُودًا ﴿٧٨﴾

on him) to leave his home town. Within a further eight years, however, the Prophet (peace be on him) had returned to Makka as victor. Thereafter, in less than another two years, the whole of the Arabian peninsula had been purged of polytheists. Anyone who lived there subsequently did so as a Muslim only.

90. This has been God's way of dealing with a people who either kill or banish a Prophet – such a people are never allowed to survive for long. They were either destroyed by God's scourge, or God caused some fierce enemy to overwhelm them, or else they were overpowered by the followers of the Prophet pertaining at the time.

91. Reference to these difficulties and hardships is followed by the command to establish Prayer. In a subtle way, this draws our attention to the fact that the patience and steadfastness required of a believer in times of such adversity can only be obtained by establishing Prayer.

92. We have taken *dulūk al-shams* to mean 'decline of the sun', and have done so even though we are aware that some Companions and Successors have interpreted it to mean sunset as well. The majority opinion, however, is that the expression signifies decline of the sun after reaching the meridian. 'Umar, 'Abd Allāh ibn 'Umar, Anas ibn Mālik, Abū Barzah al-Aslamī, Ḥasan al-Baṣrī, Sha'bī, 'Aṭā', Mujāhid, and according to one of the reports, Ibn 'Abbās, are of the same view. Imām Muḥammad al-Bāqir and Imām Ja'far al-Ṣādiq are also reported to be in favour of this interpretation. In fact, even some traditions from the Prophet (peace be on him) – albeit traditions which are not especially sound in terms of their chain of narration – also explain *dulūk*

to mean the same. (Ibn Kathīr, *Tafsīr*, comments on *Banī Isrā'īl* 17, verse 78 – Ed.)

93. *Ghasaq al-layl* is considered by some to mean the 'thickening of the night', or 'the spread of total darkness', and by others simply to mean midnight. According to the first sense, it suggests the earliest time for the *'Ishā'* Prayer and according to the second, the time limit for performing this.

94. *'Fajr'* literally means 'dawn' – the time when the light of the morning makes its first appearance after piercing the veil of night's darkness. *Qur'ān al-fajr* here signifies the *Fajr* Prayer. On certain occasions the Qur'ān uses the expression *ṣalāh* for Prayer; but on other occasions any one of several acts of *ṣalāh* has been mentioned, for example, *tasbīḥ* (glorifying God), *ḥamd* (praise), *dhikr* (remembrance), *qiyām* (standing), *rukū'* (bowing) and *sujūd* (prostration), any one of these acts standing for *ṣalāh* as a whole. This verse refers to the recitation of the Qur'ān in the *Fajr* Prayer rather than to merely reciting it during the hours of the morning. The Qur'ān, thus, indirectly suggests the different acts which comprise Prayer. Guided by these allusions, the Prophet Muḥammad (peace be on him) laid down the component parts of Prayer, and which the Muslims continue to follow to this day.

95. The statement that '*qur'ān al-fajr* – the Morning Prayer – is witnessed' means that it is witnessed by angels, a fact that has also been clearly stated in the traditions. (Al-Bukhārī, *K. Tafsīr al-Qur'ān; Sūrah Banī Isrā'īl;* al-Tirmidhī, *al-Sunan, K. al-Tafsīr, 'Bāb wa min Sūrah Banī Isrā'īl'* – Ed.) Although angels witness all Prayers, as they indeed witness all good deeds, the recitation of the Qur'ān in Morning Prayer has an importance all of its own. The reason being that in this Prayer the Prophet (peace be on him) used to prolong his recitation of the Qur'ānic verses. The Companions followed the same practice and Muslim jurists subsequently declared lengthy recitation in *Fajr* Prayer to be a 'recommended' or 'preferable' (*mustaḥabb*) act.

Incidentally, this verse also hints at the times for the five obligatory Prayers which were prescribed on the occasion of the Prophet's Ascension. According to this verse, the first Prayer – *Fajr* – should be offered before sunrise and the remaining four Prayers should be offered between the time beginning with the 'decline of the sun' through to the 'thickening of the night'. This directive was further elaborated by Gabriel who provided the Prophet (peace be on him) with information concerning the time of each Prayer. We find a tradition from Ibn 'Abbās in both Abū Dā'ūd and al-Tirmidhī which sheds light on the question.

On the authority of Ibn 'Abbās, the Prophet (peace be on him) said:

> Gabriel was twice leader of the Prayer which I offered near the Ka'bah. On the first occasion he offered the *Zuhr* Prayer when the sun had just passed the meridian no more than the thong of a shoe. Then he led the *'Aṣr*

Prayer when the shadow of everything was equal to its size. Then he led the *Maghrib* Prayer at the time when the sun had just set and a man breaks his fast. Then he led the *'Ishā'* Prayer as soon as the red glow of twilight (*shafaq*) disappeared. Then he offered the *Fajr* Prayer when the morning light had just appeared, at the time when eating becomes forbidden for him who fasts. On the second occasion he led the *Ẓuhr* Prayer when the shadow of everything was equal to its size and *'Aṣr* Prayer when the shadow of everything became double its size, and *Maghrib* Prayer at its previous time; and offered the *'Ishā'* Prayer when a third of the night had passed; and he offered the *Fajr* Prayer when there was a fair amount of light to make the earth visible. Gabriel turned to me and said: 'Muḥammad, these are the times of the Prayers as observed by the Prophets before you; the right time of each Prayer is between the two time-limits.' (Al-Tirmidhī, *al-Sunan, Abwāb al-Ṣalāh, 'Bāb mā jā' min Mawāqīt al-Ṣalāh'* – Ed.)

There are allusions to the times of Prayer in the Qur'ān itself. For example, in *Sūrah Hūd* it is said: 'And establish the Prayer at the two ends of the day and in the first hours of the night' (*Hūd* 11: 114). A similar point is made in *Sūrah Ṭā Hā*: 'And Glorify Allah, praising Him before sunrise and before sunset, and glorify Him in the watches of the night and at the end of the day' (*Ṭā Hā* 20: 130). We also learn from *Sūrah al-Rūm*: 'So give glory to Allah when you reach eventide and when you rise in the morning: to Him be praise in the heavens and the earth; and in the late afternoon and when the day begins to decline' (*al-Rūm* 30: 17–18).

One of the major considerations underlying the regulations concerning the times of Prayer is to ensure that any and all resemblance to rituals of sun-worship is excluded.

It should be borne in mind that the sun was always one of the greatest deities and that its worshippers were especially wont to offer their thanks and prayers at sunrise and sunset. Hence, to offer Prayer precisely at the time when the sun was rising or setting was prohibited. Likewise, worship of the sun was especially performed when the sun reached the meridian. It was, therefore, enjoined upon Muslims to offer the Morning Prayer before the sun had risen, and that the Prayers of the daytime be offered after the sun was past the meridian. This consideration is clearly stated by the Prophet (peace be on him) in several traditions. 'Amr ibn 'Abasah relates that when he asked the Prophet (peace be on him) about the time when Prayers should be offered, he replied:

> Offer the Morning Prayer [until the time of sunrise], then refrain from offering Prayer until the sun goes well up, for at the time when it is rising, it rises between the two horns of the Devil. This is the moment when the unbelievers prostrate themselves before it. (Muslim, *K. Salāt al-Musāfirīn wa Qaṣrihā, 'Bāb Islām 'Amr ibn 'Abasah'* – Ed.)

After mentioning the *'Aṣr* Prayer, the Prophet (peace be on him) said:

(79) And rise from sleep during the night as well,[96] an additional Prayer for you;[97] possibly your Lord will raise you to an honoured position.[98]

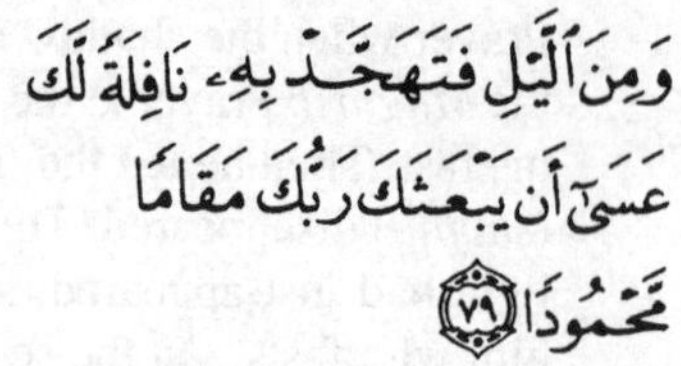

Offer the *'Aṣr* Prayer and then refrain from praying until the sun sets, for when the sun sets it sets between the two horns of the Devil; this is the time when the unbelievers prostrate themselves before it. (*Loc. cit.*)

The statement that the sun rises and sets between the horns of the Devil made in this tradition is a metaphor. The underlying reason behind the metaphor is that the Devil has made the time of sunrise and sunset a means by which he can mislead many people. In other words, when people prostrate themselves at the sight of the rising or setting sun, it seems as if Satan has brought the sun on his head and that he is carrying it away on his head. The equivocation in the statement is removed by the Prophet's own statement, viz. that the unbelievers prostrate themselves before it at that moment. This clearly explains the reason for the interdiction of Prayer at sunrise, sunset and mid-day.

96. The word *tahajjud* means to rouse oneself from sleep. To perform *tahajjud* at night signifies the act of rising from sleep during the night and then praying.

97. The word *nafl* signifies supererogation, something over and above that which is obligatory. The use of this word suggests that whereas the five Prayers mentioned earlier are obligatory, the sixth referred to here is in addition.

98. Here, it is proclaimed that God will bestow upon the Prophet (peace be on him) an exalted position in both the present world and the Next. It will be a position of eminence, and one which will evoke universal appreciation and praise. It will be in sharp contrast to the situation that was obtaining at that time when the Prophet's opponents heaped every kind of derogation, abuse and slander upon him. For the time was not far off when the whole world would reverberate with tributes paid to the Prophet (peace be on him), and these by all and sundry. This will be the exalted position of the Prophet (peace be on him) in the present world. As for the Next World, there too the Prophet (peace be on him) will be the object of everyone's praise. There he will enjoy a position of unique privilege in that God will accept his intercession. This forms an integral part of the 'exalted station' mentioned in this verse.

(80) And pray: 'My Lord! Cause me to enter wherever it be, with truth, and cause me to exit, wherever it be, with truth,[99] and support me with authority from Yourself.'[100]

(81) And proclaim: 'The truth has come, and falsehood has vanished. Surely falsehood is ever bound to vanish.'[101]

وَقُل رَّبِّ أَدْخِلْنِي مُدْخَلَ صِدْقٍ
وَأَخْرِجْنِي مُخْرَجَ صِدْقٍ وَاجْعَل
لِّي مِن لَّدُنكَ سُلْطَانًا نَّصِيرًا ﴿٨٠﴾
وَقُلْ جَاءَ الْحَقُّ وَزَهَقَ الْبَاطِلُ
إِنَّ الْبَاطِلَ كَانَ زَهُوقًا ﴿٨١﴾

99. This prayer, taught to the Prophet (peace be on him) by God, is significant. It indicates that the time of migration was close at hand. It is for this reason that he is directed to pray such that he might always adhere to the truth: if he leaves a place, he should do so for the sake of truth; and if he enters a place, he should also do so for the sake of truth.

100. The prayer consists of asking God either to endow him with authority, or to aid him by causing some governmental authority to be his supporter such that he might restore righteousness, stem the tide of lewdness and sin, and make God's law of justice prevail in a world steeped in corruption. This is the sense in which Ḥasan al-Baṣrī and Qatādah interpreted this verse. The same interpretation was adopted by such high-standing commentators on the Qur'ān as al-Ṭabarī and Ibn Kathīr. The interpretation is further corroborated by the following tradition: 'God eradicates by means of authority what He does not eradicate by means of the Qur'ān.' (Cited in Ibn Kathīr, *Tafsīr*, in the comments on *Banī Isrā'īl* 17, verses 80–1 – Ed.)

This shows that the reform which Islam seeks to bring about cannot be accomplished merely by preaching and by sermons. Accomplishment of that reform also requires the use of political power and authority. Now, since God Himself taught the Prophet (peace be on him) to pray for such authority, it is quite evident that to seek governmental power and to strive for its acquisition so as to make the true faith prevail in human life, and so as to implement the *Sharī'ah* and to enforce the punishments laid down in God's Law is not only lawful but is also both required and desirable.

It is also evident from this that those who denounce the seeking of political power as sheer worldliness are altogether mistaken. For the charge of worldliness only applies if someone seeks political power for their own personal ends. It is quite different if it is sought solely to promote the cause of the true faith. In that case, far from being an act of worldliness, it is an

(82) What We are sending down in the course of revealing the Qur'ān is a healing and a grace for those who have faith; but it adds only to the ruin of the wrong-doers.[102] ▶

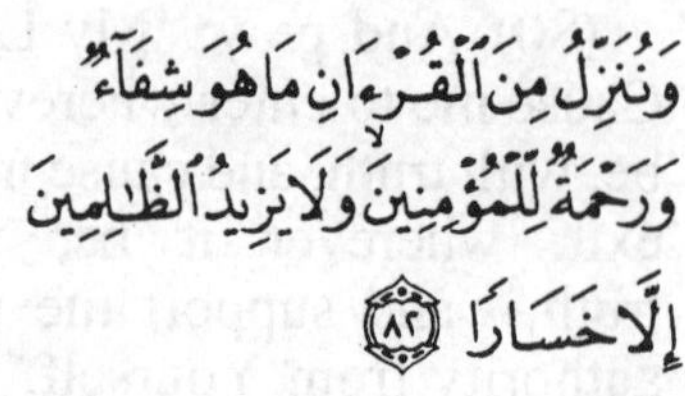

unmistakable requisite of godliness. For if obtaining a sword and waging *jihād* is not a sin, how then can it be sinful to obtain political authority to enforce the injunctions of the *Sharī'ah*?

101. This declaration came at a time when a large number of Muslims had forsaken their hearth and home in Makka and taken refuge in Abyssinia. As for the rest of the Muslims, they were living a miserable life in and around Makka, suffering from harsh persecutions. Even the life of the Prophet (peace be on him) was constantly in danger. The forces of falsehood seemed preponderant. There were no signs promising the success of the truth even in the distant future. Against this backdrop, the Prophet (peace be on him) was asked to proclaim to the unbelievers that the truth had come and that falsehood had perished. Given the situation pertaining at the time, his proclamation appeared to many people at best a tall claim, and the unbelievers simply laughed it away. Within nine years of that declaration, however, the Prophet Muḥammad (peace be on him) had entered Makka as its conqueror, destroying falsehood symbolized by the more than 360 idols which lay in the precincts of the Ka'bah. According to 'Abd Allāh ibn Mas'ūd, on the day of the conquest of Makka, as the Prophet (peace be on him) struck the idols in the Ka'bah, he repeatedly said: 'The truth has come and falsehood has perished. Indeed falsehood was destined to perish. The truth has come and falsehood shall neither make its appearance nor return.' (Al-Bukhārī, *K. al-Tafsīr, Sūrah Banī Isrā'īl, 'Bāb wa qul jā' al-Ḥaqq . . . .'* – Ed.)

102. The Qur'ān is God's mercy for those who seek to be guided by it and who follow its teachings. The Qur'ān cures such people of all the intellectual, spiritual, social and cultural maladies which bedevil their lives. As for the evil-doers who reject the Qur'ān and wilfully turn away from it, its impact is quite different. Such people are not allowed to remain in the state in which they were at the time before the Qur'ān was revealed, or when they were ignorant of the Qur'ān. The loss which they will suffer will be that much greater than anything they suffered previously. For the loss which they suffered before the Qur'ān was revealed or before they knew about it was a loss caused by ignorance. But if someone had been made aware of the Qur'ān and its message, and thus knew the distinction between truth and falsehood, then there was no

(83) Whenever We bestow favours upon man, he arrogantly turns away and draws aside; and whenever evil visits him, he is in utter despair. (84) Say (O Prophet!): 'Each one acts according to his own manner. Your Lord knows well who is best-guided to the right path.'

(85) They ask you about 'the spirit'. Say: 'The spirit comes by the command of my Lord, but you have been given only a little knowledge.'[103] ▶

وَإِذَآ أَنْعَمْنَا عَلَى ٱلْإِنسَٰنِ أَعْرَضَ وَنَـَٔا
بِجَانِبِهِۦ ۖ وَإِذَا مَسَّهُ ٱلشَّرُّ كَانَ يَـُٔوسًا
(٨٣) قُلْ كُلٌّ يَعْمَلُ عَلَىٰ شَاكِلَتِهِۦ
فَرَبُّكُمْ أَعْلَمُ بِمَنْ هُوَ أَهْدَىٰ سَبِيلًا
(٨٤) وَيَسْـَٔلُونَكَ عَنِ ٱلرُّوحِ ۖ قُلِ
ٱلرُّوحُ مِنْ أَمْرِ رَبِّى وَمَآ أُوتِيتُم
مِّنَ ٱلْعِلْمِ إِلَّا قَلِيلًا (٨٥)

excuse for him not to follow the truth. If that person continued to reject it and adamantly persisted in his effort then this means that he is not simply ignorant, but also perverse and iniquitous; he consciously loves falsehood and has an innate revulsion against the truth. Such a person is akin to those who, after becoming aware of the difference between poison and its antidote, deliberately opt for the former. In view of their awareness, such people will be considered fully responsible for their errors and will be duly punished for the sins they commit. They will suffer not on account of their prior ignorance but on account of their persistent perversity, hence the loss they will suffer is bound to be greater than that of those who are simply ignorant. This point is eloquently, albeit succinctly, expressed in the following words: 'The Qur'ān will either be an evidence in your favour, or against you.' (See Muslim, *K. al-Ṭahārah, 'Bāb Faḍl al-Wuḍū' '* – Ed.)

103. It is generally assumed that the word *rūḥ* here signifies 'life'. Some people had asked the Prophet (peace be on him) about the essence of life. In response, they are told that it comes by the command of God. We have, however, serious reservations about this view since the context of the verse does not support such an interpretation. Such an interpretation would only be apt if the verse was taken out of its context and studied in isolation, i.e. as if it was an independent statement. In fact, if we here consider *rūḥ* to mean life, the passage becomes incoherent to the point of sounding peculiar. Let us recall that just a little before this verse two categories of people are mentioned – one, those for whom the Qur'ān is both a 'healing' and a 'mercy', and two, those

(86) Had We willed, We could take away what We have revealed to you, then you would find none to help you in recovering it from Us. (87) [Whatever you have received] is nothing but grace from your Lord. Indeed His favour to you is great.[104] (88) Say: 'Surely, if men and *jinn* were to get together to produce the like of this Qur'ān, they will never be able to produce the like of it, howsoever they might help one another.'[105]

وَلَئِن شِئْنَا لَنَذْهَبَنَّ بِٱلَّذِىٓ أَوْحَيْنَآ
إِلَيْكَ ثُمَّ لَا تَجِدُ لَكَ بِهِۦ عَلَيْنَا وَكِيلًا
﴿٨٦﴾ إِلَّا رَحْمَةً مِّن رَّبِّكَ ۚ إِنَّ فَضْلَهُۥ
كَانَ عَلَيْكَ كَبِيرًا ﴿٨٧﴾ قُل لَّئِنِ
ٱجْتَمَعَتِ ٱلْإِنسُ وَٱلْجِنُّ عَلَىٰٓ أَن يَأْتُوا۟
بِمِثْلِ هَٰذَا ٱلْقُرْءَانِ لَا يَأْتُونَ بِمِثْلِهِۦ
وَلَوْ كَانَ بَعْضُهُمْ لِبَعْضٍ ظَهِيرًا ﴿٨٨﴾

who, because of their rejection of the Qur'ān, are denounced for their iniquity and ingratitude – and that soon after the present verse, the Qur'ān puts forth evidence to establish that it was a revelation from God. In this context it appears incomprehensible for a statement to be made to the effect that living beings are endowed with life by God's command.

The context of the verse in fact makes it quite clear that the word *rūḥ* here signifies either revelation or the angel who communicates revelation. The polytheists had in fact posed the question: What is the source of the Qur'ān? In reply, God directs the Prophet (peace be on him) to inform the inquirers about the origin or source of the Qur'ān – that it comes by the command of God. The knowledge and understanding of the polytheists was so poor that they were unable to see the difference between two discourses, one whose source is God and the other whose source is man.

This interpretation of the statement is preferable, first of all, because it makes sense in the context in which it occurs. Additionally, at different points in the Qur'ān when such a statement is made, recourse is made to more or less the same words. For example, in *al-Mu'min* it is stated: 'He sends revelation to any of His servants whom He pleases that He may warn of the day when they will be brought together (*al-Mu'min* 40: 15). Similarly, in *al-Shūrá* (42: 52) the same point is made: 'And thus have We, by Our command, sent a revelation to you. You did not know prior to that what was revelation and what was faith.'

Among early scholars Ibn 'Abbās, Qatādah and Ḥasan al-Baṣrī interpret the verse along similar lines. Ibn Jarīr al-Ṭabarī ascribes this view to Ibn 'Abbās on the authority of Qatādah. Strangely enough, however, he adds that Ibn 'Abbās only expressed this view secretly. In *Rūḥ al-Ma'ānī* the opinion of Ḥasan al-Baṣrī and Qatādah has been quoted in the following words: 'The *rūḥ* [here] stands for Gabriel, and the question in fact was how he [i.e. Gabriel] came down and how he conveyed revelation to the heart of the Prophet (peace be on him).' (See al-Ālūsī, *Rūḥ al-Ma'ānī,* vol. 15, p. 152, comments on *Banī Isrā'īl* 17, verse 85 – Ed.)

104. Although this statement is addressed to the Prophet (peace be on him), it is aimed at the unbelievers who had expressed the opinion that the Qur'ān had been authored either by the Prophet (peace be on him), or someone else who after authoring it had secretly passed it on to him. They are told here in no uncertain terms that the Qur'ān was not authored by the Prophet (peace be on him) but was instead bestowed upon him by none other than God Himself. Were God to deprive him of the Qur'ān, neither the Prophet (peace be on him) nor anyone else would be able to produce such a miraculous Book.

105. The same challenge occurs in the Qur'ān on three previous occasions (see *al-Baqarah* 2: 23–4; *Yūnus* 10: 38, and *Hūd* 11: 13) and later also in *al-Ṭūr* 52: 33–4). The content of all the verses referred to above is in response to the allegation of the unbelievers that the Qur'ān had been composed by the Prophet (peace be on him) and then falsely ascribed to God. All this was refuted. Additionally, one may recall in this context what had been said on an earlier occasion: 'Tell them, had Allah so willed, I would not have recited the Qur'ān to you, nor would Allah have informed you of it. I have spent a lifetime among you before this. Do you, then, not use your reason?' (*Yūnus* 10: 16).

The evidence put forward in these verses to establish that the Qur'ān is the word of God consists of three arguments:

First, it is emphasized that the Qur'ān is miraculous in respect of its language, style, manner of argument, content, and the information it provides relating to the realm that lies beyond the ken of sense-perception; in sum, that human beings are totally incapable of producing anything like it. The unbelievers had claimed that the Qur'ān had been authored by an individual, but the fact is that even if all human beings were to combine their efforts, they would still not be able to produce a Book of the Qur'ān's magnitude. In fact, those who disbelieve in the Qur'ān would fail to produce a Book like the Qur'ān even if they were to enlist the support of all men and even the *jinn* whom they regard as their deities and whose godhead the Qur'ān emphatically repudiates.

Second, it is pointed out that the Prophet Muḥammad (peace be on him) did not emerge on the public scene from nowhere. He had lived for a full forty years amidst his people. Did the unbelievers ever hear from him anything that would bear the least resemblance to the Qur'ān in style, approach and content? Now, since that was definitely not the case, how could they explain how such a phenomenal change had suddenly come about in the Prophet's discourse, in his

(89) We have explained
things for people in the Qur'ān
in diverse ways to make them
understand the Message, yet
most people obstinately persist in disbelief. (90) They
said: 'We shall not accept your
Message until you cause a
spring to gush forth for us
from the earth; (91) or that
there be a garden of palms and
vines for you and then you
cause rivers to abundantly
flow forth through them;
(92) or you cause the sky to
fall on us in pieces as you
claimed, or you bring Allah
and the angels before us, face
to face; ►

وَلَقَدْ صَرَّفْنَا لِلنَّاسِ فِي هَٰذَا ٱلْقُرْءَانِ
مِن كُلِّ مَثَلٍ فَأَبَىٰٓ أَكْثَرُ ٱلنَّاسِ إِلَّا
كُفُورًا ﴿٨٩﴾ وَقَالُوا۟ لَن نُّؤْمِنَ
لَكَ حَتَّىٰ تَفْجُرَ لَنَا مِنَ ٱلْأَرْضِ يَنۢبُوعًا
﴿٩٠﴾ أَوْ تَكُونَ لَكَ جَنَّةٌ مِّن نَّخِيلٍ
وَعِنَبٍ فَتُفَجِّرَ ٱلْأَنْهَٰرَ خِلَٰلَهَا
تَفْجِيرًا ﴿٩١﴾ أَوْ تُسْقِطَ ٱلسَّمَآءَ كَمَا
زَعَمْتَ عَلَيْنَا كِسَفًا أَوْ تَأْتِيَ بِٱللَّهِ
وَٱلْمَلَٰٓئِكَةِ قَبِيلًا ﴿٩٢﴾

---

language, diction, ideas, information, mode of thinking and style of expression? How was he able to present something as excellent and exalted as the Qur'ān?

Third, people were also reminded that the Prophet Muḥammad (peace be on him) had lived in their midst, and expressed himself on a great many subjects as well as recited to them many verses from the Qur'ān. Now, his discourse was divided into two categories: (a) the Qur'ān, and (b) the Prophet's ordinary discourse. The fact that the discourse which the Prophet (peace be on him) referred to as God's own speech – the Qur'ān – was so very different in language and style, from his own discourse, even though both were verbalized by him, was evident even at the time when the Prophet (peace be on him) lived in the midst of his compatriots, and is still evident today. Furthermore, given that a great many of the Prophet's statements and his addresses to his people are extant in the works of *Ḥadīth,* one cannot, therefore, fail to notice that the language and style of these utterances are very different from that of the Qur'ān. The difference is so pronounced that anyone who has the least sense of language and literature cannot dare to say that both the Qur'ān and the material preserved in the collections of *Hadīth* are the work of the same author. (For further elaboration, see *Towards Understanding the Qur'ān,* vol. IV, *Yūnus* 10, n. 21, pp. 19–21, and *al-Ṭūr* 52, nn. 22–7).

(93) or that there come to be for you a house of gold, or that you ascend to the sky – though we shall not believe in your ascension [to the skies] – until you bring down a book for us that we can read.' Say to them (O Muḥammad!): 'Holy is my Lord! Am I anything else than a human being, who bears a message (from Allah)?'[106]

أَوْ يَكُونَ لَكَ بَيْتٌ مِّن زُخْرُفٍ أَوْ تَرْقَىٰ فِي
السَّمَآءِ وَلَن نُّؤْمِنَ لِرُقِيِّكَ حَتَّىٰ تُنَزِّلَ
عَلَيْنَا كِتَٰبًا نَّقْرَؤُهُۥ قُلْ سُبْحَانَ رَبِّي
هَلْ كُنتُ إِلَّا بَشَرًا رَّسُولًا ﴿٩٣﴾

106. A rejoinder to the unbelievers' demands for miracles was made above in verse 59. The present verse responds, once again, to the same demand but in a somewhat different manner. The eloquence and effectiveness of this succinct rejoinder beggars description. The Prophet's enemies were wont to argue that if he was a true Messenger of God, he should make this apparent by some sign, for example, by causing a stream to gush forth or a flourishing orchard to appear with streams of water flowing through it. Or he should signal to the sky and command it to fall upon his opponents, instantly crushing them; or bring into being a palace of gold by a mere blow of his breath; or he should merely raise a cry and both God and His angels should appear before them testifying that Muḥammad had indeed been designated as His Messenger; or that he should climb up to the heavens before their very eyes and then bring forth a letter from God which they might be able to touch and read. In response to all this a comprehensive reply is being given: (verse 93) 'Say: "Holy is my Lord! Am I anything else than a human being, who bears a message (from Allah)?"' This statement suggests that the Prophet (peace be on him) claimed to be no more than a human being who had been entrusted with a message from God. Never did he claim that he himself was God. Had he claimed godhead, or omnipotence, people would have been justified in asking him to do those things that they had requested as a sign.

From the very beginning, the Prophet (peace be on him) claimed only that he had brought a message from God, and that those who wanted to test him, should do so by evaluating his message. As for those who wished to accept Islam, they should do so after carefully examining his message and satisfying themselves that it was indeed true and stood to reason. Conversely, if they decided to reject Islam, they should do so only after having carefully considered it and found it to be deficient or faulty. Likewise, if they had to

(94) Whenever guidance
came to people, nothing prevented men from believing
except that they said: 'Has
Allah sent a human being as
Messenger?'[107] (95) Say:
'Had angels been walking
about in peace on the earth,
We would surely have sent to
them an angel from the
heavens as Messenger.'[108]

وَمَا مَنَعَ ٱلنَّاسَ أَن يُؤْمِنُوٓا۟ إِذْ جَآءَهُمُ
ٱلْهُدَىٰٓ إِلَّآ أَن قَالُوٓا۟ أَبَعَثَ ٱللَّهُ بَشَرًا
رَّسُولًا ﴿٩٤﴾ قُل لَّوْ كَانَ فِى ٱلْأَرْضِ
مَلَٰٓئِكَةٌ يَمْشُونَ مُطْمَئِنِّينَ
لَنَزَّلْنَا عَلَيْهِم مِّنَ ٱلسَّمَآءِ
مَلَكًا رَّسُولًا ﴿٩٥﴾

---

decide whether the Prophet (peace be on him) was truthful or not, they should look closely at his life, his conduct, and his work. But rather than focus their attention on such relevant matters, they chose instead to demand that the Prophet (peace be on him) tear the earth asunder and make the sky crumble and fall in pieces about them. How preposterous they all are, for what have such things got to do with the message and mission of a Prophet?

107. Throughout the ages, ignorant people have entertained the misconception that it is impossible for a human being to be God's Prophet. Hence, whenever a Prophet came and people saw him living a normal human life – that he ate and drank, married, and was found to be made of the same flesh and bone as themselves – they instantly declared that he could not possibly be a Prophet for the simple reason that he too was a human being. Ironically enough, it was not unusual that with the passage of time some of the immoderate admirers of a Prophet would reject the idea of his being human. They did so by resorting to the strange argument that since he was a Prophet, he could not possibly then be human! Hence, at times such a person has been declared by some people to be God, the Son of God, or the incarnation of God. In short, the combination of humanity and prophethood in one person always appears enigmatic to those who are ignorant of the truth. (For further elaboration, see *Yā Sīn* 36, n. 11.)

108. The Messenger's task does not merely consist in transmitting his Message. He is also required to reform human life in the light of his Message, and is required to apply the principles of that message to human life, including his own. In addition, a Messenger also has to concern himself with solving the intellectual problems faced by people in their effort to grasp his Message, and to organize and train those who accept his Message so as to bring into existence a society in conformity with his teachings. Furthermore, he is required to

(96) Tell them (O Prophet!): 'Allah suffices as a witness between me and you. Allah is well aware and fully observes everything pertaining to His creatures.'[109]

(97) Whomsoever Allah guides is rightly guided; and whomsoever Allah lets go astray, you shall find none – apart from Him – who could protect him.[110] We shall muster them all on the Day of Resurrection, on their faces, blind and dumb and deaf.[111] Hell shall be their refuge. Every time its fire subsides, We will intensify for them its flame. (98) That will be their recompense because they disbelieved in Our signs and said: 'What! When we shall be reduced to bones and particles (of dust), shall we be raised again as a new creation?' ▶

قُلْ كَفَىٰ بِٱللَّهِ شَهِيدًۢا بَيْنِى
وَبَيْنَكُمْ إِنَّهُۥ كَانَ بِعِبَادِهِۦ خَبِيرًۢا
بَصِيرًا ﴿٩٦﴾ وَمَن يَهْدِ ٱللَّهُ فَهُوَ
ٱلْمُهْتَدِ وَمَن يُضْلِلْ فَلَن تَجِدَ لَهُمْ
أَوْلِيَآءَ مِن دُونِهِۦ وَنَحْشُرُهُمْ يَوْمَ
ٱلْقِيَٰمَةِ عَلَىٰ وُجُوهِهِمْ عُمْيًا وَبُكْمًا
وَصُمًّا مَّأْوَىٰهُمْ جَهَنَّمُ كُلَّمَا
خَبَتْ زِدْنَٰهُمْ سَعِيرًا ﴿٩٧﴾ ذَٰلِكَ
جَزَآؤُهُم بِأَنَّهُمْ كَفَرُوا۟ بِـَٔايَٰتِنَا
وَقَالُوٓا۟ أَءِذَا كُنَّا عِظَٰمًا وَرُفَٰتًا أَءِنَّا
لَمَبْعُوثُونَ خَلْقًا جَدِيدًا ﴿٩٨﴾

---

struggle against those who reject, oppose and attempt to subvert his cause. He has to do all this in order to overwhelm the forces of evil and corruption and bring about the reform for which he has been raised. Now, if all these tasks are to be performed in a human milieu, it is obvious that only a human being, rather than someone belonging to a different species – say an angel – can perform them.

109. God was well aware of the efforts of the Prophet (peace be on him) to make people see the truth and reform their lives. God was equally aware of the hostile campaign launched by the Prophet's opponents. And since it is God Who is the ultimate judge of all, people should remember that it is sufficient that God is aware of all the facts needed to make such judgements.

110. If the door to guidance has been shut against someone by God on account of his love for error and his adamant opposition to the truth, and if God

(99) Have they not perceived that Allah, Who has created the heavens and the earth, has the power to create the like of them? He has fixed a term for them about which there is no doubt. And yet the wrong-doers obstinately persist in disbelief.

(100) Tell them (O Prophet!): 'Even if you owned the treasures of my Lord's mercy you would have held them back for fear of spending them.' Man is indeed ever niggardly.[112]

۞ أَوَلَمْ يَرَوْاْ أَنَّ ٱللَّهَ ٱلَّذِى خَلَقَ
ٱلسَّمَٰوَٰتِ وَٱلْأَرْضَ قَادِرٌ عَلَىٰٓ أَن
يَخْلُقَ مِثْلَهُمْ وَجَعَلَ لَهُمْ أَجَلًا
لَّا رَيْبَ فِيهِ فَأَبَى ٱلظَّٰلِمُونَ إِلَّا
كُفُورًا ﴿٩٩﴾ قُل لَّوْ أَنتُمْ تَمْلِكُونَ
خَزَآئِنَ رَحْمَةِ رَبِّىٓ إِذًا لَّأَمْسَكْتُمْ
خَشْيَةَ ٱلْإِنفَاقِ ۚ وَكَانَ ٱلْإِنسَٰنُ
قَتُورًا ﴿١٠٠﴾

has allowed him to proceed along the path of error and evil which he himself wanted to pursue in the first place, then it will be impossible for anyone else to bring him back to the right path. When someone turns away from the truth and feels satisfied with falsehood, God creates the circumstances which make it possible for his hatred for truth and his satisfaction with falsehood to mount. For God does not compel those who intentionally seek error to embrace the truth. Furthermore, it is beyond the power of anyone else to change their hearts.

111. The unbelievers' lives were characterized by their refusal to perceive, heed or speak the truth. They will be raised on the Day of Resurrection with their erstwhile attitude to the truth.

112. This alludes to a statement made in the earlier part of this *sūrah* (see verse 55 above): 'Your Lord knows all who dwell in the heavens and the earth.' One of the psychological reasons why the Makkan polytheists were unable to affirm the prophethood of Muḥammad (peace be on him) was that such an affirmation clearly implied an acceptance of the Prophet's greatness. Such an attitude is understandable since people are generally disinclined to recognize the greatness of their contemporaries. In view of this common shortcoming, it is being pointed out here that those who are so predisposed to niggardliness will hardly act with liberality if they are given the keys to God's infinite treasure.

(101) We granted Moses nine clear signs.[113] Ask the Children of Israel about it: when these signs came forth, Pharaoh said to him: 'O Moses, I think that you are bewitched'[114] ▶

وَلَقَدْ ءَاتَيْنَا مُوسَىٰ تِسْعَ ءَايَٰتٍۭ بَيِّنَٰتٍ فَسْـَٔلْ بَنِىٓ إِسْرَٰٓءِيلَ إِذْ جَآءَهُمْ فَقَالَ لَهُۥ فِرْعَوْنُ إِنِّى لَأَظُنُّكَ يَٰمُوسَىٰ مَسْحُورًا ﴿١٠١﴾

113. This, again, is in response to the unbelievers' demands to perform miracles and constitutes the third rejoinder on the subject. It will be recalled that the unbelievers contended that their believing in the Prophet (peace be on him) was contingent upon the latter's performance of certain miracles. In response, they are told that in the past Pharaoh witnessed no less than nine miracles in succession. But since he was bent upon not believing, he was unable to change his views even after witnessing all those miracles. One should in any case recall Pharaoh's tragic end, the result of his persistent disbelief.

The nine clear signs of God to which this verse alludes are specifically mentioned in *al-A'rāf* (see verses 107–33). They are as follows: (i) the rod of Moses which turned into a serpent; (ii) Moses' bright hand which shone like the sun; (iii) the defeat, in public, of the magicians' sorcery; (iv) the countrywide famine; (v) the flood; (vi) the locusts; (vii) the frogs; (viii) the lice; (ix) the rain of blood. All these calamities smote Pharaoh's people in succession.

114. The Makkan polytheists would often brand the Prophet Muḥammad (peace be on him) as one afflicted by sorcery. This allegation has already been mentioned in verse 47 of the present *sūrah*: 'You are only following one who is bewitched.' Here it is being emphasized how very similar were the people of Pharaoh who had hurled exactly the same charge at Moses (peace be on him).

It is also pertinent to discuss another related issue at this stage. Some of those who reject the *Hadīth* have expressed the view that this Qur'ānic verse proves that the entire corpus of *Hadīth* is unreliable. They mention the tradition which reports that the Prophet Muḥammad (peace be on him) was once afflicted with sorcery. (See al-Bukhārī, *K. al-Ṭibb, 'Bāb al-Siḥr . . . .'* – Ed.) Yet the Qur'ān, they claim, refutes this contention.

Let us consider the matter more carefully. Here, the Qur'ān states clearly that Pharaoh's allegation that Moses (peace be on him) was affected by sorcery is false. Nevertheless, in *Ṭā Hā*, the Qur'ān says: 'Then suddenly it appeared to Moses, owing to their magic, as if their ropes and staffs were running. So Moses' heart was filled with fear' (*Ṭā Hā* 20: 66–7). The words of the verses

(102) Moses replied: 'You know well that no one but the Lord of the heavens and the earth has sent these as eye opening proofs.[115] I truly think, O Pharaoh, that you are indeed doomed.'[116] ▶

قَالَ لَقَدْ عَلِمْتَ مَآ أَنزَلَ هَٰٓؤُلَآءِ إِلَّا
رَبُّ ٱلسَّمَٰوَٰتِ وَٱلْأَرْضِ بَصَآئِرَ
وَإِنِّى لَأَظُنُّكَ يَٰفِرْعَوْنُ
مَثْبُورًا ﴿١٠٢﴾

suggest quite categorically that at that particular moment Moses was affected by sorcery. Now, were the rejecters of *Ḥadīth* to follow the logical implication of their contention, would they not be led to contending that here the Qur'ān contradicts itself and corroborates Pharaoh's allegation?

Those who raise such objections are presumably not aware of the sense in which the Makkan unbelievers and Pharaoh branded the Prophet Muḥammad and the Prophet Moses (peace be on them) respectively with sorcery. What they imagined was that some enemy had worked magic upon them, causing them to become mad, and it was under the spell of this magic that each of them claimed to be God's Messenger, and each of them came forth with a strange message. It is this which the Qur'ān refutes.

As for the possibility of a Prophet being temporarily affected by sorcery – whether that sorcery affected the whole or just a part of his body – this is not denied by the Qur'ān. Such a temporary effect of sorcery is no different from someone being hurt by a piece of rock which has been hurled at him. Now, the opponents of Moses and Muḥammad (peace be on them) did not claim that they had fallen victims to sorcery for just a few moments. And since they did not express such an opinion there was no occasion for the Qur'ān to deny their contention. For, if a Prophet is temporarily affected by magic, this is not inconsistent with the station of a Prophet. If a Prophet, like anyone else, can be affected by poison, or can suffer other bodily injuries, so too can he be affected by magic. There is no reason why this should be considered inconsistent with his office of prophethood. What is inconsistent with prophethood is that the mental faculties of a Prophet are so overpowered by magic that he begins both to say strange things and act differently under its spell. The unbelievers claimed that this is precisely what happened to Moses and Muḥammad (peace be on them). And again, it is precisely this contention which the Qur'ān emphatically refutes.

115. The Prophet Moses (peace be on him) made this statement to emphasize the fact that the calamities which befell people could only be from God. There was widespread famine across the land. Frogs in large numbers infested a vast area, covering hundreds of thousands of square miles. Food

(103) At last Pharaoh decided to uproot Moses and the Children of Israel from the land, but We drowned him together with all who were with him; (104) and thereafter We said to the Children of Israel: 'Now dwell in the land,[117] but when the promised time of the Hereafter comes, We shall bring you all together.'

(105) We have sent down the Qur'ān with the truth, and it is with the truth that it has descended. And We have not sent you but to proclaim good news and give warning.[118] ▶

فَأَرَادَ أَن يَسْتَفِزَّهُم مِّنَ الْأَرْضِ
فَأَغْرَقْنَٰهُ وَمَن مَّعَهُۥ جَمِيعًا ﴿١٠٣﴾ وَقُلْنَا
مِنۢ بَعْدِهِۦ لِبَنِىٓ إِسْرَٰٓءِيلَ ٱسْكُنُوا۟
ٱلْأَرْضَ فَإِذَا جَآءَ وَعْدُ ٱلْءَاخِرَةِ جِئْنَا
بِكُمْ لَفِيفًا ﴿١٠٤﴾ وَبِٱلْحَقِّ أَنزَلْنَٰهُ
وَبِٱلْحَقِّ نَزَلَ ۗ وَمَآ أَرْسَلْنَٰكَ إِلَّا مُبَشِّرًا
وَنَذِيرًا ﴿١٠٥﴾

---

stocks in the barns throughout the land were eaten up by weevils. Calamities such as these could not be the result of some magician's sorcery, or the manifestation of some human being's extraordinary power.

It is also significant that each calamity which befell the people did so after Moses had warned Pharaoh that such things would happen if he did not give up his obduracy. In such a case, only a lunatic or an incorrigibly obdurate person can entertain the belief that such calamities could have been brought about by anyone other than the Lord of the Universe.

116. The Prophet Moses (peace be on him) had stated quite clearly and while he was not afflicted with sorcery, that Pharaoh was doubtlessly doomed. This was evident from the latter's total obduracy, and his firm refusal to accept the truth.

117. This brings out the true moral of the narrative. The Makkan polytheists were intent on uprooting the Prophet Muḥammad (peace be on him) and the Muslims from Arabia. They are told that Pharaoh intended to do the same with the Prophet Moses (peace be on him) and the Israelites. However, what really happened was that while Pharaoh and his people were annihilated, Moses (peace be on him) and his followers became firmly established in the land which was earlier under Pharaoh's sway. Now if the Makkan unbelievers

(106) We have revealed the Qur'ān in parts that you may recite it to people slowly and with deliberation; and (for that reason) We have revealed it gradually [to suit particular occasions].[119] (107) Tell them, (O Prophet!): 'Believe in it, or do not believe'; when it is recited to those who were given the knowledge before its revelation,[120] they fall down upon their faces in prostration, (108) and say: 'Glory be to our Lord. Surely the promise of our Lord was bound to be fulfilled.'[121] (109) And they fall down upon their faces, weeping, and their humility increases when they hear recitation of the Qur'ān.[122]

وَقُرْءَانًا فَرَقْنَٰهُ لِتَقْرَأَهُۥ عَلَى ٱلنَّاسِ عَلَىٰ
مُكْثٍ وَنَزَّلْنَٰهُ تَنزِيلًا ﴿١٠٦﴾ قُلْ
ءَامِنُوا۟ بِهِۦٓ أَوْ لَا تُؤْمِنُوٓا۟ إِنَّ ٱلَّذِينَ أُوتُوا۟
ٱلْعِلْمَ مِن قَبْلِهِۦٓ إِذَا يُتْلَىٰ عَلَيْهِمْ
يَخِرُّونَ لِلْأَذْقَانِ سُجَّدًا ﴿١٠٧﴾ وَيَقُولُونَ
سُبْحَٰنَ رَبِّنَآ إِن كَانَ وَعْدُ رَبِّنَا لَمَفْعُولًا
﴿١٠٨﴾ وَيَخِرُّونَ لِلْأَذْقَانِ يَبْكُونَ
وَيَزِيدُهُمْ خُشُوعًا ۩ ﴿١٠٩﴾

chose to follow in the footsteps of Pharaoh and his people their end would be no different from theirs.

118. It is not part of a Prophet's job to somehow persuade those who are not prepared to make up their minds about what is true and what is false after they have been able to examine the teachings of the Qur'ān. It is not a Prophet's role to work wonders – to make streams of water gush forth and gardens suddenly sprout. All that he is required to do is to present the truth before people and to impress upon them that he who accepts it will benefit and he who rejects it will suffer.

119. This is in response to the detractors' charge as to why God's Message was not revealed in one piece, why it was delivered, instead, at intervals. Is God, they inquire, also in need of time to think, just like human beings, before saying something? This question has been discussed earlier at some length (see *Towards Understanding the Qur'ān,* vol. IV, *al-Naḥl* 16: 101–2 and the notes thereon, pp. 364–5), and so we need not concern ourselves further with it here.

(110) Say to them (O Prophet!): 'Call upon Him as Allah or call upon Him as al-Raḥmān; call Him by whichever name you will, all His names are good.[123] Neither offer your Prayer in too loud a voice, nor in a voice too low; but follow a middle course.'[124] (111) And say: 'All praise be to Allah Who has neither taken to Him a son, nor has He any partner in His kingdom; nor does He need, out of weakness, anyone to protect Him.'[125] So magnify Him greatly.

قُلِ ادْعُوا اللَّهَ أَوِ ادْعُوا الرَّحْمَٰنَ أَيًّا مَّا
تَدْعُوا فَلَهُ الْأَسْمَاءُ الْحُسْنَىٰ وَلَا
تَجْهَرْ بِصَلَاتِكَ وَلَا تُخَافِتْ بِهَا
وَابْتَغِ بَيْنَ ذَٰلِكَ سَبِيلًا ﴿١١٠﴾ وَقُلِ
الْحَمْدُ لِلَّهِ الَّذِي لَمْ يَتَّخِذْ وَلَدًا وَلَمْ يَكُن
لَّهُ شَرِيكٌ فِي الْمُلْكِ وَلَمْ يَكُن لَّهُ وَلِيٌّ
مِّنَ الذُّلِّ وَكَبِّرْهُ تَكْبِيرًا ﴿١١١﴾

---

120. This refers to those People of the Book who are familiar with the teachings of the Scriptures and who are conversant with its characteristic style.

121. On listening to the Qur'ān, they instantly realized that the Messenger alluded to in the Scriptures had come.

122. The Qur'ān notes this attitude of the righteous ones from among the People of the Book. (See, for instance, *Āl 'Imrān* 3: 113–15 and 199 and *al-Mā'idah* 5: 82–5.)

123. This is in response to the polytheists' objection to calling God by the name *al-Raḥmān*. They claimed that while they were familiar with the appellation Allah, there seemed no justification for using the appellation *al-Raḥmān*. Their objection was based on their unfamiliarity with this word as a personal name of God.

124. According to Ibn 'Abbās, when the Prophet Muḥammad (peace be on him) or his Companions offered Prayers in Makka or recited the Qur'ān, the unbelievers often made noises and even hurled abuse at them. (Muslim, *K. al-Ṣalāh, 'Bāb al-Tawassuṭ fī al-Qirā'ah fī al-Ṣalāh . . . .'* – Ed.) The believers

were, therefore, counselled neither to recite in such a loud voice that would attract the attention of the unbelievers who might interrupt their Prayers, nor to recite in a voice inaudible even to people close by. During the Madinan period of the Prophet's life when the situation altogether changed, there was no need to follow this injunction. However, whenever Muslims are faced with the kind of circumstances which they encountered during the Makkan period of the Prophet's life, they should follow the directive laid down here.

125. This statement is tinged with irony. The polytheists believed that God had assigned various departments or parts of His kingdom to different gods and saints. That God should have to fall back on the support of others implied that God lacked the power needed to control His dominion. It is for this reason that the Qur'ān points out here that God does not lack power so that He would be compelled to appoint deputies and assistants to help Him.

Sūrah 18

al-Kahf

(The Cave)

(Makkan Period)

Title

The title of this *sūrah* is derived from verse 10: 'When the youth sought refuge in the cave . . . .' The title simply signifies that this is the *sūrah* in which the word *kahf* (cave) occurs.

This *sūrah* marks the beginning of the group of *sūrahs* revealed in the third period of the Prophet's Makkan life. We have divided the Makkan phase of the Prophet's life into four major periods of which some details can be found in the 'Introduction' to *Sūrah al-An'ām*. (See *Towards Understanding the Qur'ān*, vol. II, pp. 211–12 – Ed.) According to this division of the Prophet's Makkan life, the third period commenced around the fifth year and continued until the tenth year of his prophethood. What sets this period apart from others is that during this period the Quraysh escalated their opposition to the Prophet (peace be on him). In the second period the opposition of the Quraysh had been largely confined to campaigns of lampoon and ridicule, of slander and abuse, and to maliciously false propaganda against the Prophet's movement. Occasionally they also tried to tempt or terrorize his followers. During the third period, however, the Makkans subjected the believers to violent suppression, ruthless torture, and to severe economic deprivation.

This inevitably prompted a considerable number of Muslims to migrate to Abyssinia. As for those Muslims that remained, including the Prophet (peace be on him) and his family, they were confined to the quarters called Sha'b Abī Ṭālib and had to face a full-scale economic and social boycott. Nonetheless, there were two people during this period because of whom at least two influential families of the Quraysh continued to protect the Prophet (peace be on him). These two persons were his uncle, Abū Ṭālib and his own wife, Khadījah. This period came to an end with the death of both of them, in the tenth year of prophethood. Shortly after, the fourth period commenced, and with it the Muslims of Makka were confronted with wide-scale persecution. Eventually all Muslims including the Prophet (peace be on him), were compelled to leave Makka.

If one reflects over the contents of this *sūrah,* it will be evident that it was most probably revealed during the beginning of the third period of the Prophet's Makkan life. It was revealed at a time when the Muslims were facing severe persecution and a little before their migration to Abyssinia. The story of the People of the Cave was narrated to these persecuted Muslims so as to raise their spirit. It was also narrated to apprise them of the sacrifices that the believers had made in the past in the cause of their faith.

Subject Matter

This *sūrah* was revealed in response to three questions which were posed by the Makkan polytheists. After consulting with the People of the Book, they had put these questions to the Prophet (peace be on him) so as to test him. As for these questions, they were as follows: Who were the People of the Cave? What is the true nature of the story of Khiḍr?* What is the story of Dhū al-Qarnayn? All these stories pertain to Judaeo-Christian history and were scarcely known to people in the Arabian peninsula. The People of the Book had selected these stories carefully so as to test whether or not any extraordinary source of knowledge was available to the Prophet (peace be on him). God subsequently provided adequate answers to their questions through the Prophet (peace be on him). What is more, He hinted at how each of the three stories was significant for understanding the situation obtaining in Makka at the time, viz. the conflict between Islam and Unbelief. The following points are of special importance:

(1) It was pointed out that the People of the Cave believed in the same monotheism which was being expounded by the Qur'ān.

---

*According to some reports (see, for instance, Ibn Hishām, *Sīrah,* vol. I, p. 30), the second question was about the nature of the soul, which had been answered in *Banī Isrā'īl* (see 17: 85 ff.). There was, however, a gap of several years between the revelation of *Sūrahs Banī Isrā'īl* and *al-Kahf.* Moreover, there are three rather than two stories related in *al-Kahf.* We are, therefore, inclined to believe that the second question concerned Khiḍr rather than spirit. Our view seems to be corroborated by an allusion in the Qur'ān itself. (For details see n. 61 below.)

Also, the situation of the People of the Cave was no different from that of the Makkan Muslims who were then being subjected to severe persecution. Likewise, the attitude towards the People of the Cave by their own people was quite similar to the attitude displayed by the Quraysh unbelievers to the Prophet (peace be on him) and his followers. Moreover, through this story the believers are instructed that even if the unbelievers are dominant and the believers oppressed, the latter should not surrender to falsehood. Instead, they should go boldly forth and strive for their cause, putting their trust in God. In this regard the Makkan unbelievers are told, *en passant,* that the story of the People of the Cave is evidence in support of the doctrine of the Hereafter. Since God had awakened the People of the Cave after a long spell of death-like slumber, it clearly shows that He has full power to raise the dead to life – a doctrine which they denied.

(2) In the course of narrating the story of the People of the Cave, the main story is set aside for a moment to mention the wrong-doing and injustice, and the humiliation and degradation which the Makkan leaders and aristocracy had perpetrated on the small, nascent Muslim community of their town. On the one hand, the Prophet (peace be on him) is directed neither to make any compromise with the perpetrators of wrong-doing and injustice, nor to pay much attention to affluent unbelievers in preference to his poor Companions. On the other hand, the affluent unbelievers of Makka are admonished to refrain from exulting in their ephemeral wealth and prosperity, and to seek instead virtues of abiding value.

(3) The story of Khiḍr and Moses was recounted in the same context. The story was narrated in such a manner that it served a two-fold purpose. On the one hand, the questions posed by the unbelievers were answered; and on the other, the suffering Muslims were comforted. The moral of the story is that man is in no position to plumb the depths of the wisdom of Providence. It is for this reason that man stands perplexed and begins to question, out of curiosity, why things should happen the way they do, sometimes considering certain events to be shockingly atrocious. If the totality of relevant facts were disclosed to him, man would know that there is good reason for things to happen the way they do.

(4) This is followed by the story of Dhū al-Qarnayn. The interlocutors, are informed that while people generally feel proud of their petty positions of power and eminence, Dhū al-Qarnayn

was singularly different. He was a great ruler and a great conqueror who controlled vast resources. And yet, none of these turned his head and he remained in a state of submission to his Creator. People foolishly think that they will enjoy life indefinitely; that their little palaces and mansions and orchards, and the resplendent life which they enjoy intensely will endure; but not Dhū al-Qarnayn. Despite the impenetrable wall that he managed to build for protective purposes, he placed all his trust in God. As long as God so willed, the wall would shield him and his people from attack. And, if and when, God willed something different, the wall would be riddled by a host of cracks and holes ensuring that it would crumble to pieces. Thus, the questions which had been put forward to test the Prophet (peace be on him) were thrown back at the unbelievers who had originally posed them. Thereafter, the main points which had been mentioned at the outset were repeated in the closing part of the *sūrah*. These points affirmed that monotheism and the Next Life are doubtlessly truths and that it is in man's own interest to believe in them, to shape his life according to those doctrines and to live with full consciousness of his accountability to God. Failure to do so will be to man's own detriment, and all his efforts will go to waste.

In the name of Allah, the Merciful, the Compassionate.

(1) Praise be to Allah, Who has revealed to His servant the Book shorn of all crookedness;[1] (2) an unerringly straight Book, meant to warn of a stern punishment from Allah, and to proclaim, to those who believe and work righteous deeds, the tiding that theirs shall be a good reward (3) wherein they shall abide for ever; (4) and also to warn those who say: 'Allah has taken to Himself a son',[2] (5) a thing of which they have no knowledge, neither they nor did their ancestors.[3] Dreadful is the word that comes out of their mouths. What they utter is merely a lie.

(6) (O Muḥammad!): If they do not believe in this message, you will perhaps torment yourself to death with grief, sorrowing over them.[4] ▶

ٱلْحَمْدُ لِلَّهِ ٱلَّذِىٓ أَنزَلَ عَلَىٰ عَبْدِهِ ٱلْكِتَـٰبَ
وَلَمْ يَجْعَل لَّهُۥ عِوَجَا ﴿١﴾ قَيِّمًا لِّيُنذِرَ
بَأْسًا شَدِيدًا مِّن لَّدُنْهُ وَيُبَشِّرَ ٱلْمُؤْمِنِينَ
ٱلَّذِينَ يَعْمَلُونَ ٱلصَّـٰلِحَـٰتِ أَنَّ
لَهُمْ أَجْرًا حَسَنًا ﴿٢﴾ مَّـٰكِثِينَ فِيهِ
أَبَدًا ﴿٣﴾ وَيُنذِرَ ٱلَّذِينَ قَالُوا۟
ٱتَّخَذَ ٱللَّهُ وَلَدًا ﴿٤﴾ مَّا لَهُم بِهِۦ مِنْ
عِلْمٍ وَلَا لِـَٔابَآئِهِمْ كَبُرَتْ كَلِمَةً
تَخْرُجُ مِنْ أَفْوَٰهِهِمْ إِن يَقُولُونَ
إِلَّا كَذِبًا ﴿٥﴾ فَلَعَلَّكَ بَـٰخِعٌ نَّفْسَكَ
عَلَىٰٓ ءَاثَـٰرِهِمْ إِن لَّمْ يُؤْمِنُوا۟ بِهَـٰذَا
ٱلْحَدِيثِ أَسَفًا ﴿٦﴾

---

1. This means that there is nothing in the Qur'ān which, being intrinsically complex and enigmatic, defies understanding. Likewise, there is nothing in the Qur'ān which is repugnant to truth and righteousness making it difficult for any truth-loving person to believe in it.

2. Those who declare that God had begotten offspring include Christians, Jews and the polytheists of Arabia.

3. That is, when the polytheists declare that someone is either God's son, or that God has taken him as His son, such statements are not based on any

(7) Surely, We have made all that is on the earth an embellishment for it in order to test people as to who of them is better in conduct. (8) In the ultimate, We shall reduce all that is on the earth to a barren plain.[5]

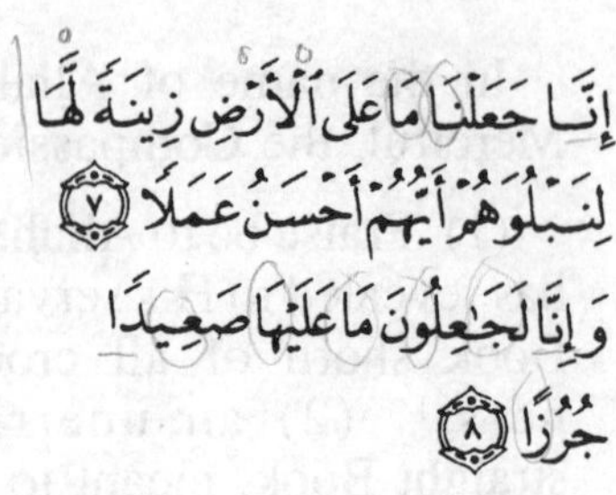

dependable knowledge of which they might feel sure. People in fact are wont to make such arbitrary statements in a fit of exaggerated devotion. Little do they realize how outrageously misleading their doctrine is. Nor do they fully recognize what blasphemy they utter, and what fabrication they foist upon God.

4. This refers to the condition of the Prophet (peace be on him) at that time. It is evident that he was not grieved primarily because of the persecution to which he and his Companions were subjected. What really grieved him and caused him intense suffering was the realization that while he sincerely wished to salvage his people from the doctrinal error and moral corruption in which they were steeped they, however, showed no readiness to get out of the rut in which they were in. He, therefore, felt convinced that his people would be seized by God's scourge. For while the Prophet (peace be on him) exerted himself day and night to save his people, they virtually insisted that God's punishment should inflict them. In a *ḥadīth,* the Prophet (peace be on him) portrays this condition in the following words:

> 'The analogy of me and of the people is this: a person who lit a fire which illuminated the area around him, but this caused moths and other insects which (are inclined to) fall into fire to fall into it. This person tried to somehow pull them away (from the fire), but they overpower him and plunge into the fire. My position is that I seek to restrain you from the fire but you plunge into it.' K. al-Riqāq, *'Bāb al-Intihā' min al-Ma'āṣī'*. (See also Muslim, *K. al-Faḍā'il, 'Bāb Shafaqat Ṣallā Allāh 'alayhi wa sallam 'alá Ummatih'* . . . – Ed.)

The verse apparently states that the Prophet (peace be on him) is so intensely concerned with the welfare of his people, the Quraysh, that he might lose his life. The verse, however, also contains a message of consolation for the Prophet (peace be on him), for it also subtly tells him that he is not to blame for the failure of his people to believe and do good. It is beyond anyone's power to turn people into believers. The Prophet (peace be on him) should, therefore,

(9) Do you think that the People of the Cave[6] and the Inscription[7] were one of Our wondrous signs?[8] (10) When those youths sought refuge in the Cave and said: 'Our Lord! Grant us mercy from Yourself and provide for us rectitude in our affairs', ▶

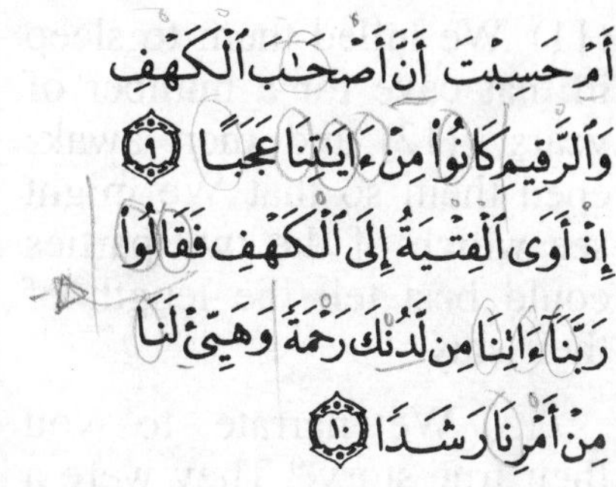

persevere in his mission: giving good tidings to those who believe, and warning those that do not of the evil consequences of disbelieving.

5. The earlier verse (i.e. verse 6) was addressed to the Prophet (peace be on him) while these two verses (i.e. verses 7–8) are addressed to the unbelievers. After saying a word of comfort to the Prophet (peace be on him), the deniers of the truth are told – albeit without addressing them directly – that the riches and pomp and grandeur of the world which fascinate them, are all transient, and are meant to test human beings. Many are misled by the opportunity to live in ease and luxury, mistakenly believing that they were created simply to enjoy the pleasures of worldly life. As a result, such people pay no heed to the counsel of sincere well-wishers. They fail to appreciate that the opportunities for enjoyment are in fact simply a means of testing how people behave. The purpose of the test is precisely to distinguish those who immerse themselves in the pleasures of life from those who remain conscious of their duty to serve their Lord and follow the right way. The day this test ends, this life of enjoyment will also be brought to a sudden close, and the earth will become merely a vast stretch of desolation.

6. In Arabic, the word *kahf* signifies a large cave, whereas the word *ghār* signifies a relatively narrow and small cave.

7. There is disagreement among scholars concerning the word *al-raqīm.* Some Companions and Successors are reported to have expressed the view that it is the name of the place where the event took place, and that it was located between Elia, i.e. the land (i.e. 'Aqabah) and Palestine. Some of the early commentators on the Qur'ān, however, are of the opinion that *al-raqīm* refers to the epitaph which was placed at the Cave as a monument to the People of the Cave. Mawlānā Abū al-Kalām Āzād has expressed his preference for the former view in his work *Tarjumān al-Qur'ān.* (See his *Tarjumān al-Qur'ān* (New Delhi, Sahatyah Academy, 1970), vol. 4, pp. 406–7 – Ed.) He considers

(11) We lulled them to sleep in that cave for a number of years (12) and then awakened them so that We might see which of the two parties could best tell the length of their stay.

(13) We narrate to you their true story.[9] They were a party of young men who had faith in their Lord, and We increased them in guidance[10] ▶

فَضَرَبْنَا عَلَىٰٓ ءَاذَانِهِمْ فِى ٱلْكَهْفِ
سِنِينَ عَدَدًا ﴿١١﴾ ثُمَّ بَعَثْنَٰهُمْ لِنَعْلَمَ
أَىُّ ٱلْحِزْبَيْنِ أَحْصَىٰ لِمَا لَبِثُوٓا۟ أَمَدًا ﴿١٢﴾
نَّحْنُ نَقُصُّ عَلَيْكَ نَبَأَهُم بِٱلْحَقِّ ۚ إِنَّهُمْ
فِتْيَةٌ ءَامَنُوا۟ بِرَبِّهِمْ وَزِدْنَٰهُمْ
هُدًى ﴿١٣﴾

---

this to be the same place as Rekem mentioned in the Bible (see *Joshua* 18: 27). Āzād also identifies this with the ancient Nabataean city of Petra. He has failed, however, to take into account the fact that Rekem was mentioned in the Bible among the cities inherited by the Benjeminites. According to the *Book of Joshua,* this was located to the west of the River Jordan and the Sea of Lot. Obviously, it would be out of the question for Petra to be located there. For the ruins of Petra were discovered in an area which was separated from the territory under the occupation of the Benjeminites by the territory of Judah and Edomia. It is for this reason that modern archaeologists are strongly disinclined to regard Petra and al-Raqīm as the same place. (See art. 'Petra' in *Encyclopaedia Britannica,* 1946 edition, vol. 17, p. 658; also art. 'Petra' in the 15th edition of *Encyclopaedia Britannica,* vol. 9, p. 339 – Ed.)

In our view, *al-raqīm* signifies epitaph, or the inscription on the epitaph rather than the name of any particular place.

8. The unbelievers are being asked whether they consider it impossible to believe that God – Who out of His power could bring the earth and the heaven into existence – would be unable to cause a group of people to remain asleep for three hundred years and then restore them to their former state – youthful and healthy – as if they had never been subjected to such a long spell of slumber? If the unbelievers were to keep in mind God's power to create such objects as the sun, the moon and the earth, they would never have considered that act at all difficult for God.

9. The earliest evidence of this story is found in the *Sermons* of the Christian priest James of Sarug, a work which is in Syriac. He was born a few years after

the death of the People of the Cave in 452 C.E. and he compiled his *Sermons* around 474 C.E.

This Syriac account reached the commentators of the Qur'ān and this explains why Ibn Jarīr al-Ṭabarī reproduced it in his *Commentary* under different chains of transmission. The same account reached Europe and was subsequently translated and summarized in Greek and Latin. Edward Gibbon provided a summarized version of the story based on these sources under the title 'The Seven Sleepers' in his *Decline and Fall of the Roman Empire*. (See Edward Gibbon, *The History of the Decline and Fall of the Roman Empire*, second edition, in six volumes, London, Murray, 1846, vol. 3, pp. 220–2.) Gibbon's account is so closely similar to the reports found in the works of Muslim commentators of the Qur'ān that both seem to have drawn on the same source. For example, the king who persecuted the People of the Cave, forcing them to retire to the cave, is called Daqyānūs, or Daqyanūs (see al-Ṭabarī's comments on this *sūrah*) or Daqyāus in Muslim sources. According to Gibbon, his name was Decius and he ruled over the Roman Empire from 249 C.E. to 251 C.E. His reign was notorious for the persecution of the followers of Jesus Christ (peace be on him). The city where the incident took place is called Afsus, or Afsaūs in Muslim sources, while Gibbon names it as Ephesus, which was the largest town and a famous Roman port on the western coast of Asia Minor. The ruins of this town can be found at a distance of some twenty to twenty-five miles from the present-day Turkish town and seaport of Izmir (Smyrna). (See Map 2.) Moreover, the Emperor during whose reign the People of the Cave woke up is referred to as Tīdhūsīs in Muslim sources (see, for instance, al-Ṭabarī's comments on the *sūrah* in his *Tafsīr* – Ed.) while, according to Gibbon, the event took place during the reign of Theodosius II who ruled over Rome from 408 to 450 C.E., after the Roman Empire's adoption of Christianity as its official religion.

The two accounts resemble each other so closely that the person sent to the town to bring food is called Yamlīkhā by Muslims and Yamblichus by Gibbon. The story, in all its details, is common to both sources. In its bare outline, the story mentions that while the disciples of Jesus Christ (peace be on him) were persecuted during the rule of Decius, the Seven Youths of Ephesus retired to the cave and finally woke up in the thirty-eighth year of the Emperor Theodosius, i.e. in 445 or 446 C.E., at a time when the entire Roman Empire had already embraced Christianity. According to this account, they remained in the Cave for about 196 years. Some Orientalists have, however, cast doubt on the Qur'ānic version on the ground that the Qur'ān specifies the period of their stay to be 309 years. (For our view on this subject, however, see n. 25 below.)

The Syriac and Qur'ānic versions of the story differ in certain respects. Gibbon had the temerity to dub the Prophet (peace be on him) as 'ignorant' on account of these differences. (See Gibbon, *The Decline and Fall of the Roman Empire, op. cit.*, vol. 3, p. 220, n. 45 – Ed.) This is bold indeed of Gibbon who himself recognizes the Syriac work to have been composed by someone in Syria some thirty or forty years after the event. It is evident that oral traditions

(14) and strengthened their hearts when they stood up and proclaimed: 'Our Lord is the Lord of the heavens and the earth. We shall call upon no other god beside Him; (for if we did so), we shall be uttering a blasphemy.' (15) (Then they conferred among themselves and said): 'These men, our own people, have taken others as gods beside Him: why do they not bring any clear evidence that they indeed are gods? Who can be more unjust than he who foists a lie on Allah? (16) And now that you have dissociated yourselves from them and from whatever they worship beside Allah, go and seek refuge in the Cave.[11] Your Lord will extend His mercy to you and will provide for you the means for the disposal of your affairs.'

وَرَبَطْنَا عَلَىٰ قُلُوبِهِمْ إِذْ قَامُوا
فَقَالُوا رَبُّنَا رَبُّ السَّمَٰوَٰتِ وَالْأَرْضِ
لَن نَّدْعُوَا مِن دُونِهِۦٓ إِلَٰهًا لَّقَدْ قُلْنَآ
إِذًا شَطَطًا ﴿١٤﴾ هَٰٓؤُلَآءِ قَوْمُنَا
اتَّخَذُوا مِن دُونِهِۦٓ ءَالِهَةً لَّوْلَا
يَأْتُونَ عَلَيْهِم بِسُلْطَٰنٍۭ بَيِّنٍ
فَمَنْ أَظْلَمُ مِمَّنِ افْتَرَىٰ عَلَى اللَّهِ
كَذِبًا ﴿١٥﴾ وَإِذِ اعْتَزَلْتُمُوهُمْ وَمَا
يَعْبُدُونَ إِلَّا اللَّهَ فَأْوُۥٓا إِلَى
الْكَهْفِ يَنشُرْ لَكُمْ رَبُّكُم مِّن
رَّحْمَتِهِۦ وَيُهَيِّئْ لَكُم مِّنْ أَمْرِكُم
مِّرْفَقًا ﴿١٦﴾

usually undergo changes in the process of transmission from one land to another. Gibbon's judgement would have made some sense had the Syriac account been fully authentic and reliable. But we know that is not the case. Hence the insistent contention that if the Qur'ānic account varies to any extent from the Syriac account the Qur'ān must be wrong can only behove those whose religious bigotry has totally overwhelmed them. (See also Appendix I.)

10. When these youths became sincere men of faith, God enhanced their guidance and enabled them to faithfully adhere to the truth. This also gave them the strength to prefer courting all kinds of dangers as opposed to timidly surrendering before the forces of falsehood.

(17) Had you looked at them in the Cave[12] it would have appeared to you that when the sun rose, it moved away from their cave to the right; and when it set, it turned away from them to the left, while they remained in a spacious hollow in the Cave.[13] This is one of the Signs of Allah. Whomsoever Allah guides, he alone is led aright; and whomsoever Allah lets go astray, you will find for him no guardian to direct him. ▶

۞ وَتَرَى ٱلشَّمْسَ إِذَا طَلَعَت تَّزَٰوَرُ
عَن كَهْفِهِمْ ذَاتَ ٱلْيَمِينِ وَإِذَا
غَرَبَت تَّقْرِضُهُمْ ذَاتَ ٱلشِّمَالِ وَهُمْ
فِى فَجْوَةٍ مِّنْهُ ذَٰلِكَ مِنْ ءَايَٰتِ ٱللَّهِ
مَن يَهْدِ ٱللَّهُ فَهُوَ ٱلْمُهْتَدِ وَمَن
يُضْلِلْ فَلَن تَجِدَ لَهُۥ وَلِيًّا مُّرْشِدًا ﴿١٧﴾

---

11. At the time when these devout youths had to flee from the towns and take shelter in the mountains, the town of Ephesus was a major centre of idolatry and magic in Asia Minor. The splendid temple to the goddess Diana, which then adorned the town, was famous the world over. (For the goddess Diana, q.v., *Encyclopaedia Britannica* – Ed.) It attracted devotees from far-flung places who took part in rites of worship there. The sorcerers, soothsayers, and amulet-writers of Ephesus were well-known; theirs was a flourishing business all over Syria, Palestine and Egypt. The Jews, who attributed their skill in this field to the Prophet Solomon (peace be on him), also had an important share in this business. (See art. 'Ephesus' in *Cyclopaedia of Biblical Literature*.)

The plight of righteous people in this atmosphere – an atmosphere charged with polytheism and superstition – was summed up in the following remark about the People of the Cave: 'For if they should come upon us, they will stone us to death or force us to revert to their faith' (*al-Kahf* 18: 20).

12. In the course of this narration, mention of the youths' collective decision to take refuge in a cave in this mountainous region such that they might avoid being subjected to lapidation or compelled apostasy has been omitted.

13. The mouth of their cave faced north, thus preventing sunlight from entering it no matter what the season. The result being that the cave remained

(18) On seeing them you would fancy them to be awake though they were asleep; and We caused them to turn their sides to their right and to their left,[14] and their dog sat stretching out its two forelegs on the threshold of the Cave. Had you looked upon them you would have certainly fled away from them, their sight filling you with terror.[15]

(19) Likewise, We roused them in a miraculous way[16] that they might question one another. One of them asked: 'How long did you remain (in this state)?' The others said: 'We remained so for a day, or part of a day.' Then they said: 'Your Lord knows better how long we remained in this state. Now send one of us to the city with this coin of ours and let him see who has the best food, and let him buy some provisions from there. Let him be cautious and not inform anyone of our whereabouts. ▶

وَتَحْسَبُهُمْ أَيْقَاظًا وَهُمْ رُقُودٌ
وَنُقَلِّبُهُمْ ذَاتَ الْيَمِينِ وَذَاتَ
الشِّمَالِ وَكَلْبُهُم بَاسِطٌ ذِرَاعَيْهِ
بِالْوَصِيدِ لَوِ اطَّلَعْتَ عَلَيْهِمْ لَوَلَّيْتَ
مِنْهُمْ فِرَارًا وَلَمُلِئْتَ مِنْهُمْ رُعْبًا
١٨ وَكَذَٰلِكَ بَعَثْنَاهُمْ
لِيَتَسَاءَلُوا بَيْنَهُمْ قَالَ قَائِلٌ مِّنْهُمْ
كَمْ لَبِثْتُمْ قَالُوا لَبِثْنَا يَوْمًا أَوْ
بَعْضَ يَوْمٍ قَالُوا رَبُّكُمْ أَعْلَمُ بِمَا
لَبِثْتُمْ فَابْعَثُوا أَحَدَكُم
بِوَرِقِكُمْ هَٰذِهِ إِلَى الْمَدِينَةِ
فَلْيَنظُرْ أَيُّهَا أَزْكَىٰ طَعَامًا
فَلْيَأْتِكُم بِرِزْقٍ مِّنْهُ
وَلْيَتَلَطَّفْ وَلَا يُشْعِرَنَّ
بِكُمْ أَحَدًا ١٩

dark and it was impossible for any passer-by to observe the inmates of the cave from outside.

14. Even if someone were to carefully peep into the cave, he would have noticed that the seven people every now and again changed their positions. This would have made any observer believe that they were simply taking a rest rather than sleeping.

(20) For if they should come upon us, they will stone us to death or force us to revert to their faith whereafter we shall never prosper.' (21) Thus did We make their case known to the people of the city[17] so that they might know that Allah's promise is true, and that there is absolutely no doubt that the Hour will come to pass.[18] But instead of giving thought to this, they disputed with one another concerning the People of the Cave, some saying: 'Build a wall over them. Their Lord alone knows best about them.'[19] But those who prevailed over their affairs[20] said: 'We shall build a place of worship over them.'[21]

إِنَّهُمْ إِن يَظْهَرُوا عَلَيْكُمْ يَرْجُمُوكُمْ
أَوْ يُعِيدُوكُمْ فِي مِلَّتِهِمْ
وَلَن تُفْلِحُوا إِذًا أَبَدًا ﴿٢٠﴾
وَكَذَٰلِكَ أَعْثَرْنَا عَلَيْهِمْ
لِيَعْلَمُوا أَنَّ وَعْدَ اللَّهِ حَقٌّ
وَأَنَّ السَّاعَةَ لَا رَيْبَ فِيهَا إِذْ
يَتَنَٰزَعُونَ بَيْنَهُمْ أَمْرَهُمْ
فَقَالُوا ابْنُوا عَلَيْهِم بُنْيَٰنًا
رَّبُّهُمْ أَعْلَمُ بِهِمْ قَالَ الَّذِينَ
غَلَبُوا عَلَىٰ أَمْرِهِمْ لَنَتَّخِذَنَّ
عَلَيْهِم مَّسْجِدًا ﴿٢١﴾

15. The presence of a handful of people in a dark cave in a mountainous area, guarded by a dog, presented such an awesome spectacle that those who observed them would have run for their lives, presumably assuming them to be robbers. This was one of the main reasons why the truth about these people remained a mystery for so long. No one simply had the courage to enter the cave and find out the truth of the matter.

16. The manner in which these youths were roused from their long slumber was no less wondrous than the manner in which they were made to sleep, beyond the reach of the whole world.

17. When one of those youths went to the city to buy food, a world of change had already taken place. Pagan Rome had long since been Christianized. Perceptible changes were evident in the language, culture, civilization and dress of the people; in sum, almost everything had changed. Similarly, this young man from the cave, who in fact belonged to a period

about two centuries earlier, also struck everybody as an oddity since his overall demeanour, his dress, and his language were all antiquated. So, when he presented a coin dating from the time of Decius, the shopkeeper was simply baffled and looked at him with dazed eyes. According to the Syriac traditions, the shopkeeper thought that his customer had obtained the coin by laying his hands on some hidden ancient treasure. The shopkeeper, therefore, drew the attention of people around him to this strange man, and eventually the youth was brought before the authorities. In the course of investigations it was discovered that the youth was one of the followers of Jesus Christ who had fled some two centuries ago for fear of his faith. This news instantly spread among the Christians of the city. A huge crowd of people, accompanied by government officials, therefore, soon went to the cave. On realizing that they had been awakened from a sleep which had lasted for two hundred years, the People of the Cave greeted their fellow-Christians, and then lay down to rest and breathed their last.

18. According to Syriac traditions, a fierce controversy was then raging on the issue of the Resurrection and the Hereafter. True, most people had embraced Christianity under the influence of the Roman Empire, and as Christians one of their articles of faith was belief in the Hereafter. Nevertheless, Roman polytheism and idolatry and Greek philosophy still had a strong hold on the population. The result was that many people either denied or were sceptical about the Hereafter. What specially reinforced this attitude about the Hereafter was the influence of the Jews. A large Jewish population was evident in Ephesus, and of these the Sadducees openly denied the Hereafter. The Sadducees put forward arguments drawn from the Torah in their contention against the Hereafter, and Christian scholars were unable to produce any powerful and persuasive arguments to refute them. In *Matthew, Mark* and *Luke* we find references to the debate between the Sadducees and Jesus (peace be on him) on the question of the Hereafter. For some reason, Jesus' contention recorded in these three Gospels is so weak that this weakness is even acknowledged by Christian scholars. (See *Matthew* 22: 23–33; *Mark* 12: 18–27 and *Luke* 20: 27–40.) Consequently this strengthened the position of the deniers of the Hereafter, so much so that even those who strongly believed in the Hereafter began to entertain doubts about it. It was precisely at this moment that the People of the Cave were aroused from their long sleep, an incident which provided incontrovertible proof of life after death.

19. The context indicates that this statement was made by a group of righteous Christians. They were of the opinion that the People of the Cave should be left to lie in the positions in which they were found and that the mouth of the cave should be sealed off by erecting a wall against the side of the cave. In other words, it was not right to go about investigating about them for their Lord knew best who they were, what their status was, and what treatment should rightly be meted out to them.

20. This refers to the rulers of the Roman Empire and the clergy of the Christian Church. They were so powerful that true Christians, who held on to the true, original doctrines of Jesus Christ, made little impression on them. By the middle of the fifth century, the Christians in general, and the Roman Catholic Church in particular, fell prey to polytheism, saint-worship and grave-worship. Shrines of saints became objects of worship and statues of Jesus, Mary and the apostles adorned the churches.

In 431 C.E., just a few years before the People of the Cave were roused from their sleep, a Synod was held in Ephesus. This Council proclaimed as official doctrine of the Christian Church that Jesus was God and Mary was the Mother of God. Keeping this historical context in mind, it seems evident that the people mentioned in the present verse as 'those who prevailed over their affairs' are those who, as opposed to the true followers of Christ, had become the leaders of the Christian masses and thus held the reins of religious and political affairs. It is these people who sought to promote polytheism, and it is they who decided that the burial site of the People of the Cave should be turned into a shrine.

21. Some Muslim scholars have taken this verse to mean the opposite of what it truly means. They argue the legitimacy of erecting mausoleums, monuments and mosques on the tombs of saints. The Qur'ān, however, considers this a bad practice and erroneous. What the Qur'ān rather suggests here is that the cave should have served as a token to strengthen belief in Resurrection and the Hereafter; that these are realities which are bound to come to pass. It is ironic that this statement was seized upon by some people as a God-sent opportunity for engaging in polytheism, as a pretext for adding to the list of saints who could be worshipped. This is quite evident from the context in which the above verse occurs. In fact even if the context were disregarded, how can one use the statement to justify building mosques at the tombs of saints for this would be in flagrant opposition to many sayings of the Prophet (peace be on him)? Several of his sayings explicitly prohibit such a practice:

> God cursed the women who visit graves, and those who construct mosques at graves, and illuminate them. (See Aḥmad ibn Ḥanbal, *Musnad,* vol. 1, p. 229; al-Tirmidhī, *Sunan, Abwāb al-Ṣalāh, 'Bāb (mā jā' fī) Karāhiyah 'an yuttakhadh 'alá al-Qabr Masjidan'*; al-Nasā'ī, *Sunan, K. al-Janā'iz, 'Bāb al-Taghlīẓ fī Ittikhādh al-Sarj 'alā al-Qubūr'*; Ibn Mājah, *Sunan, K. al-Janā'iz, 'Bāb mā jā' fī al-Nahy 'an Ziyārat al-Nisā' al-Qubūr'* – Ed.)

> Lo! Those who preceded you made the graves of their Prophets into places of worship, but I forbid you from it. (Muslim, *K. al-Masājid wa Mawāḍi' al-Ṣalāh, 'Bāb al-Nahy 'an Binā' al-Masājid 'alá al-Qubūr wa Ittikhādh al-Ṣuwar fi-hā . . . .'* – Ed.)

(22) Some will say concerning them: 'They were three and their dog, the fourth'; and some will say: 'They were five, and their dog, the sixth' – all this being merely guesswork; and still others will say: 'They were seven, and their dog, the eighth.'[22] Say: 'My Lord knows their number best. Few know their correct number. So, do not dispute concerning their number, except cursorily, and do not question anyone about them.[23] ▶

سَيَقُولُونَ ثَلَٰثَةٌ رَّابِعُهُمْ كَلْبُهُمْ
وَيَقُولُونَ خَمْسَةٌ سَادِسُهُمْ
كَلْبُهُمْ رَجْمًۢا بِٱلْغَيْبِ ۖ وَيَقُولُونَ
سَبْعَةٌ وَثَامِنُهُمْ كَلْبُهُمْ ۚ قُل رَّبِّىٓ
أَعْلَمُ بِعِدَّتِهِم مَّا يَعْلَمُهُمْ إِلَّا قَلِيلٌ ۗ
فَلَا تُمَارِ فِيهِمْ إِلَّا مِرَآءً ظَٰهِرًا وَلَا
تَسْتَفْتِ فِيهِم مِّنْهُمْ أَحَدًا ﴿٢٢﴾

God cursed the Jews and the Christians who took the graves of their Prophets as places of worship. (Al-Bukhārī, *K. al-Janā'iz, 'Bāb mā Yukrah min Ittikhādh 'alá al-Qubūr . . .'*; Muslim, *K. al-Masājid wa Mawāḍi' al-Ṣalāh; al-Nahy 'an Binā' al-Masājid 'alā al-Qubūr wa Ittikhādh al-Ṣuwar fi hā . . .*; al-Nasā'ī, *K. al-Masājid, 'Bāb al-Nahy 'an Ittikhādh al-Qubūr Masājid'*; Aḥmad ibn Ḥanbal, *Musnad,* vol. 1, p. 218 – Ed.)

Such were the people that if a pious person among them died, they constructed a temple at his grave and painted in it those portraits they will be reckoned the worst creatures on the Last Day. (See al-Nasā'ī, *Sunan, al-Masājid, 'Bāb al-Nahy 'an Ittikhādh al-Qubūr Masājid*; Aḥmad ibn Ḥanbal, *Musnad,* vol. 6, p. 51; al-Bukhārī, *K. al-Janā'iz, 'Bāb Binā' al-Masājid 'alá al-Qabr*; Muslim, *K. al-Masājid wa Mawāḍi' al-Ṣalāh, 'Bāb al-Nahy 'an Binā' al-Masājid 'alā-Qubūr . . .'* – Ed.)

In view of these clear sayings from the Prophet (peace be on him) how can any God-fearing person use the above Qur'ānic statement – a statement which simply mentions an erroneous act by Christian priests and Roman rulers – as an argument in support of such a practice?

It seems pertinent to mention here that in 1834 Reverend T. Arundell published his observations in *Discoveries in Asia Minor*. According to him, he found traces of the tomb ruins of Mary and the seven youths, i.e. the People of the Cave, on a hillock adjoining the ancient city of Ephesus.

22. This shows that at the time of the revelation of the Qur'ān, approximately three hundred years after the incident, a number of stories were in circulation among the Christians about the People of the Cave. It also shows that no authentic version of the incident was available in all its details. This is understandable since the event took place long before the invention of the printing press whereafter it would have been possible for books containing accurate information about the event to have gained general circulation. As for the time which concerns us, the main sources of information about the incident were oral ones. With the passage of time, many details inevitably became mixed up with authentic verbal reports, with the result that accounts about the incident became legendary. We note, however, that the Qur'ān does not contradict the third statement mentioned here which says that the People of the Cave numbered seven. Hence, there are some grounds for believing that their actual number was indeed seven.

23. The purpose of the statement is to emphasize the fact that the number of the People of the Cave is not a matter of much consequence. What is really important is the lesson to be drawn from their story. The story teaches that men of faith ought never to deviate from truth, nor submit to falsehood. It also teaches that men of faith ought to place their trust entirely in God rather than in worldly resources. It also teaches that even if circumstances do not seem propitious for the truth to prosper, men of faith should still proceed in the cause of the truth, placing their trust entirely in God.

The story also dispels a serious misconception. At times people are led to the false belief that the apparent complex of causal relationships, which they call the laws of nature, are absolutely inalterable. What we call laws of nature are in fact the usual ways in which God lets things happen. He is not, however, bound by any such laws and has the power to set aside or alter these so-called 'laws' and to do whatever He wills, in flagrant contravention of the usual ways in which things happen. It is not at all difficult for God to cause someone to remain asleep for two hundred years and then rouse him from it and make him feel as if he had slept for just a few hours. It is also quite easy for Him to ensure that these two hundred years are not allowed to have any effect on that person's age, appearance, and health. All in all then it is quite evident that it is easily within God's power to resurrect all the human beings who have ever lived on earth, all at once, as has been foretold by the Prophets and the Scriptures.

The actual historical facts relating to the People of the Cave also provide a very useful lesson. They show how foolish people in all ages have been in failing to derive the right lesson from God's signs which have been sent to serve as a means of guidance for them; in fact, they have often been further misguided by these signs. The miracle of the People of the Cave should have further strengthened people's faith in the Hereafter. It is a pity that this very event led people to proceed in completely the opposite direction; the net result being that they contrived yet more saints whom they could worship.

These are the main lessons and points which one ought to draw from the story of the People of the Cave. But instead of taking note of these, people often

(23) And never say about anything: "I shall certainly do this tomorrow" (24) unless Allah should will it. And should you forget, (and make such a statement), remember your Lord and say: "I expect my Lord to guide me to what is nearer to rectitude than this." '24 ▶

وَلَا تَقُولَنَّ لِشَاْىۡءٍ إِنِّي فَاعِلٌ
ذَٰلِكَ غَدًا ﴿٢٣﴾ إِلَّآ أَن يَشَآءَ
ٱللَّهُۚ وَٱذۡكُر رَّبَّكَ إِذَا نَسِيتَ
وَقُلۡ عَسَىٰٓ أَن يَهۡدِيَنِ رَبِّي
لِأَقۡرَبَ مِنۡ هَٰذَا رَشَدًا ﴿٢٤﴾

get embroiled in trivial and far-fetched questions. They ask, for example, what was the total number of the People of the Cave? What were their names? What was the colour of their dog? Such questions can only be of interest to those who concern themselves with the husk rather than with the kernel; for those interested in irrelevant details rather than in the substance. Hence God has directed His Prophet (peace be on him), and through him all believers, that even if others raise irrelevant questions, they should refrain from answering them; nor should they waste their time on academic research pertaining to such irrelevant questions. They should rather concern themselves with substantive questions. It is presumably for this reason that God did not care to reveal the true number of the People of the Cave so as not to encourage those who have a penchant for fruitless and sterile intellectual pursuits.

24. We believe this to be a parenthetical statement which is thematically linked to the preceding verse. The preceding verse states that God alone knows the exact number of the People of the Cave and that it is pointless to try to ascertain their true number. One should, therefore, avoid wasting one's time on unsubstantive matters, and should refrain from pursuits that will lead nowhere. The question is of such trivial consequence that one should not even get involved with others in such debates.

At this stage, before proceeding to the next point, both the Prophet (peace be on him) and the believers are directed not to make categorical statements as to what they would do on the morrow. For no one knows what they will in fact be able to do. One does not know at all what lies in store for the future. Nor has one absolute power to do whatever one wills. So even if one were to unintentionally make any categorical statements as to what one will be able to do on the morrow, one should be instantly conscious and remember God, and make one's statement conditional with God's will. In other words, one should state that one will do a certain thing provided God so wills. In like manner, a person does not know for sure whether the act he intends will be beneficial for him or

(25) They remained in the Cave for three hundred years; and some others add nine more years.[25] (26) Say: 'Allah knows best how long they remained in it; for only He knows all that is hidden in the heavens and the earth. How well He sees; how well He hears! The creatures have no other guardian than Him; He allows none to share His authority.'

وَلَبِثُوا۟ فِى كَهْفِهِمْ ثَلَٰثَ مِا۟ئَةٍ سِنِينَ وَٱزْدَادُوا۟ تِسْعًا ﴿٢٥﴾ قُلِ ٱللَّهُ أَعْلَمُ بِمَا لَبِثُوا۟ ۖ لَهُۥ غَيْبُ ٱلسَّمَٰوَٰتِ وَٱلْأَرْضِ ۖ أَبْصِرْ بِهِۦ وَأَسْمِعْ ۚ مَا لَهُم مِّن دُونِهِۦ مِن وَلِىٍّ وَلَا يُشْرِكُ فِى حُكْمِهِۦٓ أَحَدًا ﴿٢٦﴾

whether some other action would be conducive to greater benefit. Hence, one ought to place one's reliance on God and say that one hopes God will direct one to the right judgement.

25. This is in continuation of the statement immediately preceding the parenthetical statement: 'Some people will say that they were three in number and the fourth was their dog . . .' This part of the earlier verse connects with the present verse: 'They remained in the Cave for three hundred years and some others add nine more years.' In our opinion these figures – three hundred or three hundred and nine years – have been mentioned by way of narrating the different opinions held by people on the question. The statement, therefore, about the period of stay in the cave is not God's, but rather the varying opinions of human beings. This is substantiated by what has been said in the very next verse in which the Prophet (peace be on him) has been asked to say that God knows best how long they actually remained in the cave. Had God Himself said that they remained in the cave for three hundred and nine years, the statement which follows would be meaningless. It is for this reason that 'Abd Allāh ibn 'Abbās has expressed the view that the statement is not God's; it rather merely recounts what people said on the matter. (See al-Ālūsī, *Rūḥ al-Ma'ānī*, vol. 15, p. 252.)

(27) (O Prophet!):[26] Recite to them from the Book of your Lord what has been revealed to you, for none may change His words; (and were you to make any change in His words) you will find no refuge from Him.[27] ▶

وَٱتْلُ مَآ أُوحِيَ إِلَيْكَ مِن كِتَابِ
رَبِّكَ لَا مُبَدِّلَ لِكَلِمَٰتِهِۦ وَلَن تَجِدَ
مِن دُونِهِۦ مُلْتَحَدًا ﴿٢٧﴾

26. After concluding the story of the People of the Cave, another subject is introduced. In this discourse comments are made about the problems which the Muslims of Makka were then facing.

27. This does not in any way mean that the Prophet (peace be on him) was inclined – God forbid – to alter the Qur'ān so as to placate the Makkan unbelievers and strike a deal with them, and that God asked the Prophet (peace be on him) not to do so. The fact is that this verse is directed to the unbelievers of Makka, even though it is addressed to the Prophet Muḥammad (peace be on him) who had no authority to make any alteration of his own accord to the Book of God. His task rather consisted in faithfully transmitting what had been revealed to him by God. The unbelievers had the option to accept what he had communicated to them on God's behalf or not; and those who accepted it were required to accept it *in toto*. If they were not convinced about the Prophet's Message then they were free to reject it. They could exercise either of these two options. It was quite out of the question, however, that the religion revealed by God could, in any way, be subjected to modifications, however minor, so as to suit peoples' fancies.

This has been said in response to the unbelievers' persistent demand that the Prophet (peace be on him) should not insist on the acceptance of his message in full. They asked the Prophet (peace be on him) to make at least some allowance for their ancestral faith, for their age-old customs and usages. What they proposed was a kind of compromise, involving give and take on both sides. They suggested that such a compromise would have the benefit of averting dissension. The Qur'ān frequently recounts this demand by the unbelievers and its response too is uniformly the same. To cite just one example:

> And whenever Our clear revelations are recited to them, those who do not expect to meet Us say: 'Bring us a Qur'ān other than this one, or at least make changes in it' (*Yūnus*: 10: 15).

(28) Keep yourself content with those who call upon their Lord, morning and evening, seeking His pleasure, and do not let your eyes pass beyond them. Do you seek the pomp and glitter of the world?[28] Do not follow him[29] whose heart We have caused to be heedless of Our remembrance, and who follows his desires, and whose attitude is of excess.[30] ▶

وَاصْبِرْ نَفْسَكَ مَعَ الَّذِينَ يَدْعُونَ
رَبَّهُم بِالْغَدَوٰةِ وَالْعَشِيِّ يُرِيدُونَ
وَجْهَهُۥ وَلَا تَعْدُ عَيْنَاكَ عَنْهُمْ تُرِيدُ
زِينَةَ الْحَيَوٰةِ الدُّنْيَا وَلَا تُطِعْ مَنْ
أَغْفَلْنَا قَلْبَهُۥ عَن ذِكْرِنَا وَاتَّبَعَ هَوَىٰهُ
وَكَانَ أَمْرُهُۥ فُرُطًا ﴿٢٨﴾

28. As reported by Ibn 'Abbās, the Quraysh elites advised the Prophet (peace be on him) that they were not prepared to sit in the company of people of such low status as Bilāl, Ṣuhayb, 'Ammār, Khabbāb and Ibn Mas'ūd. Were the Prophet (peace be on him) to get rid of them then they would be willing to visit him and spend time learning about his message. (See al-Qurṭubī's comments on *al-Kahf* 18: verse 28 in his *Commentary* – Ed.)

In response, God tells the Prophet (peace be on him) that he should be content with the company of those who had gathered around him merely to seek God's pleasure, and to remember God at all times of the day and night. There was no good reason for him to choose for his company those whose claim to importance rested on their affluence in preference to his sincere and devoted followers.

Once again, even though this directive is apparently addressed to the Prophet (peace be on him), it is meant to give a message to the Quraysh elites who are being told that their affluence and the pomp and glory in which they exulted carried no weight with God and His Messenger. As compared to them, those poor ones who were sincere and ever-conscious of God, were of much greater value.

All this has a striking similarity to the exchange between the Prophet Noah (peace be on him) and the notables of his nation. The latter used to tell the Prophet Noah (peace be on him): 'We merely consider you a human being like ourselves: Nor do we find among those who follow you except the lowliest of our folk, the men who follow you without any proper reason' (*Hūd* 11: 27). To this the Prophet Noah replied: 'Nor will I drive away those who believe' (*Hūd* 11: 29). On another occasion he said: 'Nor do I say regarding those whom you look upon with disdain that Allah will not bestow any good upon them' (*Hūd* 11: 31). (See also *al-An'ām* 6: 52 and *al-Ḥijr* 15: 88.)

(29) And proclaim: 'This is the truth from your Lord. Now let him who will, believe; and let him who will, disbelieve.[31] We have prepared a Fire for the wrong-doers whose billowing folds encompass them.[32] If they ask for water, they will be served with a drink like dregs of oil[33] that will scald their faces. How dreadful a drink, and how evil an abode! (30) As for those who believe and do good We shall not cause their reward to be lost. ▶

وَقُلِ ٱلْحَقُّ مِن رَّبِّكُمْ فَمَن شَآءَ
فَلْيُؤْمِن وَمَن شَآءَ فَلْيَكْفُرْ
إِنَّآ أَعْتَدْنَا لِلظَّٰلِمِينَ نَارًا أَحَاطَ
بِهِمْ سُرَادِقُهَا وَإِن يَسْتَغِيثُوا۟
يُغَاثُوا۟ بِمَآءٍ كَٱلْمُهْلِ يَشْوِى
ٱلْوُجُوهَ بِئْسَ ٱلشَّرَابُ
وَسَآءَتْ مُرْتَفَقًا ٢٩ إِنَّ
ٱلَّذِينَ ءَامَنُوا۟ وَعَمِلُوا۟
ٱلصَّٰلِحَٰتِ إِنَّا لَا نُضِيعُ أَجْرَ
مَنْ أَحْسَنَ عَمَلًا ٣٠

29. That is, one ought not to follow a person who is heedless of God, nor submit to him, nor accept his command. Here the word 'obedience' means all this, having been used in its widest, most comprehensive sense.

30. The words used in the above verse are كَانَ أَمْرُهُ فُرُطًا . This can be translated in more than one way. One such possibility is reflected in our translation above. The verse may, however, also be understood in a slightly different sense; it can typify the person who brazenly abandons the truth, and who exceeds all moral bounds in his ruthless bid to achieve his aims. In both cases, however, the result is much the same. The lives of all those who become slaves to their base desires as a result of relegating God to oblivion become devoid of balance and proportion. To obey such a person means that one should abandon one's own sense of proportion and indulge in immoderation and stumble in all directions in one's effort to follow leaders who are not bound by any limits.

31. It is quite clear at this point as to why this statement was made after narrating the story of the People of the Cave. While recounting the events referred to above, it was mentioned that after having come to have faith in God's unity, the People of the Cave rose up and proclaimed: 'Our Lord is the Lord of the heavens and the earth' (verse 14). Moreover, they categorically refused to enter into any compromise with their people who were immersed in doctrinal error. Instead, they resolutely proclaimed: 'We shall call upon no

(31) They shall dwell in the Gardens of Eternity – Gardens beneath which streams flow. There they will be adorned with bracelets of gold,[34] will be arrayed in green garments of silk and rich brocade, and will recline on raised couches.[35] How excellent is their reward, and how nice their resting-place!'

أُوْلَٰٓئِكَ لَهُمۡ جَنَّٰتُ عَدۡنٖ تَجۡرِي مِن
تَحۡتِهِمُ ٱلۡأَنۡهَٰرُ يُحَلَّوۡنَ فِيهَا مِنۡ أَسَاوِرَ
مِن ذَهَبٖ وَيَلۡبَسُونَ ثِيَابًا خُضۡرٗا مِّن
سُندُسٖ وَإِسۡتَبۡرَقٖ مُّتَّكِـِٔينَ فِيهَا عَلَى
ٱلۡأَرَآئِكِۚ نِعۡمَ ٱلثَّوَابُ وَحَسُنَتۡ
مُرۡتَفَقًا ٣١

other god beside Him; (for if we did so), we shall be uttering a blasphemy' (verse 14).

Thus, abandoning their people and their gods, they preferred to retire to a cave despite being devoid of any support and resources. They preferred this to striking a bargain with their people at the cost of truth. Later on, when they woke up after their long slumber, the thing that truly agitated them was the possibility of their being reverted to the faith of their erring people, a possibility which seemed catastrophic to them (see verse 20).

After narrating these events the discourse now turns to the Prophet (peace be on him) even though its true purport is to impress upon the opponents of Islam that any compromise with those who associate others with God in His divinity or who deny the truth is simply out of the question. The Prophet (peace be on him) is directed to faithfully communicate the truth that had been vouchsafed to him from on high. Once he had done so, the people would be free both to accept it and see its good result, or to reject it and suffer the consequences. All those who accept the truth – even if they be young, poor resourceless, ordinary slaves or labourers – deserve to be considered as valuable as precious gems. As for those who are indifferent to God on account of their excessive devotion to their base desires, they should be considered as devoid of all worth even if they have a great deal of influence and an abundance of riches.

32. The word *surādiq* signifies the walls of a tent. In its present usage in connection with Hell, however, it seems that it denotes the extent of the reach of the flames or the heat of Hell-Fire. The verse here says that the *surādiq* of Hell-Fire encompasses the wrong-doers. Some scholars consider this expression to refer to the future, in which case it would mean that in the Hereafter the Hell-Fire would enclose them as the walls of a tent encloses the inmates of the tent. We are, however, of the opinion that the verse means that

(32) (O Muḥammad!): Propound a parable to them.[36] There were two men of whom We bestowed upon one of them two vineyards, surrounding both of them with date-palms and putting a tillage in between. (33) Both the vineyards yielded abundant produce without failure and We caused a stream to flow in their midst ▶

۞ وَاضْرِبْ لَهُم مَّثَلًا رَّجُلَيْنِ جَعَلْنَا
لِأَحَدِهِمَا جَنَّتَيْنِ مِنْ أَعْنَابٍ
وَحَفَفْنَاهُمَا بِنَخْلٍ وَجَعَلْنَا بَيْنَهُمَا
زَرْعًا ﴿٣٢﴾ كِلْتَا الْجَنَّتَيْنِ آتَتْ
أُكُلَهَا وَلَمْ تَظْلِم مِّنْهُ شَيْئًا
وَفَجَّرْنَا خِلَالَهُمَا نَهَرًا ﴿٣٣﴾

---

the wrong-doers who have rejected the truth have already been enclosed by this Hell-Fire and that it is not possible for them to escape it.

33. The word *muhla* has a number of meanings. According to some scholars, it means a residue of oil. According to others, it means lava, that is the elements of the earth which have melted under excessive heat. Others consider it to mean molten metals. Some consider it to mean pus and blood. (Cf. the meaning of *muhl,* al-Zamakhsharī, *al-Kashshāf,* comments on *al-Kahf* 18: verse 29. See also *muhl,* Ibn Manẓūr, *Lisān al-'Arab* – Ed.)

34. In ancient times kings used to wear bracelets of gold. This has been mentioned with regard to the People of Paradise to emphasize that the believers will be made to don a royal dress so as to honour them. Thus, the situation of the Hereafter will be altogether different from what it is in the present world. For in the Hereafter even those unbelievers who are highly placed in this world, including kings, will be made to suffer humiliation. On the contrary, righteous believers – even if they occupy humble positions in this world – will be shown the honour usually reserved for kings.

35. The word *arā'ik* is the plural of *arīkah,* meaning a throne shaded by a canopy. Once again, this verse underscores the truth that the honour which is accorded to royal personages will be conferred on all those who are rewarded with Paradise.

36. In order to understand the context of this parable one would do well to recall verse 28 above which was in fact revealed in response to the arrogant attitude displayed by the Quraysh chiefs. They had disdainfully refused to sit in

(34) so the owner had fruit in abundance and he said to his neighbour, while conversing with him: 'I have greater wealth than you and I am stronger than you in numbers.' (35) Then he entered his vineyard[37] and said, wronging himself: 'Surely, I do not believe that all this will never perish. (36) Nor do I believe that the Hour of Resurrection will ever come to pass. And even if I am returned to my Lord, I shall find a better place than this.'[38] ▶

وَكَانَ لَهُۥ ثَمَرٌ فَقَالَ لِصَٰحِبِهِۦ وَهُوَ
يُحَاوِرُهُۥٓ أَنَا۠ أَكۡثَرُ مِنكَ مَالًا وَأَعَزُّ
نَفَرًا ﴿٣٤﴾ وَدَخَلَ جَنَّتَهُۥ وَهُوَ
ظَالِمٌ لِّنَفۡسِهِۦ قَالَ مَآ أَظُنُّ أَن تَبِيدَ
هَٰذِهِۦٓ أَبَدًا ﴿٣٥﴾ وَمَآ أَظُنُّ ٱلسَّاعَةَ
قَآئِمَةً وَلَئِن رُّدِدتُّ إِلَىٰ رَبِّي
لَأَجِدَنَّ خَيۡرًا مِّنۡهَا مُنقَلَبًا ﴿٣٦﴾

---

the company of poor and humble believers. They had expressed their readiness to listen to the Prophet's teaching only if his assembly was cleared of these ordinary, poor believers.

It is also pertinent at this stage to consider this parable in conjunction with another in *al-Qalam,* 68: 17–33. Furthermore, it is also useful to bear in mind the following verses: *Maryam* 19: 73–4, *al-Mu'minūn* 23: 55–61, *Sabā'* 34: 36, and *Fuṣṣilat* 41: 49–50.

37. That is, he entered his orchards which he considered no less than Paradise. Small, mean people are easily puffed up by worldly successes, and they tend to believe that their achievements in this world are synonymous with Paradise. So great are these successes and attainments in their eyes that they hardly see any reason to strive for the attainment of Paradise in the Hereafter.

38. They claim that if the Next Life really does come about, then they will be even better off. For the prosperity that they enjoy in this world – at least, as they see it – is only indicative of the fact that they are God's favourites.

(37) While conversing with him his neighbour exclaimed: 'Do you deny Him Who created you of dust, then of a drop of sperm, and then fashioned you into a complete man?[39] (38) As for myself, Allah alone is my Lord, and I associate none with my Lord in His divinity. (39) When you entered your vineyard, why did you not say: "Whatever Allah wills shall come to pass, for there is no power save with Allah!"[40] If you find me less than yourself in wealth and children (40) it may well be that my Lord will give me something better than your vineyard, and send a calamity upon your vineyard from the heaven and it will be reduced to a barren waste, (41) or the water of your vineyard will be drained deep into the ground so that you will not be able to seek it out.' ▶

قَالَ لَهُۥ صَاحِبُهُۥ وَهُوَ يُحَاوِرُهُۥٓ أَكَفَرْتَ
بِٱلَّذِى خَلَقَكَ مِن تُرَابٍ ثُمَّ مِن نُّطْفَةٍ
ثُمَّ سَوَّىٰكَ رَجُلًا ﴿٣٧﴾ لَّٰكِنَّا۠ هُوَ ٱللَّهُ رَبِّى
وَلَآ أُشْرِكُ بِرَبِّىٓ أَحَدًا ﴿٣٨﴾ وَلَوْلَآ إِذْ
دَخَلْتَ جَنَّتَكَ قُلْتَ مَا شَآءَ ٱللَّهُ لَا
قُوَّةَ إِلَّا بِٱللَّهِ ۚ إِن تَرَنِ أَنَا۠ أَقَلَّ مِنكَ
مَالًا وَوَلَدًا ﴿٣٩﴾ فَعَسَىٰ رَبِّىٓ أَن يُؤْتِيَنِ
خَيْرًا مِّن جَنَّتِكَ وَيُرْسِلَ عَلَيْهَا
حُسْبَانًا مِّنَ ٱلسَّمَآءِ فَتُصْبِحَ صَعِيدًا
زَلَقًا ﴿٤٠﴾ أَوْ يُصْبِحَ مَآؤُهَا غَوْرًا فَلَن
تَسْتَطِيعَ لَهُۥ طَلَبًا ﴿٤١﴾

---

39. The person concerned did not deny the existence of God. In fact the words وَلَئِن رُّدِدتُّ إِلَىٰ رَبِّى ('. . . and even if I am returned to my Lord') (see verse 36) positively indicate that he did believe in the existence of God. Still, he was branded by his neighbour as one who denied God. The reason for this is that *kufr* does not merely consist in denying the existence of God. In addition, pride, arrogance, vainglory and the denial of the Hereafter also constitute *kufr* of God; for the faith required of man does not merely consist of affirming God's existence; it also requires affirming Him as the Master, the Lord, and the Sovereign. Whoever focuses his attention exclusively upon himself, who considers his attainments, his wealth and his high social standing not as gifts from God but the result of his own ability and effort, who thinks that his wealth will endure and that none has the power to deprive him of it, and who thinks

(42) Eventually all his produce was destroyed and he began to wring his hands in sorrow at the loss of what he had spent on it, and on seeing it fallen down upon its trellises, saying: 'Would I had not associated anyone with my Lord in His divinity.' (43) And there was no host, beside Allah, to help him, nor could he be of any help to himself. (44) [Then he knew] that all power of protection rests with Allah, the True One. He is the best to reward, the best to determine the end of things.

(45) (O Prophet!): Propound to them the parable of the present life: it is like the vegetation of the earth which flourished luxuriantly when it mingled with the water that We sent down from the sky, but after that the same vegetation turned into stubble which the winds blew about. Allah alone has the power over all things.[41] ▶

وَأُحِيطَ بِثَمَرِهِۦ فَأَصْبَحَ يُقَلِّبُ كَفَّيْهِ عَلَىٰ
مَآ أَنفَقَ فِيهَا وَهِىَ خَاوِيَةٌ عَلَىٰ عُرُوشِهَا
وَيَقُولُ يَٰلَيْتَنِى لَمْ أُشْرِكْ بِرَبِّىٓ أَحَدًا ﴿٤٢﴾
وَلَمْ تَكُن لَّهُۥ فِئَةٌ يَنصُرُونَهُۥ مِن دُونِ ٱللَّهِ
وَمَا كَانَ مُنتَصِرًا ﴿٤٣﴾ هُنَالِكَ ٱلْوَلَٰيَةُ
لِلَّهِ ٱلْحَقِّ هُوَ خَيْرٌ ثَوَابًا وَخَيْرٌ عُقْبًا ﴿٤٤﴾
وَٱضْرِبْ لَهُم مَّثَلَ ٱلْحَيَوٰةِ ٱلدُّنْيَا كَمَآءٍ
أَنزَلْنَٰهُ مِنَ ٱلسَّمَآءِ فَٱخْتَلَطَ بِهِۦ
نَبَاتُ ٱلْأَرْضِ فَأَصْبَحَ هَشِيمًا
تَذْرُوهُ ٱلرِّيَٰحُ وَكَانَ ٱللَّهُ عَلَىٰ كُلِّ شَىْءٍ
مُّقْتَدِرًا ﴿٤٥﴾

---

that he is accountable to no one – such a person in fact does not believe in God in the sense in which he is required to; that is, he does not believe in Him as his Master, Lord, and Sovereign.

40. Whatever God alone wills comes to happen, for man does not have the power to make things happen according to his wishes. Whatever man does is only by God's aid and succour.

(46) Wealth and children are an adornment of the life of the world. But the deeds of lasting righteousness are the best in the sight of your Lord in reward, and far better a source of hope. (47) Bear in mind the Day when We shall set the mountains in motion[42] and you will find the earth void and bare.[43] On that Day We shall muster all men together, leaving none of them behind.[44] ▶

ٱلْمَالُ وَٱلْبَنُونَ زِينَةُ ٱلْحَيَوٰةِ ٱلدُّنْيَا
وَٱلْبَٰقِيَٰتُ ٱلصَّٰلِحَٰتُ خَيْرٌ عِندَ
رَبِّكَ ثَوَابًا وَخَيْرٌ أَمَلًا ﴿٤٦﴾ وَيَوْمَ
نُسَيِّرُ ٱلْجِبَالَ وَتَرَى ٱلْأَرْضَ بَارِزَةً
وَحَشَرْنَٰهُمْ فَلَمْ نُغَادِرْ مِنْهُمْ أَحَدًا ﴿٤٧﴾

41. God grants life as well as death. He enables people to rise as well as causes them to fall. He causes the blossoming of the spring, and also ordains that it will be followed by autumn. Hence, if someone happens to flourish and enjoy prosperity, he ought not to be deluded into believing that this state would necessarily last for ever. It is God Who has granted man all bounties and he will be instantly deprived of them the moment God so wills.

42. This refers to the time when the present order of things will be disrupted. The earth will lose its gravitational pull and the mountains will float about as clouds. The same point has been made elsewhere in the Qur'ān: 'And you see the mountains and think that they are firmly fixed, but they shall pass by like clouds' (*al-Naml* 27: 88).

43. The earth will become devoid of all vegetation and of every structure. It will turn into a barren, desolate mass of land. This virtually reiterates what was said earlier in this *sūrah*:

> Surely, We have made all that is on the earth an embellishment for it in order to test people as to who of them is better in conduct. In the ultimate, We shall reduce all that is on the earth to a barren plain (verses 7–8).

44. This includes all human beings that have ever been born from the very early beginnings till the very last moment before the Day of Resurrection. This includes even those infants who may have lived after birth for no more than a single breath. All human beings who ever existed will be resurrected and will be brought together at the same time.

(48) They shall be brought before your Lord, all lined up, and shall be told: 'Now, indeed, you have come before Us in the manner We created you in the first instance,[45] although you thought that We shall not appoint a tryst [with Us].' (49) And then the Record of their deeds shall be placed before them and you will see the guilty full of fear for what it contains, and will say: 'Woe to us! What a Record is this! It leaves nothing, big or small, but encompasses it.' They will find their deeds confronting them. Your Lord wrongs no one.[46]

(50) And recall when We said to the angels: 'Prostrate yourselves before Adam'; all of them fell prostrate, except Iblīs.[47] He was of the *jinn* and so disobeyed the command of his Lord.[48] Will you, then, take him and his progeny as your guardians rather than Me although they are your open enemies? What an evil substitute are these wrong-doers taking!

وَعُرِضُوا۟ عَلَىٰ رَبِّكَ صَفًّا لَّقَدْ جِئْتُمُونَا
كَمَا خَلَقْنَـٰكُمْ أَوَّلَ مَرَّةٍۭ ۚ بَلْ زَعَمْتُمْ أَلَّن
نَّجْعَلَ لَكُم مَّوْعِدًا ﴿٤٨﴾ وَوُضِعَ
ٱلْكِتَـٰبُ فَتَرَى ٱلْمُجْرِمِينَ مُشْفِقِينَ
مِمَّا فِيهِ وَيَقُولُونَ يَـٰوَيْلَتَنَا مَالِ هَـٰذَا
ٱلْكِتَـٰبِ لَا يُغَادِرُ صَغِيرَةً وَلَا
كَبِيرَةً إِلَّآ أَحْصَىٰهَا ۚ وَوَجَدُوا۟
مَا عَمِلُوا۟ حَاضِرًا ۗ وَلَا يَظْلِمُ رَبُّكَ
أَحَدًا ﴿٤٩﴾ وَإِذْ قُلْنَا لِلْمَلَـٰٓئِكَةِ
ٱسْجُدُوا۟ لِـَٔادَمَ فَسَجَدُوٓا۟ إِلَّآ
إِبْلِيسَ كَانَ مِنَ ٱلْجِنِّ فَفَسَقَ
عَنْ أَمْرِ رَبِّهِۦٓ ۗ أَفَتَتَّخِذُونَهُۥ
وَذُرِّيَّتَهُۥٓ أَوْلِيَآءَ مِن دُونِى
وَهُمْ لَكُمْ عَدُوٌّۢ ۚ بِئْسَ
لِلظَّـٰلِمِينَ بَدَلًا ﴿٥٠﴾

45. At that moment it will be impressed on all those who had denied the Hereafter that what the Messengers had informed them had indeed come about. The Prophets had told people that God Who had created them in the first

instance would bring them back to life. There were many who had refused to accept this, and it is they who will be asked on the Day of Resurrection whether what they had been told by the Messengers of God about being raised back to life after death had been proven true or not.

46. No one will be wronged. It will not happen that sins which a person did not commit will find a way to his record. Nor will a person be punished in excess of his actual misdeeds. And, of course, no one who is innocent will be seized and punished without justification.

47. This is an allusion to the story of Adam and Satan. The purpose of alluding to it in the present context is to draw man's attention to a folly that he is wont to commit. That Satan is man's sworn enemy is well-known. And yet, man tends to turn away from God, Who is clement, and compassionate; man also turns away from the Prophets who are his sincere well-wishers. Ironically enough, after turning away from God and His Prophets man falls into the trap of his eternal enemy, Satan, who has always been consumed with envy of man.

48. This means that Satan did not belong to the species of angels. Instead, he was a *jinn*. Accordingly, it was possible for him to disobey God's command. The Qur'ān categorically states that the nature of angels is so constituted that they can only obey God: '. . . they do not disobey Allah and do what they are bidden' (*al-Taḥrīm* 66: 6). Likewise, the angels are elsewhere described in the Qur'ān: '. . . as never do they behave in arrogant defiance. They hold their Lord, Who is above them, in fear, and do as they are bidden' (*al-Naḥl* 16: 49–50).

In contrast to angels, the *jinn* – like human beings – are invested with free will. They are not *inherently* obedient; instead, they have the freedom to choose between belief and unbelief, between obedience and disobedience. This is the point which is spelled out clearly here: that since Iblīs (Satan) was a *jinn,* it was possible for him to choose disobedience and transgression. This clarification should put an end to the common misconceptions that Satan was an angel. (For further elaboration see *al-Ḥijr* 15: 27 and *al-Jinn* 72: 13–15.)

Here another question naturally arises. If Satan was not an angel, why does the Qur'ān state: 'And when We ordered the angels: ''Prostrate yourselves before Adam'', all of them fell prostrate, except Iblīs . . .' (*al-Baqarah* 2: 34). It must be appreciated that the command to the angels to prostrate themselves before Adam also signified that all other earthly creatures which lived in the jurisdiction of the angels should also acknowledge their subservience to man. And indeed all creatures did actually prostrate themselves before man along with the angels. Iblīs, however, refused to go along with the rest of the creatures in carrying out the order to prostrate. (For the meaning of the word Iblīs see *al-Mu'minūn* 23, n. 73.)

(51) I did not call them to witness the creation of the heavens and the earth, nor in their own creation.[49] I do not seek the aid of those who lead people astray.

(52) What will such people do on the Day when the Lord will say: 'Now call upon all those whom you believed to be My partners.'[50] Thereupon they will call upon them, but they will not respond to their call; and We shall make them a common pit of doom.[51] (53) And the guilty shall behold the Fire and know that they are bound to fall into it, and will find no escape from it.

مَّآ أَشْهَدتُّهُمْ خَلْقَ ٱلسَّمَٰوَٰتِ
وَٱلْأَرْضِ وَلَا خَلْقَ أَنفُسِهِمْ وَمَا
كُنتُ مُتَّخِذَ ٱلْمُضِلِّينَ عَضُدًا
﴿٥١﴾ وَيَوْمَ يَقُولُ نَادُوا۟ شُرَكَآءِىَ
ٱلَّذِينَ زَعَمْتُمْ فَدَعَوْهُمْ فَلَمْ
يَسْتَجِيبُوا۟ لَهُمْ وَجَعَلْنَا بَيْنَهُم
مَّوْبِقًا ﴿٥٢﴾ وَرَءَا ٱلْمُجْرِمُونَ
ٱلنَّارَ فَظَنُّوٓا۟ أَنَّهُم مُّوَاقِعُوهَا
وَلَمْ يَجِدُوا۟ عَنْهَا مَصْرِفًا ﴿٥٣﴾

49. The verse puts a straight question to man: 'What right do the satans have to be obeyed and served by men?' For, far from having any share in the creation of the heavens and the earth, they were themselves created by God.

50. This is a recurring Qur'ānic theme – that to follow someone's command and guidance other than God's amounts to associating others with God in His divinity. It is irrelevant whether one verbally brands such a being as a partner in God's divinity or not. Even if a person curses someone while following his commands in disregard of God's, he is guilty of associating him with God in His divinity. This point is best illustrated with reference to satans. As we know, everyone curses satans but at the same time follows them. The Qur'ān, therefore, charges people with associating satans with God in His Divinity. This form of polytheism is not related to belief; it is rather linked with action. The Qur'ān, nevertheless, denounces it as a form of polytheism. (For further details see *al-Nisā'* 4, nn. 91 and 145; *al-An'ām* 6, nn. 87 and 107; *al-Tawbah* 9, n. 31; *Ibrāhīm* 14, n. 32; *Maryam* 19, n. 27; *al-Mu'minūn* 23, n. 41; *al-Furqān* 25, n. 56; *al-Qaṣaṣ* 28, n. 86; *Sabā'* 34, nn. 59–63; *Yā Sīn* 36, n. 53; *al-Shūrá* 42, n. 38 and *al-Jāthiyah* 45, n. 30.)

(54) And surely We have explained matters to people in the Qur'ān in diverse ways, using all manner of parables. But man is exceedingly contentious. (55) What is it that prevented mankind from believing when the guidance came to them, and from asking forgiveness of their Lord, except that they would like to be treated as the nations of yore, or that they would like to see the scourge come upon them face to face?[52]

(56) We raise Messengers only to give good news and to warn.[53] But the unbelievers resort to falsehood in order to rebut the truth with it, and scoff at My revelations and My warnings. ▶

وَلَقَدْ صَرَّفْنَا فِي هَٰذَا الْقُرْءَانِ
لِلنَّاسِ مِن كُلِّ مَثَلٍ وَكَانَ
الْإِنسَٰنُ أَكْثَرَ شَيْءٍ جَدَلًا
﴿٥٤﴾ وَمَا مَنَعَ النَّاسَ أَن يُؤْمِنُوٓا
إِذْ جَآءَهُمُ الْهُدَىٰ وَيَسْتَغْفِرُوا
رَبَّهُمْ إِلَّآ أَن تَأْتِيَهُمْ سُنَّةُ
الْأَوَّلِينَ أَوْ يَأْتِيَهُمُ الْعَذَابُ قُبُلًا
﴿٥٥﴾ وَمَا نُرْسِلُ الْمُرْسَلِينَ إِلَّا
مُبَشِّرِينَ وَمُنذِرِينَ وَيُجَٰدِلُ
الَّذِينَ كَفَرُوا بِالْبَٰطِلِ
لِيُدْحِضُوا بِهِ الْحَقَّ وَاتَّخَذُوٓا
ءَايَٰتِي وَمَآ أُنذِرُوا هُزُوًا ﴿٥٦﴾

---

51. Commentators on the Qur'ān have given two different interpretations of this verse. One of these is reflected in our translation of the text above. The second interpretation is that God will cause enmity among them; that is, the friendship which they enjoyed among themselves during this worldly life will change into severe enmity in the Hereafter.

52. The Qur'ān has advanced all kinds of arguments and has marshalled all kinds of evidence to illuminate the truth it expounds. It has spared no device in making an appeal to peoples' hearts and minds. Since all available measures had been exhausted, it was not clear what prevented people from embracing the truth. Were people waiting to be seized by God's scourge? Would they only accept the truth the hard way?

53. This verse also has two possible meanings, both of which seem valid. In one sense, the verse means that the Messengers are sent by God for no other purpose than to apprise people of the good consequences of obeying God and

(57) Who is more wicked than the man who, when he is reminded by the revelations of his Lord, turns away from them and forgets (the consequence of) the deeds wrought by his own hands? We have laid veils over their hearts lest they understand the message of the Qur'ān, and We have caused heaviness in their ears. Call them as you may to the right path, they will not be guided ever.[54]

(58) Your Lord is All-Forgiving, full of mercy. Had He wished to take them to task for their doings, He would have hastened in sending His scourge upon them. But He has set for them a time-limit which they cannot evade.[55]

وَمَنْ أَظْلَمُ مِمَّن ذُكِّرَ بِـَٔايَٰتِ رَبِّهِۦ
فَأَعْرَضَ عَنْهَا وَنَسِىَ مَا قَدَّمَتْ يَدَاهُ ۚ
إِنَّا جَعَلْنَا عَلَىٰ قُلُوبِهِمْ أَكِنَّةً أَن
يَفْقَهُوهُ وَفِىٓ ءَاذَانِهِمْ وَقْرًا ۖ وَإِن
تَدْعُهُمْ إِلَى ٱلْهُدَىٰ فَلَن يَهْتَدُوٓا۟
إِذًا أَبَدًا ﴿٥٧﴾ وَرَبُّكَ ٱلْغَفُورُ ذُو
ٱلرَّحْمَةِ ۖ لَوْ يُؤَاخِذُهُم بِمَا
كَسَبُوا۟ لَعَجَّلَ لَهُمُ ٱلْعَذَابَ ۚ
بَل لَّهُم مَّوْعِدٌ لَّن يَجِدُوا۟ مِن
دُونِهِۦ مَوْئِلًا ﴿٥٨﴾

---

the evil consequences of disobeying Him. It is tragic that foolish people have often failed to pay heed to these warnings and seem to be bent upon inviting God's scourge upon themselves while the Messengers of God try hard to avert this.

The other meaning of the verse is that if the unbelievers wanted to witness God's scourge, they need not ask the Messenger (peace be on him) to bring it forth. For the Messengers are not sent to bring about God's scourge; they are rather raised to warn people about it.

54. If someone resorts to sheer irrationality when confronted with arguments and sincere counsel, and pits falsehood, fraud and deception against truth and evinces no readiness in recognizing that his misdeeds will have evil consequences, then God seals his heart and mind. As a result, such people become deaf to all voices calling them to truth and sanity. Instead of taking heed of sincere counsel, they obstinately continue towards self-destruction.

(59) All the townships afflicted with scourge are before your eyes.[56] When they committed wrong, We destroyed them. For the destruction of each We had set a definite term.

(60) (And recount to them the story of Moses) when Moses said to his servant: 'I will journey on until I reach the point where the two rivers meet, though I may march on for ages.'[57] ▶

وَتِلْكَ ٱلْقُرَىٰٓ أَهْلَكْنَٰهُمْ لَمَّا
ظَلَمُوا۟ وَجَعَلْنَا لِمَهْلِكِهِم مَّوْعِدًا ﴿٥٩﴾
وَإِذْ قَالَ مُوسَىٰ لِفَتَىٰهُ لَآ
أَبْرَحُ حَتَّىٰٓ أَبْلُغَ مَجْمَعَ
ٱلْبَحْرَيْنِ أَوْ أَمْضِىَ حُقُبًا ﴿٦٠﴾

They do not acknowledge that they are rushing towards the abyss of destruction until they find themselves helplessly in it.

55. God does not punish the guilty instantly. Out of infinite mercy, He grants such criminals a reasonable period of respite that they may mend themselves. Out of utter folly and ignorance, many people totally misunderstand this respite they receive from God. They tend to believe that regardless of what they do, they will not be held to account – a belief which, of course, is totally erroneous.

56. This refers to the ruins and desolation of the lands of the people of Sabā, Thamūd, Midian and Lot which lay on the trade routes of the Quraysh. All these were also well known to the other tribes of Arabia.

57. The narration of Moses' story here is meant to draw both the unbelievers' and the believers' attention to an important fact. Those who are concerned with the external aspects of things are liable to draw false conclusions from their observations. This happens because man is not aware of the wisdom underlying the events that take place under God's dispensation. One frequently witnesses that the wrong-doers prosper whereas the innocent suffer hardships; those who disobey God and commit transgression live in great affluence whereas those who obey God face adversities, and that the wicked enjoy the pleasures of worldly life whereas the virtuous live in misery. Such spectacles are quite common.

Not knowing why such things happen, doubts arise in people's minds, leading them, on occasion, to have a totally false perception of things. Those who consciously disbelieve and are immersed in the perpetration of injustice and oppression are led to conclude that they live in a disordered and chaotic world, a world which has either no sovereign, or if there is any, one who must have become senseless or unjust. Hence, they conclude that people may go about doing what they please, without fearing that they will be called to account. On the other hand, those who believe in God are heart-broken by what they see around them. It also often happens that when such believers are faced with severe tests, their faith is shaken to the core.

It was in order to enable Moses to comprehend the wisdom underlying those events which generally baffle one's understanding that God slightly lifts the curtain from the reality which governs the workings of the world. In this way Moses was able to appreciate that appearances are quite different from the reality.

The Qur'ān does not specify where and when this incident relating to Moses took place. In the *Ḥadīth,* however, we do find some information about it. For instance, there is a tradition from 'Awfī in which he reports a statement by Ibn 'Abbās according to which the incident took place after Pharaoh's drowning, and when Moses had settled his people in Egypt. (Al-Ālūsī, *Rūḥ al-Ma'ānī,* vol. 15, comments on *al-Kahf* 18, verse 60, p. 313 – Ed.) There are, however, other traditions, more authentic ones, which are found in al-Bukhārī and other collections of *Ḥadīth* which do not support the content of the tradition just mentioned. Nor do any other sources confirm that after Pharaoh's drowning, the Prophet Moses (peace be on him) ever lived in Egypt. In fact the Qur'ān makes it clear that after the exodus from Egypt, Moses spent all his life in Sinai, in the wilderness. (See *al-Mā'idah* 5: 26 – Ed.) Hence there seems no reason to accept al-'Awfī's report.

When we reflect over the details of the story, however, two points clearly emerge. Firstly, that the Prophet Moses' experience probably belongs to the early phase of his prophethood. For it is in the earlier part of their prophetic careers that Prophets stand in need of the kind of instruction given to Moses and requiring that he be exposed to certain experiences. Secondly, it also stands to reason that Moses would have been in need of such instruction at the time when the Israelites faced conditions similar to those facing the Muslims during the Makkan phase of the Prophet's life.

Because of these two reasons we presume – though the truth is known to God alone – that this story belongs to the period when the Israelites were being persecuted by Pharaoh in Egypt. At that time Pharaoh and his courtiers, in the manner of the Quraysh aristocracy, believed that they would not be held to account because God's punishment – which, as we know, is not meted out instantly – was not in sight. It is likely that the Egyptian Muslims [i.e. the followers of Moses], like their Makkan counterparts in the time of the Prophet (peace be on him) felt agitated at seeing their tormentors flourishing while they suffered grievously. How long, they asked somewhat impatiently, will this state of affairs continue? Even Moses cried out to God in these words: 'Our Lord! You bestowed upon Pharaoh and his nobles splendour and riches in the world. Our Lord! Have You done this that they may lead people astray from Your path?' (*Yūnus*: 10: 88).

If our assumption is correct, then it is probable that the Prophet Moses (peace be on him) travelled towards the Sudan and that the place referred to in the Qur'ān by the expression *majma' al-baḥrayn* (see verse 60) is located near Khartoum where the two main branches of the Nile – the Blue Nile and White Nile – converge (see Map 1.) When one traces the places through which Moses journeyed in his life, there is no other place than the one just mentioned where the two rivers meet.

The Bible is totally silent about all this. The event as such is, however, mentioned in the Talmud. The Talmudic version is, however, quite different in so far as it is attributed to Rabbi Jochanan, the son of Levi, rather than to the Prophet Moses (peace be on him). According to the same report, the other person involved in the incident was Elijah. This is the same Elijah who is considered to have been taken up alive from this world to the heavens, who was subsequently made an angel and asked to look after the affairs of the world. (See H. Polano, *The Talmud Selections,* pp. 313–16.)

Possibly, like other events of Jewish history which pre-date the exodus, this event might not have been authentically preserved. Accretions might also have adulterated the account as has happened in the case of other events. Influenced by the Talmudic account, some Muslim scholars think that the person called Moses in the Qur'ānic account is a Moses other than the Prophet Moses (peace be on him). Now, there is no reason to believe that all reports mentioned in the Talmud are reliable. Nor is there any *prima facie* reason why the Qur'ān would narrate the story of some unknown Moses at such length. On the other hand, we have authentic *ḥadīth* narrated by Ubayy b. Ka'b, in which the Prophet Muḥammad (peace be on him) mentioned Moses (peace be on him) while explaining this very story. (See al-Bukhārī, *K. Tafsīr al-Qur'ān: Sūrah al-Kahf, 'Bāb wa idh qāl Mūsá li Fatāhu . . .'* and *'Bāb Qawluh fa lammā balaghā Majma' baynihimā nasiyā Ḥūtahumā'* . . . – Ed.) In view of all this, there is no reason for any Muslim to pay attention to the Talmudic account.

The Orientalists, true to their ilk, have attempted to explore the possible sources of this Qur'ānic story as well. After strenuous efforts, they identify three possible sources from which the Prophet Muḥammad (peace be on him) may have composed the story and ascribed it to God's revelation. These sources are the *Gilgamesh* epic, the Alexandrian romance in Syriac, and the Talmudic report referred to earlier about Elijah.

It is obvious that Orientalists share a common attitude: that one may be open to all assumptions except that the Qur'ān is a revelation from God. That being definitely excluded, these scholars embark on this grand mission to dissect whatever was presented in the Qur'ān (which, in their view, was definitely the work of Muḥammad (peace be on him) rather than God) and to show how each fragment had some external source. They pursue this line of inquiry so brazenly and go to such absurd lengths that one feels instinctively repelled. Ironically, they term their bigoted pursuit scholarly research. If such biased

MAP RELATING TO THE STORY OF KHIḌR AND MOSES

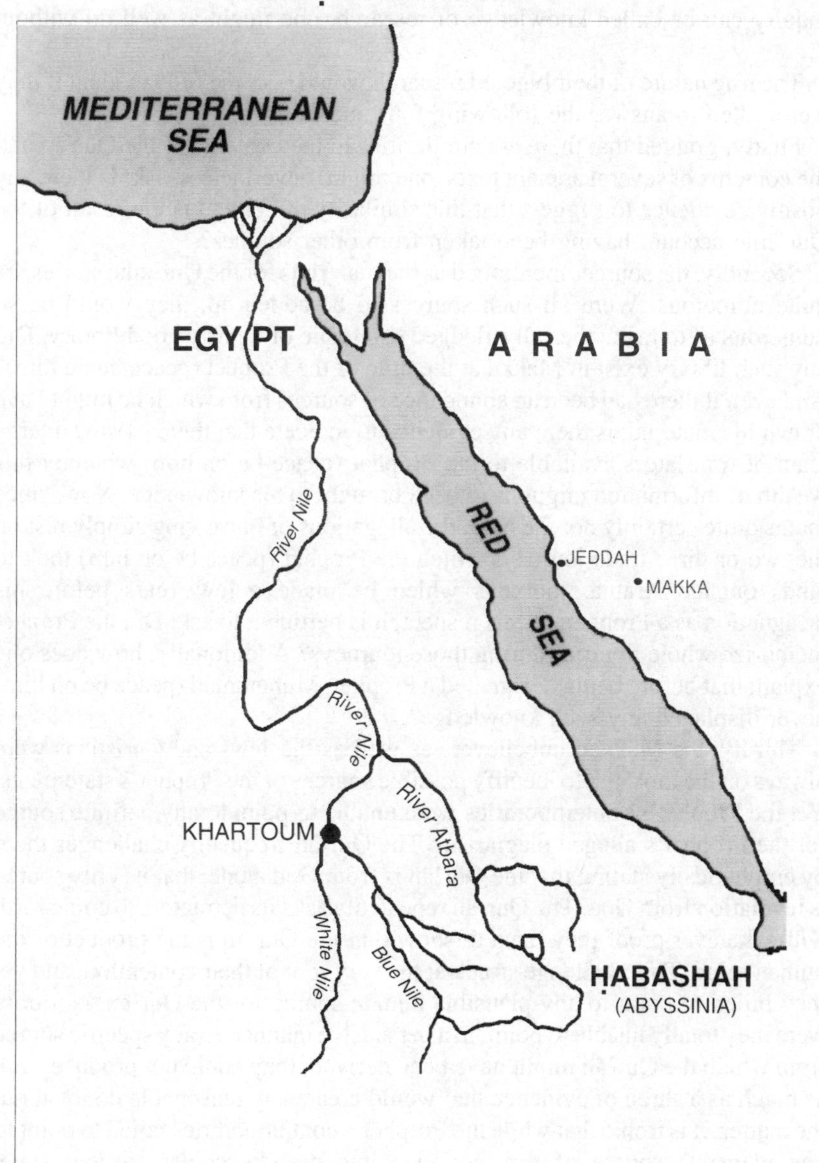

inquiry can be called knowledge or research, one might as well do without it.

The true nature of their bigoted research would become fully evident if they were asked to answer the following four questions:

Firstly, granted that there are similarities in the contents of the Qur'ān and the contents of several ancient texts, one might, nevertheless, ask: Is there any positive evidence to suggest that this similarity of content is the result of the Qur'ānic account having been taken from other sources?

Secondly, the sources mentioned as the materials for the Qur'ānic stories are quite numerous. Were all such sources to be added up, they would be so numerous as to make the fully-fledged catalogue of a fairly good library. Did any such library exist in Makka at the time of the Prophet (peace be on him)? And even if there had been an abundance of sources from which he might have drawn his material, is there any evidence to indicate that there existed a large team of translators available to the Prophet (peace be on him) whereby this wealth of information might have been brought to his knowledge. Now, since that is quite certainly not the case, the allegations of borrowing simply rest on the two or three trade journeys which the Prophet (peace be on him) took to lands outside Arabia; journeys which he made a few years before his designation as a Prophet. In this respect, it is pertinent to ask: Did the Prophet memorize whole libraries during those journeys? Additionally, how does one explain that before being designated a Prophet, Muḥammad (peace be on him) never displayed any such knowledge?

Thirdly, the Makkan unbelievers as well as the Jews and Christians were always on the look-out to identify possible sources of the Prophet's statements. Yet the Prophet's contemporaries were unable to point to any definite source for the Prophet's alleged plagiarism. The Qur'ān frequently challenges them by emphatically stating that the Qur'ān is from God alone, that its only source is revelation from God. The Qur'ān repeatedly asks its detractors to come forth with whatever proof they have to show that the Qur'ān is the product of the human mind. This challenge struck at the very root of their contention, and yet they failed to point to any plausible human source for the Qur'ān. Not only were they totally unable to point, in a persuasive manner, to any specific source from which the Qur'ān might have been derived, they could not produce even as much as a shred of evidence that would create any reasonable doubt about the matter. It is ironic that while the Prophet's contemporaries failed to point to any plausible source of the Qur'ān, some pseudo-scholars of our time, animated by inveterate hostility to Islam, have the temerity to claim – a thousand and several hundred years after the Prophet's time – the so-called sources from which the contents of the Qur'ān were derived!

The last point to consider is the following. It is not possible for anybody to deny that there exists at least the *logical possibility* that the Qur'ān might be the revealed word of God. It is logically possible that the information the Qur'ān provides about past events might indeed be true whereas those reports commonly available to us about the past might be the distorted versions of oral reports of events over the centuries, and hence unreliable. It should be noted

(61) But when they reached the point where the two rivers meet, they forgot their fish, and it took its way into the sea, as if through a tunnel. (62) When they had journeyed further on, (63) Moses said to his servant: 'Bring us our repast. We are surely fatigued by today's journey.' The servant said: 'Did you see what happened? When we betook ourselves to the rock to take rest, I forgot the fish – and it is only Satan who caused me to forget to mention it to you – so that it made its way into the sea in a strange manner.' (64) Moses said: 'That is what we were looking for.'[58] So the two turned back, retracing their footsteps, (65) and there they found one of Our servants upon whom We had bestowed Our mercy, and to whom We had imparted a special knowledge from Ourselves.[59]

فَلَمَّا بَلَغَا مَجْمَعَ بَيْنِهِمَا نَسِيَا
حُوتَهُمَا فَاتَّخَذَ سَبِيلَهُۥ فِى ٱلْبَحْرِ سَرَبًا
﴿٦١﴾ فَلَمَّا جَاوَزَا قَالَ لِفَتَىٰهُ ءَاتِنَا
غَدَآءَنَا لَقَدْ لَقِينَا مِن سَفَرِنَا
هَٰذَا نَصَبًا ﴿٦٢﴾ قَالَ أَرَءَيْتَ إِذْ أَوَيْنَآ
إِلَى ٱلصَّخْرَةِ فَإِنِّى نَسِيتُ ٱلْحُوتَ
وَمَآ أَنسَىٰنِيهُ إِلَّا ٱلشَّيْطَٰنُ أَنْ
أَذْكُرَهُۥ وَٱتَّخَذَ سَبِيلَهُۥ فِى ٱلْبَحْرِ
عَجَبًا ﴿٦٣﴾ قَالَ ذَٰلِكَ مَا كُنَّا نَبْغِ
فَٱرْتَدَّا عَلَىٰٓ ءَاثَارِهِمَا قَصَصًا
﴿٦٤﴾ فَوَجَدَا عَبْدًا مِّنْ عِبَادِنَآ
ءَاتَيْنَٰهُ رَحْمَةً مِّنْ عِندِنَا
وَعَلَّمْنَٰهُ مِن لَّدُنَّا عِلْمًا ﴿٦٥﴾

---

that this possibility was arbitrarily ruled out without any valid reason whatsoever. Having discarded this all attention was focused on one assumption alone – that the material in the Qur'ān was primarily drawn from oral reports and legends that were current in the region at the time the Qur'ān was revealed. One wonders if this can be explained by anything other than religious prejudice and bigotry.

A little reflection on the above points should convince us that much of what has been trumpeted by the Orientalists as knowledge and scholarship is far too palpably coloured by bigotry to be worthy of serious consideration by students who have embarked on a quest for the truth.

(66) Moses said to him: 'May I follow you that you may teach me something of the wisdom which you have been taught?' (67) He answered: 'You will surely not be able to bear with me. (68) For how can you patiently bear with something you cannot encompass in your knowledge?' (69) Moses replied: 'You shall find me, if Allah wills, patient; and I shall not disobey you in anything.' (70) He said: 'Well, if you follow me, do not ask me concerning anything until I myself mention it to you.'

قَالَ لَهُۥ مُوسَىٰ هَلْ أَتَّبِعُكَ عَلَىٰٓ أَن
تُعَلِّمَنِ مِمَّا عُلِّمْتَ رُشْدًا ﴿٦٦﴾
قَالَ إِنَّكَ لَن تَسْتَطِيعَ مَعِىَ صَبْرًا
﴿٦٧﴾ وَكَيْفَ تَصْبِرُ عَلَىٰ مَا لَمْ تُحِطْ
بِهِۦ خُبْرًا ﴿٦٨﴾ قَالَ سَتَجِدُنِىٓ إِن
شَآءَ ٱللَّهُ صَابِرًا وَلَآ أَعْصِى لَكَ
أَمْرًا ﴿٦٩﴾ قَالَ فَإِنِ ٱتَّبَعْتَنِى فَلَا
تَسْـَٔلْنِى عَن شَىْءٍ حَتَّىٰٓ أُحْدِثَ
لَكَ مِنْهُ ذِكْرًا ﴿٧٠﴾

---

58. Moses exclaimed that it was precisely the disappearance of the fish in the sea that was the significant indicator of the place where he would encounter the person whom he wanted to meet. This implies that Moses (peace be on him) had undertaken his journey under God's direction. It is for this reason that he was informed he would encounter certain incidents which would be of special significance. He had been foretold that the place where the fish intended for breakfast would disappear would be the meeting place between him and the person he was required to meet.

59. According to authentic traditions, this person was called Khiḍr. Hence, those reports which, under the influence of the Israelite traditions, link this story with Elijah are erroneous. It is incorrect to think that Moses met Elijah, firstly because it is opposed to the Prophet's statements on the question. (Al-Bukhārī, *K. Tafsīr al-Qur'ān: Sūrah al-Kahf, 'Bāb wa idh qāl Mūsá li Fatāhu . . .'* and *'Bāb fa lammā balaghā Majma' baynihimā . . .'* – Ed.) Secondly, Elijah was born several hundred years after the time of the Prophet Moses (peace be on him), thus casting further doubt on the likelihood of their meeting.

The Qur'ān does not specify the name of Moses' servant. According to some reports, it was Joshua, son of Nun who later succeeded the Prophet Moses (peace be on him). (See al-Bukhārī, *K. Tafsīr al-Qur'ān: Sūrah al-Kahf, 'Bāb wa idh qāl Mūsá li Fatāhu . . .'* – Ed.)

(71) Then the two went forth until, when they embarked on the boat, he made a hole in it, whereupon Moses exclaimed: 'Have you made a hole in it so as to drown the people in the boat? You have certainly done an awful thing.' (72) He replied: 'Did I not tell you that you will not be able to patiently bear with me?' (73) Moses said: 'Do not take me to task at my forgetfulness, and do not be hard on me.'

(74) Then the two went forth until they met a lad, whom he slew, whereupon Moses exclaimed: 'What! Have you slain an innocent person without his having slain anyone? Surely you have done a horrible thing.' (75) He said: 'Did I not tell you that you will not be able to patiently bear with me?' (76) Moses said: 'Keep me no more in your company if I ever question you concerning anything after this. You will then be fully justified.'

(77) Then the two went forth until when they came to a town, they asked its people for food, but they refused to play host to them. They found in that town a wall that was on the verge of tumbling down, and he buttressed it, whereupon Moses said: 'If you had wished, you could have received payment for it.' ▶

فَانطَلَقَا حَتَّىٰٓ إِذَا رَكِبَا فِي ٱلسَّفِينَةِ
خَرَقَهَاۖ قَالَ أَخَرَقۡتَهَا لِتُغۡرِقَ أَهۡلَهَا
لَقَدۡ جِئۡتَ شَيۡـًٔا إِمۡرٗا ٧١ قَالَ أَلَمۡ
أَقُلۡ إِنَّكَ لَن تَسۡتَطِيعَ مَعِيَ صَبۡرٗا
٧٢ قَالَ لَا تُؤَاخِذۡنِي بِمَا نَسِيتُ
وَلَا تُرۡهِقۡنِي مِنۡ أَمۡرِي عُسۡرٗا ٧٣
فَانطَلَقَا حَتَّىٰٓ إِذَا لَقِيَا غُلَٰمٗا فَقَتَلَهُۥ
قَالَ أَقَتَلۡتَ نَفۡسٗا زَكِيَّةَۢ بِغَيۡرِ نَفۡسٖ
لَّقَدۡ جِئۡتَ شَيۡـٔٗا نُّكۡرٗا ٧٤ ۞
قَالَ أَلَمۡ أَقُل لَّكَ إِنَّكَ لَن تَسۡتَطِيعَ
مَعِيَ صَبۡرٗا ٧٥ قَالَ إِن سَأَلۡتُكَ
عَن شَيۡءِۭ بَعۡدَهَا فَلَا تُصَٰحِبۡنِيۖ قَدۡ
بَلَغۡتَ مِن لَّدُنِّي عُذۡرٗا ٧٦ فَانطَلَقَا
حَتَّىٰٓ إِذَآ أَتَيَآ أَهۡلَ قَرۡيَةٍ ٱسۡتَطۡعَمَآ
أَهۡلَهَا فَأَبَوۡاْ أَن يُضَيِّفُوهُمَا
فَوَجَدَا فِيهَا جِدَارٗا يُرِيدُ أَن
يَنقَضَّ فَأَقَامَهُۥۖ قَالَ لَوۡ شِئۡتَ
لَتَّخَذۡتَ عَلَيۡهِ أَجۡرٗا ٧٧

(78) He said: 'This brings me and you to a parting of ways. Now I shall explain to you the true meaning of things about which you could not remain patient. (79) As for the boat, it belonged to some poor people who worked on the river, and I desired to damage it for beyond them lay the dominion of a king who was wont to seize every boat by force. (80) As for the lad, his parents were people of faith, and we feared lest he should plague them with transgression and disbelief, (81) and we desired that their Lord should grant them another in his place, a son more upright and more tender-hearted. (82) And as for the wall, it belonged to two orphan boys in the city, and under it there was a treasure that belonged to them. Their father was a righteous man and your Lord intended that they should come of age and then bring forth their treasure as a mercy from your Lord; I did not do this of my own bidding. This is the true meaning of things with which you could not keep your patience.'[60]

(83) (O Muḥammad!): They ask you about Dhū al-Qarnayn.[61] Say: 'I will give you an account of him.'[62]

قَالَ هَٰذَا فِرَاقُ بَيْنِي وَبَيْنِكَ سَأُنَبِّئُكَ
بِتَأْوِيلِ مَا لَمْ تَسْتَطِع عَّلَيْهِ صَبْرًا ﴿٧٨﴾
أَمَّا ٱلسَّفِينَةُ فَكَانَتْ لِمَسَٰكِينَ
يَعْمَلُونَ فِي ٱلْبَحْرِ فَأَرَدتُّ أَنْ أَعِيبَهَا
وَكَانَ وَرَآءَهُم مَّلِكٌ يَأْخُذُ كُلَّ سَفِينَةٍ
غَصْبًا ﴿٧٩﴾ وَأَمَّا ٱلْغُلَٰمُ فَكَانَ أَبَوَاهُ
مُؤْمِنَيْنِ فَخَشِينَآ أَن يُرْهِقَهُمَا
طُغْيَٰنًا وَكُفْرًا ﴿٨٠﴾ فَأَرَدْنَآ أَن
يُبْدِلَهُمَا رَبُّهُمَا خَيْرًا مِّنْهُ زَكَوٰةً
وَأَقْرَبَ رُحْمًا ﴿٨١﴾ وَأَمَّا ٱلْجِدَارُ
فَكَانَ لِغُلَٰمَيْنِ يَتِيمَيْنِ فِي
ٱلْمَدِينَةِ وَكَانَ تَحْتَهُۥ كَنزٌ
لَّهُمَا وَكَانَ أَبُوهُمَا صَٰلِحًا
فَأَرَادَ رَبُّكَ أَن يَبْلُغَآ أَشُدَّهُمَا
وَيَسْتَخْرِجَا كَنزَهُمَا رَحْمَةً
مِّن رَّبِّكَ وَمَا فَعَلْتُهُۥ عَنْ أَمْرِي
ذَٰلِكَ تَأْوِيلُ مَا لَمْ تَسْطِع عَّلَيْهِ
صَبْرًا ﴿٨٢﴾ وَيَسْـَٔلُونَكَ عَن ذِي
ٱلْقَرْنَيْنِ قُلْ سَأَتْلُوا عَلَيْكُم
مِّنْهُ ذِكْرًا ﴿٨٣﴾

60. This story gives rise to a difficult and complex problem which needs to be explained. Of Khiḍr's three acts, all except the third, are opposed to injunctions which, since man's inception, have always been an integral part of Divine Law. No version of the Divine Law permits man to damage things which belong to others, or to kill an innocent person. In fact such injunctions are of fundamental importance. Hence, even if a person were to learn by means of revelation (*ilhām*) that a boat will be forcibly damaged by someone in the future, or that a young person will grow into an unbeliever and commit excesses, still no one, according to all versions of Divine Law, has the right to damage that boat by making a hole in it, or to kill that innocent person.

One can of course, claim that both these acts were committed under God's command and hence the person concerned was not blameworthy. This contention, however, does not solve the problem. For the question as to who asked Khiḍr to commit those acts is not at all relevant. There is no doubt that those acts were in compliance with God's command. Khiḍr himself states [in this very verse] that it was God's mercy rather than his own volition which caused those acts. This is also confirmed by God Who clearly states that He bestowed a special knowledge upon Khiḍr (see verse 65 above). Thus, there can be absolutely no doubt that these acts were carried out in compliance with God's command. The real issue, however, is what the nature of those commands was.

It is obvious that these commands were not part of the Law revealed by God as an imperative for man. For doubtlessly the basic principles which form part of the Qur'ān or the earlier Scriptures do not permit the killing of any person who has not been convicted of a crime. Hence, the only reasonable assumption in this case is that these commands are in the nature of God's cosmic laws – laws which are merely statements of causal relationships. These laws are similar to those by which some people fall sick and then recover, which cause some to die and enable others to survive, and which lead some to their destruction but enable others to prosper.

This being the nature of the commands in the present context, it is clear that they could only have been communicated to angels. For there can be no question that the angels would violate God's commands; that is so because angels, [according to the Qur'ān], *involuntarily* carry out God's commands. (See *al-Taḥrīm* 66: 7; *al-Naḥl* 16: 49–50 – Ed.) But man's position is quite different. Whether he performs an act involuntarily in accordance with the laws of nature, or does so in accordance with some inspiration (*ilhām*) or on the basis of some special knowledge obtained from some unseen source, he will be guilty of committing a sin if his act is opposed to any of God's revealed laws. This is so because man, *qua* man, is responsible for carrying out God's commands [in the sense of imperatives]. Additionally, the principles of Divine Law do not permit anyone to violate any of God's laws on the grounds that he was directed by means of inspired knowledge or that he had discovered the rationale and wisdom of violating God's laws through some extraordinary, super-sensory means of cognition.

There is complete agreement on this point among all scholars of the

Sharī'ah. Not only that, prominent Sufis are also agreed on this point. Al-'Ālūsī has quoted extensively from the writings of prominent Sufis such as 'Abd al-Wahhāb al-Sha'rānī (d. 973 A.H./1565 C.E.), Muhī al-Dīn ibn al-'Arabī (d. 638 A.H./1234 C.E.), Mujaddid-i Alf-i Thānī (d. 1034 A.H./1625 C.E.), 'Abd al-Qādir al-Jaylānī (d. 561 A.H./1166 C.E.), Junayd al-Baghdādī (d. 297 A.H./910 C.E.), Sarī al-Saqaṭī (d. 253 A.H./867 C.E.), Abū al-Ḥusayn al-Nūrī (d. 295 A.H.), Abū Sa'īd al-Kharrāz (d. 279 A.H.), Abū al-'Abbās Aḥmad al-Dīnawarī (d. *circa* 340 A.H.) and Abū Ḥāmid al-Ghazālī (d. 550 A.H./1111 C.E.). On the basis of these quotations, al-'Ālūsī has established that according to the Sufis a person may not do anything against a law clearly laid down in the authoritative texts even if he is the recipient of an inspiration which directs him to do so. (See al-Ālūsī, *Rūḥ al-Mā'ānī,* vol. 16, pp. 16-18.)

Should we, then, assume that at least one human being – Khiḍr – was granted exemption from this rule? Or should we hold that Khiḍr was not a human being; that he was one of those creatures of God who work in consonance with God's cosmic providential Will rather than according to the injunctions of Divine Law?

It would be logical to opt for the former position if the Qur'ān had explicitly stated that the 'servant' under whom the Prophet Moses (peace be on him) was to receive this instruction was a human being. The Qur'ān, however, does not specifically describe him as a 'human being'. The word used by the Qur'ān is *'abd* which simply indicates that Khiḍr was one of the creatures or servants of God, a word that does not necessarily signify a human being. It is significant that the same expression has been used at several places in the Qur'ān for angels. (See, for example, *al-Anbiyā'* 21: 26 and *al-Zukhruf* 43: 19.)

Nor do we find in any authentic tradition mention by the Prophet (peace be on him) of Khiḍr as a human being. The most authentic traditions in this regard are those which bear the following chain of transmission: Sa'īd ibn al-Jubayr – Ibn 'Abbās or Ubayy b. Ka'b – the Prophet (peace be on him). The word that occurs in these traditions is *rajul,* and although it is used for human males, this is not exclusively the case. (For the occurrence of the word *rajul* see al-Bukhārī, *K. al-'Ilm, 'Bāb mā yustaḥabb li al-'Ālim idhā su'il ayy al-Nās A'lam . . .'* – Ed.) The Qur'ān itself uses the same word in connection with *jinn* (see *al-Jinn* 72: 6). Obviously whenever a *jinn,* an angel or any invisible being appears before man, it will also do so in human form and in this state it will also be called a human being (*bashar* or *insān*). For example, when an angel came to Maryam, the Qur'ān makes the point that it appeared before her as a human being (*Maryam* 19: 17). Hence, the statement by Muḥammad (peace be on him) that the Prophet Moses (peace be on him) found a male does not conclusively establish that Khiḍr was necessarily a human being.

The only way for us to resolve this difficulty is to consider Khiḍr not as a human being but as one of the angels of God, as a creature belonging to some other species of God's creation, one of those who act as God's agents and carry out God's will as reflected in the laws of nature and who are not bound by the *Sharī'ah*. Some earlier scholars also hold this view, which has in any case been mentioned by Ibn Kathīr in his *Tafsīr* on the authority of al-Māwardī. (See Ibn Kathīr, *Tafsīr,* comments on *al-Kahf* 18, verse 82 – Ed.)

61. The word *wa* ('and') which precedes the query about Dhū al-Qarnayn certainly connects the two parts of the verse. This makes it clear that the story of Khiḍr and Moses was also narrated in response to the questions that had been asked. This further corroborates our contention that the Makkan unbelievers put a number of questions to the Prophet (peace be on him) in order to test whether he had access to any extraordinary source of knowledge or not.

62. The identity of Dhū al-Qarnayn has long been a contentious issue. Early commentators on the Qur'ān were generally inclined to believe that it referred to Alexander. The characteristics attributed to Dhū al-Qarnayn in the Qur'ān, however, hardly apply to Alexander. In the light of the latest historical evidence, contemporary commentators on the Qur'ān are inclined to believe that Dhū al-Qarnayn signifies the Persian Emperor, Cyrus. This, in any case, seems more plausible. Nevertheless, the information available to date does not enable us to form a definitive opinion concerning Dhū al-Qarnayn's identity.

Qur'ānic statements concerning Dhū al-Qarnayn clearly bring out the following four points:

(1) The title Dhū al-Qarnayn (literally, 'The Two-Horned'), was at least familiar to the Jews. This is evident from the fact that they had instigated the Makkan unbelievers to ask the Prophet (peace be on him) about him. One must, therefore, inevitably turn to Jewish literature to find out who this person was or to establish which was the kingdom known as 'The Two-Horned'.

(2) The Qur'ānic description also makes it quite clear that Dhū al-Qarnayn must have been a great ruler as well as a conqueror for his conquests covered a vast stretch of territory extending from the east to the west and on the third side, extending either to the north or the south. There were only a few such outstanding figures before the revelation of the Qur'ān. So we must apply our search for the other characteristics of Dhū al-Qarnayn to any one of these figures.

(3) The title Dhū al-Qarnayn may aptly be used for a ruler who, being concerned with the defence of his kingdom from the assaults of Gog and Magog, had a strong protective wall constructed across a mountain pass. In order to determine who that person was, it is necessary to find out to whom the words Gog and Magog refer. It is also necessary to find out whether any such wall was ever built adjacent to the habitat of Gog and Magog; and if it was, by whom.

(4) In addition to all this, the Qur'ān describes Dhū al-Qarnayn as a God-conscious and just ruler. In fact in the Qur'ānic portrayal of him, these stand out as his dominant characteristics.

MAP REFERENCE FOR THE STORY OF DHŪ AL-QARNAYN

Let us consider the first clue regarding Dhū al-Qarnayn – that he was known to the Jews. Now the information available in Jewish sources seems to apply to Cyrus. For according to the Bible, Daniel saw the united empire of Media and Persia, before the rise of the Greeks, in the form of a two-horned ram (see *Daniel* 8: 3, 20). There was much talk of the 'two-horned' one among the Jews for it was he who shattered the Babylonian Empire to pieces and brought about the liberation of the Israelites (see *Banī Isrā'īl* 17, n. 8 above).

The second clue also seems, to a very large extent, to apply to Cyrus, though not fully. His conquests undoubtedly extended as far as Asia Minor and the Syrian coastline in the west and Balkh in the east. So far, however, we have not found any trace of a north or south expedition by Cyrus even though the Qur'ān categorically mentions a third expedition by Dhū al-Qarnayn (see verse 83 ff.). The possibility that Cyrus did undertake such an expedition, however, cannot be ruled out for according to historical sources Cyrus' empire extended as far as Caucasia in the north.

As far as the third clue is concerned, we know almost for sure that Gog and Magog were the wild tribes of Russia and northern China who were variously known as Tatars, Mongols, Huns, and Scythians who had carried out various raids against civilized lands. We also know that the bulwarks of Darband and Daryal were built in the southern regions of Caucasia so as to ensure defence against the incursions of these wild tribes. It has not been fully established historically, however, that those bulwarks were built by Cyrus.

Arriving at the last clue, this applies most to Cyrus of all the conquerors of the world. For Cyrus was widely praised for being a just ruler, so much so that even his enemies praised him for this. The Bible's *Book of Ezra* portrays him as a God-worshipping and God-fearing king who liberated the Israelites precisely by virtue of his devotion to God, and that he also ordered the Temple of Solomon in Jerusalem to be rebuilt for the worship of God.

On the basis of all the above, we would be quite justified in concluding that of all past conquerors Cyrus comes closest to the Qur'ānic description of Dhū al-Qarnayn. However, the evidence so far available to us, does not conclusively establish that Cyrus was indeed the Dhū al-Qarnayn of the Qur'ān. Nevertheless, no other conqueror comes as close to the Qur'ānic characterization of Dhū al-Qarnayn as Cyrus.

Historically speaking, Cyrus was a Persian ruler whose rise to fame began around 549 B.C. Within a few years he seized the kingdoms of Media and Lydia (Asia Minor), and later in 539 B.C. he also conquered Babylon. This made him the supreme ruler of the region, as there was no powerful kingdom left to oppose him. His subsequent conquests extended to Sind, Ṣughd (present-day Turkestan), Egypt and Libya on one side, and to Thrace, Macedonia, Caucasia and Khawarazm in the north on the other. For all practical purposes, the civilized world of the day was under his sway.

(84) We granted him power in the land and endowed him with all kinds of resources. (85) He set out (westwards) on an expedition, (86) until when he reached the very limits of where the sun sets,[63] he saw it setting in dark turbid waters;[64] and nearby he met a people. We said: ‘O Dhū al-Qarnayn, you have the power to punish or to treat them with kindness.’[65] (87) He said: ‘We will chastise him who does wrong, whereafter he will be returned to his Lord and He will chastise him grievously. (88) But as for him who believes and acts righteously, his will be a goodly reward and we shall enjoin upon him only mild commands.’

إِنَّا مَكَّنَّا لَهُۥ فِى ٱلْأَرْضِ وَءَاتَيْنَٰهُ مِن كُلِّ
شَىْءٍ سَبَبًا ﴿٨٤﴾ فَأَتْبَعَ سَبَبًا ﴿٨٥﴾
حَتَّىٰٓ إِذَا بَلَغَ مَغْرِبَ ٱلشَّمْسِ وَجَدَهَا
تَغْرُبُ فِى عَيْنٍ حَمِئَةٍ وَوَجَدَ
عِندَهَا قَوْمًا ۗ قُلْنَا يَٰذَا ٱلْقَرْنَيْنِ إِمَّآ
أَن تُعَذِّبَ وَإِمَّآ أَن تَتَّخِذَ فِيهِمْ
حُسْنًا ﴿٨٦﴾ قَالَ أَمَّا مَن ظَلَمَ فَسَوْفَ
نُعَذِّبُهُۥ ثُمَّ يُرَدُّ إِلَىٰ رَبِّهِۦ فَيُعَذِّبُهُۥ
عَذَابًا نُّكْرًا ﴿٨٧﴾ وَأَمَّا مَنْ ءَامَنَ
وَعَمِلَ صَٰلِحًا فَلَهُۥ جَزَآءً ٱلْحُسْنَىٰ ۖ
وَسَنَقُولُ لَهُۥ مِنْ أَمْرِنَا يُسْرًا ﴿٨٨﴾

---

63. The ‘limit where the sun sets’, as pointed out by Ibn Kathīr, signifies the extreme limit of the west. It does not mean the actual place where the sun sets. (See Ibn Kathīr, *Tafsīr,* comments on verse 86 – Ed.) Thus, what the verse implies is that Dhū al-Qarnayn conquered one territory after another in a westward direction until he reached the very end of the land mass and beyond which lay the sea.

64. When the sun set in that land it seemed as if it had set in the blackish, muddy waters of the sea. If we are to assume that Cyrus was indeed Dhū al-Qarnayn, then the reference would be to the western coast at the point where the Aegean Sea splits into several small gulfs. This is also supported by the Qur’ānic use of the word *‘ayn,* instead of *baḥr,* since the former word is more appropriately used to denote a lake or gulf, rather than sea.

65. The present statement does not necessarily mean that God communicated this directive to Dhū al-Qarnayn by means of revelation (*waḥy*) or

(89) Then he set out on
another expedition, (90)
until he reached the limit
where the sun rises and he
found it rising on a people
whom We had provided no
shelter from it.[66] (91) Thus
was the state of those people,
and We encompassed in
knowledge all concerning
Dhū al-Qarnayn.

(92) Then he set out on
another expedition, (93)
until when he reached a place
between the two mountains,[67]
he found beside the mountains
a people who scarcely understood anything.[68] ▶

ثُمَّ أَتْبَعَ سَبَبًا ﴿٨٩﴾ حَتَّىٰٓ إِذَا بَلَغَ
مَطْلِعَ ٱلشَّمْسِ وَجَدَهَا تَطْلُعُ عَلَىٰ
قَوْمٍ لَّمْ نَجْعَل لَّهُم مِّن دُونِهَا
سِتْرًا ﴿٩٠﴾ كَذَٰلِكَ وَقَدْ أَحَطْنَا بِمَا
لَدَيْهِ خُبْرًا ﴿٩١﴾ ثُمَّ أَتْبَعَ سَبَبًا
حَتَّىٰٓ إِذَا بَلَغَ بَيْنَ ٱلسَّدَّيْنِ ﴿٩٢﴾
وَجَدَ مِن دُونِهِمَا قَوْمًا
لَّا يَكَادُونَ يَفْقَهُونَ قَوْلًا ﴿٩٣﴾

inspiration (*ilhām*). Had that been the case, it would necessarily mean that Dhū al-Qarnayn was a *nabī* (Prophet) or *muḥaddath* (one to whom God spoke). (See Muḥammad ibn A'lā al-Thānawī, *Kashshāf Isṭilāḥāt al-Funūn* (Calcutta, 1863), vol. 2, art. *'al-Nabī'*, pp. 1358–9 – Ed.) It is quite possible that no actual communication took place and that it amounted to no more than making a statement of fact. This indeed seems more likely. For the situation obtaining at that time was that Dhū al-Qarnayn had just established his control over that territory; i.e. that the conquered nation was firmly in his grip. At this stage, God put a question to Dhū al-Qarnayn's conscience: How should he treat these helpless people? Being in full control, he could either treat them with injustice or treat them with grace and magnanimity. The situation was, thus, a test for his moral calibre.

66. Dhū al-Qarnayn went forth eastwards, conquering one land after another until he reached a territory which marked the end of the civilized world. The lands ahead were inhabited by slave nations who did not have the skill to construct houses, let alone even know how to pitch tents.

67. The Qur'ān later points out that the land beyond the two mountains was that of Gog and Magog (see verse 94). Hence the mountains mentioned in the

(94) They said: 'O Dhū al-Qarnayn, Gog and Magog[69] are spreading corruption in this land. So shall we pay you taxes on the understanding that you will set up a barrier between us and them?' (95) He answered: 'Whatever my Lord has granted me is good enough. But help me with your labour and I will erect a rampart between you and them.[70] ▶

قَالُوا۟ يَٰذَا ٱلْقَرْنَيْنِ إِنَّ يَأْجُوجَ وَمَأْجُوجَ مُفْسِدُونَ فِى ٱلْأَرْضِ فَهَلْ نَجْعَلُ لَكَ خَرْجًا عَلَىٰٓ أَن تَجْعَلَ بَيْنَنَا وَبَيْنَهُمْ سَدًّا ﴿٩٤﴾ قَالَ مَا مَكَّنِّى فِيهِ رَبِّى خَيْرٌ فَأَعِينُونِى بِقُوَّةٍ أَجْعَلْ بَيْنَكُمْ وَبَيْنَهُمْ رَدْمًا ﴿٩٥﴾

present verse are bound to have been part of the range located between the Caspian Sea and the Black Sea.

68. The language of these people was almost foreign to Dhū al-Qarnayn and his companions. Being a wild people, they neither knew any other language nor did others know theirs.

69. We stated earlier (see n. 62 above), that Gog and Magog were the wild peoples which inhabited the north-eastern region of Asia. They constantly carried out predatory raids against civilized lands, pouring over both Asia and Europe like tidal waves. In *Genesis* (see chap. 10), their ancestry is traced to Japheth, son of Noah. (This view is also shared by Muslim historians.) The *Book of Ezekiel* (see chaps. 38–9) states that their land was comprised of Meshech (presently Moscow) and Tubal (presently Tubalsek). The Jewish historian, Josephus, identifies them with the Scythians who inhabited the area lying north and east of the Black Sea. According to Jerome, the Magog lived to the north of Caucasia, near the Caspian Sea.

70. Dhū al-Qarnayn was conscious that as a ruler it was his duty to safeguard his people against predatory invaders. It was not proper for him, therefore, to impose any additional tax on his people for that purpose. The treasures of the land which had already been entrusted to him by God were sufficient to arrange for his people's defence. This defence would, however, still require that his people should provide him with physical help.

(96) Bring me ingots of iron.'
Then after he had filled up
the space between the two
mountain-sides, he said:
'[Light a fire] and ply
bellows.' When he had made
it [red like] fire, he said:
'Bring me molten copper
which I may pour on it.' (97)
Such was the rampart that Gog
and Magog could not scale,
nor could they pierce it. (98)
Dhū al-Qarnayn said: 'This is
a mercy from my Lord; but
when the time of my Lord's
promise shall come, He will
level the rampart with the
ground.[71] My Lord's promise
always comes true.'[72]

ءَاتُونِي زُبَرَ ٱلْحَدِيدِ حَتَّىٰٓ إِذَا سَاوَىٰ
بَيْنَ ٱلصَّدَفَيْنِ قَالَ ٱنفُخُوا۟ حَتَّىٰٓ إِذَا
جَعَلَهُۥ نَارًا قَالَ ءَاتُونِىٓ أُفْرِغْ عَلَيْهِ
قِطْرًا ﴿٩٦﴾ فَمَا ٱسْطَٰعُوٓا۟ أَن
يَظْهَرُوهُ وَمَا ٱسْتَطَٰعُوا۟ لَهُۥ نَقْبًا
﴿٩٧﴾ قَالَ هَٰذَا رَحْمَةٌ مِّن رَّبِّى فَإِذَا جَآءَ
وَعْدُ رَبِّى جَعَلَهُۥ دَكَّآءَ وَكَانَ وَعْدُ رَبِّى
حَقًّا ﴿٩٨﴾

---

71. The other point made by Dhū al-Qarnayn concerned the protective arrangements he had made. He said that even though he had built a strong, protective wall to the best of his ability, there was no reason to believe that it would endure for ever. As long as God willed, it would remain intact; but when the appointed time for its destruction came, nothing could avert its destruction.

The expression 'the appointed time of my Lord' is very meaningful. This refers both to the time set by God for the destruction of the wall as well as the time appointed for the death and extinction of all – i.e. the Last Day. (See also Appendix II.)

72. This marks the conclusion of Dhū al-Qarnayn's story. The story itself being narrated in response to a query put to the Prophet (peace be on him) by the Makkan unbelievers so as to test him. The Qur'ān, however, employs this story, just as it did the stories of the People of the Cave and Moses (peace be on him) and Khiḍr, to drive home a moral. The Qur'ān emphasizes that Dhū al-Qarnayn, whose glorious achievements were known to the People of the Book, was not simply a conqueror, but also someone who believed in monotheism and the Hereafter and who was just and generous in his dealings with his subjects. Moreover, Dhū al-Qarnayn was not a petty person who puffed up with pride as soon as he attained any success.

(99) And on that Day[73] We shall let some of them to surge like waves against others, and the Trumpet shall be blown. Then We shall gather them all together. (100) That will be the Day We shall place Hell before the unbelievers (101) whose eyes had become blind against My admonition and who were utterly disinclined to hear it.

(102) Do the unbelievers,[74] then, believe that they can take any of My creatures as their guardians beside Me?[75] Verily We have prepared Hell to welcome the unbelievers.

۞ وَتَرَكْنَا بَعْضَهُمْ يَوْمَئِذٍ يَمُوجُ فِي
بَعْضٍ وَنُفِخَ فِي الصُّورِ فَجَمَعْنَاهُمْ
جَمْعًا ﴿٩٩﴾ وَعَرَضْنَا جَهَنَّمَ يَوْمَئِذٍ
لِلْكَافِرِينَ عَرْضًا ﴿١٠٠﴾ الَّذِينَ
كَانَتْ أَعْيُنُهُمْ فِي غِطَاءٍ عَنْ ذِكْرِي
وَكَانُوا لَا يَسْتَطِيعُونَ سَمْعًا ﴿١٠١﴾
أَفَحَسِبَ الَّذِينَ كَفَرُوا أَنْ يَتَّخِذُوا
عِبَادِي مِنْ دُونِي أَوْلِيَاءَ إِنَّا
أَعْتَدْنَا جَهَنَّمَ لِلْكَافِرِينَ نُزُلًا ﴿١٠٢﴾

73. 'On that Day', refers to the Day of Resurrection. Dhū al-Qarnayn had alluded to the Day of Resurrection as a day that is bound to come about because God had so decided. What is being said here is in that context and is an addition to the statement made by Dhū al-Qarnayn (see verse 98 above).

74. This is the conclusion of the whole *sūrah*. In order to comprehend the context of this conclusion, one should not only consider the story of Dhū al-Qarnayn, but also the contents of the *sūrah* as a whole.

The central point of the *sūrah* is that the Prophet (peace be on him) called upon his people to give up polytheism and to embrace monotheism in its place; to give up excessive devotion to the world and to base their conduct on a strong belief in the Hereafter. The Makkan chiefs – thanks to the intoxication caused by their riches and eminence – spurned this call. Additionally, they persecuted and humiliated those righteous people who had accepted the Prophet's call. It is in this context that we ought to view the entire discourse of this *sūrah*. For these three stories which the Prophet (peace be on him) is asked about by his opponents by way of a test are narrated beautifully, and are so interwoven as to constitute an integral part of the overall discourse. With this the three stories end, and the discourse reverts to the main subject mentioned at the outset of the *sūrah* (see verses 24–59).

(103) Say (O Muḥam-
mad!): ‘Shall We tell you who
will be the greatest losers in
respect of their works? (104)
It will be those whose effort
went astray in the life of the
world,[76] and who believe
nevertheless that they are
doing good. (105) Those
are the ones who refused to
believe in the revelations of
their Lord and that they are
bound to meet Him. Hence, all
their deeds have come to
naught, and We shall assign
no weight to them on the Day
of Resurrection.[77] ▶

قُلْ هَلْ نُنَبِّئُكُم بِالْأَخْسَرِينَ أَعْمَٰلًا ﴿١٠٣﴾
الَّذِينَ ضَلَّ سَعْيُهُمْ فِي الْحَيَوٰةِ الدُّنْيَا وَهُمْ
يَحْسَبُونَ أَنَّهُمْ يُحْسِنُونَ صُنْعًا ﴿١٠٤﴾
أُوْلَٰٓئِكَ الَّذِينَ كَفَرُوا بِـَٔايَٰتِ رَبِّهِمْ
وَلِقَآئِهِۦ فَحَبِطَتْ أَعْمَٰلُهُمْ فَلَا نُقِيمُ
لَهُمْ يَوْمَ الْقِيَٰمَةِ وَزْنًا ﴿١٠٥﴾

75. Do the unbelievers still think, despite all they have been told, that it will do them any good to take God’s creatures rather than God as their patrons and guardians?

76. This verse may be interpreted in two ways, one of which is reflected in our translation above. The other meaning could be that the efforts of the unbelievers were exclusively devoted to this worldly life. In other words, whatever they did was for the purpose of gaining worldly goods and they paid no heed to God and the Hereafter. They mistook worldly life as their true objective and they set their eyes on worldly success alone. Even if they believed in the existence of God, they did not care enough to find out what would please Him. Nor did they care for the fact that one day they would return to God and would be required to render their account to Him. They considered themselves no different from animals, albeit endowed with rationality, animals possessed of absolute freedom, unencumbered with any responsibility; animals whose term in life had only one purpose – to enjoy worldly life to its full.

77. No matter how great the unbelievers’ worldly attainments might be they are bound to come to an end with the end of the world itself. All that man is

(106) Hell is their recompense for disbelieving and their jesting with My revelations and My Messengers. (107) As for those who believe and do good works, the Gardens of Paradise[78] shall be there to welcome them; (108) there they will abide for ever, with no desire to be removed from there.'[79]

(109) Say: 'If the sea were to become ink to record the Words of my Lord,[80] indeed the sea would be all used up before the Words of my Lord are exhausted, and it would be the same even if We were to bring an equal amount of ink.'

ذَٰلِكَ جَزَآؤُهُمْ جَهَنَّمُ بِمَا كَفَرُوا۟
وَٱتَّخَذُوٓا۟ ءَايَٰتِى وَرُسُلِى هُزُوًا ﴿١٠٦﴾
إِنَّ ٱلَّذِينَ ءَامَنُوا۟ وَعَمِلُوا۟ ٱلصَّٰلِحَٰتِ
كَانَتْ لَهُمْ جَنَّٰتُ ٱلْفِرْدَوْسِ نُزُلًا
﴿١٠٧﴾ خَٰلِدِينَ فِيهَا لَا يَبْغُونَ عَنْهَا
حِوَلًا ﴿١٠٨﴾ قُل لَّوْ كَانَ ٱلْبَحْرُ مِدَادًا
لِّكَلِمَٰتِ رَبِّى لَنَفِدَ ٱلْبَحْرُ قَبْلَ أَن
تَنفَدَ كَلِمَٰتُ رَبِّى وَلَوْ جِئْنَا بِمِثْلِهِۦ
مَدَدًا ﴿١٠٩﴾

intensely proud of – his grand palaces and splendid mansions, his universities and libraries, his grand highways and wondrous vehicles of transportation, his great inventions and staggering industries, his magnificent arts and sciences, his impressive museums and art galleries – will all be left behind at the time of man's death and will have absolutely no weight in God's scale. If anything is to be of enduring benefit to man in the Next Life it will be the good deeds that he has performed, acts performed according to God's directives and with the intent of seeking God's pleasure alone.

Now, if someone's objectives are confined to this worldly life and he wishes to see his efforts bear fruit in the present world alone, then it is quite obvious that all his acts will vanish with the extinction of the world. If he seeks any recompense in the Hereafter, then obviously he should seek it with regard to those acts which were performed to please God and to attain good results in the Hereafter, and which were in consonance with God's command; if a person did nothing of the sort, then all his striving in this world would have gone to waste.

78. For an explanation of this see *al-Mu'minūn* 23, n. 10.

(110) Say (O Muḥammad!): 'I am no more than a human being like you; one to whom revelation is made: "Your God is the One and Only God." Hence, whoever looks forward to meet his Lord, let him do righteous works, and let him associate none with the worship of his Lord.'

قُلْ إِنَّمَآ أَنَا۠ بَشَرٌ مِّثْلُكُمْ يُوحَىٰٓ إِلَىَّ أَنَّمَآ
إِلَٰهُكُمْ إِلَٰهٌ وَٰحِدٌ فَمَن كَانَ يَرْجُوا۟ لِقَآءَ
رَبِّهِۦ فَلْيَعْمَلْ عَمَلًا صَٰلِحًا وَلَا يُشْرِكْ
بِعِبَادَةِ رَبِّهِۦٓ أَحَدًۢا ﴿١١٠﴾

79. The inmates of Paradise could never even think of going anywhere else since one cannot imagine a better state than that of Paradise.

80. The word *kalimāt* (words) here signifies God's marvellous acts, and the excellent and wondrous manifestations of His power and wisdom.

Sūrah 19

Maryam

(Mary)

(Makkan Period)

Title

The title of this *sūrah* refers to verse 16 in which the name Mary is mentioned.

Period of Revelation

This *sūrah* was revealed before some Companions of the Prophet (peace be on him) emigrated to Abyssinia. We learn from authentic traditions that when these Muslim emigrants were summoned to the court of Negus, Ja'far al-Ṭayyār recited this very *sūrah* in his court in front of a large crowd of people. (See Aḥmad ibn Ḥanbal, *Musnad,* vol. 5, p. 291 – Ed.)

Historical Background

In the introduction to the preceding *sūrah, al-Kahf,* some of the conditions prevailing at the time when that *sūrah* was revealed have been explained. What we said there, however, is not sufficient for a full appreciation of the contents of the present *sūrah* nor for others revealed during this period. Hence it is useful to spend some time now outlining the conditions obtaining at the time.

The Quraysh chiefs attempted to suppress the Islamic movement by deriding and ridiculing the Prophet's followers, by tempting and threatening them and by making allegations against them. However, when all these means failed to achieve their desired purpose, they resorted to physical and economic pressures, to persecution and imprisonment, to subjecting the Muslims to starvation and torture so as to compel them to forsake their faith. The worst sufferers, of course, were the poor, the slaves and those who lived under the tutelage of the Quraysh. Among the worst hit were Bilāl, ʻĀmir ibn Fuhayrah, Umm ʻUbays, Zinnīrah and ʻAmmār ibn Yāsir and his parents. They were beaten mercilessly, interned for days without food and water, and were made to lie on the scorching Makkan sands with boulders placed across their chests so that they writhed in pain for hours. In similar fashion, professional Muslims were asked to work but they were thwarted by persistent delays in the payment of their wages. Thus in al-Bukhārī and Muslim the following tradition was transmitted by Ibn Aratt: 'I used to work in Makka as an ironsmith. ʻĀṣ ibn Wā'il engaged me to work for him. But when I went to collect my wages he refused to pay, saying that unless I forsook the Prophet (peace be on him) he would not pay me my wages.' (See al-Bukhārī, *K. Tafsīr al-Qur'ān, Sūrah Kāf. Ha. Yā. ʻAyn. Ṣād, 'Bāb Qawlahū: a fa ra'ayta al-ladhī kafara bi Āyātinā . . .'* – Ed.)

Likewise, efforts were made to wreck traders' business and those with a good position in society were disgraced in a number of ways. Some glimpse of this situation is afforded by Khabbāb's report. He states: 'One day while the Prophet (peace be on him) was taking rest under the shade of the Kaʻbah, I went to him and said: "O Messenger of Allah! Oppression has now reached its limit. Would you not pray to God?" On hearing this, the Prophet's face turned red and he said: "Believers before you were subjected to greater oppression. Their bones were scraped with combs of iron. Their heads were cut with saws. Yet they did not abandon their faith. Believe me, God will help accomplish this mission. There will come a day when a person will journey from Ṣanʻā' to Ḥaḍramawt and there will be no reason for him to fear anyone except God. You, however, are too impatient".' (Al-Bukhārī, *K. al-Manāqib, 'Bāb 'Alāmāt al-Nubūwwah fī al-Islām'* – Ed.)

In Rajab during the fifth year of the prophethood which corresponds to the forty-fifth year of the Elephant (most probably 615 C.E. – Ed.), the situation became almost intolerable. The Prophet (peace be on him) told his Companions: 'You may now go forth to Abyssinia, for there is a King in whose realm injustice is done to none. It is a land of truth. Stay there till God provides a way – out of your affliction.' (Ibn Hishām, *Sīrah,* vol. 1, pp. 321–2 – Ed.)

In compliance with this directive, eleven men and four women initially migrated to Abyssinia. The Quraysh pursued them as far as the coast. However, these Muslim migrants were fortunate enough to catch a boat from the port of Shu'aybah heading for Abyssinia and this enabled them to escape arrest. After a few months another group of Muslims migrated, making the total number of migrants 83 men, 11 women and 7 non-Quraysh Muslims. Only 40 Companions were now left behind with the Prophet (peace be on him) in Makka.

This emigration caused much distress throughout Makka for the migrants to Abyssinia included someone from virtually every family. If one of these migrants was someone's son, he was also someone else's son-in-law; daughters, brothers and sisters, had left their families for Abyssinia. To name just a few, there was Abū Jahl's brother, Salamah ibn Hishām; his cousins Hāshim ibn Abī Ḥudhayfah and 'Ayyāsh ibn Abī Rabī'ah and the daughter of his uncle, Umm Salamah; Abū Sufyān's daughter, Umm Ḥabībiah; Abu Ḥudhayfah, who was 'Utbah's son and Hind's brother; Suhayl ibn 'Amr's daughter, Sahlah. Also among these migrants to Abyssinia were the children of several Quraysh chiefs – their fathers the enemies of Islam. They too had forsaken their hearths and homes for the sake of their faith. Thus, there was hardly anyone in Makka who had not been affected by this emigration, and inevitably some were hardened in their hostility toward Islam as a result. By the same token, however, some people were so touched by the incident that they eventually embraced Islam. The position of 'Umar ibn al-Khaṭṭāb is a case in point for this was the first in a series of events which blunted his hostility towards Islam. According to a report narrated by Laylá bint Abī Ḥathmah, one of 'Umar's close relatives tells the following story: 'I was packing my things ready for Migration while my husband 'Āmir ibn Rabī'ah went out in connection with some errand. In the meantime 'Umar came to our house and watched me pack up. Then he said: ''O Mother of 'Abd Allāh! Are you leaving?'' I replied: ''By God, you have persecuted us a great deal. However, God's vast earth is open to us; we can migrate to some place where God will give us peace.'' 'Umar's face displayed signs of him having been moved, signs I had never seen before. He only said: ''God be with you'', and then he rushed out.' (Ibn Hishām, *Sīrah,* vol. 1, pp. 342–3 – Ed.)

After these waves of emigration, the Quraysh chiefs held consultations and resolved that 'Abd Allāh ibn Abī Rabī'ah (Abū Jahl's maternal brother) and 'Amr ibn al-'Āṣ should be sent on a mission to Abyssinia to persuade Negus to send the Muslim migrants back to Makka with the valuable gifts they were to take with them being an inducement to return their people. Umm Salamah, a wife of the Prophet (peace be on him) and one of the migrants, has narrated this event at considerable length. According to her, the two clever Quraysh envoys reached Abyssinia in pursuit of the Muslims. Their first act was to distribute lavish gifts among Negus' courtiers, asking them in return to put collective pressure on Negus to hand over the Muslim migrants. Then they called on Negus, and after presenting him with valuable gifts, they said: 'Some unripe youths of our town have fled in order to live in your land. Our notables have sent us to you with requests for their extradition. These young men have abjured our ancestral faith, but have not entered the fold of your faith. Instead, they have invented a new faith of their own.' No sooner had these Quraysh emissaries finished speaking than Negus' courtiers burst forth, saying: 'Such people must surely be returned. Their own people know best what is wrong with them. It is inappropriate to let them stay here.' Negus, however, was irritated, retorting: 'I will not return them. For I cannot betray those who escaped their country, and reposing trust in my country, have sought shelter in it. I will first investigate the truth of the charges levelled against them.' Negus, therefore, sent for the Prophet's Companions asking that they visit his court.

On receiving Negus' message, the Companions assembled together and decided, after mutual consultation, what they should say to him. Unanimously, they decided that they would faithfully expound to Negus the teachings of the Prophet (peace be on him), regardless of whether Negus expelled them or let them remain as a result. As soon as the Muslims reached the court, Negus asked: 'Why did you abandon your ancestral faith, without accepting my faith or any of the faiths of the world? What is this new faith of yours anyway?' To this, Ja'far al-Ṭayyār on behalf of the migrants, made an extemporaneous speech. He recalled the religious, moral and social ills which afflicted the Arabs during the Time of Ignorance (*Jāhilīyah,* i.e. the period prior to the advent of Islam). He then mentioned the teachings of the Prophet (peace be on him) and the persecution to which his followers were subjected in Makka. He concluded by saying that they had come to the land of Negus in the hope that the wrongs they had been subjected to would now cease.

After this speech Negus asked him to recite a part of the Book which he and the other migrants believed to have been revealed by God to their Prophet (peace be on him). Ja'far began to recite the opening part of *Sūrah Maryam* which relates to the Prophets John and Jesus (peace be on them). Negus listened to the recitation of the Qur'ān in rapt attention, and as he listened he cried, tears flowing from his eyes in such profusion that his beard grew wet. When Ja'far's recitation ceased, Negus said: 'Surely this Revelation and the Revelation of Jesus were from the same source. By God, I will not hand over these persons to you.' (Ibn Hishām, *Sīrah,* vol. 1, pp. 334–6 – Ed.)

The next day, 'Amr ibn al-'Āṣ spoke to Negus, saying: 'Just send for them and ask about their belief concerning Jesus, son of Mary. For they say something blasphemous about him.' Negus again sent for the Muslim migrants who had been able, ahead of time, to get wind of 'Amr's ruse. Once again they assembled together and discussed what they would say when asked about Jesus (peace be on him). The situation was a critical one and naturally everyone was worried. The Companions, however, decided that they would simply say what God had stated in the Qur'ān about Jesus and which had been further elaborated by God's Messenger. When they arrived at Negus' court he put to them that question which had been suggested by 'Amr ibn 'Āṣ. Without any hesitation, Ja'far al-Ṭayyār replied: 'He [Jesus] is God's servant and Messenger; a spirit and a word from God that He bestowed on the virgin Mary.' On hearing this, Negus picked up a straw from the ground and said: 'By God, Jesus was not even as much as one straw more than what you have said about him.' Negus then returned to the Quraysh the gifts they had presented him with, stating that he was not accustomed to accepting bribery, and that the Muslims might stay in his land without fear. (See Ibn Hishām, *Sīrah,* vol. 1, pp. 337–8 – Ed.)

Subject Matter

When *Sūrah Maryam* is viewed against this historical background, the first thing that strikes one about it is that God did not direct the Muslims to make any compromises in matters of faith, even in the most precarious of circumstances such as when they went to Abyssinia as a small group of helpless fugitives. Thus the Muslims were taught to place fidelity to their faith over and above everything else. Additionally, the present *sūrah* was granted to the Muslims almost in the way of a provision for their journey. For it enabled them to explain the true position about Jesus (peace be on him) – that he was a human being, a Prophet and one of God's Messengers, but certainly not God's son.

After relating the story of the Prophets John and Jesus (peace be on them) (verses 1–40), the *sūrah* then turns to narrating the story of Abraham (see verses 41–50). This, it will be noted, was directly relevant to the conditions of the day. For Abraham, too, had left his country after persecution at the hands of his father, family, and people. Thus, in effect the *sūrah* told the Makkan unbelievers that the position of the Muslim migrants resembled that of their forefather Abraham (peace be on him) and that the position of the Makkan unbelievers was similar to that of Abraham's cruel opponents who banished him from his homeland. At the same time, the Muslim migrants are assured that their migration, like Abraham's, will not prove their undoing. On the contrary, it would enable them to reach, like Abraham, greater heights of eminence. Their journey, although the culmination of much persecution, was actually a journey to success and glory. Thereafter, follows an account of other Prophets (see verses 51–65) so as to impress upon the Muslims that all Prophets expounded the same religion as that put forward by Muḥammad (peace be on him). What doctrinal differences there were between the Muslims and the so-called followers of earlier Prophets could be explained by the fact that with the passage of time the latter had gone astray. Their erroneous ways which prevailed at that time were simply the outcome of this error.

The concluding verses (verses 66–98) represent a scathing criticism of the errors of the Makkan unbelievers. Finally, the *sūrah* ends by announcing good news to the believers: despite the efforts of their enemies to harm them, they will eventually come out with flying colours and the very same people who for the moment at least opposed them, will eventually lavish their affections on them.

In the name of Allah, the Merciful, the Compassionate.

(1) *Kāf. Hā. Yā. 'Ayn. Ṣād.* (2) This is an account[1] of the mercy of your Lord to His servant Zechariah[2] (3) when he cried to his Lord in secret.

(4) He said: 'Lord! My bones have grown feeble and my head is glistening with age; yet, never have my prayers to You, my Lord, been unfruitful. (5) I fear after me evil from my kinsmen[3] and my wife is barren. So grant me an heir out of Your special grace, (6) one that might be my heir and the heir of the house of Jacob[4] and make him, Lord, one that will be pleasing to You.'

بِسْمِ ٱللَّهِ ٱلرَّحْمَٰنِ ٱلرَّحِيمِ

كٓهيعٓصٓ ١ ذِكْرُ رَحْمَتِ رَبِّكَ
عَبْدَهُۥ زَكَرِيَّآ ٢ إِذْ نَادَىٰ
رَبَّهُۥ نِدَآءً خَفِيًّا ٣ قَالَ رَبِّ إِنِّى
وَهَنَ ٱلْعَظْمُ مِنِّى وَٱشْتَعَلَ ٱلرَّأْسُ
شَيْبًا وَلَمْ أَكُنۢ بِدُعَآئِكَ رَبِّ
شَقِيًّا ٤ وَإِنِّى خِفْتُ ٱلْمَوَٰلِىَ
مِن وَرَآءِى وَكَانَتِ ٱمْرَأَتِى
عَاقِرًا فَهَبْ لِى مِن لَّدُنكَ وَلِيًّا
٥ يَرِثُنِى وَيَرِثُ مِنْ ءَالِ يَعْقُوبَ
وَٱجْعَلْهُ رَبِّ رَضِيًّا ٦

1. For comparison see *Āl 'Imrān* 3: 33 ff. where, with some minor variation, substantially the same story is recounted.

2. Zechariah, who is mentioned here, was from the family of Aaron. For an appropriate understanding of his position it is necessary to comprehend the Israelites' priestly system. After their occupation of Palestine, the Israelites entrusted the government of the land to the twelve tribes, all descended from the Prophet Jacob (peace be on him) by dividing the functions of the government between them; whereas, the religious duties were assigned to the thirteenth tribe, the Levites. Even among the Levites though, the house that was set apart to 'sanctify the most holy things . . .' and to 'burn incense before the Lord', was the house of Aaron. Other Levites were permitted to enter the Temple, but their duties were 'to assist the sons of Aaron for the service of the house of the Lord, having the care of the courts and the chambers, the cleansing of all that is holy, and any work for the service of the house of God . . .' (*I Chronicles* 23: 28). They were also required to '. . . stand every morning,

(7) (He was told): 'Zechariah, We bring you the good news of the birth of a son whose name shall be Yahya (John), one whose namesake We never created before.'[5]

(8) He said: 'My Lord! How can I have a boy when my wife is barren and I have reached an extremely old age?' (9) He answered: 'So shall it be.' Your Lord says: "It is easy for Me", and then added: "For beyond doubt, I created you earlier when you were nothing"[6] ▶

يَٰزَكَرِيَّآ إِنَّا نُبَشِّرُكَ بِغُلَٰمٍ ٱسْمُهُۥ
يَحْيَىٰ لَمْ نَجْعَل لَّهُۥ مِن قَبْلُ سَمِيًّا
﴿٧﴾ قَالَ رَبِّ أَنَّىٰ يَكُونُ لِى
غُلَٰمٌ وَكَانَتِ ٱمْرَأَتِى عَاقِرًا
وَقَدْ بَلَغْتُ مِنَ ٱلْكِبَرِ عِتِيًّا
﴿٨﴾ قَالَ كَذَٰلِكَ قَالَ رَبُّكَ هُوَ
عَلَىَّ هَيِّنٌ وَقَدْ خَلَقْتُكَ مِن قَبْلُ
وَلَمْ تَكُ شَيْـًٔا ﴿٩﴾

---

thanking and praising the Lord, and likewise at evening, and whenever burnt offerings are offered to the Lord on Sabbaths, new moons, and feast days . . .' (*I Chronicles* 23: 30–1).

The descendants of Aaron comprised 24 houses, and these performed their duties in turn. One of these was the house of Abijah whose chief was Zechariah. Whenever it was his house's turn to serve the Temple, it was Zechariah's duty to go there and burn the incense. (For further details, see *I Chronicles* 23–4 and *Luke* 1: 5 ff. – Ed.)

3. What Zechariah meant was that he did not see any suitable successor in the house of Abijah who could hold his office after his death. No one in his family had the religious and moral qualities essential for shouldering the task which had so far been entrusted to him. He perceived that future generations held little promise.

4. He was not only concerned as an individual that he should have a good successor. What is more, he was looking for someone who would inherit all the virtues of the House of Israel.

5. According to *Luke*: 'None of your kindred is called by this name' (*Luke* 1: 61).

(10) Zechariah said: 'Lord, grant me a sign.'

Said He: 'Your sign is that you shall not be able to speak to people for three nights, though you will be otherwise sound.'

(11) Thereupon Zechariah came out from the sanctuary[7] and directed his people by gestures to extol His glory by day and by night.[8]

قَالَ رَبِّ ٱجْعَل لِّيٓ ءَايَةً قَالَ
ءَايَتُكَ أَلَّا تُكَلِّمَ ٱلنَّاسَ
ثَلَٰثَ لَيَالٍ سَوِيًّا ﴿١٠﴾ فَخَرَجَ
عَلَىٰ قَوْمِهِۦ مِنَ ٱلْمِحْرَابِ
فَأَوْحَىٰٓ إِلَيْهِمْ أَن سَبِّحُوا۟
بُكْرَةً وَعَشِيًّا ﴿١١﴾

---

6. One should take particular note of this conversation between Zechariah and the angel. For it is the same statement – viz. that the creation of a child is easy for God [even when the usual causes of such a birth do not exist] – which occurs a little later in the *sūrah* when the story of Mary is recounted (see verse 17 ff.). It is obvious that the same statement although appearing in two places has the same meaning.

Zechariah asks the angel how, given he is age-stricken and his wife barren, a son can be born to him. The angel simply replies: 'So shall it be.' In other words, he tells Zechariah that notwithstanding his old age and his wife's barrenness he will be blessed with a son. In this context, the angel obviously refers to God's infinite power, God Who has brought man into existence from a state of non-existence. If God can create a being from total non-existence, how can it possibly be difficult for Him to grant a son to one who has fallen into old age and whose wife is barren?

7. For the meaning of *'miḥrāb'* see *Towards Understanding the Qur'ān*, vol. I, *Āl 'Imrān* 3, n. 36, pp. 249–50.

8. The relevant Biblical account of the event as narrated in *Luke* is reproduced below. This will enable the reader to have a comparative view of both the Qur'ānic and Biblical accounts:

> In the days of Herod, King of Judea, there was a priest named Zechariah, of the division of Abijah; and he had a wife of the daughters of Aaron, and her name was Elizabeth. And they were both righteous before God, walking in all the commandments and ordinances of the Lord blameless. But they had no child, because Elizabeth was barren, and both were advanced in years.

(12) 'O John! Hold fast the Book with all your strength.[9] We had bestowed wisdom[10] upon him while he was still a child; ▶

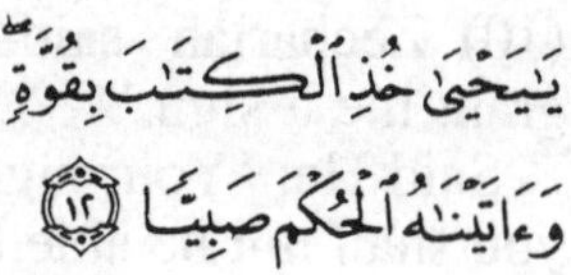

Now while he was serving as priest before God, when his division was on duty, according to the custom of the priesthood, it fell to him by lot to enter the temple of the Lord and burn incense. And the whole multitude of the people were praying outside at the hour of incense. And there appeared to him an angel of the Lord standing on the right side of the altar of incense. And Zechariah was troubled when he saw him, and fear fell upon him. But the angel said to him, 'Do not be afraid, Zechariah, for your prayer is heard, and your wife Elizabeth will bear you a son, and you shall call his name John.

And you will have joy and gladness,
and many will rejoice at his birth;
for he will be great before the Lord,
and he shall drink no wine nor strong drink,
and he will be filled with the Holy Spirit,
even from his mother's womb.
And he will turn many of the sons of Israel to the Lord their God,
and he will go before him in the spirit and power of Elijah,
to turn the hearts of the fathers to the children,
and the disobedient to the wisdom of the just,
to make ready for the Lord a people prepared.'

And Zechariah said to the angel, 'How shall I know this? For I am an old man, and my wife is advanced in years.' And the angel answered him, 'I am Gabriel, who stand in the presence of God; and I was sent to speak to you, and to bring you this good news. And behold, you will be silent and unable to speak until the day that these things come to pass, because you did not believe my words which will be fulfilled in their time.' And the people were waiting for Zechariah, and they wondered at his delay in the temple. And when he came out, he could not speak to them, and they perceived that he had seen a vision in the temple; and he made signs to them and remained dumb (*Luke* 1: 5–22).

9. The Qur'ānic narrative does not mention certain details of John's story – his birth under God's special command, and his attainment of youth. Omitting all this, the Qur'ān mentions the mission entrusted to John (peace be on him) when he attained maturity. This mission is referred to in just a single sentence

(13) and We also endowed him with tenderness[11] and purity; and he was exceedingly pious (14) and cherishing to his parents. Never was he insolent or rebellious. (15) Peace be upon him, the day he was born, and the day he will die, and the day he will be raised up alive.'[12]

وَحَنَانًا مِّن لَّدُنَّا وَزَكَوٰةً وَكَانَ
تَقِيًّا ﴿١٣﴾ وَبَرًّا بِوَٰلِدَيْهِ وَلَمْ يَكُن
جَبَّارًا عَصِيًّا ﴿١٤﴾ وَسَلَٰمٌ عَلَيْهِ
يَوْمَ وُلِدَ وَيَوْمَ يَمُوتُ وَيَوْمَ يُبْعَثُ
حَيًّا ﴿١٥﴾

---

on the occasion of his designation to the office of prophethood. That mission consisted of adhering to the Torah and to making efforts to ensure that the Israelites did the same.

10. The word *ḥukm* connotes the power of making the right decision, the ability to apply the principles of faith to changing circumstances, and the capacity to comprehend the teachings of the faith both in letter and spirit. It also connotes the ability to arrive at correct judgements, and to have the authority from God to judge things.

11. The Qur'ān uses the word *ḥanān,* which roughly denotes the love and compassion characteristic of mothers. (See *ḥnn* in Ibn Manẓūr, *Lisān al-'Arab* – Ed.) The idea is that John's compassion for God's creatures was comparable to a mother's compassion for her children.

12. The Biblical account of Prophet John's life and work can be found in different parts of the Bible. In what follows below we have attempted to develop an integral image of John with the help of these various statements, hoping that the statement made about him in the Qur'ān, both here and in *Sūrah Āl 'Imrān,* will be thereby further explicated.

According to *Luke,* John (peace be on him) was older than Jesus (peace be on him) by six months. His mother and Jesus' mother were close relatives. John was designated to prophethood when he was about 30 years old. According to the Book of *John,* it was in Jordan that he commenced his prophetic mission, inviting people to turn to God in penitence. He told people: 'I am the voice of one crying in the wilderness: ''Make straight the way of the Lord'', as the prophet Isaiah said' (*John* 1: 23).

According to *Mark,* John asked people to repent and baptized those who did so. This meant that he would have people repent and then take baptism in order that they become clean both in body and soul. A large number of people both in Judea and Jerusalem became his devotees and went to him for baptism (*Mark* 1: 4–5). He, therefore, came to be known as John the Baptist. The Israelites in general recognized him as a Prophet (*Matthew* 21: 26). Jesus (peace be on him) said of him: 'Truly, I say to you, among those born of women there has risen no one greater than John the Baptist' (*Matthew* 11: 11).

John (peace be on him) wore a garment made of camel's hair and had a leather girdle around his waist. His staple diet consisted of locusts and honey (*Matthew* 3: 4). Leading such an ascetic life, John would proclaim: 'Repent, for the kingdom of heaven is at hand' (*Matthew* 3: 2). This meant that Jesus' prophethood and the mission were close at hand. John is, therefore, known as Jesus' *irhāṣ* (precursor). (For the meaning of *irhāṣ* see *Lisān al-'Arab,* q.v. *r h ṣ* – Ed.) The Qur'ān makes the same point: 'Allah gives you good tidings of John who shall confirm a command of Allah' (*Āl 'Imrān,* 3: 39).

John (peace be on him) urged people to pray and fast. (For the praying and fasting of John's followers see *Matthew* 9: 14; *Luke* 3: 3, 5: 33 and 11: 1.) He also said: 'He who has two coats, let him share with him who has none; and he who has food, let him do likewise' (*Luke* 3: 11). Tax collectors asked him, 'Teacher, what shall we do?' And he said to them: 'Collect no more than is appointed you.' Soldiers also asked him: 'And we, what shall we do?' and he said to them: 'Rob no one by violence or by false accusation, and be content with your wages.' (See *Luke* 3: 12–14.)

When the Pharisees and Sadducees, people immersed in evil ways, came to him for baptism, he retorted: 'You brood of vipers! Who warned you to flee from the wrath to come? . . . and do not presume to say to yourselves, "We have Abraham as our father" . . . . Even now the axe is laid to the root of the trees; every tree therefore that does not bear good fruit is cut down and thrown into the fire' (*Matthew* 3: 7–10).

The ruler of the day, in whose domain John carried out his mission was a Jew by the name of Herod. Herod, however, was immersed in the ways of the Romans with the net result that corruption and immorality spread far and wide; indeed, Herod himself was so perverse that he had Herodias, his brother's wife, live with him in his house. John reproached Herod at this, raising his voice in protest at such incestuous behaviour. Before long Herod had John arrested, casting him into prison. But at the same time Herod knew that John was a pious and truthful person and honoured him in his heart on that account. He also held him in some awe as a result of his influence on the public. Herodias, however, burned with rage against John; the moral consciousness which he aroused inevitably meant that women of her ilk were stigmatized. Hence, she wanted John beheaded. The whole story is ably narrated in *Matthew*:

> . . . Herod had seized John and bound him and put him in prison, for the sake of Herodias, his brother Philip's wife; because John said to him, 'It is not lawful for you to have her.' And though he wanted to put him to death, he feared the people, because they held him to be a prophet. But when Herod's birthday came, the daughter of Herodias danced before the company, and pleased Herod, so that he promised with an oath to give her

(16) (O Muḥammad!): Recite in the Book the account of Mary,[13] when she withdrew from her people to a place towards the east; (17) and drew a curtain, screening herself from people,[14] whereupon We sent to her Our spirit and he appeared to her as a well-shaped man. (18) Mary exclaimed: 'I surely take refuge from you with the Most Compassionate Lord, if you are at all God-fearing.'

وَٱذۡكُرۡ فِي ٱلۡكِتَٰبِ مَرۡيَمَ
إِذِ ٱنتَبَذَتۡ مِنۡ أَهۡلِهَا مَكَانٗا
شَرۡقِيّٗا ١٦ فَٱتَّخَذَتۡ مِن
دُونِهِمۡ حِجَابٗا فَأَرۡسَلۡنَآ إِلَيۡهَا
رُوحَنَا فَتَمَثَّلَ لَهَا بَشَرٗا سَوِيّٗا
١٧ قَالَتۡ إِنِّيٓ أَعُوذُ بِٱلرَّحۡمَٰنِ
مِنكَ إِن كُنتَ تَقِيّٗا ١٨

whatever she might ask. Prompted by her mother, she said, 'Give me the head of John the Baptist here on a platter.' And the king was sorry; but because of his oaths and his guests he commanded it to be given; he sent and had John beheaded in the prison, and his head was brought on a platter and given to the girl, and she brought it to her mother. (*Matthew* 14: 3–11. See also *Mark* 6: 17–29; *Luke* 3: 19–20.)

13. For comparison see *Towards Understanding the Qur'ān,* vol. I, *Āl 'Imrān* 3, n. 42, pp. 251–2 and vol. II, *al-Nisā'* 4, nn. 190–1, pp. 105–7.

14. We learn from *Sūrah Āl 'Imrān* (see verse 35 ff.) that Mary's mother had vowed that Mary would be solely consecrated to the worship of God. In keeping with this vow, Mary was taken to Jerusalem where Zechariah was to look after her. It is also stated there that Mary retreated to a sanctuary in Jerusalem. Here, we are told that the location of that sanctuary was in the eastern part of Jerusalem.

Following a custom of her time, Mary concealed herself from other people by means of a drawn curtain. It is also pertinent at this point to show the error of those who, out of consideration for the Biblical account, have expressed the view that the 'eastern location' mentioned in the present verse, is Nazareth. This, however, is patently wrong. For Nazareth is situated to the north of Jerusalem not to the east of it.

(19) He said: 'I am just a message-bearer of your Lord, come to grant you a most pure boy.'

(20) Mary said: 'How can a boy be born to me when no man has even touched me, nor have I ever been unchaste?'

(21) The angel said: 'Thus shall it be. Your Lord says: "It is easy for Me; and We shall do so in order to make him a sign for mankind[15] and a mercy from Us. This has been decreed." '

قَالَ إِنَّمَآ أَنَا۠ رَسُولُ رَبِّكِ لِأَهَبَ
لَكِ غُلَٰمًا زَكِيًّا ﴿١٩﴾ قَالَتْ
أَنَّىٰ يَكُونُ لِي غُلَٰمٌ وَلَمْ يَمْسَسْنِي
بَشَرٌ وَلَمْ أَكُ بَغِيًّا ﴿٢٠﴾ قَالَ
كَذَٰلِكِ قَالَ رَبُّكِ هُوَ عَلَيَّ
هَيِّنٌ وَلِنَجْعَلَهُۥٓ ءَايَةً لِّلنَّاسِ
وَرَحْمَةً مِّنَّا وَكَانَ أَمْرًا
مَّقْضِيًّا ﴿٢١﴾

---

15. We have earlier discussed the significance of the angel's statement: 'So shall it be', in response to Zechariah's exclamation (see n. 6 above). The angel's utterance obviously does not mean that some human being would have physical contact with her whereby she would give birth to a son. It will be recalled – as we have pointed out – that Zechariah also expressed his amazement at the possibility of a child being born to him in his very old age and when his wife was barren. Significantly, the response of the angel on both counts was exactly the same: 'So shall it be.' Obviously, then, the meaning at both the places is bound to be the same. Likewise, in *Sūrah al-Dhāriyāt* the angel gives Abraham the good news of the birth of a son. On hearing this, Abraham's wife too exclaims incredulously how would a barren old woman such as herself give birth to a child. To this the angel says the same: 'So shall it be' (see *al-Dhāriyāt* 51: 28–30). The meaning then is crystal clear; Sarah would give birth to a son despite her old age and barrenness.

Now, were we to take the Qur'ānic statement here to mean that someone would have physical contact with Mary as a result of which she would give birth in the manner of all other women, then the statements which follow would become meaningless. For if the birth were to take place according to the known process of procreation, why should the angel say: 'Your Lord says: "This is easy for Me; and We shall do so in order to make him a sign for mankind, and a mercy from Us . . ." ' (verse 21). The word *āyah* ('sign') in this context definitely signifies 'miracle'. The same is corroborated by the following part of the verse: 'That is easy for Me . . .' Thus, what is being said here can only

(22) Then she conceived him and withdrew with him to a far-off place.[16] (23) Then the birth pangs drove her to the trunk of a palm-tree and she said: 'Oh, would that I had died before this and had been all forgotten.'[17] (24) Thereupon the angel at the foot of her cried out: 'Grieve not, for your Lord has caused a stream of water to flow beneath you. ▶

۞ فَحَمَلَتْهُ فَانتَبَذَتْ بِهِۦ مَكَانًا قَصِيًّا ﴿٢٢﴾ فَأَجَآءَهَا ٱلْمَخَاضُ إِلَىٰ جِذْعِ ٱلنَّخْلَةِ قَالَتْ يَٰلَيْتَنِى مِتُّ قَبْلَ هَٰذَا وَكُنتُ نَسْيًا مَّنسِيًّا ﴿٢٣﴾ فَنَادَىٰهَا مِن تَحْتِهَآ أَلَّا تَحْزَنِى قَدْ جَعَلَ رَبُّكِ تَحْتَكِ سَرِيًّا ﴿٢٤﴾

mean one thing – that this child's birth would be a miracle which God wanted to place before the Israelites. The details that follow make the miraculous character of Jesus (peace be on him) even more evident.

16. The Qur'ānic expression 'a far-off place' occurs with reference to Bethlehem. It was natural for Mary to move away from her place of confinement in Jerusalem to Bethlehem. She was, as we all know, the daughter of the most pious Israelite family – the house of Aaron – and she had consecrated herself exclusively to a life of devotion and worship. But then suddenly, she became pregnant. Had she stayed on in Jerusalem and her pregnancy been discovered, her life would have been made miserable by all kinds of people – whether by members of her own family or by other Israelites. Hence, Mary simply left her place of worship, hoping that at least until the birth of her child, she would be spared public denunciation, slander and scandalization.

The event itself is strong evidence proving that Jesus (peace be on him) was indeed born without a father. For had Mary been a married woman and had she become pregnant by her husband, there was no reason for her to abandon all her relatives and head to a far-off place merely to give birth to her child.

17. This verse enables one to gauge Mary's suffering and anguish. If one remembers the gravity of the situation, it is easy to grasp that she did not utter these words because of intense labour pains. Rather, what tormented her was the awkward situation in which she found herself, and she did not know how she was going to come out of it. For up until then she had somehow been able to hide her pregnancy. But once the child was born she could no longer hide the situation. The consoling words of the angel: 'grieve not' (verse 24), also indicate why Mary had uttered those anguished words. For, the psychology of

(25) Shake the trunk of the palm-tree towards yourself and fresh and ripe dates shall fall upon you. (26) So eat and drink and cool your eyes; and if you see any person say to him: Verily I have vowed a fast to the Most Compassionate Lord, and so I shall not speak to anyone today.'[18]

(27) Then she came to her people, carrying her baby. They said: 'O Mary! You have committed a monstrous thing. (28) O sister of Aaron![19] Your father was not an evil man, nor was your mother an unchaste woman.'[19a]

وَهُزِّىٓ إِلَيْكِ بِجِذْعِ ٱلنَّخْلَةِ تُسَٰقِطْ
عَلَيْكِ رُطَبًا جَنِيًّا ﴿٢٥﴾ فَكُلِى وَٱشْرَبِى
وَقَرِّى عَيْنًا فَإِمَّا تَرَيِنَّ مِنَ ٱلْبَشَرِ
أَحَدًا فَقُولِىٓ إِنِّى نَذَرْتُ لِلرَّحْمَٰنِ
صَوْمًا فَلَنْ أُكَلِّمَ ٱلْيَوْمَ إِنسِيًّا
﴿٢٦﴾ فَأَتَتْ بِهِۦ قَوْمَهَا تَحْمِلُهُۥ
قَالُوا۟ يَٰمَرْيَمُ لَقَدْ جِئْتِ شَيْـًٔا
فَرِيًّا ﴿٢٧﴾ يَٰٓأُخْتَ هَٰرُونَ مَا كَانَ
أَبُوكِ ٱمْرَأَ سَوْءٍ وَمَا كَانَتْ
أُمُّكِ بَغِيًّا ﴿٢٨﴾

---

a married woman who gives birth to her first child is well known. Even when she writhes in unbearable pain, she is far removed from grief and sorrow.

18. Mary was asked to say nothing concerning the baby. If anyone raised an accusing finger at the child's birth, it would be for God to explain the reality of the matter. (It may be recalled that this type of fast – a fast involving abstinence from speech – was quite customary among the Israelites.)

This directive is also suggestive of the true reason for Mary's disconcertion. It is also worth considering why a married woman giving birth to her first child would have resorted to a fast of silence.

19. This may be interpreted in two ways. Taken literally, it may mean that Mary had a brother named Aaron. Alternatively, in accordance with Arabic idiom, it may be taken to mean that she was a member of Aaron's house. For, according to the known Arabic linguistic tradition, a person is referred to as the brother of the tribe to which he belongs. If a person belongs to Muḍar, he is at times addressed as: 'O brother of Muḍar', or as 'O brother of Hamadān', if he belongs to Hamadān.

There are reasons to support each of these two interpretations. As for the first, there are traditions from the Prophet (peace be on him) saying so. (See, for instance al-Tirmidhī, *Sunan, Abwāb al-Ṣalāh 'an Rasūl Allāh, 'Bāb mā jā'*

(29) Thereupon Mary pointed to the child. They exclaimed: 'How can we speak to one who is in the cradle, a mere child?'[20]

فَأَشَارَتْ إِلَيْهِ قَالُوا كَيْفَ نُكَلِّمُ مَن كَانَ فِي الْمَهْدِ صَبِيًّا ﴿٢٩﴾

---

anna man adhdhan fa huwa yuqīm' – Ed.) As for the second, it seems to be supported by the context. For the event gave rise to such a commotion among the people that it can hardly be considered to be simply the case of the virgin sister of some unknown person called Aaron who returned home with a new-born baby. What enraged the public was that the apparently scandalous incident involved a girl who belonged to the most highly pious Israelite family – the house of Aaron. In principle, when there is a tradition which can be traced back to the Prophet (peace be on him), no other interpretation is admissible. However, when we consider the actual words of the tradition concerned – in Muslim, al-Nasā'ī and al-Tirmidhī – it becomes clear that they necessarily mean that Mary had a brother named Aaron. In the report narrated by Mughīrah ibn Shu'bah, it is stated that a Christian from Najrān raised the objection that the Qur'ān spoke of Mary as Aaron's sister while Aaron had passed away centuries before her. Mughīrah ibn Shu'bah was unable to provide any satisfactory explanation and so he placed the matter before the Prophet (peace be on him). The Prophet (peace be on him) said: 'Why did you not tell them that the Israelites used to name their children after Messengers and other righteous persons.' (Muslim, *K. al-Ādāb, 'Bāb al-Nahy 'an al-takannī bi Abī al-Qāsim . . .'*, and al-Tirmidhī, *Sunan, K. Tafsīr al-Qur'ān, 'Bāb wa min Sūrat Maryam'* – Ed.) What this statement suggests is that the objection could have been resolved in that manner and that instead of cutting a sorry figure, Mughīrah could have given a satisfactory answer by responding in such a way.

19a. Those who deny the miraculous birth of Jesus (peace be on him) can hardly explain the people's uproar when Mary returned to them with her baby. Nothing else but the birth of a child to an unmarried girl could explain such outraged feelings.

20. Some of those who have been engaged in distorting the meaning of the Qur'ān have been inclined to put the following interpretation on this verse: 'What, should we talk to him who is merely a child of yesterday?' They, thus, hold that this conversation took place at a time when Jesus was in his youth. The elderly Israelites were contemptuously disinclined to talk with him who was so much younger than themselves; someone who not long ago used to lie in his cradle before their very eyes.

Anyone who cares to consider the verse in its correct context, however, will

(30) The child cried out: 'Verily I am Allah's servant. He has granted me the Book and has made me a Prophet (31) and has made me blessed wherever I might be and has enjoined upon me Prayer and *Zakāh* (purifying alms) as long as I live; (32) and has made me dutiful to my mother.[20a] He has not made me oppressive, nor bereft of God's blessings. (33) Peace be upon me the day I was born and the day I will die, and the day I will be raised up alive.'[21]

قَالَ إِنِّي عَبْدُ ٱللَّهِ ءَاتَىٰنِيَ ٱلْكِتَٰبَ
وَجَعَلَنِي نَبِيًّا ﴿٣٠﴾ وَجَعَلَنِي مُبَارَكًا
أَيْنَ مَا كُنتُ وَأَوْصَٰنِي بِٱلصَّلَوٰةِ
وَٱلزَّكَوٰةِ مَا دُمْتُ حَيًّا ﴿٣١﴾
وَبَرًّۢا بِوَٰلِدَتِي وَلَمْ يَجْعَلْنِي
جَبَّارًا شَقِيًّا ﴿٣٢﴾ وَٱلسَّلَٰمُ عَلَيَّ
يَوْمَ وُلِدتُّ وَيَوْمَ أَمُوتُ
وَيَوْمَ أُبْعَثُ حَيًّا ﴿٣٣﴾

---

instantly realize that this interpretation is simply absurd. It also becomes obvious that recourse has been made to this far-fetched interpretation merely because of the disinclination of the persons concerned to affirm miracles. However, such people have allowed themselves to disregard the fact that such objections were made at the time of Jesus' birth and not when he had grown into a young man. Moreover, there are other Qur'ānic verses (see *Āl 'Imrān* 3: 46 and *al-Mā'idah* 5: 113) which mention Jesus (peace be on him) as uttering these words while he was a baby and in his cradle. We learn from *Āl 'Imrān* 3: 46, that the angel, while giving the good news of the coming birth of a son to Mary also said that Jesus would speak to people both while in his cradle and as a youth. In *Sūrah al-Mā'idah* 5: 113, God Himself tells Jesus that he will speak to people while still in his cradle as well as during his youth.

20a. It is significant here that Jesus is not mentioned as one who is dutiful to his parents, but rather as one who is only dutiful to his mother. This itself suggests that he did not have a father. Evidence which further corroborates this is that Jesus is invariably referred to in the Qur'ān as 'Jesus, son of Mary'.

21. The 'sign' referred to above is the person of the Prophet Jesus (peace be on him) who was presented as a miracle before the Israelites. Before punishing

(34) This is Jesus, the son of Mary; and this is the truth about him concerning which they are in doubt. (35) It does not behove Allah to take for Himself a son. Glory be to Him! When He decrees a thing He only says: 'Be' and it is.[22]

ذَٰلِكَ عِيسَى ٱبْنُ مَرْيَمَ قَوْلَ
ٱلْحَقِّ ٱلَّذِى فِيهِ يَمْتَرُونَ ﴿٣٤﴾
مَا كَانَ لِلَّهِ أَن يَتَّخِذَ مِن وَلَدٍ
سُبْحَٰنَهُۥٓ إِذَا قَضَىٰٓ أَمْرًا فَإِنَّمَا
يَقُولُ لَهُۥ كُن فَيَكُونُ ﴿٣٥﴾

---

the Israelites for their persistent wickedness and corruption, God wanted to make things indubitably clear so that they were left with no excuses for their errors. This was done in the following manner. A God-fearing and devout girl of the house of Aaron who had been set apart for a life of devotion in Jerusalem and who had been under the care and guidance of Zechariah, became – by God's will – pregnant while she was still a virgin. All this was with a particular design in mind. The purpose being that when she appeared with a child in her lap, creating a huge uproar within the nation, and when virtually the entire Israelite nation, in a state of anger and disgust, thronged around Mary, God made the baby speak to them. Thereafter, when that same child had attained maturity and claimed to be a Prophet, thousands could testify to the earlier miracle they themselves had witnessed, i.e. Jesus (peace be on him) speaking from his cradle. Now, if those people still refused to recognize him as a Prophet, and instead of dutifully following him, charged him with being a criminal and sought to crucify him, they should be dealt a punishment more severe than that meted out to all other peoples. (For further details see *Towards Understanding the Qur'ān,* vol. I, *Āl 'Imrān* 3, nn. 44–53, pp. 252–60; and vol. II, *al-Nisā'* 4, nn. 212–13, pp. 116–17; see also *al-Anbiyā'* 21, nn. 88–90 below, and *al-Mu'minūn* 23, n. 43.)

22. The thrust of the argument so far clearly reveals that the Christian belief in Jesus is false. Although John was born in a miraculous manner, this birth did not make him God's son. Similarly, although Jesus too was born by means of another miracle, this in no way provided any reason for considering him to be God's son. Jesus' birth was no more miraculous than John's and there are no grounds for referring to John as God's son. Remember that according to reports which are accepted by Christians, both John and Jesus were born miraculously. In *Luke,* both miracles are described in terms which bear close resemblance to the Qur'ānic version of the miracles. Hence, the Christian exaltation of Jesus as God's son is simply an act of doctrinal exaggeration which is shorn of all justification.

وَإِنَّ ٱللَّهَ رَبِّي وَرَبُّكُمْ فَٱعْبُدُوهُ هَٰذَا
صِرَٰطٌ مُّسْتَقِيمٌ ﴿٣٦﴾ فَٱخْتَلَفَ
ٱلْأَحْزَابُ مِنۢ بَيْنِهِمْ فَوَيْلٌ لِّلَّذِينَ
كَفَرُوا۟ مِن مَّشْهَدِ يَوْمٍ عَظِيمٍ ﴿٣٧﴾
أَسْمِعْ بِهِمْ وَأَبْصِرْ يَوْمَ يَأْتُونَنَا
لَٰكِنِ ٱلظَّٰلِمُونَ ٱلْيَوْمَ فِى ضَلَٰلٍ
مُّبِينٍ ﴿٣٨﴾ وَأَنذِرْهُمْ يَوْمَ ٱلْحَسْرَةِ
إِذْ قُضِىَ ٱلْأَمْرُ وَهُمْ فِى غَفْلَةٍ وَهُمْ
لَا يُؤْمِنُونَ ﴿٣٩﴾ إِنَّا نَحْنُ نَرِثُ
ٱلْأَرْضَ وَمَنْ عَلَيْهَا وَإِلَيْنَا
يُرْجَعُونَ ﴿٤٠﴾

(36) (Jesus had said): 'Indeed Allah is my Lord and your Lord, so serve Him alone. This is the straight way.'[23] (37) But different parties[24] began to dispute with one another. A dreadful woe awaits on that great Day for those that reject the truth. (38) How well shall they hear and how well shall they see on the Day they come to Us! But today the evil-doers are in manifest error. (39) (O Muḥammad!): Warn those who are steeped in heedlessness and are obstinately rejecting the truth that the Day shall come when things will be finally decided and they shall be left with utter remorse. (40) Ultimately, We shall inherit the earth and whatever is on it; to Us shall they be returned.[25]

23. The Christians are told that Jesus' message was the same as that of all other Prophets before him. He called people to serve none but the One True God. It was they, the Christians, who made Jesus – a servant of God – into God, and associated someone other than God in His divinity. This was merely an innovation of the Christians themselves, an innovation with which Jesus, whom they claimed to follow, had nothing to do with. (For further details see *Towards Understanding the Qur'ān,* vol. I, *Āl 'Imrān* 3, n. 68, pp. 267–8 and vol. II, *al-Mā'idah* 5, nn. 100, 101 and 103, pp. 180–5, 186–7; and *al-Zukhruf* 43, nn. 57–8.)

24. Reference is made here to the various Christian sects which hold mutually differing views.

(41) (O Muḥammad!): Recite in the Book the account of Abraham.[26] Most surely he was a man of truth, a Prophet. (42) (And remind people) when he said to his father: 'Father! Why for do you worship that which neither sees nor hears, and which can be of no avail to you? (43) Father, a knowledge that has not reached you has come to me. So follow me that I may guide you to a straight way. (44) Father, do not serve Satan,[27] for Satan has indeed been a persistent rebel against the Most Compassionate Lord. (45) Father, I fear that a punishment from the Most Compassionate Lord might strike you and you may end up as one of Satan's companions?'

وَاذْكُرْ فِي الْكِتَٰبِ إِبْرَٰهِيمَ إِنَّهُ كَانَ
صِدِّيقًا نَّبِيًّا ﴿٤١﴾ إِذْ قَالَ لِأَبِيهِ يَٰٓأَبَتِ
لِمَ تَعْبُدُ مَا لَا يَسْمَعُ وَلَا يُبْصِرُ وَلَا
يُغْنِي عَنكَ شَيْـًٔا ﴿٤٢﴾ يَٰٓأَبَتِ إِنِّي
قَدْ جَآءَنِي مِنَ الْعِلْمِ مَا لَمْ
يَأْتِكَ فَاتَّبِعْنِيٓ أَهْدِكَ صِرَٰطًا
سَوِيًّا ﴿٤٣﴾ يَٰٓأَبَتِ لَا تَعْبُدِ
الشَّيْطَٰنَ إِنَّ الشَّيْطَٰنَ كَانَ
لِلرَّحْمَٰنِ عَصِيًّا ﴿٤٤﴾ يَٰٓأَبَتِ
إِنِّيٓ أَخَافُ أَن يَمَسَّكَ عَذَابٌ
مِّنَ الرَّحْمَٰنِ فَتَكُونَ
لِلشَّيْطَٰنِ وَلِيًّا ﴿٤٥﴾

25. This concludes the discourse as addressed to the Christians. For a proper understanding of its significance, one should recall the historical background to this *sūrah* as stated in its introductory section (see pp. 139–43 above). The present discourse was revealed at a time when the oppressed Makkan Muslims were making their way towards Abyssinia to seek refuge in that Christian dominion. The purpose of revelation of this discourse, therefore, seems to have been to enable the Muslims to come forward with this official and authoritative statement whenever questions about the Islamic standpoint on Jesus might arise.

Additionally, the discourse seeks to establish the fact that Islam teaches Muslims not to make any compromise in matters relating to truth. The religious fervour of these righteous Muslim migrants to Abyssinia is all the more remarkable since they expressed the true doctrinal position about Jesus before the court of a Christian Emperor at a time when that court was strongly inclined to accept a bribe to hand them over to their enemies. It was obvious to the

(46) The father said: 'Abraham, have you turned away from my gods? If you do not give this up, I shall stone you to death. Now begone from me for ever.'

(47) Abraham answered: 'Peace be upon you. I shall seek pardon for you from my Lord.[27a] My Lord has always been kind to me. (48) I shall withdraw from you and all that you call upon beside Allah. I shall only call upon my Lord. I trust the prayer to my Lord will not go unanswered.'

قَالَ أَرَاغِبٌ أَنتَ عَنْ ءَالِهَتِي
يَٰٓإِبْرَٰهِيمُ لَئِن لَّمْ تَنتَهِ لَأَرْجُمَنَّكَ
وَٱهْجُرْنِي مَلِيًّا ﴿٤٦﴾ قَالَ سَلَٰمٌ
عَلَيْكَ سَأَسْتَغْفِرُ لَكَ رَبِّيٓ إِنَّهُۥ
كَانَ بِي حَفِيًّا ﴿٤٧﴾ وَأَعْتَزِلُكُمْ
وَمَا تَدْعُونَ مِن دُونِ ٱللَّهِ
وَأَدْعُوا۟ رَبِّي عَسَىٰٓ أَلَّآ أَكُونَ
بِدُعَآءِ رَبِّي شَقِيًّا ﴿٤٨﴾

Muslims that their forthright criticism of the Christian doctrine might enrage Negus and that as a result he might return them to the ruthless Makkan unbelievers. Notwithstanding the precariousness of their situation, they showed remarkable strength of faith and showed not even the slightest hesitation in speaking the truth.

26. From here onwards, the discourse is addressed to the Makkans who had compelled their own sons, brothers and all manner of relatives to leave their hearths and homes for the simple reason that they worshipped the One True God. The plight of these Muslims resembled that of the Prophet Abraham (peace be on him) who had earlier been forced by his father, and by his kith and kin, to say adieu to his homeland. The reason for recounting the Prophet Abraham's (peace be on him) story to the exclusion of other Prophets, is that the Quraysh considered Abraham (peace be on him) to be their patriarch, bragging about their descent from him in order to reinforce their pre-eminence throughout the whole of Arabia.

27. The Qur'ān says: 'Do not serve Satan.' This was said even though Abraham's father and his people worshipped idols. The statement – 'do not serve Satan' – is made because those people followed the behests of Satan. We, thus, learn that worship does not only mean a set of rituals, but also covers obedience. Another point that emerges from this statement is that if a person

(49) Thereupon after Abraham withdrew from his people and all whom they served beside Allah, We bestowed upon him Isaac and Jacob and made each of them a Prophet; (50) and We bestowed on them Our mercy, and granted them a truly lofty renown.[28]

(51) And recite in the Book the account of Moses. He was a chosen person,[29] a Messenger, a Prophet.[30] ▶

فَلَمَّا ٱعْتَزَلَهُمْ وَمَا يَعْبُدُونَ مِن دُونِ
ٱللَّهِ وَهَبْنَا لَهُۥٓ إِسْحَٰقَ وَيَعْقُوبَ وَكُلًّا
جَعَلْنَا نَبِيًّا ﴿٤٩﴾ وَوَهَبْنَا لَهُم مِّن
رَّحْمَتِنَا وَجَعَلْنَا لَهُمْ لِسَانَ صِدْقٍ
عَلِيًّا ﴿٥٠﴾ وَٱذْكُرْ فِى ٱلْكِتَٰبِ
مُوسَىٰٓ إِنَّهُۥ كَانَ مُخْلَصًا وَكَانَ رَسُولًا
نَّبِيًّا ﴿٥١﴾

---

unreservedly obeys someone, he is guilty of worshipping him even if he lavishes curses upon him. This is quite obvious given that human beings have never declared Satan to be the object of their devotional worship. On the contrary, they have always cursed him. (For further explanation see *al-Kahf* 18, nn. 49–50 above.)

27a. For further elaboration see *Towards Understanding the Qur'ān,* vol. III, *al-Tawbah* 9, n. 112, pp. 262–3.

28. This is intended to console and comfort the Muslim migrants who had been forced to forsake their homeland. They are being told that when Abraham surrendered his ties with his family, he courted no disaster. On the contrary, he eventually attained a much higher position. Likewise, the migration of the Prophet's followers will not bring about their ruination. Rather they will rise to heights of eminence which the Makkan unbelievers could not even have dreamed of before the advent of Islam.

29. The word *mukhlaṣ* used here denotes he who had been selected by God as exclusively His own.

30. The word *rasūl* literally means 'the one sent'. For this reason it is used to denote 'the envoy, the message-bearer, the emissary, the ambassador'. In the Qur'ān it is employed for angels who are entrusted by God with some special mission, or for those human beings who are assigned the task of communicating His Message to His creatures.

(52) We cried out to him from the right side of the Mount,[31] and We drew him near to Us by communing to him in secret,[32] (53) and out of Our mercy We appointed his brother Aaron, a Prophet (that he may assist him).

وَنَٰدَيْنَٰهُ مِن جَانِبِ ٱلطُّورِ ٱلْأَيْمَنِ وَقَرَّبْنَٰهُ نَجِيًّا ﴿٥٢﴾ وَوَهَبْنَا لَهُۥ مِن رَّحْمَتِنَآ أَخَاهُ هَٰرُونَ نَبِيًّا ﴿٥٣﴾

Lexicographers disagree as to the exact meaning of the word *nabī*. Some consider it to be the derivative of the verb *naba'a* and denotes 'to give news' and hence the word *nabī* means someone who brings news. Others consider it to be derived from *nabū,* meaning height and elevation. (Cf. al-Thānawī, *Kashshāf Iṣṭilāḥāt al-Funūn,* vol. II, art. *al-nabī,* pp. 1358–9 – Ed.) Accordingly, *nabī* is a person who holds a high, elevated position. Quoting the authority of al-Kisā'ī, al-Azharī has put forward an altogether different source – *nabī'a,* meaning 'way'. Thus, a *nabī* is someone who directs to the way that leads to God. (See al-Azharī, *Tahdhīb al-Lughah* (Cairo, 1967), vol. 15, p. 486 – Ed.)

In sum, when someone is called *rasūl nabī* it either means a 'Messenger of high standing', a 'Messenger who brings news from God', or a 'Messenger who directs people to the way leading to God'.

So far as the two words – *nabī* and *rasūl* – are concerned, they are generally used in the Qur'ān as equivalents. We note that on some occasions a person is referred to simply as *rasūl* (Messenger) whereas on others he is called *nabī* (Prophet). On yet further occasions, both words are used in conjunction with each other for the same person. There are also instances where the two words are employed in such a manner which distinguishes between a Prophet and a Messenger in respect of their status or the nature of their assignment. For instance, in *Sūrah al-Ḥajj* it is said: 'Never did We send a Messenger or a Prophet before you except . . .' (*al-Ḥajj* 22: 52). This clearly indicates that the Messenger and the Prophet represent two distinct entities. As a result, commentators on the Qur'ān have engaged in serious discussions about the nature of these differences between a Prophet and a Messenger. The fact, however, remains that these scholars have failed to persuasively establish the precise nature of any difference between a Messenger and a Prophet. All that can be said with certainty is that the word Messenger (*rasūl*) has a more restrictive connotation than the word Prophet (*nabī*). Hence, while every Messenger is a Prophet, every Prophet does not enjoy the status of a Messenger. In other words, the word *'rasūl'* (Messenger) is used for those great figures who had been assigned duties of greater significance than those

(54) And recite in the Book the account of Ishmael! He was ever true to his promise, and was a Messenger, a Prophet. (55) He enjoined his household to observe Prayer and to give *Zakāh* (purifying alms); and his Lord was well pleased with him.

(56) And recite in the Book the account of Idrīs.[33] He was a man of truth, a Prophet; (57) and We exalted him to a lofty position.[34]

وَٱذۡكُرۡ فِي ٱلۡكِتَٰبِ إِسۡمَٰعِيلَۚ إِنَّهُۥ كَانَ
صَادِقَ ٱلۡوَعۡدِ وَكَانَ رَسُولٗا نَّبِيّٗا ﴿٥٤﴾
وَكَانَ يَأۡمُرُ أَهۡلَهُۥ بِٱلصَّلَوٰةِ وَٱلزَّكَوٰةِ
وَكَانَ عِندَ رَبِّهِۦ مَرۡضِيّٗا ﴿٥٥﴾ وَٱذۡكُرۡ
فِي ٱلۡكِتَٰبِ إِدۡرِيسَۚ إِنَّهُۥ كَانَ صِدِّيقٗا
نَّبِيّٗا ﴿٥٦﴾ وَرَفَعۡنَٰهُ مَكَانًا عَلِيًّا ﴿٥٧﴾

---

assigned to mere Prophets. This point is further corroborated by the tradition reported by Aḥmad ibn Ḥanbal from Abū Umāmah, and by Ḥākim, from Abū Dharr. According to this tradition Muḥammad (peace be on him) was asked about the number of Messengers. He replied that they were 313 or 315 in number, whereas when asked about the number of Prophets, he mentioned their number to be 124,000. (See Aḥmad ibn Ḥanbal, *Musnad,* vol. 5, p. 266; al-Ḥākim al-Nayshābūrī, *al-Mustadrak* (Riyadh), vol. 2, p. 597 – Ed.) Although the chains of transmission of this *ḥadīth* are weak, it has been reported in such a variety of ways and to such a great extent, that this weakness is compensated for.

31. The right side of Mount Ṭūr (i.e. Sinai) refers to its eastern side. The Prophet Moses (peace be on him) on his way from Midian to Egypt, took the route which passes the southern side of the Mount. Were anyone to look at the Mount from its southern side, the east would be to his right and the western side would be to his left. Hence, it is with context to the Prophet Moses' vantage-point that the eastern side is mentioned as lying to the right. Devoid of that reference, it is quite obvious that a mountain as such can neither have any right side nor any left.

32. For further explanation see *Towards Understanding the Qur'ān,* vol. II, *al-Nisā'* 4, n. 206, pp. 114–15.

33. There is some disagreement concerning Prophet Idrīs (Enoch) (peace be on him). Whilst some scholars regard him as an Israeli Prophet, the majority of scholars believe that Enoch lived at a time prior even to that of the Prophet

Noah (peace be on him). There are authentic *ḥadīth* to help us establish the historicity of the Prophet Enoch (peace be on him). However, there seems to be some indication at one place in the Qur'ān that he did appear before the time of Noah (peace be on him):

> These are the Prophets upon whom Allah bestowed His favour from the seed of Adam, and from the seed of those whom We carried (in the Ark) with Noah, and from the seed of Abraham and Israel (verse 58).

Of the Messengers mentioned here, John, Jesus and Moses are descendants of Israel, and Ishmael, Isaac and Jacob are descendants of Abraham, and Abraham is a descendant of Noah. This leaves only Idrīs and it is to him alone that the expression 'descendant of Adam' might be applied. It should also be pointed out that commentators on the Qur'ān generally believe that the Biblical figure of Enoch is identical with the Prophet called Idrīs in the Qur'ān. The Biblical account of Enoch is narrated as follows:

> When Enoch had lived sixty-five years, he became the father of Methuselah. Enoch walked with God after the birth of Methuselah three hundred years . . . Enoch walked with God; and he was not, for God took him (*Genesis* 5: 21–4).

Israelite traditions in the Talmud describe Enoch in greater detail. These traditions state that at some time before the advent of the Prophet Noah (peace be on him), people had taken to evil ways, and that it was then that God's angel cried out the following to Enoch, who up until then had lived in seclusion and who was devoted to a life of asceticism:

> 'Arise, go forth from thy solitude and walk among the people of the land. Teach them the way they should go, and instruct them in the actions they should perform.' And Enoch did as the Lord commanded him. He walked among the people and taught them the ways of the Creator, assembling them together and addressing them in earnestness and truth . . . And Enoch reigned over the human race for three hundred and fifty-three years. In justice and righteousness he ruled, and peace blessed the land during all this period. (*The Talmud Selections,* pp. 18–21.)

34. The statement here simply means that God granted Enoch a high position. Under the influence of Israelite traditions, however, many Muslims have come to believe that God raised him to the heavens. So far as the Bible is concerned, it only claims that he disappeared. The Talmudic account, however, is embellished with a great many details. It ends with the following statement: 'And on the seventh day Enoch ascended to heaven in a whirlwind, with chariot and horses of fire.' (*The Talmud Selections,* p. 21.)

(58) These are the Prophets upon whom Allah bestowed His favour from the seed of Adam, and from the seed of those whom We carried (in the Ark) with Noah, and from the seed of Abraham and Israel. They were those whom We guided and chose (for an exalted position). They were such that when the words of the Most Compassionate Lord were recited to them, they fell down in prostration, weeping.

(59) They were succeeded by a people who neglected the Prayers[35] and pursued their lusts.[36] They shall presently meet with their doom, (60) except those who repent and believe and act righteously. Such shall enter Paradise and shall not be wronged at all. ▶

أُوْلَٰٓئِكَ ٱلَّذِينَ أَنۡعَمَ ٱللَّهُ عَلَيۡهِم مِّنَ
ٱلنَّبِيِّـۧنَ مِن ذُرِّيَّةِ ءَادَمَ وَمِمَّنۡ
حَمَلۡنَا مَعَ نُوحٖ وَمِن ذُرِّيَّةِ إِبۡرَٰهِيمَ
وَإِسۡرَٰٓءِيلَ وَمِمَّنۡ هَدَيۡنَا وَٱجۡتَبَيۡنَآۚ
إِذَا تُتۡلَىٰ عَلَيۡهِمۡ ءَايَٰتُ ٱلرَّحۡمَٰنِ
خَرُّواْۤ سُجَّدٗا وَبُكِيّٗا ۩ ﴿٥٨﴾
۞فَخَلَفَ مِنۢ بَعۡدِهِمۡ خَلۡفٌ
أَضَاعُواْ ٱلصَّلَوٰةَ وَٱتَّبَعُواْ
ٱلشَّهَوَٰتِۖ فَسَوۡفَ يَلۡقَوۡنَ غَيًّا
﴿٥٩﴾ إِلَّا مَن تَابَ وَءَامَنَ وَعَمِلَ
صَٰلِحٗا فَأُوْلَٰٓئِكَ يَدۡخُلُونَ ٱلۡجَنَّةَ
وَلَا يُظۡلَمُونَ شَيۡـٔٗا ﴿٦٠﴾

35. They either gave up observing Prayers, or became indifferent or negligent to them. In fact, negligence and abandoning Prayer are the very first step in a people's slide towards their decline. For Prayer is the primary link between man and God. Prayer keeps a person constantly in touch with God, during all hours of the day and night. Prayer prevents a person from moving away from a life of devotion, worship and obedience of Him. As soon as this bond is broken, man increasingly begins to draw away from God. This may even happen to such an extent that not only is man's relationship with God reduced to naught on a practical level but also on an intellectual level. It is for this reason that the Qur'ān expounds here a general rule: that the corruption in a nation which originally followed a Prophet began the moment that nation abandoned Prayer.

36. Following one's lusts and desires rather than truth and justice naturally results from the weakening of one's God-consciousness. When a person

(61) Theirs shall be everlasting Gardens which the Most Compassionate Lord has promised His servants in a realm which is beyond the ken of sense perception.[37] Surely His promise shall be fulfilled. (62) They shall not hear in it anything vain; they shall hear only what is good;[38] and they shall have their provision in it, morning and evening. (63) Such is the Paradise which We shall cause those of Our servants who have been God-fearing to inherit.

جَنَّٰتِ عَدۡنٍ ٱلَّتِي وَعَدَ ٱلرَّحۡمَٰنُ
عِبَادَهُۥ بِٱلۡغَيۡبِۚ إِنَّهُۥ كَانَ وَعۡدُهُۥ
مَأۡتِيّٗا ٦١ لَّا يَسۡمَعُونَ فِيهَا لَغۡوًا
إِلَّا سَلَٰمٗاۖ وَلَهُمۡ رِزۡقُهُمۡ فِيهَا
بُكۡرَةٗ وَعَشِيّٗا ٦٢ تِلۡكَ ٱلۡجَنَّةُ
ٱلَّتِي نُورِثُ مِنۡ عِبَادِنَا مَن كَانَ
تَقِيّٗا ٦٣

becomes heedless of God and abandons Prayer, he comes increasingly into the grip of his own carnal desires. Eventually, he becomes impervious to all God's commands despite the fact that these had earlier shaped his morality and conduct. Instead, bit by bit, he begins to follow, all those ways which conform to his own likes and dislikes.

37. This refers to the Gardens promised to the believers by God, Gardens which are beyond the ken of their senses.

38. The word used here – *salām* – denotes that which is free from all flaws and imperfections. Of the numerous blessings bestowed on man in Paradise, one of these will be that he will not encounter anything vulgar, stupid or filthy. The prevailing atmosphere in Paradise will be one of elegance and decency, and all its inmates will be people possessed of good taste. Hence, all those who abide in Paradise will hear neither abuse nor slander nor obscenity. Their ears will hear only those things which are good and decent. The import of this great blessing can only be appreciated by people whose tastes have not been impaired. Such persons can well appreciate what a torture it is for a person of good taste to be placed in a milieu where he is exposed to lies, slander, mischievous statements, obscenity and vulgarity.

(64) (The angels will say): '(O Muḥammad!):[39] We descend not except by the command of your Lord. To Him belongs all that is before us and all that is behind us, and all that is in-between. Your Lord is not forgetful in the least. (65) He is the Lord of the heavens and the earth and all that is in-between. Serve Him, then, and be constant in serving Him.[40] Do you know anyone that might be His compeer?'[41]

وَمَا نَتَنَزَّلُ إِلَّا بِأَمْرِ رَبِّكَ لَهُۥ مَا بَيْنَ
أَيْدِينَا وَمَا خَلْفَنَا وَمَا بَيْنَ ذَٰلِكَ
وَمَا كَانَ رَبُّكَ نَسِيًّا ﴿٦٤﴾ رَّبُّ
ٱلسَّمَٰوَٰتِ وَٱلْأَرْضِ وَمَا بَيْنَهُمَا
فَٱعْبُدْهُ وَٱصْطَبِرْ لِعِبَٰدَتِهِۦ هَلْ
تَعْلَمُ لَهُۥ سَمِيًّا ﴿٦٥﴾

39. This whole paragraph is in fact a parenthetical statement which marks the conclusion of one discourse and which serves as a prelude to another. The style adopted here suggests that this *sūrah* was revealed some time after the Prophet (peace be on him) and his Companions had gone through trying circumstances, whereby they constantly waited for revelation to guide and comfort them. This time-gap in revelation, therefore, distressed them greatly. It was against this background that Gabriel came down to the Prophet (peace be on him) along with a retinue of other angels. First of all he proclaimed that command which was urgently required under the circumstances, but before proceeding further, he said something which at once explained his prolonged absence: he spoke words of comfort from God as well as an exhortation to the believers to remain patient and restrained.

What is said above is not only borne out by internal evidence, it is also corroborated by several traditions which have been quoted by al-Ṭabarī, Ibn Kathīr and al-'Ālūsī, the author of *Rūḥ al-Ma'ānī,* in their works of Qur'ānic exegesis.

40. Believers are directed to steadfastly adhere to God's service and to bear all the sufferings which they might encounter with patience. They are told that if there occurs any delay in providing them with support and comfort they should not lose heart. An obedient believer is required to be content in all circumstances with God's Will and to persevere, with full determination in the task assigned to him as God's servant.

(66) Man is prone to say:
'Shall I be raised to life after
I die?' (67) Does man not
remember that We created
him before when he was
nothing. (68) By your Lord,
We will surely muster them
and the devils together.[42] Then
We will surely bring them all,
on their knees, around Hell,
(69) and then We will draw
aside from each party those
who were most rebellious
against the Most Compassionate Lord,[43] (70) and
then We shall know well all
those most worthy to be cast in
Hell. (71) There is not one
of you but shall pass by Hell.[44]
This is a decree which your
Lord will fulfil. (72) Then
We shall deliver those that
feared Allah and leave the
wrong-doers there on their
knees.

وَيَقُولُ ٱلْإِنسَٰنُ أَءِذَا مَا مِتُّ لَسَوْفَ
أُخْرَجُ حَيًّا ﴿٦٦﴾ أَوَلَا يَذْكُرُ
ٱلْإِنسَٰنُ أَنَّا خَلَقْنَٰهُ مِن قَبْلُ وَلَمْ يَكُ
شَيْـًٔا ﴿٦٧﴾ فَوَرَبِّكَ لَنَحْشُرَنَّهُمْ
وَٱلشَّيَٰطِينَ ثُمَّ لَنُحْضِرَنَّهُمْ حَوْلَ
جَهَنَّمَ جِثِيًّا ﴿٦٨﴾ ثُمَّ لَنَنزِعَنَّ مِن
كُلِّ شِيعَةٍ أَيُّهُمْ أَشَدُّ عَلَى ٱلرَّحْمَٰنِ
عِتِيًّا ﴿٦٩﴾ ثُمَّ لَنَحْنُ أَعْلَمُ بِٱلَّذِينَ
هُمْ أَوْلَىٰ بِهَا صِلِيًّا ﴿٧٠﴾ وَإِن مِّنكُمْ
إِلَّا وَارِدُهَا كَانَ عَلَىٰ رَبِّكَ حَتْمًا
مَّقْضِيًّا ﴿٧١﴾ ثُمَّ نُنَجِّى ٱلَّذِينَ
ٱتَّقَوا۟ وَّنَذَرُ ٱلظَّٰلِمِينَ فِيهَا
جِثِيًّا ﴿٧٢﴾

---

41. The word *samī* means namesake or homonym. The purpose of the statement is to emphasize that God alone is the One True God, and no one else holds that position. And if indeed there is no other god – and they know that is the case – there is no other than Him to worship and serve.

42. This refers to those devils under whose evil influence the unbelievers regarded the life in this world as the only life and thereby denied the Next Life where all will be called to account.

43. This alludes to the leaders of the groups that defied God's commands.

(73) When Our clear reve-
lations are recited to those
who deny the truth they are
wont to say to those who have
faith: 'Which of the two
groups has a better status and
whose assemblies are grander?'[45] (74) How numerous
are the peoples We destroyed
before them – those that were
more resourceful and grander
in outward appearance! (75)
Say: 'The Most Compassionate
Lord grants respite to those
who stray into error, until they
behold what they had been
threatened with, either God's
chastisement [in the world] or
the Hour (of Resurrection)' –
then they fully know whose
station is worse, and who is
weaker in hosts! ▶

وَإِذَا تُتْلَىٰ عَلَيْهِمْ ءَايَٰتُنَا بَيِّنَٰتٍ قَالَ
الَّذِينَ كَفَرُوا لِلَّذِينَ ءَامَنُوٓا أَيُّ
الْفَرِيقَيْنِ خَيْرٌ مَّقَامًا وَأَحْسَنُ
نَدِيًّا ﴿٧٣﴾ وَكَمْ أَهْلَكْنَا قَبْلَهُم
مِّن قَرْنٍ هُمْ أَحْسَنُ أَثَٰثًا وَرِءْيًا
﴿٧٤﴾ قُلْ مَن كَانَ فِي الضَّلَٰلَةِ
فَلْيَمْدُدْ لَهُ الرَّحْمَٰنُ مَدًّا حَتَّىٰٓ إِذَا
رَأَوْا مَا يُوعَدُونَ إِمَّا الْعَذَابَ
وَإِمَّا السَّاعَةَ فَسَيَعْلَمُونَ
مَنْ هُوَ شَرٌّ مَّكَانًا وَأَضْعَفُ
جُندًا ﴿٧٥﴾

44. The word *wārid,* according to some traditions, signifies 'one who enters'. (Aḥmad ibn Ḥanbal, *Musnad,* vol. 3, pp. 328–9 – Ed.) These traditions, however, are not backed up by a chain of authentic narrations going back to the Prophet (peace be on him). Moreover, this interpretation is contrary to the teachings of the Qur'ān and a large number of authentic traditions which exclude righteous believers from entering Hell. Furthermore, this view is not supported by lexical evidence for indeed *warūd* does not mean entrance. What is meant by this verse, therefore, is that everyone will pass by Hell; yet, as stated in the following verse, the pious will be saved from entering it, while the wrong-doers will be hurled into it. (See al-Tirmidhī, *Sunan, K. Tafsīr al-Qur'ān, 'Bāb wa min Sūrat Maryam'*; Muslim, *K. al-Īmān, 'Bāb Adná Ahl al-Jannah Manzilatan fī hā'* – Ed.)

45. This was a fallacious argument which the unbelievers often put forward, claiming that it was they rather than the believers upon whom God's bounties were lavished. They audaciously asked: 'Who has more stately houses to live in – the believers or us? Who enjoy higher standards of living –

(76) (On the contrary), Allah increases in guidance[46] those who follow the right way. Lasting acts of righteousness are better in the sight of your Lord as reward and conducive to a better end.

(77) Have you seen him who rejects Our signs and said: 'Surely I shall continue to be favoured with riches and children.'[47] (78) Has he obtained knowledge of the Unseen, or has he taken a covenant with the Most Compassionate Lord? (79) By no means! We shall write down all what he says;[48] and We shall greatly prolong his chastisement. (80) And We shall inherit all the resources and hosts of which he boasts, and he will come to Us all alone.

وَيَزِيدُ ٱللَّهُ ٱلَّذِينَ ٱهْتَدَوْا۟
هُدًى ۗ وَٱلْبَٰقِيَٰتُ ٱلصَّٰلِحَٰتُ
خَيْرٌ عِندَ رَبِّكَ ثَوَابًا وَخَيْرٌ مَّرَدًّا
٧٦ أَفَرَءَيْتَ ٱلَّذِى كَفَرَ
بِـَٔايَٰتِنَا وَقَالَ لَأُوتَيَنَّ مَالًا
وَوَلَدًا ٧٧ أَطَّلَعَ ٱلْغَيْبَ أَمِ
ٱتَّخَذَ عِندَ ٱلرَّحْمَٰنِ عَهْدًا ٧٨
كَلَّا ۚ سَنَكْتُبُ مَا يَقُولُ
وَنَمُدُّ لَهُۥ مِنَ ٱلْعَذَابِ مَدًّا
٧٩ وَنَرِثُهُۥ مَا يَقُولُ وَيَأْتِينَا
فَرْدًا ٨٠

---

the believers or us? Whose assemblies are more splendid and grandiose – the believers or ours? How is it possible, they asked, that those who follow the truth suffer such a miserable lot whilst those who follow falsehood – as you fancy – prosper? (For details, see *al-Kahf* 18, nn. 37–8 above.)

46. That is, that whenever adherents to the truth are put to the test, God grants them the ability to judge correctly and to follow the right path. God also protects them from evil and from error. They are constantly helped by God's guidance which enables them to proceed ahead along the right path.

47. This represents the characteristic mode of thinking of the unbelievers who happen to be well-off and prosperous. Such people tend to impress upon believers that no matter what they claim about the waywardness of unbelievers or say about them being struck down by God's punishment, the fact remains that they seem better-off than the believers. Such people also contend that there

(81) They have taken other gods beside Allah that they may be a source of strength for them.[49] (82) By no means! They shall soon deny their worship[50] and shall become their adversaries instead.

(83) Do you not see that We have sent devils upon the unbelievers who greatly incite them (to oppose the truth)? (84) Therefore, do not hasten (in seeking a scourge against them). We are counting their days.[51] (85) The Day shall soon come when We shall bring together the God-fearing to [Us] the Most Compassionate Lord, as honoured guests; ▶

وَاتَّخَذُوا مِن دُونِ اللَّهِ آلِهَةً
لِّيَكُونُوا لَهُمْ عِزًّا ﴿٨١﴾ كَلَّا ۚ
سَيَكْفُرُونَ بِعِبَادَتِهِمْ وَيَكُونُونَ
عَلَيْهِمْ ضِدًّا ﴿٨٢﴾ أَلَمْ تَرَ أَنَّا أَرْسَلْنَا
الشَّيَاطِينَ عَلَى الْكَافِرِينَ تَؤُزُّهُمْ
أَزًّا ﴿٨٣﴾ فَلَا تَعْجَلْ عَلَيْهِمْ ۖ إِنَّمَا
نَعُدُّ لَهُمْ عَدًّا ﴿٨٤﴾ يَوْمَ نَحْشُرُ
الْمُتَّقِينَ إِلَى الرَّحْمَٰنِ وَفْدًا ﴿٨٥﴾

---

is every reason to believe that what is happening to them – the unbelievers of the present – will also happen in the future. These people are wont to say exultantly: ‘Look at my riches, at my power and position, at the eminence achieved by my offspring: do these show that I have been cursed by God?’ Such thoughts were not merely those of just a few stray Makkan unbelievers, but rather such illusions were entertained by every tribal chief, by every eminent Makkan.

48. Such boastful remarks will further compound his crimes, and he will have to pay the price for such outrageous utterances.

49. The word used in this verse is *‘izzāh* which conveys the meaning of bringing honour and glory. According to Arabic usage, the word denotes one who is so powerful that none will dare try to harm him. (See *‘izz* in Ibn Manẓūr, *Lisān al-‘Arab* – Ed.) The idea that someone can be the cause of honour and glory for another person means that the former is so effective a supporter of the other that no enemy will even entertain evil designs against him.

50. On the Day of Judgement the gods which men have contrived will be utterly powerless and they will declare that they never asked anyone to worship

(86) and We shall drive the
guilty ones to Hell as thirsty
animals. (87) On that Day
none will have the power to
intercede for them except
those who received a sanction
from the Most Compassionate
Lord.[52]

(88) They claim: 'The Most
Compassionate Lord has taken
a son to Himself.' (89) Surely you have made a monstrous
statement. (90) It is such a
monstrosity that heavens
might well-nigh burst forth at
it, the earth might be cleaved,
and the mountains fall (91)
at their ascribing a son to the
Most Compassionate Lord.
(92) It does not behove the
Most Compassionate Lord that
He should take a son. (93)
There is no one in the heavens
and the earth but he shall come
to the Most Compassionate
Lord as His servant. ▶

وَنَسُوقُ ٱلْمُجْرِمِينَ إِلَىٰ جَهَنَّمَ وِرْدًا
﴿٨٦﴾ لَّا يَمْلِكُونَ ٱلشَّفَٰعَةَ إِلَّا مَنِ
ٱتَّخَذَ عِندَ ٱلرَّحْمَٰنِ عَهْدًا ﴿٨٧﴾
وَقَالُوا۟ ٱتَّخَذَ ٱلرَّحْمَٰنُ وَلَدًا ﴿٨٨﴾
لَّقَدْ جِئْتُمْ شَيْـًٔا إِدًّا ﴿٨٩﴾
تَكَادُ ٱلسَّمَٰوَٰتُ يَتَفَطَّرْنَ
مِنْهُ وَتَنشَقُّ ٱلْأَرْضُ وَتَخِرُّ ٱلْجِبَالُ
هَدًّا ﴿٩٠﴾ أَن دَعَوْا۟ لِلرَّحْمَٰنِ وَلَدًا
﴿٩١﴾ وَمَا يَنۢبَغِى لِلرَّحْمَٰنِ أَن يَتَّخِذَ
وَلَدًا ﴿٩٢﴾ إِن كُلُّ مَن فِى
ٱلسَّمَٰوَٰتِ وَٱلْأَرْضِ إِلَّآ ءَاتِى
ٱلرَّحْمَٰنِ عَبْدًا ﴿٩٣﴾

them; they will also say that they were not even aware of the existence of those who were foolish enough to worship them.

51. The Muslims were asked not to get impatient at the excesses the unbelievers committed. For the time for them to be struck by God's punishment had drawn near; they had gone just too far, exceeding all limits. The term granted to them by God was all but over, and one only had to wait a little while before they would be seized by God's scourge.

52. The verse seems to suggest two things regarding intercession. Firstly, it will be possible only to intercede for those in whose favour God allows intercession. Secondly, intercession will only be made by those whom God

(94) Verily He encompasses
them and has counted them
all. (95) On the Day of
Resurrection each one of them
will come to Him singly.

(96) Indeed the Most Com-
passionate Lord will soon
create enduring love for those
who believe and do righteous
works.[53] (97) Therefore, We
have revealed the Qur'ān in
your tongue and made it easy to
understand that you may give
glad tidings to the God-fearing
and warn a contentious people.
(98) How numerous are the
peoples that We destroyed
before them! Do you perceive
any one of them, or hear even a
whisper of them?

لَّقَدْ أَحْصَىٰهُمْ وَعَدَّهُمْ عَدًّا ﴿٩٤﴾
وَكُلُّهُمْ ءَاتِيهِ يَوْمَ ٱلْقِيَـٰمَةِ فَرْدًا
﴿٩٥﴾ إِنَّ ٱلَّذِينَ ءَامَنُوا۟ وَعَمِلُوا۟
ٱلصَّـٰلِحَـٰتِ سَيَجْعَلُ لَهُمُ
ٱلرَّحْمَـٰنُ وُدًّا ﴿٩٦﴾ فَإِنَّمَا يَسَّرْنَـٰهُ
بِلِسَانِكَ لِتُبَشِّرَ بِهِ
ٱلْمُتَّقِينَ وَتُنذِرَ بِهِۦ قَوْمًا لُّدًّا
﴿٩٧﴾ وَكَمْ أَهْلَكْنَا قَبْلَهُم مِّن
قَرْنٍ هَلْ تُحِسُّ مِنْهُم مِّنْ أَحَدٍ
أَوْ تَسْمَعُ لَهُمْ رِكْزًۢا ﴿٩٨﴾

---

permits to do so. Such are the words of the verse that they seem to embrace both elements.

The one who conforms to the first statement is one who has faith and lives a good life in devotion to God, one who is deserving of God's pardon and forgiveness. As for the second statement, it means that God will let it be known who may intervene, and it is only they, no one else, who will be able to intercede. This should dispel the illusions of those who look with great hope at some people, feeling sure that they will intercede on their behalf. What will actually happen is that no one except those whom God permits to intercede will be able to utter even a single word in His presence.

53. The believers throughout Makka were at that time subjected to the most abject humiliation. Here they are being told that that situation will not endure. Soon they will become God's favourites, the heroes of all mankind, on account of their moral excellence. People will involuntarily be attracted to them. People will simply adore them, bowing to them in respect. As for their opponents, they are doomed to ignominy. Leadership which rests on sin and transgression, on arrogance and trickery, can never win the hearts of people;

the most that it can do is force them into outward obedience. Conversely, those who invite people to the right way and are themselves invested with honesty, veracity, sincerity and good morals, are bound to win over hearts in the end even if they provoke revulsion at the outset. It is simply impossible for those who lack honesty and sincerity to impede their path for long.

Sūrah 20

Ṭā Hā

(Makkan Period)

Period of Revelation

This *sūrah* was revealed around the same time as that of *Sūrah Maryam*. Furthermore, it was probably revealed during the period when the migration to Abyssinia took place, or a little later. What is beyond doubt, however, is that it was revealed before 'Umar ibn al-Khaṭṭāb embraced Islam.

The most authentic and widely-circulated tradition about 'Umar's acceptance of Islam is as follows: When 'Umar set out to kill the Prophet Muḥammad (peace be on him), on the way he met someone who was aware of what 'Umar intended. This person asked 'Umar to first set his own house in order; the stranger was alluding to the fact that 'Umar's own sister and brother-in-law had already embraced Islam. Upon hearing this 'Umar rushed to his sister's house. His sister, Fāṭimah bint al-Khaṭṭāb and his brother-in-law, Sa'īd ibn Zayd, were at that moment studying a scroll (*ṣaḥīfah*) of the Holy Book under the direction of Khabbāb ibn Aratt. Although Fāṭimah had hidden her copy of the Scripture as soon as she saw 'Umar approaching, 'Umar had nonetheless overheard his sister and brother-in-law reciting something. He immediately began to interrogate them both and even resorted to beating Sa'īd ibn Zayd. When his sister tried to protect her husband, 'Umar also ruthlessly attacked her, causing a skull injury to Fāṭimah's head. Despite all this both his sister and brother-in-law, advised 'Umar in no uncertain terms that they had embraced Islam and were determined to adhere to it, and this regardless of how he treated them.

'Umar, however, was so moved by the sight of his sister's profuse bleeding that he asked her and her husband to show him what they had been reciting. Before Fāṭimah agreed to show 'Umar the scroll, she obtained a solemn promise from him to the effect that he would not tear it into shreds. She also subsequently told him that he could touch the Scripture but only after he had washed himself properly. Accordingly, 'Umar took a bath and then began to read the scroll. Inscribed on that was *Sūrah Ṭā Hā*. As he read through this *sūrah* 'Umar exclaimed: 'What a remarkable discourse!' On hearing this Khabbāb ibn Aratt, who had kept himself hidden throughout the various exchanges, came out and said: 'By God, I believe God has chosen you for spreading the message of His Prophet (peace be on him) for I heard him pray yesterday: "O God! Strengthen Islam through (Abū Jahl) or 'Umar ibn al-Khaṭṭāb." So, turn to God, O 'Umar!' 'Umar needed nothing more to persuade him that he should embrace Islam. Immediately thereafter, and accompanied by Khabbāb ibn Aratt, 'Umar sought out the Prophet (peace be on him) and in this way accepted Islam. These events took place shortly after the migration of some of the Prophet's Companions to Abyssinia (fifth year of prophethood/615 C.E.). (For the story of 'Umar's acceptance of Islam see Ibn Hishām, *Sīrah,* vol. 1, pp. 342–6 – Ed.)

Subject Matter

This *sūrah* opens with the emphatic statement that the Qur'ān was not revealed so as to place an unbearable burden upon the Prophet (peace be on him) (see verse 2). Rather the Prophet (peace be on him) was assured that he was not expected to accomplish impossible tasks. He was not required to cause rivers of milk to flow from rocks; nor was he required to compel those who were bent upon rejecting the truth to accept Islam, nor to make those, who had no propensity for faith, to suddenly have faith. Instead the Qur'ān is simply an admonition and a reminder which is intended to be of help to those who fear God, those who wish to escape God's punishment and be guided to the right way. The Qur'ān is the Speech of the Lord of the heavens and earth, He alone has dominion over them. These are established facts, irrespective of whether one accepts them or rejects them.

These introductory statements are followed by the story of the Prophet Moses (peace be on him). On the face of it, it is an historical narrative in which no allusion is made to the circumstances obtaining at that time. However, the circumstantial setting in which this story was narrated, makes it particularly significant for the Makkans. Even when nothing is stated directly, the message is nonetheless implicitly clear.

Before elaborating upon this further, it is useful to remember that there were a considerable number of Jews in Arabia at this time. They were generally held in great esteem since their intellectual pre-eminence was recognized throughout Arabia. As a result of this and because of the influence of Christian Rome and Abyssinia, Moses (peace be on him) was generally recognized by the Arabs as a Prophet of God. Bearing this in mind, let us now try to understand the main teachings which the *sūrah* seeks to convey to the Makkans:

1. God's appointment of someone as a Prophet does not involve proclamation of the same via pompous public ceremonies, the blowing of trumpets and the playing of music. None of the Prophets of the past, including Moses (peace be on him) were appointed with any fanfare. So why were some people surprised when Muḥammad (peace be on him) suddenly appeared among them claiming to be a Prophet unaccompanied by any public proclamation to that effect from the heavens; i.e. without any angels descending on the earth and going about ceremoniously proclaiming his prophethood? Such an attitude is strange. Perhaps there would have been some reason to be surprised at this if such a practice had been followed in the designation of earlier Prophets, but there was no such precedent.
2. The teaching of the Prophet Muḥammad (peace be on him) consisted of affirming monotheism and the After-life. These were exactly the same teachings which God had vouchsafed upon Moses at the time he was appointed a Prophet.
3. There is also another point of similarity between the Prophets Muḥammad and Moses (peace be on both). Muḥammad was the sole standard-bearer of the truth among the Quraysh. He pursued his mission even though he had neither material resources nor political power to support him. In this regard, he resembled Moses whom God had commanded to go to a tyrannical ruler, Pharaoh, so as to urge him to give up his transgression. Strange indeed are the ways of God. On his way, Moses meets a fellow traveller journeying from Midian to Egypt, who tells him to go and confront the mightiest ruler of the time. Moses (peace be on him) was asked to do this yet he had no army at his disposal to support him. The only assistance that was provided him, and that in response to his request for support, was the company of his brother, Aaron.
4. The Makkans tried to create doubts in the minds of others, raised objections, and resorted to false allegations, fraudulent tactics and

oppressive measures against the Prophet Muḥammad (peace be on him). All these bore much resemblance to the means employed by Pharaoh against Moses (peace be on him). It was for anyone to guess as to who would eventually prevail – the vastly resourceful Pharaoh or the Prophet Moses who, by comparison, was devoid of resources. Implicit in this statement was a note of consolation for the Muslims. They are asked not to feel disheartened if, in sharp contrast to their opponents, the unbelieving albeit immensely resourceful Quraysh, the Muslims find themselves lacking in material resources. For it is the cause which enjoys God's support that will ultimately triumph. At the same time, the Muslims are also told, by reference to the Egyptian magicians, how truth captivates peoples' hearts and minds. When this truth dawned upon the magicians, they instantly embraced it. Even fear of Pharaoh's ruthless reprisals was insufficient to swerve them from their faith.

5. Finally, an incident from the history of the Israelites is put before the believers in order to show them how false gods and idols are usually invented, and that God's Prophets do not tolerate anything pertaining to polytheism and idolatry. So if Muḥammad (peace be on him) launched his opposition against polytheism and idolatry, there was nothing novel about this. All other Prophets had done the same in their times.

Thus, through the story of the Prophet Moses (peace be on him), our attention is drawn to all those points on which the Prophet (peace be on him) and the Makkan unbelievers were at odds. What follows is a short sermon, in which it is emphasized that the Qur'ān is a reminder and a good counsel revealed in the believers' own language – Arabic – so as to enable them to properly comprehend it. If they turn away from it, then they will only bring ruin upon themselves.

The story of Adam (peace be on him) is also recounted, this time to emphasize the fact that the path pursued by the unbelievers is, in fact, that of Satan. One might at times be deluded by Satan because of one's own momentary weakness – something that is hard for man to consistently overcome. But the right course for man is the one that his forefather, Adam, adopted. Once Adam was made aware of his mistake, he clearly acknowledged it, repented, and reverted to God's servitude. So should every man do the same. However, if someone persists in error even after becoming conscious of it, and refuses to give up this error because of sheer adamance and despite receiving good counsel, then this would be an act as stupid as deliberately burning one's own fingers.

No one except he who refuses to give up his error will suffer the consequences of that folly.

In the end, the Prophet (peace be on him) and the believers are asked not to be hasty, not to be impatient with those who deny the truth. For God does not punish a people as soon as they commit disbelief. He rather grants them sufficient time to mend their ways. The Prophet (peace be on him) and the believers should persevere, tolerating the excesses of their people, and continuing to give them the right counsel.

In this regard, the believers are urged to hold fast to Prayers so that they might develop patience, forbearing, contentment, and satisfaction with God's Will, and learn the habit of critical self-examination – all of them vital qualities for serving the truth.

No one except he who refuses to give up his error will suffer the consequences of that folly.

In the end, the Prophet (peace be on him) and the believers are asked not to be hasty, nor to be impatient with those who deny the truth, for God does not punish a people as soon as they commit disbelief. He rather grants them sufficient time to mend their ways. The Prophet (peace be on him) and the believers should persevere, tolerating the excesses of their people, and continuing to give them the right counsel.

In this regard, the believers are urged to hold fast to Prayers so that they might develop patience, forbearing, contentment and satisfaction with God's Will, and learn the habit of critical self-examination – all of them vital qualities for serving the truth.

In the name of Allah, the Merciful, the Compassionate.

(1) *Ṭā Hā*. (2) We did not reveal the Qur'ān to you to cause you distress; (3) it is only a reminder for him who fears Allah;[1] (4) a revelation from Him Who created the earth and the high heavens. (5) The Most Compassionate Lord is settled on the Throne (of the universe).[2] (6) To Him belongs all that is in the heavens and all that is in the earth, and all that is in between, and all that is beneath the soil. (7) Whether you speak out aloud, (or in a low voice) He knows what is said secretly, and even that which is most hidden.[3] (8) Allah is He beside Whom there is no god. His are the most excellent names.[4]

طه ﴿١﴾ مَآ أَنزَلْنَا عَلَيْكَ ٱلْقُرْءَانَ
لِتَشْقَىٰٓ ﴿٢﴾ إِلَّا تَذْكِرَةً لِّمَن
يَخْشَىٰ ﴿٣﴾ تَنزِيلًا مِّمَّنْ خَلَقَ
ٱلْأَرْضَ وَٱلسَّمَٰوَٰتِ ٱلْعُلَى ﴿٤﴾
ٱلرَّحْمَٰنُ عَلَى ٱلْعَرْشِ ٱسْتَوَىٰ
﴿٥﴾ لَهُۥ مَا فِى ٱلسَّمَٰوَٰتِ وَمَا فِى
ٱلْأَرْضِ وَمَا بَيْنَهُمَا وَمَا تَحْتَ
ٱلثَّرَىٰ ﴿٦﴾ وَإِن تَجْهَرْ بِٱلْقَوْلِ
فَإِنَّهُۥ يَعْلَمُ ٱلسِّرَّ وَأَخْفَى ﴿٧﴾ ٱللَّهُ
لَآ إِلَٰهَ إِلَّا هُوَ لَهُ ٱلْأَسْمَآءُ
ٱلْحُسْنَىٰ ﴿٨﴾

---

1. If this statement is read in conjunction with the previous one, the purpose of it becomes quite clear. What is emphasized here is that God did not reveal the Qur'ān in order that the Prophet (peace be on him) might accomplish something that is impossible to achieve. The Prophet (peace be on him) is not required to make those who had consciously decided not to accept the truth believe in it. Nor is he required to imbue faith in people whose hearts have been sealed against acceptance of that faith. The Qur'ān was revealed simply as a reminder and as an admonition so that those who feared God might take heed. The Prophet (peace be on him) need not pursue those who have no fear of God and who are not the least bit concerned with distinguishing between right and wrong.

2. The Lord of the universe did not retreat into retirement once the universe was created. Far from it: He continues to govern the universe and to exercise

(9) Has the story of Moses reached you? (10) When he saw a fire[5] and said to his family: 'Hold on! I have just perceived a fire; perhaps I will bring a brand from it for you, or I will find some guidance at the fire (about the way to follow).'[6]

وَهَلْ أَتَىٰكَ حَدِيثُ مُوسَىٰٓ ﴿٩﴾
إِذْ رَءَا نَارًا فَقَالَ لِأَهْلِهِ ٱمْكُثُوٓا۟
إِنِّىٓ ءَانَسْتُ نَارًا لَّعَلِّىٓ ءَاتِيكُم مِّنْهَا
بِقَبَسٍ أَوْ أَجِدُ عَلَى ٱلنَّارِ هُدًى ﴿١٠﴾

control over His seemingly infinite dominion. In short, He is not only the Creator of the universe, but also its Sovereign, and its actual Ruler.

3. It is not necessary for the believers to always bemoan their sufferings to God; He is well aware of the acts of wickedness and mischief which their opponents employ against them. He is even aware of those grievances which lay concealed in their hearts, unarticulated.

4. To say that God has the best names amounts to saying that God has the best attributes.

5. This happened when the Prophet Moses (peace be on him), after his years of exile in Midian, was on his way back to Egypt with his wife whom he had married there. (The events which took place prior to this are described in *Sūrah al-Qaṣaṣ* 28: 3–38 – Ed.) In its bare outline, the story narrated there runs thus: after Moses killed a Copt, he feared that he would be arrested. Hence his departure from Egypt and his taking refuge in Midian. (See *al-Qaṣaṣ,* verse 15 ff. – Ed.)

6. It appears that this occurred on a wintry night. Moses (peace be on him) was crossing the southern part of the Sinaitic peninsula when he saw a fire in the distance. He decided to venture over to the place where he saw the fire in the hope that he would either be able to obtain some fire that would keep his family warm during the night, or at least gain directions for the journey ahead. Ironically, he went to that spot expecting to find the way to his destination in this world, only to find a way that was far more valuable – the way to success and felicity in the Hereafter.

(11) When he came to it, a voice cried out to him: 'Moses, Verily I am your Lord! (12) Take off your shoes.[7] You are in the sacred valley, Tuwā![8] ▶	فَلَمَّآ أَتَىٰهَا نُودِيَ يَٰمُوسَىٰٓ ﴿١١﴾ إِنِّيٓ أَنَا۠ رَبُّكَ فَٱخۡلَعۡ نَعۡلَيۡكَ إِنَّكَ بِٱلۡوَادِ ٱلۡمُقَدَّسِ طُوٗى ﴿١٢﴾

7. These words uttered by God, probably led the Jews to believe that it was unlawful to perform this Prayer with their shoes on. It was in order to remove this misunderstanding that the Prophet Muḥammad (peace be on him) said: 'Act in ways contrary to those of the Jews for they do not offer the Prayer with shoes and leather socks on.' (Abū Dā'ūd, *Sunan, K. al-Ṣalāh, 'Bāb al-Ṣalāh fī al-Na'l'* – Ed.) This does not mean that one must necessarily offer the Prayer with one's shoes on. What is meant by the *ḥadīth* is that it is lawful to pray with one's shoes on. Hence, the Islamic position on the question is that Muslims may pray in both ways: either with their shoes on or off. A tradition has been reported by 'Amr ibn al-'Āṣ to the effect that he saw the Prophet (peace be on him) offering Prayers in both manners, i.e. on one occasion with his shoes on and on another with his shoes off. (See Abū Dā'ūd, *Sunan, K. al-Ṣalāh, 'Bāb al-Ṣalāh fī al-Na'l'* – Ed.)* It has also been reported both in the *Musnad* of Aḥmad ibn Ḥanbal and in the *Sunan* of Abū Dā'ūd on the authority of Abū Sa'īd al-Khudrī that the Prophet (peace be on him) said: 'When any of you comes to the mosque he should have a look at his shoes and clean them by rubbing them against the earth if they are soiled with filth, and offer Prayers with your shoes on.' (See Abū Dā'ūd, *loc. cit.*; and Aḥmad ibn Ḥanbal, *Musnad,* vol. 3, p. 92 – Ed.) The same tradition, narrated by Abū Hurayrah, records the following saying by the Prophet (peace be on him): 'If any of you treads over filth with his shoes, the earth suffices to clean it.' (Abū Dā'ūd, *Sunan, K. al-Ṭahārah, 'Bāb (fī) al-Adhá yuṣīb al-Na'l'* – Ed.) According to Umm Salamah, the Prophet (peace be on him) said that if one's shoes were soiled with filth, one's subsequent walking on the earth would purify them. (See Abū Dā'ūd, *loc. cit.* – Ed.)

In view of the large number of such traditions, several jurists such as Abū Ḥanīfah, Abū Yūsuf, Awzā'ī and Isḥāq ibn Rāhawayh are of the opinion that shoes that are soiled by filth are inevitably purified by the earth as a result of one's walking. There is one report each from Aḥmad ibn Ḥanbal and Shāfi'ī in support of this doctrine. The generally known view of Shāfi'ī, however, is opposed to this practice. Presumably Shāfi'ī considered praying with shoes on

*The author has mentioned 'Amr ibn al-Āṣ as the narrator of this tradition. In Abū Dā'ūd, however, the name of the narrator of the tradition we have cited here is 'Amr ibn Shu'ayb – Ed.

(13) I Myself have chosen you; therefore, give ear to what is revealed. (14) I am Allah. There is no god other than Me. So serve Me and establish Prayer[9] to remember Me. ▶

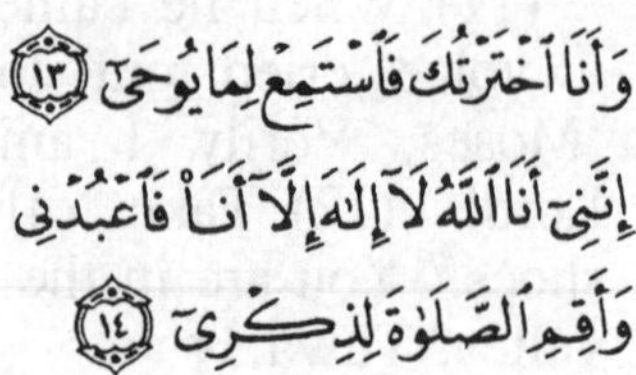

as being inconsistent with the reverence required for the act of Prayer and it is on this count that he asked people not to offer Prayers in that manner. It is generally understood, however, that Shāfi'ī did not believe that shoes which had become soiled with filth were purified by rubbing them against the earth.

In this respect it is worth mentioning that in the time of the Prophet (peace be on him) the mosque floor was not even covered with a thatch mat. It was simply covered with pebbles. Hence, it would not be appropriate for anyone today, basing themselves on the practice followed in the time of the Prophet (peace be on him), to walk on the floor of a mosque with his shoes on. One may, however, pray with one's shoes on in open areas or on grass. As for those who insist that even while offering the Funeral Prayer a person must necessarily take his shoes off, in our opinion they are simply ignorant of the relevant rules.

8. It is generally believed that Ṭuwā was the name of this valley. Some scholars, however, are of the view that the expression *al-wād al-muqaddas Tuwá* means the valley that was temporarily made sacred.

9. This indicates the main purpose of the Prayer: that man may not become oblivious of God, that the glittering allurements of this world may not make him impervious to the basic fact that he is God's servant, that man may not remain under the illusion that he is free to do as he pleases. Prayer is the most potent means of keeping this consciousness fresh in man's mind; it enables him to maintain a strong, vibrant relationship with God. Prayer weans man away, many times a day, from the ordinary hum-drum existence of daily life; it orients him towards God.

Some scholars have interpreted this verse to mean that man should offer Prayers so that God may, in turn, also remember him as has been said elsewhere in the Qur'ān: 'So remember Me; I will remember you' (*al-Baqarah* 2: 152).

Incidentally, this verse also provides the ground-work for the ruling that if one forgets to offer Prayer, one should offer it immediately one remembers such an omission. A *ḥadīth* reported by Anas ibn Mālik says: 'The Prophet (peace be on him) said: ''One who forgets to perform Prayers should do so

(15) The Hour of Resurrection is coming. I have willed to keep the time of its coming hidden so that everyone may be recompensed in accordance with his effort.[10] (16) Let him who does not believe in it and follows his lusts not turn your thought away from it, lest you are ruined. (17) And what is in your right hand, O Moses?'[11]

إِنَّ ٱلسَّاعَةَ ءَاتِيَةٌ أَكَادُ أُخْفِيهَا
لِتُجْزَىٰ كُلُّ نَفْسٍۭ بِمَا تَسْعَىٰ ﴿١٥﴾
فَلَا يَصُدَّنَّكَ عَنْهَا مَن لَّا يُؤْمِنُ
بِهَا وَٱتَّبَعَ هَوَىٰهُ فَتَرْدَىٰ ﴿١٦﴾
وَمَا تِلْكَ بِيَمِينِكَ
يَـٰمُوسَىٰ ﴿١٧﴾

whenever he recalls it. Nothing else is required to be done.'' ' (See al-Bukhārī, *K. al-Mawāqīt, 'Bāb man nasiya Ṣalātan fa li yuṣallī . . .'*; Muslim, *'K. al-Masājid wa Mawāḍi' al-Ṣalāh'*; Aḥmad ibn Ḥanbal, *Musnad,* vol. 3, p. 269 – Ed.) Another *ḥadīth* of similar import narrated by Abū Hurayrah is recorded in Abū Dā'ūd and al-Nasā'ī. (See al-Nasā'ī, *Sunan, K. al-Mawāqīt, I'ādah man nāma 'an al-Ṣalāh . . .*; Muslim, *K. al-Masājid wa Mawāḍi' al-Ṣalāh, 'Bāb Qaḍā' al-Ṣalāh al-Fā'itah . . .'*; Abū Dā'ūd, *K. al-Ṣalāh, 'Bāb fī man nāma 'an al-Ṣalāh . . .'* – Ed.) Abū Qatādah reports that when the Prophet (peace be on him) was asked by people what they should do if they overslept the time of Prayers, the Prophet replied: 'There is no sin if one is asleep. Sin is incurred when one does not pray while one is awake. If any of you forgets [to pray] or is asleep [at the time of Prayers], you should offer Prayers when you wake up or when you remember.' (See al-Tirmidhī, *Abwāb al-Ṣalāh, 'Bāb mā jā' fī al-Nawm 'an al-Ṣalāh'*; Abū Dā'ūd, *Sunan, K. al-Ṣalāh, 'Bāb fī man nāma 'an al-Ṣalāh aw nasiyahā'*; al-Nasā'ī, *K. al-Mawāqīt, 'Fī man nāma 'an al-Ṣalāh'* – Ed.)

10. The doctrine of the Hereafter is the second most important doctrine in Islam, the doctrine next in importance to monotheism. This is a basic truth, revealed to all the Prophets in different periods of history, a truth which they were all required to expound. The present verse states both the nature and purpose of this doctrine. The Last Day will come to pass so that man may be recompensed for what he has done. The time of its coming, however, has been kept hidden so as to test people. Those who are, to any extent, concerned with the Hereafter will remain ever fearful lest the Last Day suddenly takes place; this, in itself, is likely to deter them from committing evil. By contrast, those who are fully immersed in worldly pursuits will be inclined to consider the Hereafter a remote possibility.

(18) Moses answered: 'This is my staff. I lean on it (when I walk), and with it I beat down leaves for my flock, and I have many other uses for it.'[12]

(19) He said: 'Moses, throw it down.'

(20) So he threw it down, and lo! it was a rapidly moving snake. (21) He said: 'Seize it and have no fear. We shall restore it to its former state. (22) And place your hand in your arm-pit, it will come forth shining white, although unharmed.[13] This is another sign of Allah; (23) for We shall show you some of Our greatest signs. (24) And go to Pharaoh now for he has transgressed all bounds.'

قَالَ هِىَ عَصَاىَ أَتَوَكَّؤُا۟ عَلَيْهَا
وَأَهُشُّ بِهَا عَلَىٰ غَنَمِى وَلِىَ فِيهَا
مَـَٔارِبُ أُخْرَىٰ ﴿١٨﴾ قَالَ أَلْقِهَا
يَـٰمُوسَىٰ ﴿١٩﴾ فَأَلْقَىٰهَا فَإِذَا هِىَ
حَيَّةٌ تَسْعَىٰ ﴿٢٠﴾ قَالَ خُذْهَا
وَلَا تَخَفْ سَنُعِيدُهَا سِيرَتَهَا
ٱلْأُولَىٰ ﴿٢١﴾ وَٱضْمُمْ يَدَكَ إِلَىٰ
جَنَاحِكَ تَخْرُجْ بَيْضَآءَ مِنْ غَيْرِ
سُوٓءٍ ءَايَةً أُخْرَىٰ ﴿٢٢﴾ لِنُرِيَكَ
مِنْ ءَايَـٰتِنَا ٱلْكُبْرَى ﴿٢٣﴾ ٱذْهَبْ
إِلَىٰ فِرْعَوْنَ إِنَّهُۥ طَغَىٰ ﴿٢٤﴾

11. This question was not asked for the sake of soliciting information. For God knew well that Moses had a rod in his hand. The purpose of the question was to make Moses fully conscious of what he was carrying in order that he might appreciate the astonishing manifestations of God's power that he was about to witness.

12. Moses could simply have said that it was a rod. However, the lengthy reply which he gave provides an interesting clue to his state of mind. It is understandable that if out of good luck a person meets a distinguished person, he tries to prolong his conversation with the same. This is because such a meeting represents both a pleasure and an honour. (In Moses' case, the desire to prolong the conversation naturally arose because he was in the presence of none other than God Himself – Ed.)

13. Although Moses' hand would become as bright as the sun, this would happen without causing him any harm. The Biblical account of the miracle of

(25) Moses said: 'Lord! Open my breast for me;[14] (26) and ease my task for me; (27) and loosen the knot from my tongue (28) so that they may understand my speech;[15] ▶

قَالَ رَبِّ ٱشْرَحْ لِى صَدْرِى ﴿٢٥﴾ وَيَسِّرْ لِىٓ أَمْرِى ﴿٢٦﴾ وَٱحْلُلْ عُقْدَةً مِّن لِّسَانِى ﴿٢٧﴾ يَفْقَهُوا۟ قَوْلِى ﴿٢٨﴾

the bright hand, however, is somewhat different and has also found its way into Muslim works of Qur'ānic Exegesis. According to the Biblical account, when Moses took his hand out of his arm-pit, it looked as though it belonged to a leper. When he put it back into his arm-pit, it was restored to its original, healthy state. (See *Exodus,* 4: 6 – Ed.) The Talmud, too, describes the miracle in a similar fashion.

The rationale behind all this being that since Pharaoh suffered from leprosy, a fact which he had concealed from others, Moses was granted the capacity to produce this particular miracle so as to impress upon him that this disease could be as instantly cured as it had arisen. This view, however, does not seem plausible for more than one reason. First, it seems inconsistent with good taste that a Messenger of God would be sent to an emperor's court with a miracle which pertains to a disease as repulsive as leprosy. Even if we were to consider it plausible that Moses would have been endowed with such a miracle, it still seems worth asking what the significance of such a miracle would be? For, if Pharaoh was afflicted with leprosy, this miracle would only be meaningful to him; it would have made no impact on his courtiers. It seems appropriate, therefore, to adhere to the view we have expressed, namely that when this miracle was performed Moses' hand looked as bright as the sun, so much so that it dazzled all onlookers. Many of the earlier commentators of the Qur'ān have adopted this very view of the miracle. (See the comments on verse 22 in the *Commentaries* of Ibn Kathīr, al-Qurṭubī, al-Ṭabarī, al-Rāzī, and al-Ālūsī – Ed.)

14. Moses prayed that he might be granted the inner strength and courage required to shoulder his responsibilities; as a sequel he was being entrusted with a great mission which called for enormous courage and fortitude. Hence, he prayed that God might invest him with patience, fortitude, forbearance, fearlessness, firm determination, and the like: qualities that were essential for the furtherance of his mission.

15. According to the Bible, Moses said: 'Oh, my Lord, I am not eloquent, either heretofore or since thou hast spoken to thy servant; but I am slow of speech and of tongue' (*Exodus* 4: 10). The Talmud contains a lengthy account

(29) and appoint for me, from my household, someone who will help me bear my burden – (30) Aaron, my brother.[16] ▶

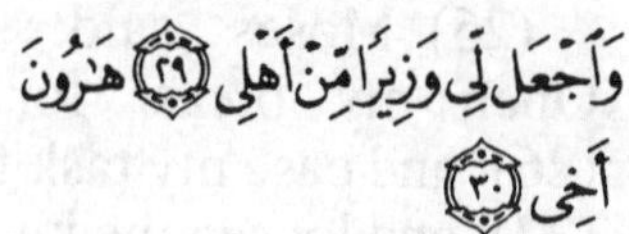

to the effect that when Moses was being brought up as a child in Pharaoh's house, he wore Pharaoh's crown. This led to inquiries about whether the child had done so deliberately or if it was merely a childish prank. It was finally resolved, however, that the child be presented with a piece of gold and a ball of fire. Both these objects were placed before Moses and he grasped the ball of fire and put it into his mouth. Although onlookers managed to save his life, it nonetheless caused Moses to stammer for the rest of his life. (See *The Talmud Selections,* pp. 127–8 – Ed.)

This story, derived from Israelite sources, has crept into the Muslim works of Qur'ānic exegesis. (See al-Qurṭubī, comments on verse 27 – Ed.) The whole account, however, seems downright irrational. For, even if one accepts that the child held the ball of fire in his palm, it would nonetheless have been impossible for him to put it into his mouth. Any child who tries to hold a piece of fire in his hand is bound to throw it away as soon as he feels its intense, burning heat. It would, therefore, simply be impossible for him to put it into his mouth.

As for the present Qur'ānic account concerning Moses, all that it says is that Moses was conscious of being ineloquent. He also feared that if he had to speak in the course of discharging his duties as a Prophet, he would perhaps be overcome by his impediment especially as he had no prior public speaking experience. Therefore, he prayed that God may endow him with eloquence that he might express himself effectively. It may be recalled that on one occasion Pharaoh ridiculed Moses for his inability to speak well: 'He is a contemptible wretch who can scarcely express himself clearly' (*al-Zukhruf* 43: 52). It was Moses' own consciousness of this weakness which had made him pray to God to appoint his brother Aaron as his helper: 'And my brother Aaron, he is more eloquent in speech than I. Send him with me as a helper' (*al-Qaṣaṣ* 28: 34).

It seems that later on Moses overcame this weakness, developing as he did an effective public speaking ability. His speeches of later time, found both in the Bible and the Qur'ān, provide ample testimony to his outstanding capacity as a speaker. It does not stand to reason that God should appoint someone who stammered to the office of Messenger. Messengers have always been the best specimens of humanity, outstanding in all respects – their facial features, personality, and other abilities bearing this out. Both their external appearances and their inner qualities have always attracted peoples' hearts and minds. Never has God raised a Messenger who suffered from a physical deformity which would reduce him to an object of ridicule or contempt.

(31) Strengthen me through him, (32) and let him share my task; (33) that we may abundantly extol Your glory; (34) and may remember You much. (35) Verily, You have always watched over us.'

(36) He said: 'Moses, your petition is granted. (37) We have again bestowed Our favour upon you.[17] (38) Recall, when We indicated to your mother through inspiration: (39) "Put him into a chest and then throw him in the river. The river will throw him up on the shore, and then an enemy of Mine and an enemy of his will take him." And I spread My love over you in order that you might be reared in My sight. ▶

اَشْدُدْ بِهِۦٓ أَزْرِى ﴿٣١﴾ وَأَشْرِكْهُ فِىٓ أَمْرِى
﴿٣٢﴾ كَىْ نُسَبِّحَكَ كَثِيرًا ﴿٣٣﴾ وَنَذْكُرَكَ
كَثِيرًا ﴿٣٤﴾ إِنَّكَ كُنتَ بِنَا بَصِيرًا ﴿٣٥﴾
قَالَ قَدْ أُوتِيتَ سُؤْلَكَ يَٰمُوسَىٰ ﴿٣٦﴾
وَلَقَدْ مَنَنَّا عَلَيْكَ مَرَّةً أُخْرَىٰٓ ﴿٣٧﴾
إِذْ أَوْحَيْنَآ إِلَىٰٓ أُمِّكَ مَا يُوحَىٰٓ ﴿٣٨﴾
أَنِ اقْذِفِيهِ فِى التَّابُوتِ فَاقْذِفِيهِ فِى
الْيَمِّ فَلْيُلْقِهِ الْيَمُّ بِالسَّاحِلِ يَأْخُذْهُ
عَدُوٌّ لِّى وَعَدُوٌّ لَّهُۥ وَأَلْقَيْتُ عَلَيْكَ
مَحَبَّةً مِّنِّى وَلِتُصْنَعَ عَلَىٰ عَيْنِىٓ ﴿٣٩﴾

16. According to the Bible, Aaron was three years older than Moses.

17. God reminds Moses of the numerous favours that had been bestowed on him from his birth up until the current moment. These favours are mentioned in greater detail in *Sūrah al-Qaṣaṣ*. (See *al-Qaṣaṣ* 28: 7–35 – Ed.) What is stated here amounts to no more than an allusion to these favours so as to make Moses conscious of the mission for which he was born, for which he had been brought up under governmental care, and which was being entrusted to him at that particular moment.

(40) Recall, when your sister went along, saying: "Shall I direct you to one who will take charge of him?" Thus We brought you back to your mother so that her heart might be gladdened and she might not grieve. Moses, recall when you slayed a person. We delivered you from distress and made you go through several trials. Then you stayed for several years among the people of Midian, and now you have come at the right moment as ordained. (41) I have chosen you for My service. (42) So go forth, both you and your brother, with My signs, and do not slacken in remembering Me. (43) Go both of you to Pharaoh, for he has transgressed all bounds, (44) and speak to him gently, perhaps he may take heed or fear (Allah).'[18]

(45) The two said:[18a] 'Lord! We fear he may commit excesses against us, or transgress all bounds.'

إِذْ تَمْشِيٓ أُخْتُكَ فَتَقُولُ هَلْ
أَدُلُّكُمْ عَلَىٰ مَن يَكْفُلُهُۥ فَرَجَعْنَٰكَ
إِلَىٰٓ أُمِّكَ كَيْ تَقَرَّ عَيْنُهَا وَلَا تَحْزَنَ
وَقَتَلْتَ نَفْسًا فَنَجَّيْنَٰكَ مِنَ ٱلْغَمِّ
وَفَتَنَّٰكَ فُتُونًا فَلَبِثْتَ سِنِينَ فِيٓ
أَهْلِ مَدْيَنَ ثُمَّ جِئْتَ عَلَىٰ قَدَرٍ
يَٰمُوسَىٰ ﴿٤٠﴾ وَٱصْطَنَعْتُكَ
لِنَفْسِي ﴿٤١﴾ ٱذْهَبْ أَنتَ وَأَخُوكَ
بِـَٔايَٰتِي وَلَا تَنِيَا فِي ذِكْرِي ﴿٤٢﴾
ٱذْهَبَآ إِلَىٰ فِرْعَوْنَ إِنَّهُۥ طَغَىٰ ﴿٤٣﴾
فَقُولَا لَهُۥ قَوْلًا لَّيِّنًا لَّعَلَّهُۥ يَتَذَكَّرُ
أَوْ يَخْشَىٰ ﴿٤٤﴾ قَالَا رَبَّنَآ إِنَّنَا نَخَافُ
أَن يَفْرُطَ عَلَيْنَآ أَوْ أَن يَطْغَىٰ ﴿٤٥﴾

18. A person abandons evil and turns to the right path for one of two reasons. Either he is convinced of the right way because of someone's persuasion, or he takes heed as a result of himself becoming conscious of the disastrous consequences of his evil actions.

18a. It would appear that this incident relates to the time when Moses had already reached Egypt and when Aaron had begun to assist him in his mission.

(46) He said: 'Have no fear. I am with you, hearing and seeing all. (47) So, go to him, and say: "Behold, both of us are the Messengers of your Lord. Let the Children of Israel go with us, and do not chastise them. We have come to you with a sign from your Lord; and peace shall be for him who follows the true guidance. (48) It has been revealed to us that chastisement awaits those who called the lie to the truth and turned away from it." '[19]

قَالَ لَا تَخَافَآ إِنَّنِي مَعَكُمَآ أَسْمَعُ
وَأَرَىٰ ﴿٤٦﴾ فَأْتِيَاهُ فَقُولَآ إِنَّا رَسُولَا
رَبِّكَ فَأَرْسِلْ مَعَنَا بَنِيٓ إِسْرَٰٓءِيلَ
وَلَا تُعَذِّبْهُمْ قَدْ جِئْنَٰكَ بِـَٔايَةٍ مِّن
رَّبِّكَ وَٱلسَّلَٰمُ عَلَىٰ مَنِ ٱتَّبَعَ ٱلْهُدَىٰٓ
﴿٤٧﴾ إِنَّا قَدْ أُوحِيَ إِلَيْنَآ أَنَّ ٱلْعَذَابَ
عَلَىٰ مَن كَذَّبَ وَتَوَلَّىٰ ﴿٤٨﴾

Presumably before proceeding to Pharaoh, both Moses and Aaron had made their fears about the evil that might befall them known to God.

19. The Qur'ānic account of the incident should be read in conjunction with those accounts in the Bible and the Talmud. This comparative study will clearly reveal the differences in the images of the Prophets as portrayed in the Qur'ān and in the Jewish religious tradition. According to the Bible, God told Moses: 'Come, I will send you to Pharaoh that you may bring forth my people, the sons of Israel, out of Egypt.' But Moses said to God: 'Who am I that I should go to Pharaoh, and bring the sons of Israel out of Egypt?' (*Exodus* 3: 10–11). Subsequently, even though God tried at length to persuade Moses of the same, encouraged him, and endowed him with miracles, Moses still said: 'Oh, my Lord, send, I pray, some other person' (*Exodus* 4: 13).

The Talmudic account goes a step further. It states that the argument between God and Moses continued for seven days. God insisted on Moses accepting the prophetic mission whereas Moses declined to do so on the grounds of his speech impediment. Finally, God said that it was His will that Moses become a Prophet. To this Moses replied that God had sent angels to save Lot, had assigned five angels when Hagar left the house of Sarah, so why was He, then, asking him to leave Egypt along with His favourite children (the Israelites)? This so enraged God that He made Aaron a party to Moses' prophetic office, and denied priesthood to the house of Moses by transferring it to the descendants of Aaron. (See *The Talmud Selections*, p. 142 ff. – Ed.) In

(49) Pharaoh[20] said: 'Moses! Who is the Lord of the two of you?'[21]

(50) He said: 'Our Lord is He[22] Who gave everything its form and then guided it.'[23]

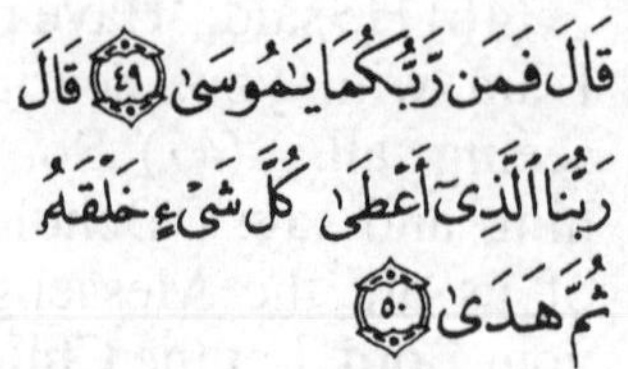

view of this clear discrepancy between the two versions it seems bold, indeed, for some scholars to claim that the Bible and the Talmud were the main sources from which the Qur'ānic stories were derived.

20. Here the Qur'ān omits certain details of the story: in particular, how Moses arrived at Pharaoh's court and how he explained his teachings to him. These details are mentioned earlier in *al-A'rāf* 7: 108; and can also be found in *al-Shu'arā'* 26: 10–33; *al-Qaṣaṣ* 28: 28–40; and *al-Nāzi'āt* 79: 15–36. For necessary information about Pharaoh see *Towards Understanding the Qur'ān*, vol. III, *al-A'rāf* 7, n. 85, p. 64.

21. Of the two brothers, Moses was the main person entrusted with the task of expounding the truth. Hence Pharaoh addressed Moses rather than Aaron. Another possible reason why Pharaoh addressed Moses rather than Aaron may be that Pharaoh wanted to deprive Aaron of the opportunity to use his rhetorical skills, the implication being that he wished to take advantage of Moses' handicap when it came to public speaking.

The purpose of the question posed by Pharaoh was to emphasize the fact that since he was sovereign of Egypt and its people, Moses had no business setting up anyone other than him as their Lord. He alone, so Pharaoh believed, could be Lord of Egypt and of the Egyptians. *Sūrah al-Nāzi'āt* records Pharaoh's claim: 'I am your highest Lord' (79: 24). The Qur'ān also records elsewhere that Pharaoh publicly addressed his whole court, saying: 'My people! Do I not possess kingship of Egypt and are these rivers not flowing under me?' (*al-Zukhruf* 43: 51). On another occasion Pharaoh vaingloriously boasted before his courtiers: 'O chiefs! I know no deity of yours other than myself. O Hāmān! Light me a kiln to bake bricks out of clay and construct a lofty palace that I might climb up to the god of Moses' (*al-Qaṣaṣ* 28: 38). Elsewhere, the Qur'ān mentions that Pharaoh rebuked Moses, saying: 'If you take anyone other than me as a deity, I shall cast you into prison' (*al-Shu'arā'* 26: 29). This does not mean that Pharaoh was the only object of the Egyptian people's worship. We have already noted that Pharaoh's claim to be sovereign was grounded in his belief that he was the incarnation of the sun-god, Ra.

It has also been established historically that the national cult of the Egyptians consisted of the worship of many gods and goddesses. Hence, in point of fact, Pharaoh did not claim to be the 'only object of worship'. He rather claimed, on a practical level, divine political lordship over the people of Egypt, and on a theoretical level, political lordship over all mankind. He was totally unprepared to accept the notion that any Superior Being could be regarded as the Lord, as One over and above him, or that anyone could come forward as His authorized representative and claim the authority to command and ask all, including Pharaoh, to obey the same.

Some people have been misled into believing that Pharaoh denied the existence of God, or that he laid claim to being God himself. According to the Qur'ān, however, Pharaoh believed that someone else governed the world above. If one reads carefully the Qur'ānic verses *al-Mu'min* 40: 28–34 and *al-Zukhruf* 43: 53, it is evident that Pharaoh did not deny the existence of God, nor that of angels. What he could not accept, however, was that God should have any authority to interfere with his political overlordship, or that any of God's Messengers should claim the right to command him. (For further elaboration see *al-Qaṣaṣ* 28, n. 53.)

22. The thrust of Moses' statement is that he accepted God as his Lord in every sense of the term. He alone is the Provider, the Master, the Lord, the Sovereign. In sum, Moses was not prepared to accept anyone other than God as his Lord.

23. All that exists in the world, whatever its shape, is the creation of God alone. Everything derives its form and texture, its power and ability, and all its properties from God alone. Man's limbs – hands, legs, and so on – were all created on a pattern best suited to make them properly serviceable. God created everything – minerals, air, water, light, in short, everything – and gave it the particular shape required for it to play the role assigned to it in the overall scheme of things.

Now God did not simply create each thing on a certain pattern and leave it at that; rather, He taught each created being how it should function and fulfil the purpose for which it had been created. It is God Who taught the fish to swim and the birds to fly, the plants to blossom and the soil to produce vegetation. In sum, He not only created but also provided guidance to everything in the universe as to how it should function.

In the above sentence, which is crisp, pithy and rich, Moses not only mentions God Who is the object of his worship, but also explains why he accepted Him as his Lord and why none else could be acknowledged to be so. The statement embodies both the thesis and its supporting argument. The fact is that Pharaoh and all his subjects owe their lives to God and none of them can survive even for a moment unless the different parts of their bodies function in accordance with the guidance that comes from God. In view of the above, Pharaoh's claim that he was the Lord of his subjects and the latter's acceptance of Pharaoh as their Lord, both appear no more than an act of folly, a ludicrous joke.

(51) Pharaoh asked: 'Then, what is the state of the former generations?'[24]

(52) Moses said: 'Its knowledge is with my Lord, recorded in the Book. My Lord does not err, nor does He forget.'[25] ▶

قَالَ فَمَا بَالُ الْقُرُونِ الْأُولَىٰ ﴿٥١﴾
قَالَ عِلْمُهَا عِندَ رَبِّي فِي كِتَابٍ لَّا يَضِلُّ رَبِّي وَلَا يَنسَى ﴿٥٢﴾

Furthermore, in this statement Moses subtly makes the case for his own prophethood, an office, as we have seen, which Pharaoh rejected. Implicit in Moses' statement is the point that since God is the Guide of the whole universe, One Who directs everything in accordance with its needs and conditions, it is befitting of Him alone that He provides the guidance to mankind. Since man cannot be guided in the same way as animals are, the best way to help man is for the choicest of their number to be selected by God and asked to make an appeal to their fellow mens' rational faculties and in this manner show them the right way.

24. Pharaoh here points out that if it was God, as Moses claimed, Who created everything to perfection and Who guided it to its role, and if there really was no Lord other than God, then this clearly also meant that the ancestors of yore who had worshipped deities other than God were in error. Were they really in error and deserved God's punishment? Were they all – their venerable ancestors – dumb, stupid people?

This was the only response which Pharaoh could afford to put forth in reply to Moses' argument. It was a response based either on ignorance, or mischief, or both. For it is indeed possible that Moses' assertion, which implied that his ancestors were in error, incensed him. At the same time, it is quite possible that Pharaoh's intent in making the above statement was to incite people against Moses by appealing to their natural feelings of love and veneration for their ancestors. This weapon has frequently been used by the opponents of the truth throughout the different periods of history, and on many occasions it proved effective in provoking ignorant people against the proponents of truth. At the time when these Qur'ānic verses were revealed, this very weapon was being constantly employed against the Prophet Muḥammad (peace be on him). It is, therefore, especially relevant to mention Pharaoh's subterfuge against Moses here.

25. Moses' reply is full of wisdom, providing a good lesson for those who wish to propagate the truth and who wish to do so wisely. Pharaoh's intent, as

(53) He[26] it is Who spread the earth for you; and made in it paths for you, and sent down water from the sky, and then through it We brought forth many species of diverse plants. ▶

ٱلَّذِى جَعَلَ لَكُمُ ٱلْأَرْضَ مَهْدًا
وَسَلَكَ لَكُمْ فِيهَا سُبُلًا وَأَنزَلَ
مِنَ ٱلسَّمَآءِ مَآءً فَأَخْرَجْنَا بِهِۦٓ
أَزْوَٰجًا مِّن نَّبَاتٍ شَتَّىٰ ٥٣

noted earlier, was probably to incite the prejudice and hostility of his audience against Moses, and, through them, the prejudice and hostility of the people at large. Moses could indeed have replied that their ancestors were in error, bound to be cast into Hell; but such a reply, regardless of its truth, would have served Pharaoh's cause rather than that of Moses.

Instead, Moses replied with the utmost wisdom, saying something which was at once true but which also frustrated Pharaoh's evil designs. He pointed out that howsoever their ancestors might have behaved, they had now completed their term of life and returned to God, and he, Moses, had no means of knowing the fullness of their actions nor the intent behind those actions so as to enable him to judge them. But the record of all the acts they committed during their lives was with God Who knew well all that they did and Who was also well aware of the motives behind those actions. For nothing escapes God's eye nor does anything fade from His memory. It is for God, and God alone, to judge them. Indeed He alone has the requisite knowledge to do so. None need worry as to what the attitude of their predecessors was to life nor what manner of ultimate fate lay in store for them. People should be concerned, instead, with themselves: they should examine their own attitude to life and consider what kind of ultimate fate they are likely to meet as a result.

26. It would appear that Moses' response concludes with the end of verse 52. The passage which follows, i.e. from verse 53 to verse 55 consists of an admonition.

The Qur'ān is full of instances where statements are made about past incidents or about future events. Such statements are followed either by a few sentences of exhortation to piety and righteousness, or by explanation or elaboration of those statements. The style of the text, on such occasions, indicates whether the statement in question was made by a human being or by God.

(54) So eat yourself and pasture your cattle. Surely there are many signs in this for men of understanding.[27] (55) From this very earth We created you, and to the same earth We shall cause you to return, and from it We shall bring you forth to life again.[28]

(56) Indeed We showed Pharaoh Our signs, all of them, but he declared them to be false and rejected them.[29] ▶

It is useful to remember that this particular statement not only relates to the immediately preceding verse ('My Lord does not err, nor does He forget'), but also to Moses' entire statement which opens with the words: 'He [Moses] said: "Our Lord is He Who gave everything its form and then guided it" ' (verse 50).

27. Those who are guided in their quest for the truth by sound reason are assisted by signs from God and they are able therewith to find the way to the truth. For these signs convince such people that this universe has a Lord and that He alone, and none else, governs and controls it.

28. Inevitably every human being has to pass through these three stages. The first stage extends from his birth to his death; the second is from his death to the Last Day; and the third is the Last Day and the Resurrection and thereafter. According to the above verse, all these three stages relating to man will take place on earth.

29. God's signs mentioned here refer to those signs both in the natural phenomena and in men's lives, as well as to the miracles granted Moses (peace be on him). The Qur'ān also mentions several successive speeches made by Moses on different occasions in order to explain his message to Pharaoh, as it does the several miracles performed in succession and which Pharaoh was made to witness.

(57) He said: 'Have you come to us to drive us out of our land by your sorcery?[30] (58) Now we shall confront you with a sorcery like your own. So appoint a day when both of us might meet face to face in an open space; an appointment which neither we nor you shall fail to keep.'

قَالَ أَجِئْتَنَا لِتُخْرِجَنَا مِنْ أَرْضِنَا بِسِحْرِكَ يَـٰمُوسَىٰ ﴿٥٧﴾ فَلَنَأْتِيَنَّكَ بِسِحْرٍ مِّثْلِهِۦ فَٱجْعَلْ بَيْنَنَا وَبَيْنَكَ مَوْعِدًا لَّا نُخْلِفُهُۥ نَحْنُ وَلَآ أَنتَ مَكَانًا سُوًى ﴿٥٨﴾

30. 'Sorcery' here refers to the miracle of the rod and to Moses' shining hand. Details of these miracles are mentioned in *al-A'rāf* and *al-Shu'arā'* and refer to a miracle which Moses performed during his first meeting with Pharaoh when the latter's court was in full attendance. This particular miracle totally unnerved Pharaoh, a fact which can be gauged by his response: 'Have you come to drive us out of our land by your sorcery' (verse 57).

Never before in the history of mankind, either before Moses' and Pharaoh's time or after it, was a magician able to establish his domination over a country by dint of his magic. In Pharaoh's own land there were numerous magicians who went about demonstrating their magical feats and asking people for money in return. Hence Pharaoh's statements that Moses was a magician, and that he constituted a threat to Pharaoh's dominion only bespoke of his nervousness and bewilderment. The fact seems to be that Pharaoh was cognizant of Moses' persuasive and well-argued discourse as well as of his impressive miracles. It would also appear that at this stage Pharaoh had begun to seriously believe that both his courtiers and the common people of his realm were being favourably impressed by Moses. He, therefore, had to resort to lies and fraudulent practices in an attempt to arouse his people's latent prejudices. He, therefore, argued that what Moses had demonstrated were simply magical feats rather than miracles; tricks which any magician of his realm could perform – transmuting a rod into a serpent. He also attempted to incite his people's anger against Moses by saying in effect: 'Look, Moses brands your ancestors to be ill-guided; as those who deserve to be cast into Hell-Fire. Beware of him! He is no Prophet, but merely hungers for power. He merely wants the Israelites to be able to seize power from the Copts and rule over this country as in the time of Joseph.' By resorting to such a stratagem Pharaoh tried to undermine Moses' mission. (For further details see *Towards Understanding the Qur'ān,* vol. III, *al-A'rāf* 7, nn. 87–90, pp. 65–8 and vol. IV, *Yūnus* 10, n. 75, p. 56 respectively).

(59) Moses said: 'The appointment to meet you is on the Day of the Feast, and let all people come together before noon.'[31]

قَالَ مَوْعِدُكُمْ يَوْمُ ٱلزِّينَةِ وَأَن يُحْشَرَ
ٱلنَّاسُ ضُحًى ﴿٥٩﴾ فَتَوَلَّىٰ فِرْعَوْنُ
فَجَمَعَ كَيْدَهُۥ ثُمَّ أَتَىٰ ﴿٦٠﴾

(60) Pharaoh went back and concerted all his stratagem and returned for the encounter.[32]

At this point it is also worth mentioning that the ruling classes, throughout all times, have maligned the votaries of truth, accusing them of hungering for power, misconstruing all their activities as being directed to that sole objective. (For some relevant instances see *al-A'rāf* 7: 110 and 123; *Yūnus* 10: 78 and *al-Mu'minūn* 23: 2.)

31. Pharaoh believed that his magicians would be able to nullify the impression created in the minds of his people by Moses' miracles. He, therefore, commanded his magicians to perform their wondrous feats, turning rods and ropes into serpents and the like. He fully believed that once such feats had been performed, Moses' miracles would lose all their effect. So when Pharaoh himself suggested an encounter between Moses and the magicians, Moses was able to seize this opportunity to demonstrate the difference between sorcery and miracles. Hence Moses readily agreed, further adding that instead of fixing a special time and place for that purpose, the festival that was about to take place be made use of since it would attract people from all over the country. Moses preferred the encounter to take place before all those who were expected to attend the festival, and during broad daylight, so that no ambiguity concerning the question in dispute would remain thereafter.

32. Pharaoh and his courtiers considered this encounter to be of crucial importance. Messengers were sent to all parts of the country to summon all skilled magicians to the capital. Likewise, efforts were made to attract the maximum number of people in order that they might witness the magicians' feats. It was hoped that the people's minds would thus be disabused of the favourable impression that had been formed of Moses on account of his miracles. Furthermore, Pharaoh and his supporters publicly claimed that the survival of their faith would depend on the performance of these magicians. If they were victorious, their faith would prevail; if not, Moses would triumph. (See *al-Shu'arā'* 26: 34–51.)

(61) (At the time of the encounter) Moses said[33] to them: 'Woe to you! Do not invent falsehoods against Allah[34] lest He destroy you with a scourge. Surely those who invent lies shall come to grief.'

قَالَ لَهُم مُّوسَىٰ وَيْلَكُمْ لَا تَفْتَرُوا۟ عَلَى ٱللَّهِ كَذِبًا فَيُسْحِتَكُم بِعَذَابٍ ۖ وَقَدْ خَابَ مَنِ ٱفْتَرَىٰ ﴿٦١﴾

At this stage one ought to recall that the religion of the Egyptian royalty and elites was perceptibly different from that adhered to by the general public; their respective deities and temples were different as were their rituals. Likewise, there was considerable diversity in their beliefs regarding Life-after-Death, a question considered of great importance in Egypt. (See Arnold Toynbee, *A Study of History,* abridgement by D.C. Somerwell (London, Oxford University Press, 1962), pp. 31–2 – Ed.) Moreover, as a result of earlier changes in Egyptian religious life, some sections of the local population had begun to prefer, or at least had developed a susceptibility towards, monotheistic as opposed to polytheistic doctrines. This is evident from the fact that the Israelites and their local co-religionists constituted at least ten per cent of the population. Moreover, barely 150 years previously Amenophis or Akhnaton (1377–1360 B.C.) had brought about a religious revolution in Egypt. As a result of this revolution, only a single deity, Aton was worshipped whereas other deities were discarded. True, this revolution was subsequently reversed with the help of the same political power which had caused it. Nevertheless, the results of this revolution had some bearing on the peoples' minds. If one bears these facts in mind, it is that much easier to understand the panic which seized Pharaoh on this occasion.

33. It is pertinent to recall that this was not addressed to the general public who had to decide whether Moses performed miracles or magical feats. Instead, Moses said this in the course of his address to Pharaoh and his courtiers who had accused Moses of being no more than a magician.

34. The people concerned were asked not to fabricate a lie against God; to refrain from calling Moses' miracle a feat of magic, and from calling a true Messenger of God a magician, one much given to lying. (See *al-Qaṣaṣ* 28: 4 – Ed.)

(62) Thereupon they wrangled among themselves about the matter and conferred in secret.[35] (63) Some of them said:[36] 'These two are magicians, who want to drive you out of your land with their magic and to destroy your excellent way of life.[37] (64) So muster all your stratagem and come forth in a row.[38] Whoever prevails today shall triumph.'

فَتَنَٰزَعُوٓاْ أَمۡرَهُم بَيۡنَهُمۡ وَأَسَرُّواْ
ٱلنَّجۡوَىٰ ﴿٦٢﴾ قَالُوٓاْ إِنۡ هَٰذَٰنِ
لَسَٰحِرَٰنِ يُرِيدَانِ أَن يُخۡرِجَاكُم
مِّنۡ أَرۡضِكُم بِسِحۡرِهِمَا وَيَذۡهَبَا
بِطَرِيقَتِكُمُ ٱلۡمُثۡلَىٰ ﴿٦٣﴾ فَأَجۡمِعُواْ
كَيۡدَكُمۡ ثُمَّ ٱئۡتُواْ صَفّٗاۚ وَقَدۡ
أَفۡلَحَ ٱلۡيَوۡمَ مَنِ ٱسۡتَعۡلَىٰ ﴿٦٤﴾

35. This shows that they had begun to feel weakened from within. They realized that what Moses had performed was not magic. Hence, they faced Moses in the encounter with considerable trepidation and reluctance, and when that encounter began, their resolve simply dissipated.

The disagreement in Pharaoh's ranks, to which the present verse refers possibly pertains to the time and venue of the encounter. They probably disagreed among themselves about whether the encounter should take place on the occasion of the great national festival and which would be attended by a large number of people from all parts of the land, and which would also take place in broad daylight enabling all to witness it. Some people in Pharaoh's ranks seem to have been opposed to the idea, thinking that if they suffered a public defeat and people became aware of the difference between miracles and magic, then it would be extremely difficult to avoid a crushing defeat.

36. This statement, in all probability, was made by those extremist members of Pharaoh's court who were willing to go to any lengths in order to defeat Moses. The zealous followers of Pharaoh thought it advisable to go vigorously ahead, give up all circumspection, and plunge into a direct encounter, come what may. Those who were mature, however, and had a better understanding of things were reluctant to proceed in a direction that would force them into a headlong confrontation with Moses.

37. Their position rested on two points. First, if the magicians succeeded in changing rods into serpents, this would impress upon the crowd that Moses was no more than a magician. Moreover, by fanning the fire of chauvinistic

(65) The magicians[39] said: 'Moses, will you throw down or shall we be the first to throw?'

(66) Moses replied: 'No, let it be you to throw first.' Then suddenly it appeared to Moses, owing to their magic, as if their ropes and staffs were running.[40] (67) So Moses' heart was filled with fear. ▶

قَالُواْ يَٰمُوسَىٰٓ إِمَّآ أَن تُلۡقِيَ وَإِمَّآ أَن نَّكُونَ
أَوَّلَ مَنۡ أَلۡقَىٰ ﴿٦٥﴾ قَالَ بَلۡ أَلۡقُواْۖ فَإِذَا
حِبَالُهُمۡ وَعِصِيُّهُمۡ يُخَيَّلُ إِلَيۡهِ مِن
سِحۡرِهِمۡ أَنَّهَا تَسۡعَىٰ ﴿٦٦﴾ فَأَوۡجَسَ فِي
نَفۡسِهِۦ خِيفَةٗ مُّوسَىٰ ﴿٦٧﴾

---

prejudice, they wanted to persuade the ruling classes that Moses' victory would mean the former's downfall and the extinction of their splendid way of life. They, thus, infused fear into the hearts and minds of influential members of the Egyptian society, advising that Moses' rise to power would sound the death-knell of their own culture. Their arts, their attractive civilization, their varied entertainments, the unfettered freedom of their womenfolk (of which we find a conspicuous example in the story of the Prophet Joseph) (see *Yūsuf* 12: 3–32 – Ed.); in sum, all the essentials of a life in pursuit of pleasure, would be destroyed. What would be left would be a life of cold and stark piety; a life so insufferable that it would be preferable for men of good taste to die rather than continue living.

38. The plan was to put up a united front against Moses. For, if during the encounter there was any sign of disagreement or reluctance, or if the magicians began to whisper amongst themselves, their awe would be lost and the onlookers would gain the impression that they were unsure about their abilities.

39. The Qur'ān omits details in that the magicians had been issued directives to take part in the contest against Moses.

40. According to *al-A'rāf*: 'Moses said: ''You throw''. So when they threw [their rods], they [i.e. the magicians] enchanted the eyes of the people and struck them with awe . . .' (*al-A'rāf* 7: 116).

The present verse makes it clear that the magicians' sorcery had not only affected the general public, but also to a certain degree even Moses (peace be on him). It was not only his eyes which experienced the effects of their sorcery but even his mind felt inclined to believe that these rods and ropes were serpents in a state of motion.

(68) We said to him: 'Have no fear;[41] for it is you who will prevail. (69) And throw down what is in your right hand; it will swallow up all that they have wrought.[42] They have wrought only a magician's stratagem. A magician cannot come to any good, come whence he may.' (70) Eventually the magicians were impelled to fall down prostrate[43] and said: 'We believe in the Lord of Moses and Aaron.'[44]

قُلْنَا لَا تَخَفْ إِنَّكَ أَنتَ ٱلْأَعْلَىٰ ﴿٦٨﴾ وَأَلْقِ مَا فِى يَمِينِكَ تَلْقَفْ مَا صَنَعُوٓا۟ ۖ إِنَّمَا صَنَعُوا۟ كَيْدُ سَٰحِرٍ ۖ وَلَا يُفْلِحُ ٱلسَّاحِرُ حَيْثُ أَتَىٰ ﴿٦٩﴾ فَأُلْقِىَ ٱلسَّحَرَةُ سُجَّدًا قَالُوٓا۟ ءَامَنَّا بِرَبِّ هَٰرُونَ وَمُوسَىٰ ﴿٧٠﴾

41. It would appear that no sooner had Moses (peace be on him) said: 'throw', the magicians instantly threw their rods and ropes towards him momentarily making Moses feel as if hundreds of serpents were speeding towards him. There is nothing strange about the fact that such a spectacle would have momentarily stunned Moses. For a human being remains a human being even if he is also a Prophet. It is further possible that Moses feared that the magicians' feats were so similar to his own miracles that many people would indeed be led towards false beliefs.

It is worth noting that the Qur'ān here indicates that even Prophets are vulnerable to magical effects just like any other human being. Magicians do not have the power to deprive a Messenger of God of his Messengership, nor to interrupt the revelations made to him, nor to cause him to go astray. But it is nevertheless possible that magic might temporarily have some effect on the powers of a Messenger. This refutes the position of those who, when they come across the traditions which mention that the Prophet Muḥammad (peace be on him) was affected by magic, find the idea that a Messenger of God can be affected by magic so outrageous that they not only reject the particular *ḥadīth* in question, but also go so far as to deny the authenticity of the whole corpus of *Ḥadīth*.

42. It is possible that the miraculously-created python swallowed all the rods and ropes which appeared in the form of serpents. However, the words used in the above verse and at other places in the Qur'ān while relating this

story, seem to suggest that the miraculously-created python did not actually swallow the serpents, but simply nullified the effect of the magic which had made the rods and ropes mistakenly appear to the onlookers as serpents. In the relevant verses the actual words used in the Qur'ān (see *al-A'rāf* 7: 117 and *al-Shu'arā'* 26: 45) are تَلْقَفُ مَا يَأْفِكُونَ which means that it began to swallow up their false devices. In the present *sūrah,* the words are تَلْقَفْ مَا صَنَعُوٓا, meaning: 'it will swallow up all that they have wrought' (verse 69). Now the false devices which they had contrived did not consist of fake rods and serpents, but rather consisted of the magic which had made those objects look like serpents. We, therefore, believe that in whichever direction the python went, it swallowed up the rods and ropes throwing them back in such a manner that everything reverted to its original form.

43. When Pharaoh's magicians observed the miraculous impact of Moses' rod, they were readily convinced that it was a genuine miracle, and had nothing to do with magic. Instantly and involuntarily, they fell down in prostration, as if someone had forcibly thrown them to the ground.

44. Everyone present in the arena knew the purpose of the encounter. No one thought that it was a mere magical tournament between Moses and the magicians in order to establish who had the greater powers. For it was common knowledge that Moses presented himself as the Messenger of God, the Lord and Creator of the earth and the heavens, rather than as a magician. It was also widely known that Moses performed the miracle of his rod as proof of his claim to Messengership rather than as an indication of his superior magical powers. Conversely, by publicly inviting the magicians to confront Moses, Pharaoh had wanted to prove that the transformation of a rod into a python was merely a magical trick by Moses rather than a miracle. In other words, Pharaoh's magicians and all those present were fully aware of the distinction between miracles and sorcery. What was at stake, therefore, was whether Moses' performance was some form of sorcery, or whether it was a miracle which could be shown only with God's special help. This explains why the magicians, once defeated did not say: 'We accept that Moses is much more skilled than we are.' Rather, the incident persuaded them to affirm that Moses was a genuine Messenger of God, the Lord of the universe, with the result that they exclaimed: 'We believe in the Lord of Moses and Aaron' (verse 70).

This enables us to gauge the tremendous impact this defeat of Pharaoh's magicians would have had on the general public and across the whole country. For Pharaoh had arranged for this tournament to take place at the largest festival in the land, in the hope that when people from all parts of the country would see for themselves that there was nothing unique in Moses' miracle, that it was something which could be performed by any magician, it would irreparably damage Moses' claim and position. The tables were, however, turned when Pharaoh's own magicians affirmed, in the presence of a huge crowd hailing from every corner of the empire, that Moses did not perform any magical trick; that his performance was indeed a miracle which only a Messenger of God could achieve.

(71) Pharaoh said: 'What! Did you believe in Him even before I permitted you to do so? Surely, he must be your chief who taught you magic.[45] Now I will certainly cut off your hands and your feet on opposite sides,[46] and will crucify you on the trunks of palm-trees;[47] and then you will come to know which of us can inflict sterner and more lasting torment.'[48]

قَالَ ءَامَنتُمْ لَهُۥ قَبْلَ أَنْ ءَاذَنَ لَكُمْ إِنَّهُۥ
لَكَبِيرُكُمُ ٱلَّذِى عَلَّمَكُمُ ٱلسِّحْرَ
فَلَأُقَطِّعَنَّ أَيْدِيَكُمْ وَأَرْجُلَكُم
مِّنْ خِلَٰفٍ وَلَأُصَلِّبَنَّكُمْ فِى جُذُوعِ
ٱلنَّخْلِ وَلَتَعْلَمُنَّ أَيُّنَآ أَشَدُّ عَذَابًا
وَأَبْقَىٰ ٧١

---

45. *Surah al-A'rāf* mentions that Pharaoh conceded the point. Furthermore, his statement: 'This is a trick which you have planned in the city to drive out its rulers' (*al-A'rāf* 7: 123) elaborates upon Pharaoh's accusation that the magicians were guilty not only of hatching a conspiracy against him, but also that Moses was their chief. Pharaoh further accused the magicians that they had feigned defeat at the behest of their master, Moses; that is, they had not been truly defeated. Pharaoh also contended that the whole thing had been pre-planned so that Moses' supremacy could be paraded as proof of his Messengership which in turn would lead to political upheaval in the land.

46. This refers to the mode of punishment: that their right foot and left hand be cut off, or vice versa.

47. The ancient method of crucifixion or hanging was to either fix a long pole in the ground or to use the trunk of a tree for the same purpose. Another piece of wood would then be tied across it at the top. The culprit was then taken up and his hands nailed to the pole; in this manner he was left hanging for hours to die a slow, painful death. The dead body of such a person was left in this state so that others might draw a lesson from his tragic end.

48. Conscious that he was fighting a losing battle, Pharaoh resorted to this artifice. By threatening them with a dreadful punishment, he aimed to force his magicians to confess that they had acted in collusion with Moses and that they had hatched a conspiracy against the state. Nonetheless, their firm resolve and courage, now that they had embraced the truth, frustrated even this last

(72) The magicians ans-
wered: 'By Him Who has
created us, we shall never
prefer you to the truth after
manifest signs have come to
us.[49] So decree whatever you
will. Your decree will pertain,
at the most, to the present
life of the world. (73) We
believe in our Lord that He
may forgive us our sins and
also forgive us the practice of
magic to which you had
compelled us. Allah alone is
the Best and He alone will
abide.' (74) The truth is[50]
that Hell awaits him who
comes to his Lord laden with
sin; he shall neither die in it
nor live.[51] ▶

قَالُوا۟ لَن نُّؤْثِرَكَ عَلَىٰ مَا جَآءَنَا مِنَ
ٱلْبَيِّنَٰتِ وَٱلَّذِى فَطَرَنَا ۖ فَٱقْضِ مَآ أَنتَ
قَاضٍ ۖ إِنَّمَا تَقْضِى هَٰذِهِ ٱلْحَيَوٰةَ
ٱلدُّنْيَآ ﴿٧٢﴾ إِنَّآ ءَامَنَّا بِرَبِّنَا لِيَغْفِرَ لَنَا
خَطَٰيَٰنَا وَمَآ أَكْرَهْتَنَا عَلَيْهِ مِنَ
ٱلسِّحْرِ ۗ وَٱللَّهُ خَيْرٌ وَأَبْقَىٰٓ ﴿٧٣﴾ إِنَّهُۥ
مَن يَأْتِ رَبَّهُۥ مُجْرِمًا فَإِنَّ لَهُۥ جَهَنَّمَ
لَا يَمُوتُ فِيهَا وَلَا يَحْيَىٰ ﴿٧٤﴾

desperate attempt by Pharaoh. The magicians' readiness to face such dreadful punishment convinced everyone that the charge of conspiracy levelled against them was little more than a political manoeuvre. Everyone was convinced that the magicians sincerely believed that Moses was truly a Prophet.

49. This verse may also be translated as follows: 'We shall never accord you precedence over the evident signs which have come to us, nor over Him Who brought us into existence.'

50. This remark is from God and supplements the magicians' statement. The style of the sentence makes it quite evident that it could not have been made by the magicians.

51. Such a person will remain suspended between life and death. He will not meet his death which would have ended his suffering and misery, nor will he experience the joy of living, which would have made him realize that life was preferable to death. He will be disgusted with life but will remain unable to

(75) But he who comes to Him with faith and righteous works shall be exalted to high ranks; (76) and shall live for ever in everlasting Gardens beneath which rivers flow. Such will be the reward of those who purify themselves.

(77) Most certainly We revealed to Moses:[52] 'Proceed with My servants in the night and strike for them a dry path in the sea.[53] Have no fear of being overtaken, nor be afraid of treading through the sea.'

وَمَن يَأْتِهِۦ مُؤْمِنًا قَدْ عَمِلَ ٱلصَّٰلِحَٰتِ
فَأُو۟لَٰٓئِكَ لَهُمُ ٱلدَّرَجَٰتُ ٱلْعُلَىٰ ﴿٧٥﴾
جَنَّٰتُ عَدْنٍ تَجْرِى مِن تَحْتِهَا ٱلْأَنْهَٰرُ
خَٰلِدِينَ فِيهَا ۚ وَذَٰلِكَ جَزَآءُ مَن
تَزَكَّىٰ ﴿٧٦﴾ وَلَقَدْ أَوْحَيْنَآ إِلَىٰ
مُوسَىٰٓ أَنْ أَسْرِ بِعِبَادِى فَٱضْرِبْ
لَهُمْ طَرِيقًا فِى ٱلْبَحْرِ يَبَسًا لَّا تَخَٰفُ
دَرَكًا وَلَا تَخْشَىٰ ﴿٧٧﴾

---

find the solace of death. He would very much like to die, but God will not oblige him. Of all the chastisements in Hell, detailed in the Qur'ān, this is the most awesome.

52. After describing this encounter between Moses and the magicians, detailed information of the incidents which occurred during the Israelites' long stay in Egypt are omitted. (For these see *al-A'rāf* 7: 130–47; *Yūnus* 10: 83–92; *al-Mu'min* 40: 23–50; and *al-Zukhruf* 43: 46–56.)

53. God finally appointed a night on which all the believers, both Israelite and non-Israelite, had to embark on the exodus. For these believers the Qur'ān uses the comprehensive expression 'My servants'. After assembling at the appointed venue, they set out in the form of a caravan. Since there was no Suez Canal at that time, the area lying between the Red Sea and the Mediterranean Sea lay open. The entire area was dotted with military camps and, hence, to travel through it was quite dangerous. Moses, therefore, chose the route leading to the Red Sea. He probably intended to reach the Sinaitic Peninsula by traversing the coastal line. Pharaoh's huge army, however, was in pursuit of the believers, and it came upon them while they were still on the Red Sea coast.

We learn from the description in *Sūrah al-Shu'arā'* (26: 61–3), that this caravan of migrants was vulnerable to attack because Pharaoh's army was

(78) Pharaoh pursued them with his hosts, but they were fully overwhelmed by the sea.[54] (79) Pharaoh led his people astray; he did not guide them aright.[55]

فَأَتْبَعَهُمْ فِرْعَوْنُ بِجُنُودِهِۦ فَغَشِيَهُم مِّنَ ٱلْيَمِّ مَا غَشِيَهُمْ ﴿٧٨﴾ وَأَضَلَّ فِرْعَوْنُ قَوْمَهُۥ وَمَا هَدَىٰ ﴿٧٩﴾

poised on one side whilst the sea was on the other. It was at this juncture that God directed Moses, 'to strike the sea with your rod' (*al-A'rāf* 7: 160 and *al-Shu'arā'* 26: 63). The sea, as the Qur'ān says, 'split up [into two]', (*al-Shu'arā'* 26: 63). Thus, the Israelites were provided with a safe passage. In fact what happened was even more significant for that portion lying between the two parts became, as the current verse says, a dry path, providing a safe route for Moses and his followers.

The manner in which the Qur'ān mentions this event leaves no doubt that it is a miracle. The Qur'ānic description provides no justification for those who claim that the event was caused by a wind storm or by the ebb and flow of the tide. This was clearly not the case. For neither a wind storm nor the recession of the tide would cause the water to stand in the form of high walls; nor does wind storm or recession of the tide cause a dry road to emerge in the midst of the sea by the splitting of water into two parts. (For further details see *al-Shu'arā'* 26, n. 47.)

54. In *al-Shu'arā'* it is said: 'We told Moses by inspiration: Strike the sea with your rod. So it split up, and each part became like a huge, firm mass of mountain. And We made the other party approach there. We delivered Moses and all who were with him but We drowned the others' (*al-Shu'arā'* 26: 64–6). This verse clearly states that soon after the Israelites had crossed the Red Sea, Pharaoh and his army entered the same road which had divided it (verses 63–7). Likewise, in *Sūrah al-Baqarah* it is said that the Israelites observed, from the safety of the other shore, the drowning of Pharaoh's people (*al-Baqarah* 2: 50). Similarly, one learns from *Sūrah Yūnus* that whilst Pharaoh was drowning, he cried out: 'I believe that there is no God but Allah in Whom the children of Israel believe, and I am also one of those who submit to Allah' (*Yūnus* 10: 90). Pharaoh's acceptance of faith while he was in the throes of death was, however, unacceptable to God. Pharaoh was told: 'Now you believe, although you disobeyed earlier and were one of the mischief-makers. We shall now save your corpse that you may serve as a warning for all posterity, although many men are heedless of Our signs' (*Yūnus* 10: 91–2).

55. Here a subtle warning is given to the Makkan unbelievers, for they are told that their leaders had been directing them to the same wrong path to which Pharaoh had earlier led his people. They must now realize that just as Pharaoh led his people in the wrong direction, their own leaders were also doing the same.

With the conclusion of this story it is now appropriate to compare the Qur'ānic and Biblical versions for such a study will demonstrate how false the contention is that the Qur'ānic stories of the past are derived from Israelite sources. In the Bible, details of this story are to be found in *Exodus*. The following elements are especially noteworthy:

1. It is said that the miracle of the rod was granted to Moses (*Exodus* 4: 2–5) and that he was directed: 'to take the rod in his hand, with which to show signs' (4: 17). Later on, the same rod inexplicably comes into Aaron's possession and he then begins to use it to perform miracles. (See Chapter 7 onwards.)
2. The account of the first meeting between Moses and Pharaoh as described in *Exodus,* Chapter 5, is absolutely silent about the debate that had ensued between Moses and Pharaoh on the issue of the Oneness and absolute Lordship of God. The Bible simply records that Pharaoh said: 'Who is the Lord, that I should heed his voice and let Israel go? I do not know the Lord . . .' (5: 2). Moses and Aaron gave only the following insipid reply: 'The God of the Hebrews has met with us . . .' (5: 3).
3. The whole story of the magicians is narrated in a few drab sentences:

   And the Lord said to Moses and Aaron, 'When Pharaoh says to you, ''Prove yourselves by working a miracle'', then you shall say to Aaron, ''Take your rod and cast it down before Pharaoh, that it may become a serpent.'' So Moses and Aaron went to Pharaoh and did as the Lord commanded. Aaron cast down his rod before Pharaoh and his servants, and it became a serpent. Then Pharaoh summoned the wise men and the sorcerers; and they also, the magicians of Egypt, did the same by their secret arts. For every man cast down his rod, and they became serpents. But Aaron's rod swallowed up their rods. Still Pharaoh's heart was hardened, and he would not listen to them; as the Lord had said (*Exodus* 7: 8–13).

4. If one compares the Biblical and Qur'ānic statements, one cannot help feeling that the Biblical passage is totally bereft of any spiritual dimension to the story. What is more surprising is that the encounter took place on the day of the festival when the magicians acknowledged their defeat and thereafter accepted faith. This is the very heart of the story, and the Biblical version makes no mention of it at all.
5. According to the Qur'ān, Moses had asked for the deliverance and freedom of the Israelites whereas the Biblical version states that he said:

(80) Children of Israel![56] We saved you from your enemy and made a covenant with you[57] on the right side of the Mount[58] and sent down on you manna and quails,[59] ▶

يَٰبَنِيٓ إِسۡرَٰٓءِيلَ قَدۡ أَنجَيۡنَٰكُم مِّنۡ عَدُوِّكُمۡ
وَوَٰعَدۡنَٰكُمۡ جَانِبَ ٱلطُّورِ ٱلۡأَيۡمَنَ وَنَزَّلۡنَا
عَلَيۡكُمُ ٱلۡمَنَّ وَٱلسَّلۡوَىٰ ٨٠

'. . . let us go, we pray, a three days' journey into the wilderness, and sacrifice to the Lord, our God . . .' (*Exodus* 5: 3).

6. A detailed account of the exodus of the Israelites from Egypt and Pharaoh's drowning occurs in Chapters 11–14 of *Exodus*. Some of its details are useful and provide some elaboration upon the Qur'ānic account. Yet, this account is also marked by some bizarre statements. For example, Moses is asked to lift up his rod and stretch out his hand over the sea and divide it so that the people of Israel may cross the dry route through the Red Sea (*Exodus* 14: 16). It should also be noted that by this time the rod had reverted to Moses. A little later, however, it is said: 'Moses stretched out his hand over the sea; and the Lord drove the sea back by a strong east wind all night and made the sea dry land, and the waters were divided. And the people of Israel went into the midst of the sea on dry ground, the waters being a wall to them on their right hand and on their left' (*Exodus* 14: 21–2). It is not clear whether this was a miracle or a natural phenomenon. If it was a miracle, it would have resulted from Moses striking the sea with his rod as the Qur'ān has stated. On the other hand, if it was caused by natural factors, it is hard to explain how an easterly wind running in the middle of the sea could have divided it into two and thus caused the water to settle on both sides in the form of high walls, leaving dry ground in the middle. Does it stand to reason that gusts of wind have such unusual effects?

The Talmudic account differs from the Biblical one and is closer to the Qur'ānic account. Nevertheless, if one compares the Qur'ānic and Talmudic accounts, it is readily discernible that while the Qur'ānic account is based directly on revelation, the Talmudic account is derived from an accumulation of oral traditions. Inevitably, over the course of many centuries, these traditions suffered much distortion. (For further details see H. Polano, *The Talmud Selections*, pp. 150–4.)

(81) saying: 'Partake of the good things that We have provided for you, but do not transgress lest My scourge fall upon you; for he upon whom My wrath falls is ruined. ▶

كُلُوا۟ مِن طَيِّبَٰتِ مَا رَزَقْنَٰكُمْ
وَلَا تَطْغَوْا۟ فِيهِ فَيَحِلَّ عَلَيْكُمْ
غَضَبِى ۖ وَمَن يَحْلِلْ عَلَيْهِ
غَضَبِى فَقَدْ هَوَىٰ ﴿٨١﴾

56. Here, details of how the Israelites crossed the sea and arrived at the foot of Mount Sinai are omitted. These details are, however, mentioned in *al-A'rāf* 7: 138–98. There, among other things, the Qur'ān also states that soon after their departure from Egypt, when the Israelites saw a temple in the Sinaitic Peninsula, they asked for a false deity. (See *Towards Understanding the Qur'ān,* vol. III, *al-A'rāf* 7, n. 98, pp. 74–5.)

57. One learns from *al-Baqarah* 2: 51 and *al-A'rāf* 7: 142 that God had fixed a period of forty days to bestow His Law on the Israelites. It was after this period had elapsed that God's commandments, inscribed on tablets, were granted to the Prophet Moses (peace be on him).

58. That is, on the eastern side of Mount Sinai.

59. Details regarding manna and quails figure in *Towards Understanding the Qur'ān,* vol. I, *al-Baqarah* 2, n. 73, p. 76 and vol. III, *al-A'rāf* 7, n. 119, pp. 88–91. According to the Bible, it was after their departure from Egypt when the Israelites were in the wilderness between Elim and Sinai, their reserves exhausted and starvation staring them in the face, that manna and quails were sent down to them. This special arrangement whereby food was provided to the Israelites continued for a full forty years, until they reached the townships of Palestine (*Exodus,* Chapter 16; *Numbers* 11: 7–9; and *Joshua* 5: 12). *Exodus* has the following account of manna and quails:

> In the evening quails came up and covered the camp; and in the morning dew lay round about the camp. And when the dew had gone up, there was on the face of the wilderness a fine, flake-like thing, fine as hoarfrost on the ground. When the people of Israel saw it, they said to one another, 'What is it?' For they did not know what it was (*Exodus* 16: 13–15).
>
> Now the house of Israel called its name manna; it was like coriander seed, white, and the taste of it was like wafers made with honey (*Exodus* 16: 31).

(82) But I am indeed Most Forgiving[60] to him who repents and believes and does righteous works and keeps to the right way.

(83) But, O Moses![61] What has made you come in haste from your people?[62] (84) He said: 'They are close behind me, and I hastened to You, Lord, that You may be pleased with me.'

وَإِنِّي لَغَفَّارٌ لِّمَن تَابَ وَءَامَنَ وَعَمِلَ صَٰلِحًا ثُمَّ ٱهْتَدَىٰ ﴿٨٢﴾ ۞ وَمَآ أَعْجَلَكَ عَن قَوْمِكَ يَٰمُوسَىٰ ﴿٨٣﴾ قَالَ هُمْ أُو۟لَآءِ عَلَىٰٓ أَثَرِى وَعَجِلْتُ إِلَيْكَ رَبِّ لِتَرْضَىٰ ﴿٨٤﴾

In *Numbers* it is further explained:

> The people went about and gathered it [manna], and ground it in mills or beat it in mortars, and boiled it in pots, and made cakes of it; and the taste of it was like the taste of cakes baked with oil. When the dew fell upon the camp in the night, the manna fell with it (*Numbers* 11: 8–9).

This was also a miracle. Hence, when the Israelites managed to secure natural resources for their subsistence, this arrangement was discontinued. Interestingly, neither quails nor manna can be found in abundant supply in the region any longer. Curious people have thoroughly scoured the area where, according to the Bible, the Israelites spent forty years in the wilderness. Despite their vigorous searches, they have not succeeded in tracing any manna. Some unscrupulous businessmen, well-versed in hoodwinking people, however, have made money by selling sweets which they claim are made of manna.

60. God pardons people but certain conditions are required for the granting of that pardon from Him. The first of these is *tawbah* (repentance), which means that man should give up his transgressions, disobedience, polytheism and unbelief – all things that displease God. The second condition is to have faith – that is, to sincerely believe in God and His Messenger, and the Book and the Hereafter. The third condition is righteous conduct; that is, to act in accordance with the directives of God and His Messenger (peace be on him). The fourth condition is constancy in following the right way and a conscious effort not to revert to the wrong path.

61. Just a little before (see verse 80 and nn. 57–8 above), it was mentioned that the Israelites had asked to stay in the land to the right of Mount Sinai, and

(85) Said He: 'Verily We tested your people in your absence and the Sāmirī[63] led them astray.'

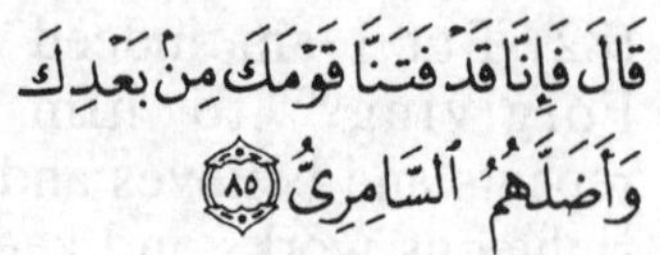

were promised that after a lapse of forty days they would receive God's commandments.

The narrative, which had been interrupted by a parenthetical statement (see verses 81–2), is resumed from the current verse.

62. It appears from this sentence that Moses' eagerness for an encounter with God, meant that he went ahead of his people. Before the caravan could reach the right side of Mount Sinai, the place promised to the Israelites, Moses had already left on his solo journey and stood in God's presence. What transpired there between God and His chosen servant, Moses, is recounted in *al-A'rāf* 7: 143–5. Moses pleaded that he might be enabled to have a glimpse of God, and God replied that Moses would be unable to do so. Then God cast His effulgence on the mountain and it was broken into pieces. This sight caused Moses to fall into unconsciousness. Later, God's commandments were given to Moses on tablets.

All these events took place on that occasion. Here, reference is made only to one event – that the Israelites fell prey to calf-worship. The purpose of this particular narrative is to emphasize to the Makkans how agitated God's Prophets become when they notice anything relating to polytheism raising its head.

63. Al-Sāmirī was not the proper name of that person. The last letter *yā* of the word clearly indicates an affiliation, either to a race, a tribe, or to a place. Moreover, the prefix *al* here indicates that the person referred to was one particular Sāmirī, implying that there were many other people bearing that appellation because of their particular tribal, racial or habital affiliation – and that it was only he from among the Israelites who was responsible for the spread of calf-worship.

In order to explain what the Qur'ān says here no further information seems to be required. However, this particular matter has been deemed to be of great significance by Christian missionaries and especially by some Orientalists who have gone to great lengths to cast aspersions on the Qur'ān. According to them, what is said here betrays – God forbid – the grievous ignorance of the Qur'ān's author.

They contend that Samaria, the capital of the ancient kingdom of Israel, was built in 925 B.C., several centuries after this event, [implying, thereby, that the word al-Sāmirī is an anachronism]. Moreover, several centuries after this a hybrid people – a cross breed of Israelites and non-Israelites – appeared on the

(86) Moses returned to his people full of wrath and grief, and said: 'My people! Has your Lord not made good an excellent promise to you?[64] And has a long time passed since those promises were fulfilled?[65] Or was it to incur the wrath of your Lord that you broke your promise with me?'[66]

فَرَجَعَ مُوسَىٰٓ إِلَىٰ قَوۡمِهِۦ غَضۡبَٰنَ أَسِفٗاۚ قَالَ يَٰقَوۡمِ أَلَمۡ يَعِدۡكُمۡ رَبُّكُمۡ وَعۡدًا حَسَنًاۚ أَفَطَالَ عَلَيۡكُمُ ٱلۡعَهۡدُ أَمۡ أَرَدتُّمۡ أَن يَحِلَّ عَلَيۡكُمۡ غَضَبٞ مِّن رَّبِّكُمۡ فَأَخۡلَفۡتُم مَّوۡعِدِي ٨٦

scene and were named Samaritans. These critics point out that along with other polytheistic innovations, worship of the golden calf was in vogue among the Samaritans. They claim that the Prophet (peace be on him) got wind of it from the Jews, and linked it with the time of the Prophet Moses (peace be on him), but invented the story that the worship of the golden calf was introduced by a Samaritan.

They level similar charges against Hāmān whom the Qur'ān mentions as one of Pharaoh's ministers. Both Christian missionaries and Orientalists identify Hāmān as a courtier of the Persian King, Cyrus, who did indeed share the same name. Using this assumption, they argue that the current Qur'ānic statement is further proof of the ignorance of the Qur'ān's author. Such a contention can only be sustained if one were to believe that in olden times there existed only one person, tribe or place, with a particular name; if that were indeed the case, the possibility of there being two or more people, tribes or places bearing the same name, is altogether excluded.

The fact, however, is that the Sumerians were a well-known ancient nation who held sway over Iraq and the areas surrounding it during the time of Abraham (peace be on him). It seems quite likely then for people belonging to this nation, or to any branch of it, to have been known as Sāmirīs in Egypt during the time of Moses (peace be on him). Let us also consider the origin of Samaria on account of which the people of northern Palestine later became known as Samarians or Samaritans. We further learn from the Bible that an Israelite ruler purchased a hill from a person named Shemer and that he later built his capital there. Since the owner of the hill was called Shemer, the place came to be known as Samaria after his name (*I Kings* 16: 24). This clearly shows that even before there were a people called Samarians, it was common for people to have the name Shemer. That being the case, how can one rule out the possibility that the name Sāmirī was used for a race or tribe because of their

(87) They answered: 'We did not break our promise with you out of our own volition; but we were laden with the load of the people's ornaments, and we simply threw them down (into the fire),[67] and the[68] Sāmirī also threw down something, ▶

قَالُوا۟ مَآ أَخْلَفْنَا مَوْعِدَكَ بِمَلْكِنَا وَلَٰكِنَّا حُمِّلْنَآ أَوْزَارًا مِّن زِينَةِ ٱلْقَوْمِ فَقَذَفْنَٰهَا فَكَذَٰلِكَ أَلْقَى ٱلسَّامِرِيُّ ﴿٨٧﴾

---

affinity with a person bearing that name, or that, for the same reason, some place might have been called Samaria.

64. This part of the Qur'ānic verse may also be translated as follows: 'Had Your Lord not made a good promise to you?' The translation we have adopted above in the text, however, means that the Israelites had received all the bounties promised to them by their Lord: in other words, God enabled them to leave Egypt in safety. He also liberated them from bondage; He annihilated their enemies and provided them with food and shelter when they were in the desert and when they occupied the mountainous region. Had these promises not been fulfilled?

Let us now consider the alternative translation that we suggested at the beginning of this note. Were we to adopt this then the verse would mean that God had promised to grant them Law and Guidance. Did this not amount to promising them a mighty good?

65. This verse may also be translated as: 'Did the fulfilment of the promise take long in coming [that they grew impatient]?'

The translation we prefer suggests that it was not long before that God had conferred great favours upon them; how, then, had they forgotten God's beneficence so quickly? Not many centuries earlier they had been delivered from their state of suffering and misery. Why, then, should their present prosperity intoxicate them into forgetting God's favours?

If we adopt the alternative translation, the verse would mean that God did not take long to fulfil His promise of granting them Guidance, which they might have construed as an excuse for breaking their covenant with their Lord.

66. This refers to the promise which each community makes to its Messenger – that it will obey him, will steadfastly adhere to the guidance he had brought, and will worship no one other than the One True God.

67. This was the excuse offered by those who had been lured by the Sāmirī. Their contention was that they had simply thrown away their jewellery without intending to make a calf from the same that they would then worship. Nor had they any idea what people intended to do with their jewellery. Whatever happened after that was such that they were involuntarily pushed towards polytheism.

The Israelites said: '. . . we were laden with the load of the people's ornaments.' This could simply mean that in keeping with their custom, the Egyptians, both males and females, wore heavy jewellery, and that this had become an intolerable burden for them, the Israelites, during their sojourn in the wilderness, and consequently they did not know what to do with it. The Bible, however, states that both the males and females of every Israeli household borrowed jewellery from their Egyptian neighbours on the night when they embarked on their migration. This quite obviously implies that just before embarking on a sacred journey they swindled their neighbours out of their possessions. It is outrageous enough that the common Israelites were, according to the Biblical narrative, guilty of a brazenly immoral act. What makes the event much more outrageous is that, according to the narrative, the act was carried out at Moses' behest, a Prophet, and that he acted on a directive from God. The relevant passages in *Exodus* read as follows:

> [God said to Moses]: 'Go and gather the elders of Israel together, and say to them, . . . and when you go, you shall not go empty, but each woman shall ask of her neighbour, and of her who sojourns in her house, jewelry of silver and of gold, and clothing, and you shall put them on your sons and on your daughters; thus you shall despoil the Egyptians' (*Exodus* 3: 16, 21–2).
>
> The Lord said to Moses . . . 'Speak now in the hearing of the people, that they ask, every man of his neighbour and every woman of her neighbour, jewelry of silver and of gold'. And the Lord gave the people favour in the sight of the Egyptians (*Exodus* 11: 1–3).
>
> The people of Israel had also done as Moses told them, for they had asked of the Egyptians jewelry of silver and of gold, and clothing; and the Lord had given the people favour in the sight of the Egyptians, so that they let them have what they asked. Thus they despoiled the Egyptians (*Exodus* 12: 35–6).

It is regrettable that some commentators on the Qur'ān have uncritically drawn on the Biblical narrative in explaining this verse. This has led many Muslims to mistakenly believe that the heavy burden of jewellery which the Israelites were carrying was in fact the burden of the 'spoils' that they had accumulated.

The part of the verse: '. . . and we threw them down', in our view means that when the people became tired of carrying the heavy burden of their jewellery, they decided, after mutual consultation, to pool all of it in one place. After recording the weight of each individual's contribution of gold and silver

(88) and brought out of them (from the molten gold) the effigy of a calf that lowed.' The people cried out: 'This is your deity and the deity of Moses, whom Moses has forgotten.' (89) Did they not see that it did not return a word to them, and had no power either to hurt them or to cause them any benefit.

(90) Certainly Aaron had said to them even before (the return of Moses): 'My people, you were fallen into error because of the calf. Surely your Lord is Most Compassionate; so follow me and obey my command.' (91) But they answered: 'By no means shall we cease to worship it until Moses returns to us.'[69]

فَأَخْرَجَ لَهُمْ عِجْلًا جَسَدًا لَّهُۥ
خُوَارٌ فَقَالُوا۟ هَٰذَآ إِلَٰهُكُمْ
وَإِلَٰهُ مُوسَىٰ فَنَسِىَ ﴿٨٨﴾ أَفَلَا
يَرَوْنَ أَلَّا يَرْجِعُ إِلَيْهِمْ قَوْلًا وَلَا
يَمْلِكُ لَهُمْ ضَرًّا وَلَا نَفْعًا ﴿٨٩﴾
وَلَقَدْ قَالَ لَهُمْ هَٰرُونُ مِن قَبْلُ
يَٰقَوْمِ إِنَّمَا فُتِنتُم بِهِۦ ۖ وَإِنَّ
رَبَّكُمُ ٱلرَّحْمَٰنُ فَٱتَّبِعُونِى وَأَطِيعُوٓا۟
أَمْرِى ﴿٩٠﴾ قَالُوا۟ لَن نَّبْرَحَ عَلَيْهِ
عَٰكِفِينَ حَتَّىٰ يَرْجِعَ إِلَيْنَا
مُوسَىٰ ﴿٩١﴾

---

to the lot, all the jewellery was melted down and made into bricks and rods, so as to make it possible to load it onto donkeys and oxen. It was in compliance with this collective decision that all the Israelites brought their jewellery, depositing it in a common pool.

68. If one reads carefully the words: '. . . and we threw them down' (verse 87), one will appreciate that at this point the statement of the Israelites comes to an end. Whatever details follow are from God rather than from the Israelites. It seems that the actual incident can best be described as follows: Unaware of the outrageous idolatry that was to take place, the Israelites threw their jewellery into a large heap. The Sāmirī was part of this crowd, and he later offered his services to melt the jewellery down. He was able to resort to some strange devices and was able to produce a golden calf which lowed like a cow. The Sāmirī thus deceived his people, although he claimed that he was in no way to blame: he had done nothing more than melt down the metals. As for the golden calf, he had no part in making it; it came into being by itself.

69. Unlike the Qur'ān which stresses that Aaron had no share in deifying the calf, the Bible affirms that it was indeed he who committed the cardinal sin of fashioning and deifying the calf:

> When the people saw that Moses delayed to come down from the mountain, the people gathered themselves together to Aaron, and said to him, 'Up, make us gods, who shall go before us; as for this Moses, the man who brought us up out of the land of Egypt, we do not know what has become of him.' And Aaron said to them, 'Take off the rings of gold which are in the ears of your wives, your sons, and your daughters, and bring them to me.' So all the people took off the rings of gold which were in their ears, and brought them to Aaron. And he received the gold at their hand, and fashioned it with a graving tool, and made a molten calf; and they said, 'These are your gods, O Israel, who brought you up out of the land of Egypt!' When Aaron saw this, he built an altar before it; and Aaron made proclamation and said, 'Tomorrow shall be a feast to the Lord' (*Exodus* 32: 1–5).

It is possible that this false report gained currency among the Israelites because the Sāmirī's proper name may have been Aaron; if that was the case then at some later date it could have led to confusion resulting in his being mistaken for Aaron, the Prophet. Christian missionaries and Orientalists of today, however, insist that this provides positive evidence of an erroneous statement in the Qur'ān. This though is all rather odd, for Christians painted a bad image of the Prophet Aaron, an image of one who had deified the calf. Ironically enough, the Qur'ānic narrative absolves him of this and it is faulted for that very reason! This is the state of their obduracy. Such people fail to realize that their view is contradicted by the Bible itself. For after the event, according to the Bible:

> . . . Moses stood in the gate of the camp, and said: 'Who is on the Lord's side? Come to me.' And all the sons of Levi gathered themselves together to him. And he said to them, 'Thus says the Lord God of Israel, "Put every man his sword on his side, and go to and fro from gate to gate throughout the camp, and slay every man his brother, and every man his companion, and every man his neighbour."' And the sons of Levi did according to the word of Moses; and there fell of the people that day about three thousand men. And Moses said, 'Today you have ordained yourselves for the service of the Lord, each one at the cost of his son and of his brother, that he may bestow a blessing upon you this day.' On the morrow Moses said to the people, 'You have sinned a great sin. And now I will go up to the Lord; perhaps I can make atonement for your sin.' So Moses returned to the Lord and said, 'Alas, this people have sinned a great sin; they have made for themselves gods of gold. But now, if thou wilt forgive their sin – and if not, blot me, I pray thee, out of thy book which thou has written.' But the Lord said to Moses, 'Whoever has sinned against me, him will I blot out of my book. But now go, lead the people to the place of which I

(92) (After rebuking his people) Moses turned to Aaron and said: 'Aaron! What prevented you, when you saw them going astray, (93) from following my way? Have you disobeyed my command?'[70] ▶	قَالَ يَٰهَٰرُونُ مَا مَنَعَكَ إِذْ رَأَيْتَهُمْ ضَلُّوٓا۟ ﴿٩٢﴾ أَلَّا تَتَّبِعَنِ ۖ أَفَعَصَيْتَ أَمْرِى ﴿٩٣﴾

> have spoken to you; behold, my angel shall go before you. Nevertheless, in the day when I visit, I will visit their sin upon them.' And the Lord sent a plague upon the people, because they made the calf which Aaron made (*Exodus* 32: 26–35).

This leaves the question of why Aaron was spared unanswered. Had he initiated this evil, he would not have been exonerated. Nor would the Levites have said to Moses: 'God has commanded to put to the sword all who were guilty of calf-worship, why should anyone be spared. What kind of justice is it? You commanded us to slay our brothers, companions and neighbours, but you refrained from slaying your brother Aaron even though he is the chief culprit.' Contrary to what one would have expected, Moses returned to the Lord, saying: 'Alas, this people have sinned a great sin; they have made for themselves gods of gold. But now, if thou wilt forgive their sin – and if not, blot me, I pray thee, out of thy book which thou hast written.' But the Lord said to Moses, 'Whoever has sinned against me, him will I blot out of my book' (*Exodus* 32: 31–3). Now, it is common knowledge that Aaron's name was not blotted out. On the contrary, the highest positions – the duties of the sanctuary and priesthood – were conferred upon his house (See *Numbers* 18: 1–7).

Does this evidence from the Bible not contradict the statements made elsewhere on the subject in the Bible itself, and does it not also corroborate what the Qur'ān has said in this regard?

70. 'Command' here refers to Moses' directive to Aaron when he delegated the leadership of the Israelites to Aaron in his absence as he headed to the Mount. According to the Qur'ān: 'And Moses said to Aaron, his brother: "Take my place among my people, act righteously, and do not follow the path of those who create mischief" ' (*al-A'rāf* 7: 142).

(99) (O Muḥammad!)[75] Thus do We recount to you the events of the past, and We have bestowed upon you from Ourself an admonition.[76] ▶

كَذَٰلِكَ نَقُصُّ عَلَيْكَ مِنْ أَنۢبَآءِ مَا قَدْ سَبَقَ ۚ وَقَدْ ءَاتَيْنَٰكَ مِن لَّدُنَّا ذِكْرًا ﴿٩٩﴾

scholars to explain it away with their bizarre interpretations. It is also important to remember that in the very next verse Moses reproaches the Sāmirī in the most vehement of terms. This clearly indicates that Moses did not accept the Sāmirī's version even for a moment.

74. Not only was the Sāmirī branded as an outcast prohibited from maintaining any social relations, he was also directed to constantly announce his outcast status so that everyone knew that he could not be touched – in the same way that everyone avoided contact with lepers. It is significant that the Bible lays down the following stringent code for people to stay away from lepers:

> The leper who has the disease shall wear torn clothes and let the hair of his head hang loose, and he shall cover his upper lip and cry, 'Unclean, unclean'. He shall remain unclean as long as he has the disease; he is unclean; he shall dwell alone in a habitation outside the camp (*Leviticus* 13: 45–6).

This leads one to think that God perhaps afflicted the Sāmirī with leprosy by way of punishment. It is also possible that God wanted people to abhor and shun he who was afflicted with moral leprosy, treating it as no less contemptible than physical leprosy. Hence, the Sāmirī was directed to warn all and sundry that he suffered from a serious moral disease which had defiled him and rendered him unworthy of all contact.

75. Thus concludes the story of Moses. Thereafter, the *sūrah* reverts to the main subject with which it opened. Before proceeding further, however, it is useful to cast another glance at the verses at the beginning of this *sūrah*, those which precede the story of the Prophet Moses (peace be on him). This will help the reader appreciate the *sūrah*'s main theme and help him understand the reason why Moses' story is narrated at such length.

76. This refers to the Qur'ān and reiterates the remark made in the *sūrah*'s opening verse. That is that it was not revealed in order to cause hardship to the Prophet (peace be on him) but was rather revealed to serve as a reminder, a good counsel, and an admonition for anyone who fears God.

Two further points regarding the Prophets are underscored in this surah. First, although the Prophets were subjected to all kinds of hardships and their enemies constantly attempted to hurt and destroy them, God nevertheless always helped them through His extraordinary ways. Second, all the Prophets subscribed to a single faith: the same faith that was expounded by the Prophet Muhammad (peace be on him). This faith is the true faith of humanity, and all other religions represent schisms and distortions caused by men who have strayed from the truth.

In conclusion it is emphasized that man's salvation lies only in following the way of life expounded by the Prophet Muhammad (peace be on him). Those who follow it will be successful in God's reckoning and judgement in the Next Life and they will inherit the earth. Those who reject the way of life expounded by the Prophet, however, will face the most tragic consequences of that rejection in the Hereafter. God, in His compassion, had informed people of all this through His Prophet (peace be on him) and long before they would necessarily face Judgement. How foolish were those who looked upon the Prophet as a nuisance instead of gratefully recognizing God's mercy in sending him to them!

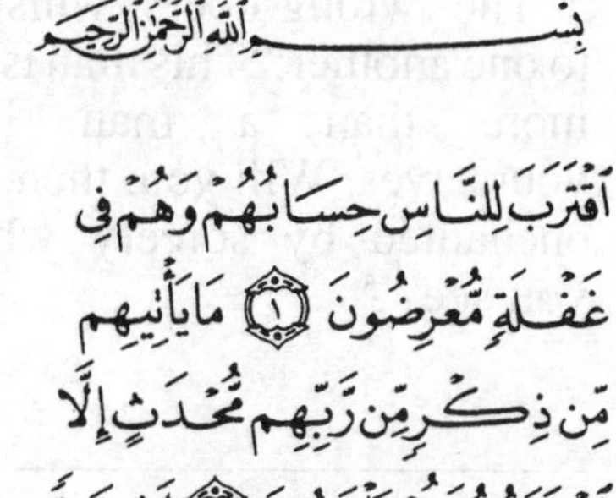

(94) Aaron answered: 'Son of my mother! Do not seize me with my beard, nor by (the hair of) my head.[71] I feared that on returning you might say: "You sowed discord among the Children of Israel, and did not pay heed to my words." '[72]

(95) Moses said: 'What, then, is your case, O Sāmirī?'

(96) He answered: 'I saw what the people did not see. So I took a handful of dust from the trail of the messenger, and I flung it (into the fire). Thus did my mind prompt me.'[73] ▶

قَالَ يَبْنَؤُمَّ لَا تَأْخُذْ بِلِحْيَتِي
وَلَا بِرَأْسِيٓ إِنِّي خَشِيتُ أَن تَقُولَ
فَرَّقْتَ بَيْنَ بَنِيٓ إِسْرَٰٓءِيلَ وَلَمْ
تَرْقُبْ قَوْلِي ﴿٩٤﴾ قَالَ فَمَا
خَطْبُكَ يَٰسَٰمِرِيُّ ﴿٩٥﴾ قَالَ
بَصُرْتُ بِمَا لَمْ يَبْصُرُواْ بِهِۦ
فَقَبَضْتُ قَبْضَةً مِّنْ أَثَرِ
ٱلرَّسُولِ فَنَبَذْتُهَا
وَكَذَٰلِكَ سَوَّلَتْ
لِي نَفْسِي ﴿٩٦﴾

---

71. In translating the above verse we have made allowance for the higher status of Moses as God's Messenger. We have also taken into consideration the fact that although Aaron was Moses' elder brother, nevertheless Moses had a higher status among the Prophets than him.

72. Aaron's reply does not mean that the maintenance of unity in the ranks of the people was of greater importance than their adherence to the truth. Nor that unity, even if it had been brought about by common acceptance of polytheism, is preferable to national disunity even if it is caused by distinguishing between truth and falsehood. If anyone interprets this verse in this sense, it would be nothing short of distorting the Qur'ānic message. For a better understanding of the point made by Aaron the following verse should be read in conjunction with it: 'My mother's son, the people overpowered me and almost killed me. So let not my enemies gloat over me, and do not number me among the wrong-doing folk' (*al-A'rāf* 7: 150).

On reading both verses together, the picture that emerges is one whereby Aaron tried his best to prevent his people from falling into calf-worship, but they reacted with great hostility towards him and were even intent on his death. Fearing that civil strife might break out before Moses returned, Aaron remained silent. He did so lest Moses rebuked him, complaining as to why he had not waited for him; if he was not in a position to control things, why had he let things escalate to the extent that it was totally out of his hands? The last part of this verse, (*al-A'rāf* 7: 150), also seems to suggest that Moses and Aaron had a number of enemies in the ranks of the Israelites.

73. In interpreting this verse, commentators on the Qur'ān fall into two distinct groups each resorting to far-fetched ideas in their attempts to understand it. According to one group, which comprises the majority of the traditional commentators on the Qur'ān, the correct interpretation of the verse is that as the Sāmirī saw Gabriel passing, he picked up a handful of dust from the earth which bore Gabriel's footprint. As this miraculous dust was poured over the image of the calf, it began to low as if it were alive. (See the comments on verse 96 in the *Commentaries* of al-Qurṭubī, Ibn Kathīr, and al-Ālūsī – Ed.) This interpretation, however, is not borne out by what the Qur'ān itself says on the subject. For the Qur'ān simply mentions the explanation offered by the Sāmirī when he was subjected to stern questioning from Moses. It is beyond us as to how and why these commentators took it to be the Qur'ān's own view.

The other group understands the Sāmirī's statement quite differently. It takes the view that the Sāmirī observed a flaw in the Prophet Moses (peace be on him) or in his message, a flaw which had not been discerned by others. He, therefore, followed in Moses' footsteps up to a certain stage but, thereafter, he abandoned that course. This interpretation was first approvingly quoted by Abū Muslim al-Iṣfahānī. Later, it was adopted by Fakhr al-Dīn al-Rāzī. (See al-Rāzī's comments on verse 96 in his *Commentary* – Ed.) At the present time, commentators on the Qur'ān with a modernistic orientation are generally inclined to prefer it.

These commentators, however, forget that the Qur'ān was neither revealed in an obscure language nor was it couched in enigmas and riddles. On the contrary, it was revealed in plain and clear Arabic so that an ordinary speaker of that language might be able to comprehend it using standard Arabic literary idiom. Now, no Arab who considers the words used by the Sāmirī would be convinced that they mean what these commentators claim them to mean. As for the method adopted by some of these commentators in this connection, they would take note of the various meanings of a word in its different usages, select one of these as the correct meaning and then arbitrarily insist upon this even if it occurred in a passage where an average Arabic-speaker would understand it to signify something totally different. Such an attitude does not attest to the linguistic competence of these scholars. If anything, their efforts can be termed as exercises in linguistic jugglery. It is not difficult to gauge how these modern Qur'ānic commentators would react if others were to interpret their writings in the same manner as they interpreted the Qur'ān. How would they feel if someone picked up a dictionary of their language, and arbitrarily chose one of the many possible meanings of the words they used in their writings, and interpreted all their writings accordingly? Perhaps just a few instances of such an arbitrary exercise would outrage them. People are wont to resort to far-fetched interpretations of the Qur'ān when they feel convinced, in their

(97) Moses said: 'Be gone, then. All your life you shall cry: "Untouchable".[74] There awaits a term for your reckoning that you cannot fail to keep. Now look at your god that you devotedly adored: We shall burn it and scatter its remains in the sea. (98) Your God is none else than Allah, beside Whom there is no god. His knowledge embraces everything.'

قَالَ فَٱذْهَبْ فَإِنَّ لَكَ فِى
ٱلْحَيَوٰةِ أَن تَقُولَ لَا مِسَاسَۖ وَإِنَّ
لَكَ مَوْعِدًا لَّن تُخْلَفَهُۥۖ وَٱنظُرْ إِلَىٰٓ
إِلَٰهِكَ ٱلَّذِى ظَلْتَ عَلَيْهِ عَاكِفًاۖ
لَّنُحَرِّقَنَّهُۥ ثُمَّ لَنَنسِفَنَّهُۥ فِى ٱلْيَمِّ
نَسْفًا ﴿٩٧﴾ إِنَّمَآ إِلَٰهُكُمُ ٱللَّهُ
ٱلَّذِى لَآ إِلَٰهَ إِلَّا هُوَۚ وَسِعَ كُلَّ
شَىْءٍ عِلْمًا ﴿٩٨﴾

---

heart of hearts, that the straightforward meaning of a verse is not good enough for them; or when they find that there is evidence of some lack of circumspection, they then feel like resorting to linguistic jugglery to offset that.

If the reader can free himself from this kind of thinking and consider the verse in its correct context, he will readily grasp that the Sāmirī was a mischievous person who deliberately and craftily contrived a nefarious plan. He made the golden calf and further made it low like a calf with the result that the ignorant and gullible Israelites were misled into accepting erroneous beliefs. But that was not all. He also had the temerity to invent a story to conceal his actions and narrated the same to Moses. He claimed that he saw what others could not see. He also claimed that he was able to achieve his wondrous feat with the help of a handful of dust from the footprint of the 'Messenger'. The term 'Messenger' could refer to Gabriel, which is how the earlier commentators have understood the word. It could, however, also have been used by the Sāmirī to denote Moses, which demonstrates just how crafty he was. For such a statement, suggesting that even Moses' footprint could produce miracles, was designed to flatter the Prophet (peace be on him). The Sāmirī may well have thought that if he could win Moses over by recourse to such flattery, the latter might begin to trust him, using his services in his effort to impress upon people how great he was, and how great the miracles were that he could perform.

The Qur'ān mentions the whole affair as being the Sāmirī's version made up by him in order to hoodwink others, rather than as the Qur'ānic version of the event. Hence there is no reason to believe that these verses contain anything that does not reflect well on the Qur'ān; it does not require the efforts of

(99) (O Muḥammad!)[75] Thus do We recount to you the events of the past, and We have bestowed upon you from Ourself an admonition.[76] ▶

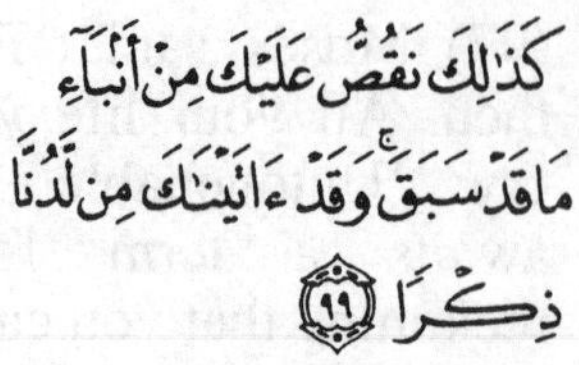

scholars to explain it away with their bizarre interpretations. It is also important to remember that in the very next verse Moses reproaches the Sāmirī in the most vehement of terms. This clearly indicates that Moses did not accept the Sāmirī's version even for a moment.

74. Not only was the Sāmirī branded as an outcast prohibited from maintaining any social relations, he was also directed to constantly announce his outcast status so that everyone knew that he could not be touched – in the same way that everyone avoided contact with lepers. It is significant that the Bible lays down the following stringent code for people to stay away from lepers:

> The leper who has the disease shall wear torn clothes and let the hair of his head hang loose, and he shall cover his upper lip and cry, 'Unclean, unclean'. He shall remain unclean as long as he has the disease; he is unclean; he shall dwell alone in a habitation outside the camp (*Leviticus* 13: 45–6).

This leads one to think that God perhaps afflicted the Sāmirī with leprosy by way of punishment. It is also possible that God wanted people to abhor and shun he who was afflicted with moral leprosy, treating it as no less contemptible than physical leprosy. Hence, the Sāmirī was directed to warn all and sundry that he suffered from a serious moral disease which had defiled him and rendered him unworthy of all contact.

75. Thus concludes the story of Moses. Thereafter, the *sūrah* reverts to the main subject with which it opened. Before proceeding further, however, it is useful to cast another glance at the verses at the beginning of this *sūrah,* those which precede the story of the Prophet Moses (peace be on him). This will help the reader appreciate the *sūrah*'s main theme and help him understand the reason why Moses' story is narrated at such length.

76. This refers to the Qur'ān and reiterates the remark made in the *sūrah*'s opening verse. That is that it was not revealed in order to cause hardship to the Prophet (peace be on him) but was rather revealed to serve as a reminder, a good counsel, and an admonition for anyone who fears God.

(100) He who turns away
from it will surely bear a
heavy burden on the Day of
Resurrection; (101) and will
abide under this burden for
ever. Grievous shall be the burden on this Day of Resurrection,[77] (102) the Day when
the Trumpet shall be sounded,[78] and We shall muster the
sinners, their eyes turned blue
with terror.[79] (103) They
shall whisper among them-
selves: 'You stayed on the
earth barely ten days.'[80] ▶

مَنْ أَعْرَضَ عَنْهُ فَإِنَّهُ يَحْمِلُ يَوْمَ
الْقِيَامَةِ وِزْرًا ﴿١٠٠﴾ خَالِدِينَ فِيهِ
وَسَاءَ لَهُمْ يَوْمَ الْقِيَامَةِ حِمْلًا ﴿١٠١﴾
يَوْمَ يُنفَخُ فِي الصُّورِ وَنَحْشُرُ
الْمُجْرِمِينَ يَوْمَئِذٍ زُرْقًا ﴿١٠٢﴾
يَتَخَافَتُونَ بَيْنَهُمْ إِن لَّبِثْتُمْ
إِلَّا عَشْرًا ﴿١٠٣﴾

---

77. The first point to be emphasized here is that anyone who turns away from the Qur'ān and refuses to be guided by it, hurts none but himself. Such a person will not be able to hurt the Prophet (peace be on him), let alone God Who had raised him. A person's turning away from the Qur'ān amounts to acting with enmity towards his own self.

The other point made in this verse is that anyone who receives the message of the Qur'ān and yet still refuses to believe in it, will not escape punishment in the Hereafter. The words used here have a universal connotation; they are not specifically addressed to any particular community, country or period of time. Since the Qur'ān will always be available for the guidance of mankind, the people whom it reaches will have the option either to accept it or reject it; either to follow it or decline to do so. Those who accept it will enjoy its good results which are described later (see verse 112 below). As for those who reject it, they will be subjected to the grievous end described in the present verse.

78. Here mention is made of the Trumpet which will be sounded before the Day of Resurrection; an instrument similar to today's bugle which is sounded in order to assemble or discharge soldiers or to issue directions to them. In order to explain things relating to the universe, God has recourse to more or less the very same words which are employed by human beings in connection with the order of things in human life. The purpose behind using these words and phrases is to enable people to have an approximate grasp of reality. Words and expressions used in the Qur'ān should not, however, be taken to mean that the things involved in God's order of the universe are exactly the same as in

human life nor that they can be generally understood by those words and expressions in current parlance. From the earliest times, whenever people have wanted to make an important public announcement or to summon people to a gathering, they have resorted to the blowing of trumpets or bugles or to some such device. God tells us that a similar instrument will be blown on the Last Day. The first blowing of the Trumpet will cause everyone to die whereas the second blowing of the Trumpet will bring about the resurrection of all. Consequently, people will rush along from all parts of the earth and will gather together in the Grand Assembly. For further details see *al-Naml* 27, n. 106.

79. The word used here – *zurq* – is a plural form of *azraq*. (See *al-Mu'jam al-Wasīṭ,* q.v., vol. 1, p. 39.) Some people interpret this to mean that out of terror all human beings will turn a bluish white. Because of fear, their blood would dry up and it would seem as if no blood is left in their veins, making them look very pale. Other scholars are of the opinion that the horror will turn their eyes a bluish white; the sense of horror will seize them, causing their eyes to petrify. For, when anyone's eyes lose their lustre, their eyelids tend to become whiter.

80. This may also mean: '[since death until now] you have hardly spent ten days'. The Qur'ān frequently states that on the Day of Resurrection people will believe that the span of their worldly life was very short. Likewise, they will believe that the time between their death and the Last Day was extremely short:

> Allah will ask: 'What number of years did you stay on earth?' They will say: 'We stayed a day or part of a day. But ask those who keep account' (*al-Mu'minūn* 23: 112–13).

At another place it is said:

> On the Day when the Hour of Reckoning will take place the transgressors will swear that they remained no more than an hour; thus were they used to being deluded! But those endued with knowledge and faith will say: 'Indeed you remained in this state, according to God's decree, till the Day of Resurrection; and this is that Day of Resurrection; but you were not aware' (*al-Rūm* 30: 55–6).

What these verses seek to emphasize is that man will believe that the time he spent both in the world and in *barzakh* (the intermediary stage between one's death and the Last Day) was very short. When people will come face to face with the Hereafter, they will realize, to their utmost dismay, that they had made no preparations for the Next Life. They will look back at their life in the world and will have a strong sense of regret and remorse on account of the fact that they ruined their everlasting life in the Hereafter for the sake of a short-term worldly life. They will consider the time span between their death and the Last

(104) We know well[81] what they will say to one another; We also know that even the most cautious in his estimate will say: 'You lived in the world no more than a day.' (105) They ask you[82] concerning the mountains: 'Where will they go?' Say: 'My Lord will scatter them like dust, (106) and leave the earth a levelled plain (107) in which you shall find no crookedness or curvature.[83] ▶

نَحْنُ أَعْلَمُ بِمَا يَقُولُونَ إِذْ يَقُولُ
أَمْثَلُهُمْ طَرِيقَةً إِن لَّبِثْتُمْ إِلَّا
يَوْمًا ﴿١٠٤﴾ وَيَسْـَٔلُونَكَ عَنِ ٱلْجِبَالِ
فَقُلْ يَنسِفُهَا رَبِّى نَسْفًا ﴿١٠٥﴾
فَيَذَرُهَا قَاعًا صَفْصَفًا ﴿١٠٦﴾
لَّا تَرَىٰ فِيهَا عِوَجًا وَلَآ أَمْتًا ﴿١٠٧﴾

Day to be very short for they excluded the Life to Come from the range of possibilities. In fact, they never took the Qur'ānic account of the Hereafter seriously. They lived in this world with false notions and they breathed their last holding on to these. So when they will suddenly rise from their state of death and will find themselves trudging along at the sound of the Trumpet in the world of the Hereafter, panic will seize them. In that state of panic, they will try to form an estimate of the time that elapsed from their becoming unconscious in some hospital or when their ship was sunk on the sea, etc. They will be unable to appreciate that they were now dead and face to face with the Next Life, a life which they had once laughed away as both absurd and preposterous. Hence, they will remain under the illusion that they had simply lain unconscious for a few hours or a few days after which they had woken up. They will think that they have reached some place where, because of some huge accident, everyone is rushing in one and the same direction. It is not unlikely that when the people of our own time wake up in the Hereafter they will mistake the sound of the Trumpet for an air-raid siren.

81. This parenthetical statement is aimed at dispelling any doubt that might arise in the minds of some of the addressees of this discourse. For people are wont to wonder how the Qur'ān was narrating a conversation that will take place on the Day of Reckoning.

82. This is another parenthetical statement, one in response to a query put forth by someone in the audience. It would appear that when this *sūrah* was being recited as a revealed discourse before a group of people, someone might mockingly have quipped: 'This is what will happen on the Last Day! Everyone

will be rushing along on a levelled plain. One wonders where all these vast mountains will disappear to!'

In order to grasp the context of this question, the reader should bear in mind the locale – Makka – where these verses were first recited. Makka resembles an aqueduct, surrounded by high mountains. It is likely that the inquirer might have referred to these very mountains – those around Makka – when he posed his query. The response from on High was that the mountains would be razed to the ground and would be reduced to tiny particles of sand, which would then be blown about in the manner that dust is blown about. The earth would then be flattened and all its ups and downs removed. It would appear as a levelled floor without any curvature or depression.

83. The shape the earth will assume on the Last Day is identified in several places in the Qur'ān. For example, in *al-Inshiqāq* it is said: 'When the earth is flattened out' (*al-Inshiqāq* 84: 3). In *al-Infiṭār*: 'When the oceans are burst forth' (*al-Infiṭār* 82: 3), which presumably means that the ocean-beds will be cleft and all their water will be absorbed by the recesses of the earth. In *al-Takwīr*: 'When the oceans boil over with swell' (*al-Takwīr* 81: 6). The present verse states: 'They ask you concerning the mountains: Say: ''My Lord will uproot them and scatter them like dust, and leave the earth a levelled plain in which you shall find no crookedness or curvature'' ' (*Ṭā Hā* 20: 105–7). If we consider these verses together the image of the Last Day that is conjured up is one where the earth would be reshaped, the oceans filled up, the mountains razed, the unevenness that we see today removed, and the forests cleared away, reducing the earth to a levelled plain. This change will occur as hinted at in the verse: 'The Day when the heavens and the earth will be altogether changed...' (*Ibrāhīm* 14: 48).

It will be on this levelled earth that the Grand Assembly of the Hereafter, in which everyone will be called to account, will be held. Thereafter the earth will be subjected to another change, which will give it its final and everlasting shape: 'They will say: ''Praise be to Allah, Who has truly fulfilled His promise to us, and has given us this land in heritage. We may dwell in the Garden as we will. What an excellent reward for the righteous!'' ' (*al-Zumar* 39: 74).

We thus know that the whole earth will be changed into Paradise, to be inhabited by the pious and righteous servants of God. The whole earth will then become one country; the mountains, oceans, rivers and deserts which presently divide the earth into numerous countries and states will cease to exist, for these geographical divisions have created discord among mankind. It is worth noting that among the Companions and Successors, Ibn 'Abbās and Qatādah also subscribe to the view that Paradise will be on this earth. (See al-Ālūsī, vol. 27, p. 27 – Ed.) They interpret the following verse: 'Near the Lote-tree beyond which none may pass. Near it is the Garden of Abode' (*al-Najm* 53: 14–15), to mean that the Garden [i.e. Paradise] will be that part of the earth which at present is the abode of the souls of martyrs. (See al-Qurṭubī's comments on the verse *al-Zumar* 39: 73 in his *Commentary*. See also al-Ālūsī, vol. 27, pp. 50–1 – Ed.)

(108) On that Day people shall follow straight on to the call of the summoner, no one daring to show any haughtiness. Their voices shall be hushed before the Most Compassionate Lord, so that you will hear nothing but a whispering murmur.[84] (109) On that Day intercession shall not avail save of him whom the Most Compassionate Lord permits, and whose word of intercession is pleasing to Him.[85] ▶

يَوْمَئِذٍ يَتَّبِعُونَ الدَّاعِيَ لَا
عِوَجَ لَهُ ۖ وَخَشَعَتِ الْأَصْوَاتُ
لِلرَّحْمَٰنِ فَلَا تَسْمَعُ إِلَّا هَمْسًا
﴿١٠٨﴾ يَوْمَئِذٍ لَّا تَنفَعُ الشَّفَاعَةُ
إِلَّا مَنْ أَذِنَ لَهُ الرَّحْمَٰنُ وَرَضِيَ
لَهُ قَوْلًا ﴿١٠٩﴾

84. The word used here – *hams* – signifies a low, faint sound such as a whisper, or of the movement of steps, or of speaking in a subdued voice, or the movement of camels. (Q.v., Ibn Manẓūr, *Lisān al-'Arab* – Ed.) The verse, thus, says that on the Last Day everyone will be seized by a great awe, and, hence, nothing will remain except the sound caused by peoples' steps or whispers of conversation in subdued voices.

85. This verse may be translated in two ways. One follows our text above. An alternative is: 'No intercession will be of any avail on the Day unless the Most Compassionate Lord grants it to be made in favour of someone and is pleased to hear the word [of intercession].' The words of the verse are encompassing and legitimately cover both renderings. For, indeed, the Last Day will be so awesome that no one will dare utter a single word let alone intercede on anyone else's behalf. Only those who enjoy God's permission to speak will be able to intercede and to say a good word for those for whom they have been permitted to intercede.

Both these points are emphasized at several different places in the Qur'ān and in quite unambiguous terms. For example, there is: 'Who is there who might intercede with Him save with His leave?' (*al-Baqarah* 2: 255). The same idea is stated elsewhere: 'That Day the Spirit and the angels will stand forth in ranks and none shall speak except any who is permitted by the Merciful, and he will say what is right' (*al-Naba'* 78: 38). At the same time the Qur'ān also says: 'They offer no intercession except for those with whose intercession He is pleased and who stand in awe out of fear for Him' (*al-Anbiyā'* 21: 28).

(110) He knows all that is ahead of them and what is behind them, while the others do not know fully.[86] ▶

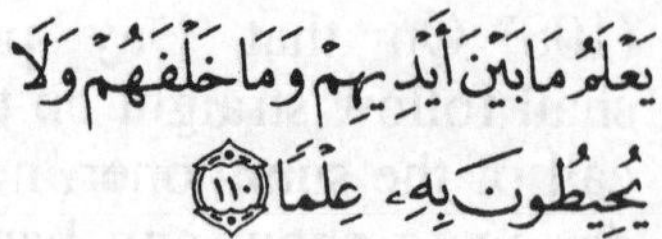

Likewise it is said: 'How numerous are the angels in the heavens! Their intercession will avail nothing until Allah permits it and in favour of whomsoever He wills and is pleased' (*al-Najm* 53: 26).

86. This explains the reasons for placing restrictions on intercession. Regardless of whether someone is an angel, or a Messenger, or a saint, nobody knows – indeed nobody – the full record of another person's deeds, of those activities which kept them preoccupied during their lives. No one fully knows what is truly creditable about a person or what makes him blameworthy. God, however, has full knowledge of the past record as well as the present state of all beings. He knows precisely the extent of the goodness of those who are good. Likewise, He knows the wickedness of those who are wicked. Only He knows whether someone deserves to be pardoned, and if so whether fully or in part. Neither angels nor Prophets nor any saints can be given a free hand to intercede on behalf of those whom they might like to. It is well known that even if an ordinary government officer begins to intercede on behalf of, or make recommendations in favour of, his relatives and friends his department would be ruined. How very catastrophic, then, would it be if the Lord of the heavens and the earth were to decide about people on grounds of intercession of others. For the record of those on whose behalf they intercede are not available to them. It is also well known that even when conscientious government officers are approached with a request that they forgive or provide favours to someone working under them, they too do not accept the pleas of those intercessors unreservedly. In fact, they are more likely to point out the weaknesses or incompetence of the persons concerned, and express their inability to concede to such requests.

When we remember these facts relating to our worldly life, it is abundantly clear how very sound, reasonable and just the principle concerning intercession mentioned here is. The door to intercession with God, however, is not completely closed. Those who were kind to others in this world will also have the opportunity to act with the same kindness in the Next World. However, before such persons actually intercede on behalf of others they will be required to seek God's permission to do so, and will only be able to intercede in favour of those for whom God's permission has been granted. Moreover, even those who are granted such permission will only be able to say, in the words of the Qur'ān, that which is right (see *al-Naba'* 78: 38). No one will be able to make any intercession which is utterly unjustified. It will not be

(111) All faces shall be humbled before the Ever-Living, the Self-Subsisting Lord, and he who bears the burden of iniquity will have failed; (112) but whosoever does righteous works, being a believer, shall have no fear of suffering wrong or loss.'[87]

(113) (O Muḥammad!): Thus have We revealed this as an Arabic Qur'ān[88] and have expounded in it warning in diverse ways so that they may avoid evil or become heedful.[89]

۞ وَعَنَتِ ٱلْوُجُوهُ لِلْحَيِّ ٱلْقَيُّومِ
وَقَدْ خَابَ مَنْ حَمَلَ ظُلْمًا ﴿١١١﴾
وَمَن يَعْمَلْ مِنَ ٱلصَّٰلِحَٰتِ وَهُوَ
مُؤْمِنٌ فَلَا يَخَافُ ظُلْمًا وَلَا
هَضْمًا ﴿١١٢﴾ وَكَذَٰلِكَ أَنزَلْنَٰهُ
قُرْءَانًا عَرَبِيًّا وَصَرَّفْنَا فِيهِ مِنَ
ٱلْوَعِيدِ لَعَلَّهُمْ يَتَّقُونَ أَوْ يُحْدِثُ
لَهُمْ ذِكْرًا ﴿١١٣﴾

---

possible, for instance, for someone who has done wrong to hundreds of people in the world to find some saint attempting to obtain his release by pleading with God on the grounds that the culprit was his favourite.

87. Every judgement in the Hereafter will be based on merit. Anyone who has acted with injustice, whether by failing to give the due he owes God, or to God's creatures, or to himself, will certainly not be able to avert punishment by recourse to intercession. On the other hand, those who have faith and act righteously – and we emphasize, those who combine the two – will have no reason to fear that any injustice will be done to them: that they will be punished for something of which they are not guilty. Nor will they be denied the reward for their good deeds.

88. That is, the Qur'ān abounds in good teachings and sound counsels. What is said here refers to the whole of the Qur'ān rather than merely to these particular verses. This observation should be especially considered in conjunction with the statement made at the beginning of the *sūrah* (see verse 1) and those verses about the Prophet Moses at the conclusion of his story (see verses 98–9). The purpose of this observation is to underscore the superb qualities of the Qur'ān which was sent down by God as His special favour, qualities because of which it has been characterized as *Tadhkirah* (Reminder) and *Dhikr* (Remembrance).

(114) Exalted is Allah, the True King![90] Hasten not with reciting the Qur'ān before its revelation to you is finished, and pray: 'Lord! Increase me in knowledge.'[91]

فَتَعَٰلَى ٱللَّهُ ٱلْمَلِكُ ٱلْحَقُّ وَلَا تَعْجَلْ
بِٱلْقُرْءَانِ مِن قَبْلِ أَن يُقْضَىٰٓ
إِلَيْكَ وَحْيُهُۥ وَقُل رَّبِّ زِدْنِى
عِلْمًا ﴿١١٤﴾

89. They are asked to wake up from their apathy and to remember the lesson they had thus far forgotten. They are also asked to reflect on how they have been directed to erroneous paths, and the heavy price they will pay for pursuing them.

90. Such statements are usually made in the Qur'ān while winding up a discourse, the purpose being to conclude with a celebration of God. The context and the style here indicate that the current discourse has come to an end and that a new one starts with verse 115: 'Most certainly We had given Adam a command before . . . .' What seems most likely is that the two discourses were revealed on two separate occasions which, at God's behest, were subsequently combined into one *sūrah*. The reason for bringing the two discourses together is that their subjects are very similar as we shall see later. (See n. 92 below – Ed.)

91. The previous subject ended with the statement: 'Exalted is Allah, the True King'. Thereafter, the angel, before departing, apprises the Prophet (peace be on him) of something he had noted in the course of communicating the revealed message to the Prophet (peace be on him). Presumably the angel did not wish to disturb him while he was in the process of receiving this revelation. Once that task had been completed, the angel drew the Prophet's attention to what he had noticed. Evidently, while receiving the revelation, the Prophet (peace be on him) had repeated the words of the message in order to fully retain them in his memory. This was bound to distract him from receiving the message for his mental concentration would have been affected. It was necessary, therefore, that the Prophet (peace be on him) should be apprised of the right manner of receiving the revelation, and that he be directed not to try to memorize the revelation before the process of receiving it was complete.

This seems to indicate that this part of *Sūrah Ṭā Hā* belongs to the early period of revelation. For it is in the early period that the Prophet (peace be on him) was not accustomed to receiving the revelation, so that on more than one occasion he did what is mentioned here. Whenever this occurred, the Prophet's attention was drawn to it. We find, for instance, that in *al-Qiyāmah* the discourse is interrupted by the following parenthetical statement: 'Move not

(115) Most certainly We[92] had given Adam a command[93] before, but he forgot. We found him lacking in firmness of resolution.[94] (116) Recall when We said to the angels: 'Prostrate yourselves before Adam'; all prostrated themselves save Iblīs. He refused. ▶

وَلَقَدْ عَهِدْنَآ إِلَىٰٓ ءَادَمَ مِن قَبْلُ فَنَسِىَ وَلَمْ نَجِدْ لَهُۥ عَزْمًا ﴿١١٥﴾ وَإِذْ قُلْنَا لِلْمَلَٰٓئِكَةِ ٱسْجُدُوا۟ لِءَادَمَ فَسَجَدُوٓا۟ إِلَّآ إِبْلِيسَ أَبَىٰ ﴿١١٦﴾

your tongue concerning the Qur'ān to make haste therewith. It is for Us to collect it and to promulgate it. So when We have promulgated it, follow its recital as promulgated. Then it is for Us to explain it' (*al-Qiyāmah* 75: 16–19). Similarly, in another *sūrah* the Prophet (peace be on him) is assured that God will enable him to remember it. 'We shall cause you to recite and then you shall not forget' (*al-A'lá* 87: 6).

As the Prophet (peace be on him) became adept at receiving the revelation, such occurrences ceased. This explains why we encounter no such remarks in the later *sūrahs*.

92. As we noted earlier, this marks the beginning of a fresh discourse, one which was revealed some time after the previous discourse. In view of the closeness of the subject matter of the two discourses, they were put together in one *sūrah*. Several subjects, however, seem common to both discourses:

(1) That the Qur'ān basically expounds the same teachings which had been given to mankind at the very advent of its existence. The Qur'ān is essentially a renewal of the lesson which man had originally been taught, a renewal that had been promised by God. It was in order to renew this that God's revealed guidance was communicated to human beings on many occasions prior to the revelation of the Qur'ān.

(2) Satan constantly causes man to forget this lesson. Man has thus shown, from the beginning, his propensity to be misled. His first lapse is evident from the lapse of Adam and Eve because of their heedlessness and forgetfulness. That, however, was not a solitary incident. Man's entire history is replete with such lapses. Man, therefore, needs to be constantly reminded.

(3) That man's true success and failure are contingent upon the attitude he adopts towards God's revealed guidance was impressed upon him from the very beginning. Hence, the Qur'ān emphasized that if man follows God's guidance, he will remain secure from falling into error and

suffering, but that if he acts otherwise he will suffer both in the present world and in the Next. What is being said today through the Qur'ān is merely a reiteration of what man was told long ago.

(4) Man has often been misled by Satan, his eternal enemy. This was due to man's propensity to forgetfulness or because of his weak resolve. Man may possibly be forgiven for this weakness provided he realizes his mistake, mends his behaviour, gives up his defiance of God, and reverts to obeying Him. This kind of weakness is one thing, but it is quite different if man deliberately decides to transgress from God's command, and so follow Satan's dictates – something which men like Pharaoh and the Sāmirī did. There is no question of any forgiveness in such cases. Anyone who embarks upon that course is bound to meet the same end as that which overtook Pharaoh and the Sāmirī.

93. Although the story of Adam (peace be on him) was narrated earlier in *al-Baqarah, al-A'rāf, al-Ḥijr, Banī Isrā'īl* and *al-Kahf,* it is resumed once again in this *sūrah*. This, in fact, is the seventh occasion that Adam's story is narrated in the Qur'ān. On each occasion, the narrative has a different context; accordingly, the details of each story have been set out in a different fashion. We find in certain instances that details incidental to the story but which are directly related to the theme of the *sūrah* are described in one place but omitted at another. Likewise, the style varies from place to place. For a full understanding of the story and its meaning, one should recall the entire narrative as documented in different places throughout the Qur'ān. We have, however, attempted to highlight, wherever the story is narrated, the underlying meaning and purpose of each fragment of the same.

94. Adam did not disobey God out of pride and deliberate rebelliousness. His fault rather lay in not paying sufficient attention to God's directive, in being forgetful and weak in his resolve. His disobedience did not stem from a conscious contention on his part that he had the right to act as he pleased, that God had no business telling him what to do and what not to do. What lay at the heart of Adam's lapse was that he did not try hard enough to retain the command he was required to follow; in essence, he forgot what he had been told. Later, when Satan attempted to mislead him, his resolve to follow God's command proved to be weak – he did not remember the warning given to him in advance, nor did he remember the admonition which we shall refer to shortly. As a result, he was unable to firmly face inducements.

That 'Adam lacked firm resolution' is interpreted by some scholars to mean that Adam did not have the resolve to obey God. In other words, they suggest that the Qur'ānic statement underscores their belief that Adam's lapse was not a result of any resolve to disobey God, but rather resulted from his negligence. This seems a rather far-fetched explanation. For had this been the purpose, the verse would simply have read لَمْ نَجِدْ لَهُ عَزْمًا عَلَى الْعِصْيَانِ whereas the Qur'ān simply says لَمْ نَجِدْ لَهُ عَزْمًا . The words employed make it quite clear that what is being referred to here is that man lacks the firm resolution to carry out God's

(117) Then We said:[95] 'Adam! He is an enemy to you and to your wife.[96] So let him not drive both of you out of Paradise[97] and plunge you into affliction. ▶	فَقُلْنَا يَٰٓـَٔادَمُ إِنَّ هَٰذَا عَدُوٌّ لَّكَ وَلِزَوْجِكَ فَلَا يُخْرِجَنَّكُمَا مِنَ ٱلْجَنَّةِ فَتَشْقَىٰٓ ﴿١١٧﴾

command. Moreover, if the statement is placed in its current context, it is clear that it is not aimed at exonerating Adam from blame. In fact the purpose of the statement is to identify that human weakness which manifested itself in the mistake Adam committed. It was because of this weakness that not only Adam but also his progeny constantly fell prey to Satan's machinations.

Furthermore, if one studies this verse without any prior assumptions, one is bound to conclude that the Qur'ān simply states that Adam did not possess firm resolve or have any strong intention of obeying God's command. Any alternative interpretation can only be considered by those who believe that it is improper to ascribe sin and disobedience to Adam, and hence some other explanation ought to be explored. The same opinion is expressed by al-Ālūsī in his commentary on the verse. It is evident that this interpretation does not instantly come to one's mind, nor does it fit in with the context. (*Rūh al-Ma'ānī,* vol. 16, p. 243 – Ed.)

95. Here the command that was given Adam, viz. that he should not eat the fruit of a certain tree, has not been stated clearly. It is, however, mentioned at several other places in the Qur'ān. Since the import of this verse is to identify how man is misled by his enemy despite God's forewarning and how this weakness compels him to act against his own interests, God summarily mentions only the warning given to Adam, and the command itself.

96. Satan's enmity was manifest at the very outset. Adam and Eve had themselves seen how Satan had refused to prostrate himself before them: 'I am better than he. You created me from fire and him you created from clay' (*al-A'rāf* 7: 12 and *Ṣād* 38: 76). On another occasion he said:

> 'Shall I prostrate myself before him whom you created of clay?' He then continued: 'Look! This is he whom you have honoured above me! If You will grant me respite till the Day of Resurrection, I shall uproot the whole of his progeny barring only a few' (*Banī Isrā'īl* 17: 61–2).

Satan made no attempt to conceal his jealousy of man. In fact he expressed it quite openly and asked God for a respite to prove, by misguiding man, that he

(118) (In Paradise) neither are you hungry nor naked; (119) nor face thirst or scorching heat.’[98] (120) But Satan seduced him,[99] saying: ‘Adam! Shall I direct you to a tree of eternal life and an abiding kingdom?’[100] ▶

إِنَّ لَكَ أَلَّا تَجُوعَ فِيهَا وَلَا تَعْرَىٰ ﴿١١٨﴾
وَأَنَّكَ لَا تَظْمَؤُا فِيهَا وَلَا تَضْحَىٰ
﴿١١٩﴾ فَوَسْوَسَ إِلَيْهِ ٱلشَّيْطَٰنُ
قَالَ يَٰٓـَٔادَمُ هَلْ أَدُلُّكَ عَلَىٰ شَجَرَةِ
ٱلْخُلْدِ وَمُلْكٍ لَّا يَبْلَىٰ ﴿١٢٠﴾

---

was not worthy of the honour of God’s vicegerency that had been bestowed on him. Satan’s challenge in this respect is referred to in *al-A‘rāf, al-Ḥijr, Banī Isrā’īl* 17: 62–6 and *Ṣād* 38: 82–3. Thus, when God told Adam that Satan was his enemy it was not something beyond verification for Adam because both he and Eve had seen Satan act as would an enemy and both had heard him express his jealousy.

97. Thus, both Adam and Eve are clearly told that if they fall under Satan’s sway, they will not be able to abide in Paradise and will be deprived of the bounties to be enjoyed there.

98. This spells out the plight which would follow Adam after his expulsion from Paradise. Here, there is no mention of the highest and perfect bounties to be enjoyed in Paradise; instead, only four important bounties are stated, namely the provision of food, water, clothing and shelter. These basic amenities are available in Paradise without any effort. But Adam and Eve are told that as a result of their violation of God’s command under the influence of Satan they will be deprived of even these basic amenities, let alone those other greater bounties to be had in Paradise. They will only be able to obtain these basic necessities by hard toil and sweat. Bread will not come to them unless they work hard for it. Similarly, the demands of earning a livelihood will consume their time and energy, leaving little time for the pursuit of life’s higher goals.

99. The Qur’ān says here that it was Adam, rather than Eve, who was first misled by Satan. Although it has been said in *al-A‘rāf* (7: 20) that both of them were misled, the focus of Satan’s effort was nonetheless to mislead Adam. By contrast the Biblical version lays the blame squarely at Eve’s door. (See *Genesis,* Chapter 3.)

(121) Then the two of them ate the fruit of that tree and their shameful parts became revealed to each other, and they began to cover themselves with the leaves from the Garden.[101] Thus Adam disobeyed his Lord, and strayed into error.[102] ▶

فَأَكَلَا مِنْهَا فَبَدَتْ لَهُمَا سَوْءَٰتُهُمَا وَطَفِقَا يَخْصِفَانِ عَلَيْهِمَا مِن وَرَقِ ٱلْجَنَّةِ وَعَصَىٰٓ ءَادَمُ رَبَّهُۥ فَغَوَىٰ ﴿١٢١﴾

100. Further details about Satan urging Adam and Eve to disobey God can be found in *al-A'rāf* (7: 20): 'He said: "Your Lord has forbidden you to approach this tree only to prevent you from becoming angels or immortals." '

101. In other words, as Adam and Eve disobeyed God, they were deprived of the comforts and amenities automatically available to them in Paradise under the special scheme of things obtaining there. They were first deprived of clothing. Later, the arrangement to provide food, water and shelter without any effort on their part was discontinued. For it would only be when they would feel hungry, that they would realize the bounty of satiety of which they had been deprived, and so on and so forth. What affected them first, however, was their nudity since they were stripped forthwith of their garments of Paradise.

102. One should understand at this point the exact weakness betrayed by Adam. He recognized God as his Creator and Lord and believed in Him with all his heart. He was also vividly conscious of the comforts available to him in Paradise. He also knew, on the basis of first-hand experience, Satan's jealousy and enmity towards him. Additionally, God had also forewarned Adam that Satan would try his utmost to mislead him, and if he fell prey to his machinations, he should be prepared to face the consequences of the same. Satan had also openly said, in Adam's very presence, that he would concentrate all his efforts towards misleading man and bringing about his ruination. Despite all this, when Satan appeared before Adam as a sincere counsellor, as a true well-wisher, he was able to seduce Adam with the promise of eternal life. Adam proved altogether unequal to Satan and could not withstand his temptations and so conveniently fell into the trap which had been laid for him. Adam still had his faith in God, and he did not question at all that he was under an obligation to obey God's command. It was merely a transient urge, which had been aroused by Satan's prompting, that caused him to lose his

(122) Thereafter, his Lord
exalted him,[103] and accepted
his repentance, bestowed
guidance upon him,[104] (123)
and said: 'Get down, both of
you, [i.e. man and Satan], and
be out of it; each of you shall
be an enemy to the other.
Henceforth if there comes to
you a guidance from Me, then
whosoever follows My guidance shall neither go astray
nor suffer misery. ▶

ثُمَّ ٱجْتَبَٰهُ رَبُّهُۥ فَتَابَ عَلَيْهِ وَهَدَىٰ
﴿١٢٢﴾ قَالَ ٱهْبِطَا مِنْهَا جَمِيعًۢا
بَعْضُكُمْ لِبَعْضٍ عَدُوٌّ فَإِمَّا
يَأْتِيَنَّكُم مِّنِّى هُدًى
فَمَنِ ٱتَّبَعَ هُدَاىَ فَلَا يَضِلُّ
وَلَا يَشْقَىٰ ﴿١٢٣﴾

---

self-control. As a result he fell from his elevated position to commit God's disobedience. It is Adam's 'forgetfulness' and 'lack of firm resolve' to which reference is made at the beginning of Adam's story as narrated here (see verse 115). This weakness has existed from man's very beginning and has remained with him throughout the passage of time.

103. Unlike Satan, however, Adam was not banished from a state of grace. God did not let him remain in the state into which he had fallen as a result of his disobedience; instead, He pulled him out of the morass into which he had become enmeshed, pardoned him and selected him for a special service to His cause.

One can see then the distinction that a master must make in response to two kinds of attitudes even when each is erroneous. One demands the treatment that the master metes out to a servant who has consciously rebelled and who has done so out of vanity and arrogance: this treatment is deserved by Satan and all those who wilfully defy God. The second kind of treatment is that which should be meted out to a servant who, while being fully loyal, lapses into disobedience as a result of negligence or lack of firm resolve, a servant who feels ashamed of himself as soon as he comes to realize what he has done. Both Adam and Satan were, therefore, treated differently. For Adam and Eve had confessed their sins and cried out: 'Our Lord! We have wronged ourselves. If You do not forgive us, and do not have mercy on us, we shall surely be among the losers' (*al-A'rāf* 7: 23).

104. Not only did God pardon them, He also showed Adam and Eve the right path for the future and instructed them on how they should follow that path.

(124) But whoever turns away from this Admonition from Me shall have a straitened life,[105] and We shall raise him blind on the Day of Resurrection,[106] ▶	وَمَنْ أَعْرَضَ عَن ذِكْرِى فَإِنَّ لَهُۥ مَعِيشَةً ضَنكًا وَنَحْشُرُهُۥ يَوْمَ ٱلْقِيَٰمَةِ أَعْمَىٰ ﴿١٢٤﴾

105. This verse says that the unrighteous will have a wretched life in this world. This does not mean that all those who are unrighteous will necessarily face poverty. What is meant is that such people will be unable to find peace and contentment. Someone may be a millionaire, and yet their life will be plagued by discontent and restlessness. Likewise, even the ruler of a vast empire may be intensely unhappy and suffer mental agonies. For it is quite possible that the success of such men has been brought about by blatantly evil means with the net result that they suffer great mental pain. Even when they reproach their consciences this only adds to their suffering. Such men will always remain in conflict with their consciences and everything around them will deprive them of true peace and happiness.

106. This marks the conclusion of Adam's story. If one reads this story carefully, as narrated here and elsewhere in the Qur'ān, it leads to the belief that true vicegerency of the earth was initially conferred upon Adam in Paradise. Paradise may have been located in the heavens or it may have been here on this earth. Being God's vicegerent, Adam enjoyed an abundance of provisions including food, drink, clothing, and shelter, with angels at his beck and call to do his bidding. During this period Adam did not have to worry about his day-to-day personal needs; instead his energy was conserved for the higher requirements of his vicegerency.

Before granting Paradise to man for his permanent settlement, it was necessary for God to test Adam's mettle so as to bring his strengths and weaknesses into the open. Accordingly, a test was arranged, the conclusion to which demonstrated that Adam was susceptible to temptations, was unable to firmly adhere to his commitments, and was liable to forgetfulness and negligence. Thereafter, Adam and his children were entrusted with provisional or probationary, rather than permanent vicegerency. This probation will end on the Last Day. However, God also decided to deprive Adam of the gratuitous provisions for his livelihood during this period of probation; a privilege he had enjoyed earlier in Paradise. So, up until the Next Life, man is required to strive to make his living. He will, however, continue to enjoy, as before, control over the earth and earthly creatures. The point of all this was to test whether man, who had been invested with free will, obeyed God or not, and to see, whenever he suffered a lapse resulting from negligence, whether or not he would mend his ways and return to the right path after being reminded and warned and instructed. The final decision about man, whether he has been obedient to God or disobedient, will be made later.

So far as man's tenure of this worldly life is concerned – and this is the period which covers his probationary vicegerency – God maintains a full and detailed record of it. Those who are declared successful in the light of this record, will be endowed with permanent vicegerency on the Day of Judgement in addition to receiving immortality and abiding dominion. (It may be recalled that Satan had lured man into error by promising him immortality.) It is at this stage that the whole of this earth will be turned into Paradise and will be given over to those righteous servants of God who were obedient to Him during the term of their probationary vicegerency, and who, whenever they lapsed into sin, soon reverted to obedience.

Those who look upon Paradise as an infinite opportunity to eat, and laze in indolence are cherishing a false notion. Instead there will be ample opportunity in Paradise for man to make constant progress, without suffering any regression. In Paradise he will occupy himself with God's vicegerency, and will do so with the full assurance that there will be no possibility for him to suffer any failure. It is impossible, however, to imagine what kind of progress man will make and the tasks he will perform. To imagine these things is as difficult as it would be for a child to imagine, during his childhood, the happiness and bliss of matrimonial life. The Qur'ān, therefore, refers only to those pleasures of Paradise which resemble the pleasures available to man in the present world.

It will not be altogether irrelevant at this point to cast a glance at the Biblical version of the story of Adam and Eve:

> Then the Lord God formed man of dust from the ground, and breathed into his nostrils the breath of life; and man became a living being. And the Lord God planted a garden in Eden, in the east; and there he put the man whom he had formed. [He planted] the tree of life also in the midst of the garden, and the tree of the knowledge of good and evil.
>
> The Lord God took the man and put him in the garden of Eden to till it and keep it. And the Lord God commanded the man, saying, 'You may freely eat of every tree of the garden; but of the tree of the knowledge of good and evil you shall not eat, for in the day you eat of it you shall die.
>
> And the man and his wife were both naked, and were not ashamed.
>
> Now the serpent was more subtle than any other wild creature that the Lord God had made. He said to the woman, 'Did God say, "You shall not eat of any tree of the garden"? ' And the woman said to the serpent, 'We may eat of the fruit of the trees of the garden; but God said, "You shall not eat of the fruit of the tree which is in the midst of the garden, neither shall you touch it, lest you die." ' But the serpent said to the woman: 'You will not die. For God knows that when you eat of it your eyes will be opened, and you will be like God, knowing good and evil.' So when the woman

saw that the tree was good for food, and that it was a delight to the eyes, and that the tree was to be desired to make one wise, she took of its fruit and ate; and she also gave some to her husband, and he ate. Then the eyes of both were opened, and they knew that they were naked; and they sewed fig leaves together and made themselves aprons.

And they heard the sound of the Lord God walking in the garden in the cool of the day, and the man and his wife hid themselves from the presence of the Lord God among the trees of the garden. But the Lord God called to the man, and said to him, 'Where are you?' And he said, 'I heard the sound of thee in the garden, and I was afraid, because I was naked; and I hid myself.' He said, 'Who told you that you were naked? Have you eaten of the tree of which I commanded you not to eat?' The man said, 'The woman whom thou gavest to be with me, she gave me fruit of the tree and I ate.' Then the Lord God said to the woman, 'What is this that you have done?' The woman said, 'The serpent beguiled me, and I ate.' The Lord God said to the serpent,

'Because you have done this,
  cursed are you above all cattle,
  and above all wild animals;
upon your belly you shall go,
  and dust you shall eat
  all the days of your life.
I will put enmity between you and the woman,
  and between your seed and her seed;
he shall bruise your head
  and you shall bruise his heel.'

To the woman he said,

'I will greatly multiply your pain in child bearing;
  in pain you shall bring forth children,
yet your desire shall be for your husband,
  and he shall rule over you.'

And to Adam he said,

'Because you have listened to the voice of your wife,
  and have eaten of the tree
of which I commanded you,
  "You shall not eat of it",
cursed is the ground because of you;
  in toil you shall eat of it all the days of your life;
thorns and thistles it shall bring forth to you;
  and you shall eat the plants of the field.
In the sweat of your face
  you shall eat bread

(125) whereupon he will say: ''Lord! Why have you raised me blind when I had sight in the world?'' (126) He will say: ''Even so it is. Our signs came to you and you ignored them. So you shall be ignored this Day.'' '[107] ▶

قَالَ رَبِّ لِمَ حَشَرْتَنِيٓ أَعْمَىٰ وَقَدْ
كُنتُ بَصِيرًا ﴿١٢٥﴾ قَالَ كَذَٰلِكَ
أَتَتْكَ ءَايَٰتُنَا فَنَسِيتَهَا وَكَذَٰلِكَ
ٱلْيَوْمَ تُنسَىٰ ﴿١٢٦﴾

> till you return to the ground,
> for out of it you were taken;
> you are dust,
> and to dust you shall return.'
>
> The man called his wife's name Eve, because she was the mother of all living. And the Lord God made for Adam and for his wife garments of skins, and clothed them.
>
> Then the Lord God said, 'Behold, the man has become like one of us, knowing good and evil; and now, lest he put forth his hand and take also of the tree of life, and eat, and live for ever' – therefore, the Lord God sent him forth from the garden of Eden (*Genesis* 2: 7–9, 15–17, 25 and 3: 1–23).

Those who proclaim loud and long that the Qur'ānic stories are borrowed from the Bible would be well advised to compare the Biblical version given above with the Qur'ānic account.

107. Transgressors will pass through different states during the interregnum, beginning with their new life commencing on the Day of Resurrection up until their entry into Hell. These states are also described at several different places in the Qur'ān. For example, the transgressors are told: 'You were heedless of this; now have We removed your veil and sharp is your sight on this Day' (*Qāf* 50: 22). Elsewhere the Qur'ān refers to another state through which they will pass: '. . . He is merely granting them respite until a Day when their eyes shall continue to stare in horror, when they shall keep pressing ahead in haste, their heads lifted up, their gaze directed forward, unable to look away from what they behold, their hearts utterly void' (*Ibrāhīm* 14: 42–3). Yet another state is described as follows: 'On the Day of Resurrection We shall produce for him his scroll, in the shape of a wide open book, [saying:] ''Read your scroll; this Day you are sufficient to take account of yourself'' ' (*Banī Isrā'īl* 17: 13–14).

(127) Thus do We requite him who transgresses and does not believe in the signs of your Lord [during the life of the world];[108] and surely the punishment of the Hereafter is even more terrible and more enduring.

(128) Did they not find any guidance[109] [from history], in the fact that We destroyed many nations in whose ruined dwelling-places they now walk about. Surely there are many signs in them for men of wisdom.[110] ▶

وَكَذَٰلِكَ نَجْزِي مَنْ أَسْرَفَ وَلَمْ يُؤْمِنْ
بِـَٔايَـٰتِ رَبِّهِۦ ۚ وَلَعَذَابُ ٱلْـَٔاخِرَةِ أَشَدُّ
وَأَبْقَىٰٓ ﴿١٢٧﴾ أَفَلَمْ يَهْدِ لَهُمْ كَمْ أَهْلَكْنَا
قَبْلَهُم مِّنَ ٱلْقُرُونِ يَمْشُونَ فِى
مَسَـٰكِنِهِمْ ۗ إِنَّ فِى ذَٰلِكَ لَـَٔايَـٰتٍ
لِّأُو۟لِى ٱلنُّهَىٰ ﴿١٢٨﴾

The verse under study also sketches a similar state. It appears that God will enable the transgressors to foresee the terrible scenes of the Last Day and the dire consequences of their misdeeds. They will, however, only be able to see this much but no more. In other respects they will be like the blind, unable to find their way: they will not enjoy the assistance of anyone to help them walk nor will they even possess a stick to help them feel their way. Instead, they will stumble at every step, not knowing in which direction to proceed, absolutely ignorant of what lies ahead of or behind them. This condition is summed up in the Qur'ān as follows: 'Allah will say: ". . . Our signs came to you and you ignored them. So you shall be ignored this Day" ' (*Ṭā Hā* 20: 126).

The underlying idea is that no attention will be paid to the unbelievers; their state of suffering and perplexity will be altogether ignored. No one will come forward to lend them a supporting hand nor will there be anyone to fulfil their needs for them, or to look after them.

108. This is a reference to the 'wretched life' which is the lot, in this world, of all those who reject God's Book – 'the Remembrance' – and its teachings. This will be in addition to the miserable fate that lies in store for them in the Next Life.

109. This refers to the Makkans to whom the Qur'ānic message was then addressed.

(129) Were it not for a word, already gone from your Lord, the decree (of their destruction) would have come to pass. (130) So bear patiently with what they say. Glorify your Lord, praising Him before sunrise and before sunset, and glorify Him in the watches of the night and at the ends of the day[111] that you may attain to happiness.[112] ▶

وَلَوْلَا كَلِمَةٌ سَبَقَتْ مِن رَّبِّكَ لَكَانَ
لِزَامًا وَأَجَلٌ مُّسَمًّى ﴿١٢٩﴾ فَاصْبِرْ عَلَىٰ
مَا يَقُولُونَ وَسَبِّحْ بِحَمْدِ رَبِّكَ قَبْلَ
طُلُوعِ الشَّمْسِ وَقَبْلَ غُرُوبِهَا وَمِنْ
آنَاءِ اللَّيْلِ فَسَبِّحْ وَأَطْرَافَ النَّهَارِ
لَعَلَّكَ تَرْضَىٰ ﴿١٣٠﴾

---

110. These signs are found in man's history, in archaeological finds, in the totality of man's experience.

111. Since God did not want to destroy them at that particular moment, and since a term had been earmarked for them by God, the Prophet (peace be on him) is asked to bear with their misdeeds during the term granted to them by God. He is also asked to persist in preaching his message and reminding people of their duties, and to disregard all the unpleasant things which they may say to him. It is from Prayers that one draws the necessary strength to endure opposition and hostility. Being of vital importance, Prayers must be properly observed according to the time-schedule prescribed for them.

'Glorify your Lord, praising Him before sunrise and before sunset' means the observance of Prayer. It is noteworthy that a little later it is said: 'Enjoin prayer on your household, and do keep observing it' (verse 132).

This verse also indicates the timings of Prayer: *Fajr* Prayer before sunrise, *'Aṣr* Prayer before sunset, and *'Ishā'* and *Tahajjud* Prayers in the hours of the night. As to the 'ends of the day', they can, at most, be three in number: in the morning, at midnight, and in the evening. Hence 'the sides of the day' refer to *Fajr, Ẓuhr* and *Maghrib* Prayers. (For further details see *Hūd* 11, n. 113; *Banī Isrā'īl* 17, nn. 91–7; *al-Rūm* 30, n. 25 and *al-Mu'min* 40, n. 74.)

112. There are two possible meanings of this verse and it is quite probable that both of them are meant. In one sense, the verse urges the Prophet (peace be on him) to feel contented with his present state wherein he has to endure a number of unpalatable things. It also urges him to reconcile himself to the fact that, for the moment the oppressors and wrong-doers will not be punished and that they will be allowed, for a short while longer, to strut about the earth, oppressing the proponents of truth. According to the alternative meaning of the

(131) Do not turn your eyes covetously towards the embellishments of worldly life that We have bestowed upon various kinds of people to test them. But the clean provision[113] bestowed upon you by your Lord is better and more enduring. (132) Enjoin Prayer on your household,[114] and do keep observing it. We do not ask you for any worldly provision; rather, it is We Who provide you. The ultimate end is for piety.[115]

وَلَا تَمُدَّنَّ عَيْنَيْكَ إِلَىٰ مَا مَتَّعْنَا بِهِۦٓ
أَزْوَٰجًا مِّنْهُمْ زَهْرَةَ ٱلْحَيَوٰةِ ٱلدُّنْيَا
لِنَفْتِنَهُمْ فِيهِ ۚ وَرِزْقُ رَبِّكَ خَيْرٌ وَأَبْقَىٰ
﴿١٣١﴾ وَأْمُرْ أَهْلَكَ بِٱلصَّلَوٰةِ
وَٱصْطَبِرْ عَلَيْهَا ۖ لَا نَسْـَٔلُكَ رِزْقًا ۖ نَّحْنُ
نَرْزُقُكَ ۗ وَٱلْعَٰقِبَةُ لِلتَّقْوَىٰ ﴿١٣٢﴾

verse, the Prophet (peace be on him) is urged to do as he was directed because his efforts would soon bear fruit and this would gladden his heart. This idea is expressed at several different junctures in the Qur'ān. For example: '. . . possibly your Lord will raise you to an honoured position' (*Banī Isrā'īl* 17: 79). In like manner: 'Soon will your Lord give you that wherewith you shall be well-pleased' (*al-Ḍuḥá* 93: 5).

113. We have translated the word *rizq* here as meaning 'clean provision'. For any unlawful earning cannot be a clean provision from God. The purpose of the directive is to impress upon the Prophet (peace be on him) and his Companions that they should not feel envious of the iniquitous who hoarded their unlawful wealth. There is no reason why the artificial sheen of wealth and power should lure the believers. Whatever little they earn as a result of their sweat and toil is much better for honest and righteous people since it conduces to their good in both worlds – the present and the Next.

114. The believers are told to enjoin upon their children not to feel heart-broken at the fact that their miserable state is in sharp contrast to the pomp and luxury of unbelieving swindlers. Instead, they should be urged to regularly observe Prayers. This is likely to change their perspective on life, their values, and the focus of their attentions; a change that will make them satisfied with their lawfully earned livelihood, even if it be meagre. All this will lead them to prefer a virtuous life ensuing from faith and godliness to a life of luxury and self-indulgence arising out of sin, disobedience and excessive worldliness.

(133) They ask: 'Why does
he not bring us a (miraculous)
sign from his Lord? Has there
not come to them a Book
containing the teachings of
the previous scriptures?'[116]
(134) Had We destroyed
them through some calamity
before his coming, they would
have said: 'Our Lord! Why did
You not send any Messenger
to us that we might have
followed Your signs before
being humbled and disgraced?' (135) Tell them, (O
Muḥammad!): 'Everyone is
waiting for his end.[117] Wait,
then, and you will soon know
who are the people of the
Right Way; those who have
true guidance.'

وَقَالُوا لَوْلَا يَأْتِينَا بِـَٔايَةٍ مِّن رَّبِّهِۦٓ
أَوَلَمْ تَأْتِهِم بَيِّنَةُ مَا فِي ٱلصُّحُفِ
ٱلْأُولَىٰ ﴿١٣٣﴾ وَلَوْ أَنَّآ أَهْلَكْنَـٰهُم
بِعَذَابٍ مِّن قَبْلِهِۦ لَقَالُوا رَبَّنَا
لَوْلَآ أَرْسَلْتَ إِلَيْنَا رَسُولًا
فَنَتَّبِعَ ءَايَـٰتِكَ مِن قَبْلِ أَن
نَّذِلَّ وَنَخْزَىٰ ﴿١٣٤﴾ قُلْ
كُلٌّ مُّتَرَبِّصٌ فَتَرَبَّصُوا
فَسَتَعْلَمُونَ مَنْ أَصْحَـٰبُ
ٱلصِّرَٰطِ ٱلسَّوِيِّ وَمَنِ
ٱهْتَدَىٰ ﴿١٣٥﴾

115. When a man observes Prayers, it does not benefit God. It is only he who prays who derives any benefit from it. That benefit consists of piety which will be a means to his success both in this world and in the Next.

116. It was nothing short of a miracle that a person from among them, an unlettered person, had come forth with a Book which embodied the quintessence of the Scripture teachings. Not only did it bring together all the guidance embodied in the Scriptures, it also explained their content in such a manner that could now be comprehended by men of even ordinary understanding.

117. Since the rise of this movement in Makka everyone in and around the town were concerned as to what its ultimate end would be.

Sūrah 21

Al-Anbiyā'

(The Prophets)

(Makkan Period)

Title

The title here is not derived from any particular verse of this *sūrah*. Rather, the *sūrah* is called *al-Anbiyā'* ('The Prophets') because several Prophets are mentioned during the course of it. Even then the choice of title would seem to be deliberately designed to mark it out from other *sūrahs* as opposed to giving an indication of its contents.

Period of Revelation

Looking at the theme and style of this *sūrah,* it appears that it was revealed in the middle of the Makkan period which, according to our scheme of periodization, equates to the phase of the Prophet's life in Makka. It does not seem to have been revealed against the background of those severe conditions conspicuous in those *sūrahs* revealed during the very last phase of the Prophet's Makkan life.

Subject Matter

Central to this *sūrah* is the ongoing struggle between the Prophet Muḥammad (peace be on him) and the leaders of the Quraysh. The revelations herein being a rejoinder to the doubts and objections expressed about the Prophet's claim to Messengership and his call to believe in the Oneness of God and in the Hereafter. Additionally, the unbelievers are denounced for their machinations against the Prophet (peace be on him). They are also reprimanded for the indifference and apathy with which they greeted the Prophet's call. Finally, they are made to realize that the Prophet (peace be on him), was not a nuisance and affliction but rather represented a blessing for them.

The main themes covered in the discourse are as follows:

(1) The Makkan unbelievers' misconception that a human being cannot be a Messenger of God, and their ensuing rejection of the Prophet (peace be on him) as one is refuted in great detail.

(2) The unbelievers are censured in concise and yet highly forceful terms for proffering different, and often contradictory objections against the Prophet (peace be on him), and for constantly shifting their own standpoint on such questions.

(3) The unbelievers view this worldly life as nothing but play and jest; they further believe that life will end without man being held to any account and without him receiving any recompense for his deeds. Since this misconception lay at the very heart of their indifference and apathy to the Prophet's call, it is effectively countered in this *sūrah*.

(4) Weighty and convincing arguments are put forward to jolt the unbelievers out of their insistence on associating others with God in His Divinity, and their aversion to the doctrine that there is none but the One True God. Since this was the main bone of contention between the Makkan unbelievers and the Prophet (peace be on him) this *sūrah* sets out a variety of persuasive arguments in support of God's Oneness and in opposition to those who associate others with God in His Divinity.

(5) Although the Makkan unbelievers had repeatedly decried the Prophet (peace be on him), calling him a liar, they had not been subjected to any Divine scourge. This led them to believe that the Prophet's claim to be God's Messenger was altogether false, and that the threats of Divine Punishment were all hollow. Part of this *sūrah* is devoted to refuting this mistaken notion.

(6) A number of incidents from the lives of the Prophets are recounted so as to bring home the point that all the Messengers raised by God, in whatever period of human history, were simply human beings; barring those characteristics exclusive to Prophets, they were similar to other human beings in all other respects. To be sure, they did not have one iota of a share in God's Divinity. On the contrary, whenever they realized that they themselves stood in need of help, they had no other option but to pray to God for His guidance.

Two further points regarding the Prophets are underscored in this *sūrah*. First, although the Prophets were subjected to all kinds of hardships and their enemies constantly attempted to hurt and destroy them, God, nevertheless, always helped them through His extraordinary ways. Second, all the Prophets subscribed to a single faith, the same faith that was expounded by the Prophet Muḥammad (peace be on him). This faith is the true faith of humanity, and all other religions represent schisms and dissensions caused by men who have strayed from the truth.

In conclusion it is emphasized that man's salvation lies only in following the way of life expounded by the Prophet Muḥammad (peace be on him). Those who follow it will be successful in God's reckoning and judgement in the Next Life and they will inherit the earth. Those who reject the way of life expounded by the Prophets, however, will face the most tragic consequences of that rejection in the Hereafter. God, in His compassion, had informed people of all this through His Prophet (peace be on him) and long before they would necessarily face Judgement. How foolish were those who looked upon the Prophet as a nuisance, instead of gratefully recognizing God's mercy in sending him to them!

In the name of Allah, the Merciful, the Compassionate.

(1) The time of people's reckoning has drawn near,[1] and yet they turn aside in heedlessness.[2] (2) Whenever any fresh admonition comes to them from their Lord,[3] they barely hear it and remain immersed in play, (3) their hearts set on other concerns.[4]

اقْتَرَبَ لِلنَّاسِ حِسَابُهُمْ وَهُمْ فِي
غَفْلَةٍ مُّعْرِضُونَ ﴿١﴾ مَا يَأْتِيهِم
مِّن ذِكْرٍ مِّن رَّبِّهِم مُّحْدَثٍ إِلَّا
اسْتَمَعُوهُ وَهُمْ يَلْعَبُونَ ﴿٢﴾ لَاهِيَةً
قُلُوبُهُمْ

---

1. This means that the Day of Resurrection is near. The Day is not far away when people will be made to appear before God to render an account of themselves. The advent of the Prophet Muḥammad (peace be on him) has ushered in the last phase of human history; as compared to earlier phases, mankind is now closer to its eventual end. The Prophet (peace be on him) himself confirmed this. According to one *ḥadīth,* he pointed to two of his fingers and said: 'I and the Hour are [close to each other] like these two fingers.' The statement implies that there would be no further divine revelation between Muḥammad (peace be on him) and the Day of Resurrection; people were closer to the Last Day than ever before. It was, thus, time for people to heed Muḥammad's (peace be on him) call as no other guide, warner and announcer of good news would be raised for mankind.

2. People do not take heed of God's warning. They are so immersed in this heedlessness that they are incapable of thinking seriously about what their end will be let alone paying attention to the Messenger who has come to warn them.

3. Each new *sūrah* of the Qur'ān, revealed to the Prophet Muḥammad (peace be on him) and recited to the people, represents a piece of good counsel and admonition.

4. The words used here may be interpreted in more than one way. We have opted for the interpretation to be found in the above translation, wherein we take 'jest' to refer to life as a whole. Hence, the verse means that because of the unbelievers' indifference to God and the Hereafter, they treat their lives merely as sport and jest rather than as a serious affair. Alternatively, the verse means

The wrong-doers whisper to one another: 'This man is no more than a man like yourselves. Will you, then, be enchanted by sorcery while you see?'[5]	وَأَسَرُّوا۟ ٱلنَّجْوَى ٱلَّذِينَ ظَلَمُوا۟ هَلْ هَـٰذَآ إِلَّا بَشَرٌ مِّثْلُكُمْ ۖ أَفَتَأْتُونَ ٱلسِّحْرَ وَأَنتُمْ تُبْصِرُونَ ﴿٣﴾

that people do not listen to the Qur'ān with the serious attention that it deserves; they rather take it as a jest.

5. This verse may be translated in either the present or the future tense, and both translations would be correct. It is the chiefs of the Quraysh who whisper among themselves for they are driven by a passionate concern to somehow counter the Prophet's mission. They rejected outright his claim to be a Prophet. They did so on the grounds that he was like any other human being: he ate and drank and went about the markets, and had a family of his own. They wondered what was so different about him that he stood out from others and merited a special relationship with God. They were cognizant, however, of the fact that the Prophet – by means of his personality and teachings – had a spellbinding effect on people. Whoever listened attentively to what he said, or had a chance to be close to him, immediately lost his heart to him. They, therefore, held that it was wise not to have any interaction with the Prophet (peace be on him), for getting close to him amounted to falling under his spell.

Ibn Isḥāq (d. 152), the earliest biographer of the Prophet (peace be on him), mentions several incidents where the unbelievers accused the Prophet (peace be on him) of sorcery. 'Utbah ibn Rabī'ah the father-in-law of Abū Sufyān and the father of Hind, approached the Quraysh chiefs, saying: 'Should you like, I will call on Muḥammad and try to persuade him.' This happened after Hamzah embraced Islam and when the number of the Prophet's Companions continued to rise, a development which seriously perturbed the Quraysh chiefs. They, the Quraysh chiefs, agreed that 'Utbah should try to dissuade Muḥammad from his course for they had full confidence in him. Accordingly 'Utbah visited the Prophet (peace be on him) and said to him: 'O my nephew! You know well the position you enjoy among us. In terms of pedigree you come from a noble family. So why have you brought down such a calamity on your people? You have caused division in the whole community. You speak ill of their faith and their deities. You brand our deceased ancestors with unbelief and error. Nephew! If you seek your supremacy in the world through all this, we will raise money and give you such an amount that you will become the wealthiest person. If you are keen to acquire chiefdom, we will make you our chief. If you seek kingship, we will appoint you our ruler. And if you suffer from some

And with David We subjected the mountains, and the birds; they celebrated the praise of Allah.[71] It was We Who did all this. ▶	وَسَخَّرْنَا مَعَ دَاوُۥدَ ٱلْجِبَالَ يُسَبِّحْنَ وَٱلطَّيْرَ ۚ وَكُنَّا فَٰعِلِينَ ﴿٧٩﴾

are absent from the Qur'ān and cannot be corroborated on the authority of the Prophet Muḥammad (peace be on him) in *Ḥadīth,* it cannot be said with certainty, therefore, what the authoritative Islamic position on the question is.

This accounts for the variety of opinions of Hanafī, Shāfi'ī, Mālikī and other Muslim jurists on the question of whether the owner of the goats should be penalized if his herd damages a field; and what penalty if any is to be levied, i.e. the quantum and mode of such a penalty.

Mention of this particular incident as it relates to David and Solomon just goes to emphasize that even though Prophets are endowed by God with extraordinary powers and abilities, they still remain human beings and do not partake of His Divinity. In this particular case, when God did not provide any guidance to David through revelation, the father's own decision was incorrect. On the other hand, God provided Solomon with the right decision. This is significant in so far as both David and Solomon were Prophets. It is also noteworthy that both these Prophets have been referred to as individuals endowed with great personal qualities, conferred upon them by God, but this did not make them equal to God.

Incidentally, the above verse also establishes that if two judges rule on a case and find differently, and regardless that only one judgement is correct, both judges will be considered vindicated in their rulings provided they have the necessary qualifications, knowledge and experience, needed for judging that case. This point is elaborated upon in traditions from the Prophet (peace be on him). In a tradition on the authority of 'Amr ibn al-'Ās it is reported that the Prophet (peace be on him) said: 'If a magistrate judges, exerting himself to the full, and arrives at the right judgement he will receive twice the reward whereas if he judges, exerting himself to the full, but errs in his judgement, he will receive a single reward.' (See Abū Dā'ūd and Ibn Mājah.) A tradition from Buraydah mentions that the Prophet (peace be on him) said: 'Judges are of three kinds: one of them will go to Paradise while the other two will go to Hell. He who discerns the truth and decides the case accordingly, will go to Paradise. However, he who discerns the truth and yet decides otherwise will go to Hell. Likewise, those judges who decide cases without the necessary knowledge will also go to Hell.' (See Abū Dā'ūd, *Sunan, K. al-Aqḍiyah, 'Bāb fī al-Qāḍīukhṭī'* '; Ibn Mājah, *Sunan, K. al-Aḥkām, 'Bāb al-Ḥākim yajtahid fa yuṣīb al-Ḥaqq'* – Ed.)

(80) It was We Who taught him the art of making coats of mail for your benefit so that it may protect you from each other's violence.[72] Do you, then, give thanks?[73] ▶

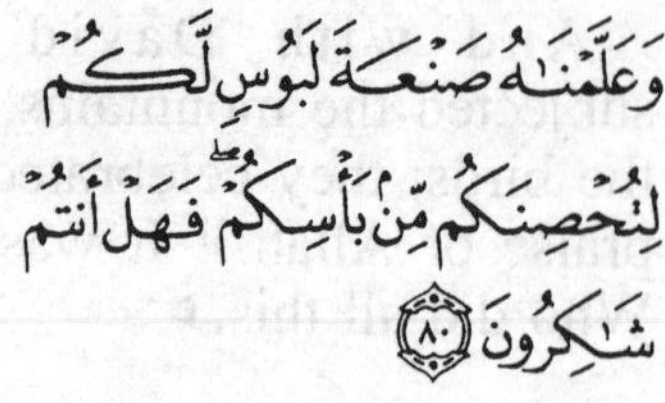

71. The words used here are مَعَ دَاوُدَ (with David) rather than لِدَاوُدَ ('for David'). In other words, the mountains and the birds, along with David, were made subservient; not that the mountains and birds were subservient to David. As a result, the mountains and the birds together with David celebrated the glory of God. The same point has been made elsewhere in the Qur'ān: 'It is We Who made the mountains subservient along with him: they celebrate Our praise at eventide and at the break of the day, and the birds were mustered together, each turning [to Allah]' (*Ṣād* 38: 18–19). This is further explained by another verse: 'We commanded the mountains to celebrate Our glory with him; and also the birds' (*Sabā'* 34: 10).

The point which emerges from those passages is that when the Prophet David was saying his hymns, the mountains echoed with his loud, melodious voice, causing the birds to suspend their flight just as if his voice had cast a spell upon them. This notion is further borne out by the following *ḥadīth*: 'Once, when Abū Mūsá al-Ash'arī, who had an exceptionally melodious voice was reciting the Qur'ān, the Prophet Muḥammad (peace be on him) passed by and stopped at hearing the recitation. He listened to him for a while, and when he [i.e. Abū Mūsá] had finished, the Prophet exclaimed: "He has a portion of David's melodies"'.

72. This point is further elaborated upon in *Sūrah Sabā'*: 'We made the iron soft for him [David] and commanded him: make coats of mail, balancing well the rings of the chain armour' (*Sabā'* 34: 10–11). Thus we learn that God granted David complete mastery over iron, especially for military purposes.

In the light of the historical and archaeological information these verses can be explained as follows: The Iron Age began somewhere between 1200 B.C. and 1000 B.C. which was the time of the Prophet David. The Hittites, inhabitants of Syria and Asia Minor, who had their hey-day during the period 2000 B.C. to 1200 B.C., were the first to invent techniques for melting and manufacturing iron; an expertise which they kept a closely-guarded secret. The iron that was thus made was, however, extremely expensive – like gold and silver – and consequently the requisite techniques were not widely used. Later on, the Philistines also acquired this knowledge but they too kept it a

(81) And We subdued the strongly raging wind to Solomon which blew at his bidding towards the land We have blessed.[74] We know everything. ▶

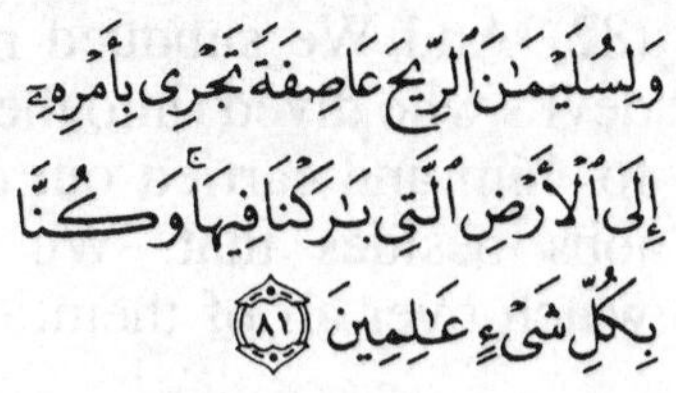

closely-guarded secret. Before Saul's accession to the throne, the Hittites and Philistines had continually defeated the Israelites and had almost driven them out of Palestine. According to the Bible, one of the factors which had ensured their superiority was their use of chariots and other weapons manufactured from iron (*Joshua* 17: 16; *Judges* 1: 19 and 4: 2–3). When Saul, under God's command, became ruler in 1020 B.C., he crushed the Hittites and Philistines and recovered a major portion of Palestine. The Prophet David (1004 B.C.–965 B.C.) extended the Israelite domain to the rest of Palestine to Transjordan and a major part of Syria.

It was during this period that smelting techniques, thus far only known to the Hittites and Philistines, were disclosed. Within a short period of time, other techniques of iron-manufacturing produced inexpensive iron, as a result of which iron products were manufactured and commonly used. Edom, in the southern part of Palestine, is immensely rich in iron ore. Recent archaeological excavations show at several places remnants of furnaces obviously used for melting and moulding iron. Indeed a furnace excavated near Ezion-Geber, a port on the Gulf of Aqaba in the days of the Prophet Solomon, appears to have been built on the very same principles which are employed to this day in blast furnaces. Quite naturally, David would have used this discovery of iron for military purposes since it was armour manufactured from this metal which in the then recent past, had created such difficulties for the Israelites.

73. For further details about David see *al-Baqarah* 2: 251, and *Banī Isrā'īl* 17, nn. 7 and 63.

74. This is elaborated elsewhere in the Qur'ān thus: 'And We subjected the wind to Solomon: its early morning stride was a month's journey, and its evening stride was a month's journey' (*Sabā'* 34: 12). Alternatively: 'We subjected the wind to him to flow gently to his order, whithersoever he willed' (*Ṣād* 38: 36).

We, thus, know that the Prophet Solomon (peace be on him) was granted control over the wind and that this greatly facilitated his voyages to places lying as far as a month's sea journey away; the wind favouring him both on his outward as well as return journeys. We learn both from Biblical sources and from modern researches that Solomon (peace be on him) embarked on large-scale naval expeditions. His fleet sailing from Ezion-Geber through the

(82) And We subdued many devils who dived (into the sea) for him and carried out other jobs besides that. We kept watch over all of them.[75]	وَمِنَ ٱلشَّيَـٰطِينِ مَن يَغُوصُونَ لَهُۥ وَيَعۡمَلُونَ عَمَلٗا دُونَ ذَٰلِكَۖ وَكُنَّا لَهُمۡ حَـٰفِظِينَ ﴿٨٢﴾

Red Sea to Yemen, and to countries lying to the south and east of his empire. Similarly, another of Solomon's fleets, called Tharashish in the Bible, operated at ports on the Mediterranean Sea and in Western countries.

The furnace which Solomon had built at Ezion-Geber for melting and moulding iron ore was substantial – no other furnace of like size has so far been discovered anywhere in Eastern Asia or the Middle East. Archaeologists believe that the ore used in this furnace was brought from the iron and copper mines of 'Araban in Edom. The iron and copper ore melted in this furnace was used for ship-building and for other purposes. This would, thus, seem to explain the meaning of the Qur'ānic verse: 'And We caused molten copper to flow for Solomon' (*Sabā'* 34: 12).

This historical background also enables us to grasp what is meant by Solomon's 'mastery over the wind'. Sea voyages in those days were totally dependent upon favourable winds. And with God's special favour Solomon's fleet always enjoyed favourable winds. If Solomon enjoyed control over the wind so that he could order it to move in the direction he wished, as is implied in the Qur'ānic statement تَجۡرِي بِأَمۡرِهِۦ ('it blew at his bidding', verse 81) this could only have been conferred upon him by God – such a task not being difficult for God. Furthermore, since God Himself granted Solomon this authority, it need not vex us here.

75. The point is thus elaborated in *Sūrah Sabā'*: 'There were *jinns* that worked in front of him by the permission of his Lord and if any of them turned aside from God's command, God made him taste of the penalty of the Blazing Fire. They worked for him as he desired, making arches, images, basons as large as reservoirs, and cooking cauldrons fixed in their places: "Work you, sons of David, with thanks; but few of My servants are grateful!" Then, when We decreed Solomon's death, nothing showed them his death except a little worm of the earth, which kept gnawing away at his staff; so when he fell down, the *jinn* saw plainly that if they had known the unseen, they would not have tarried in the humiliating penalty' (*Sabā'* 34: 12–14).

This verse makes it quite plain that the satans who had been made subservient to the Prophet Solomon (peace be on him) and who performed many tasks for him, were, in fact, *jinn*. They were the same *jinn* who, according to the beliefs of Arab polytheists, had knowledge of those realms beyond

(83) We bestowed (the same wisdom, judgement and knowledge) upon Job.[76] Recall, when he cried to his Lord: 'Behold, disease has struck me and You are the Most Merciful of those that are merciful.'[77] ▶

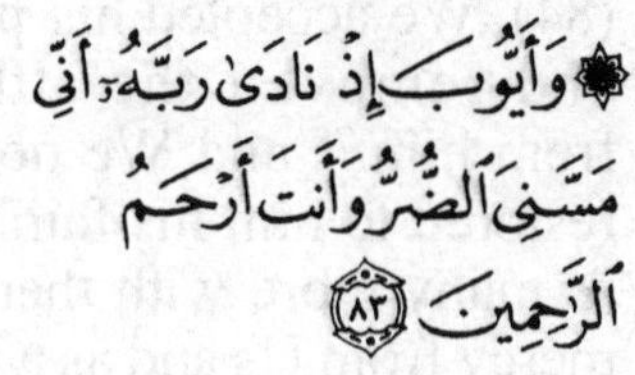

sense-perception. If one studies the Qur'ān with open eyes, and with a mind free of all biases and preconceived notions, it is clear what the Qur'ān means when it uses the term 'satans' without any qualification, what those creatures are whom it refers to as *jinn*. It is also clear what kind of *jinn* were considered by the polytheists of Arabia to possess knowledge of those realms beyond sense-perception.

Modern commentators on the Qur'ān have gone to extreme lengths to prove that the *jinn* and satans who had been put under the Prophet Solomon's control were in fact men from neighbouring nations. The words of the Qur'ān, however, exclude all such far-fetched interpretations. Additionally, wherever this story is recounted in the Qur'ān, it occurs in a context and a style which leaves no grounds for such an interpretation. If the masons employed by Solomon were indeed human beings, then what prompted the Qur'ān to mention those same masons in such an exceptional manner? For man's ability to erect buildings, ranging from the pyramids of ancient Egypt to the skyscrapers of present-day New York, is well-known. And if it is human beings who are referred to here as *jinn*, what prince or business tycoon has not enjoyed the services of such '*jinn*' and 'satans'?

76. There is much controversy surrounding who Job was, when he lived, and to which nation he belonged. Researchers of the present times advance a variety of views. Some consider him to be an Israelite, some an Egyptian, while yet others regard him as an Arab. Some are of the opinion that he lived at a time which preceded that of Moses, others that he was a contemporary of the Prophets David and Solomon, and still others that he belonged to an even later period.

These scholars' conjectures are based on the *Book of Job*, part of the Bible, and are on their differing views about the language, style and contents to be found in that Book. Barring this, there is no other historical evidence for such speculation. As for the *Book of Job* itself, it is marked by many contradictions and inconsistencies. Moreover, its content varies from the Qur'ān to such an extent that the two cannot be reconciled with each other. We are unable,

(84) We accepted his prayer and removed the affliction from him,[78] and We not only restored to him his family but as many more with them as a mercy from Us and as a lesson to the worshippers.[79]

فَٱسْتَجَبْنَا لَهُۥ فَكَشَفْنَا مَا بِهِۦ مِن ضُرٍّ وَءَاتَيْنَٰهُ أَهْلَهُۥ وَمِثْلَهُم مَّعَهُمْ رَحْمَةً مِّنْ عِندِنَا وَذِكْرَىٰ لِلْعَٰبِدِينَ ﴿٨٤﴾

therefore, to trust the *Book of Job*. The only plausible evidence to be found is that contained in the *Book of Isaiah* and the *Book of Ezekiel*, as these books are relatively more reliable from an historical viewpoint. Isaiah lived in the eighth century and Ezekiel in the tenth century B.C. It is certain, therefore, that Job lived either in the ninth century B.C. or earlier. In so far as his origins are concerned, it would appear from *al-Nisā'* 4: 163 and *al-An'ām* 6: 84 that Job was an Israelite. However, the contention of Wahb ibn al-Munabbih that Job was a descendant of Esau, son of the Prophet Isaac cannot be altogether dismissed. (See al-Ṭabarī, *Ta'rīkh,* vol. 1, p. 226 – Ed.)

77. This supplication is marked by unusual sublimity and refinement. Job mentions his suffering in the merest of words and then concludes by simply saying: 'You are the Most Merciful of those that are merciful.' He gives vent to no grievance or complaint; expresses no desire to be fulfilled, no demand to be met. The very style of the supplication suggests that it was made by an extremely patient, content, gracious and self-respecting person; but who, being overwhelmed with suffering, was compelled to utter a few words and no more. The situation seems similar to that of a dignified and self-respecting person who, long afflicted by starvation, happens to meet someone magnanimous, and to whom he simply says: 'I am extremely hungry and you are kind and generous.' He utters these words under the compulsion of his starvation, but is able to say no more. But the succinctness of the expression renders the statement very powerful, extremely rich in meaning.

78. From *Sūrah Ṣād* one learns (see verse 38: 42 ff.) that God told Job: 'Strike [the ground] with your foot. Here is cool water to wash and to drink' and so, as soon as Job struck the ground with his foot, God caused a natural spring to flow for him. Its water had a special medicinal property which cured Job when he either drank of it or bathed in it. This mode of treatment provides some clue as to Job's illness, suggesting as it does some sort of severe skin disorder. This view is also corroborated by the Bible which mentions that Job was afflicted with 'loathsome sores from the sole of his foot to the crown of his head'. (See *Job* 2: 7.)

79. The Prophet Job's story as narrated in the Qur'ān shows him as the embodiment of patience and perseverance. It also emphasizes that his life was a model for the pious and the devout. On the other hand, the account of his life in the Bible (see the *Book of Job*) conjures up an entirely different image – a picture of one who levels nothing but complaint against God. Job is mentioned as saying: 'Let the day perish wherein I was born' (*Job* 3: 3). 'Why did I not die at birth, come forth from the womb and expire?' (*Job* 3: 11). He is ever ready to complain against God: 'O that my vexation were weighed, and all my calamity laid in the balances! For then it would be heavier than the sand of the sea; therefore my words have been rash. For the arrows of the Almighty are in me, my spirit drinks their poison; the terrors of God are arrayed against me' (*Job* 6: 2–4). Additionally, 'If I sin, what do I do to thee, thou watcher of men? Why hast thou made me thy mark? Why have I become a burden to thee? Why dost thou not pardon my transgression and take away my iniquity?' (*Job* 7: 20–1). Job further says: 'I will say to God, Do not condemn me; let me know why thou dost contend against me. Does it seem good to thee to oppress, to despise the work of thy hands, and favour the designs of the wicked?' (*Job* 10: 2–3).

Three of Job's friends try to console him and urge him to be patient, and to submit to God's will. Yet all this has no effect on him. Reacting to their exhortation, he lambasts God once again and fails to see any wisdom or purpose in his suffering. He simply regards it as a calamity, a calamity striking a righteous and pious person like himself. He takes strong exception to that arrangement whereby the wrong-doers seemingly prosper whereas the pious suffer. Recounting his own good deeds, he then turns to the sufferings, which in his view, God inflicted upon him. He openly challenges God to explain why he is subjected to this kind of treatment. His outburst against God reaches such a crescendo that Job's friends desert him. When these three friends no longer respond to Job's diatribe against his Creator, the fourth person, so far a silent listener, intervenes and severely rebukes Job, for Job holds himself to be in the right, instead of God. Job's speech is interrupted by God whereafter we encounter a verbal debate between the two (see *Job*, chaps. 10, 16, 32, 41 and 42).

It is hard to believe, while reading these passages, that the account pertains to the same Job who has been presented in the Qur'ān as a paragon of patience, and whose life was considered instructive for all those who are devout.

What is especially bewildering about the account in the Bible's *Book of Job* is that its early part says one thing, the middle part something else, and the concluding part something totally different again; there is no consistency between its different parts. The opening part presents Job as pious and God-fearing, as basically a good person who, apart from these qualities, was also extremely wealthy to the extent of being the richest man in the East. Once God's son, accompanied by Satan, called on God, and during this meeting God took pride in His servant, Job. To this Satan responded by saying that Job could not be other than God's grateful servant for He had after all blessed him so immensely, but would Job be the same if God were to snatch away his possessions. Satan argued that Job would disown God if this were the case.

Satan, therefore, threw down a challenge to God on this count. God accepted the challenge and delegated all authority to Satan, authorizing him to do whatever pleased him, but cautioning him against doing anything against Job's person. Satan deprived Job of everything, including his family. Although this rendered Job alone and penniless, it still did not distract him. Instead, he 'fell upon the ground and worshipped', saying: 'Naked I came from my mother's womb, and naked shall I return; the Lord gave, and the Lord has taken away; blessed be the name of the Lord' (*Job* 1: 20–1). Yet another encounter took place in the heavens, and this attended by the son of God and Satan. God took this opportunity to assail Satan, telling him that Job had proved his mettle. Again Satan challenged God, saying that if Job were to be afflicted by extreme physical suffering, he would then disown and blaspheme against God. God, once again authorized Satan to go ahead with his machinations, asking him only to spare Job's life. On his return, Satan afflicted Job, 'with loathsome sores from the sole of his foot to the crown of his head' (*Job* 2: 7). Job's wife said to him: 'Do you still hold fast your integrity? Curse God, and die' (*Job* 2: 9). To this, he replied: 'You speak as one of the foolish women would speak. Shall we receive good at the hand of God, and shall we not receive evil?' (*Job* 2: 10).

The above account provides a summary of the first two chapters of the *Book of Job*. The third chapter, however, opens with a marked change in tone and tenor, and this continues until Chapter 42. These chapters provide a long account of Job's impatience, of bitter complaint and allegation against God, thus proving that God's estimate of Job, as identified in the earlier part of the *Book of Job*, was false whereas Satan's view was true. Chapter 42 concludes with Job seeking God's pardon after engaging in a prolonged conflict with Him. Job, did not, however, seek God's pardon out of his thanks to and trust in God. He was, rather, moved to seek God's pardon because he was severely rebuked by Him. In response to all this God removes all Job's afflictions and blesses him. Whilst studying the last part of the *Book of Job*, one cannot help but feel that neither God nor Job stood up to Satan's challenge. God compelled Job to seek His pardon and readily accepted his repentance so that He would not suffer Satan's humiliation.

The contents of the *Book of Job* eloquently attest, therefore, that it is neither God's work, nor even that of Job's. It was not even written during Job's life-time; rather, centuries later, someone wrote a legendary story about Job. The main characters of the story – Job, Eliphaz Temanite, Bildad the Shuhite, Zophar the Neamatite, Elihu the son of Barachel the Buzite – come from the author's own world-view and not historical reality. The poetic and literary qualities of the *Book of Job* may certainly be praised; there are, however, no grounds to consider the work as 'Scriptures', as one of the heavenly books. This work is no more a true mirror of Job's character than is the legendary tale of Joseph and Zelicha a true mirror of Joseph's character. Perhaps it is even less so. At most, all that can be said is that the accounts in the preliminary and concluding parts of the work have an element of historical truth. These elements must have reached the author either via oral traditions current in his time or through works which are now extinct.

(85) And (We bestowed the same favour), upon Ishmael, Idrīs[80] and Dhū al-Kifl,[81] for they were all patient men. (86) And We admitted them into Our mercy, for they were of the righteous.

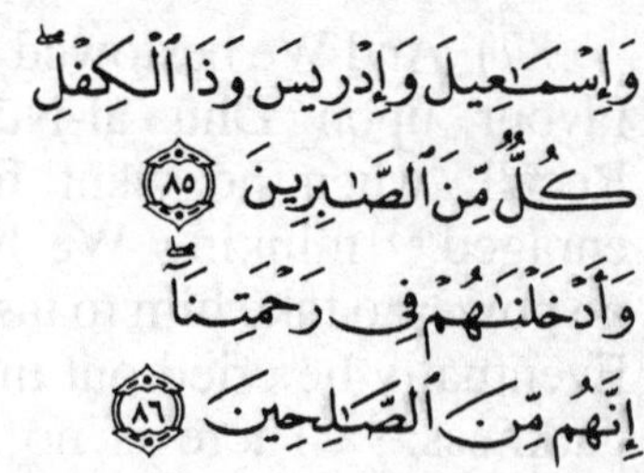

80. For further details see *Maryam* 19, n. 33 above.

81. Dhū al-Kifl literally means 'a man of good luck'; good luck not in terms of worldly benefits but rather in the sense of possessing moral excellence and so receiving reward from God in the Hereafter. Dhū al-Kifl was also the title rather than the proper name of the person concerned. The Qur'ān mentions him twice and on both occasions it is the title rather than the name that is mentioned.

Commentators on the Qur'ān have presented a myriad of opinions about the identity of Dhū al-Kifl and about the period during which he lived. Some are of the opinion that Dhū al-Kifl is the equivalent of Zechariah.* Others are of the opinion that he was Ilyās (Elijah); still others consider him to be Joshua the son of Nun, and even successor to Elisha,† or Job's son who later became a Prophet and bore the name of Bishr. Al-Ālūsī has expressed the following view: 'The Jews claim that he was the Prophet Ezekiel who was honoured with prophethood during the captivity of the Israelites in 597 B.C. He performed his mission as a Prophet in a town close to the Chebar river.' (See his *Rūḥ al-Mā'anī,* vol. 17, p. 82 – Ed.)

In view of this great diversity of opinions, it is difficult to be certain who Dhū al-Kifl exactly was. Qur'ānic commentators of recent times are inclined to the view that he was in fact Ezekiel. We, however, have failed to find any firm grounds in support of this view. Nevertheless, if any good evidence to this effect were to become available one would like to support it. This is so since the description of Ezekiel in the *Book of Ezekiel* seems to confirm the characterization of Dhū al-Kifl in this verse – viz. his being patient and righteous. Ezekiel was made a captive by Nebuchadnezzar before the fall of Jerusalem. Nebuchadnezzar also established a colony of exiles by the river Chebar calling it Tel Aviv, and it was here, in 594 B.C. that Ezekiel was designated a Prophet. He was then 30 years of age.

*This is patently wrong as we shall show later.
†This, again, is erroneous since in *Sūrah Ṣād* the two are mentioned as separate persons.

(87) And We bestowed Our favour upon Dhū al-Nūn.[82] Recall, when he went forth enraged,[83] thinking We have no power to take him to task.[84] Eventually he cried out in the darkness:[85] 'There is no god but You. Glory be to You! I have done wrong.' ▶

وَذَا ٱلنُّونِ إِذ ذَّهَبَ مُغَٰضِبًا فَظَنَّ أَن لَّن نَّقۡدِرَ عَلَيۡهِ فَنَادَىٰ فِي ٱلظُّلُمَٰتِ أَن لَّآ إِلَٰهَ إِلَّآ أَنتَ سُبۡحَٰنَكَ إِنِّي كُنتُ مِنَ ٱلظَّٰلِمِينَ ﴿٨٧﴾

For a full 22 years he continuously warned the captive Israelites as well as the self-indulgent inhabitants and rulers of Jerusalem of the need to heed the truth. His devotion to his mission may be gauged from the report that in the ninth year of his mission his wife, whom he called the 'delight of his eyes', passed away. When people came to offer their condolences, he made use of this occasion to warn them of God's impending chastisement (*Ezekiel* 24: 15–27). It seems pertinent to point out here that the *Book of Ezekiel* is one of the few books in the Bible which seems to have been truly revealed by God.

82. Reference is made here to the Prophet Jonah (peace be on him). At some places in the Qur'ān he is mentioned by his proper name and at others only his title, 'Dhū al-Nūn' (the man of the fish) is used. This title does not mean that he was engaged in catching or selling fish, but rather indicates the fish which with God's leave, devoured him, as has been described in *al-Ṣāffāt* (37: 142). (For further details see *Towards Understanding the Qur'ān,* vol. IV, *Yūnus* 10, nn. 98–100, pp. 66–8, and *al-Ṣāffāt* 37, nn. 77–8.)

83. Angry with his people, Jonah suddenly upped and left them. He did so before receiving God's command to emigrate – a command that would have provided him with the necessary justification for relinquishing the duties he had been assigned.

84. Believing that his people would soon be afflicted with God's chastisement, Jonah decided to find a refuge that would save him from this. This in itself was not objectionable, but what was objectionable, was that a Prophet should leave his post without God's permission.

85. Darkness here refers to that darkness in the belly of the fish, further compounded by the darkness of the sea.

(88) Thereupon We accepted his prayer, and delivered him from grief. Thus do We save the believers.

(89) And We bestowed favour upon Zechariah, when he cried to his Lord: 'Lord! Leave me not solitary [without any issue]. You are the best Inheritor.' (90) So We accepted his prayer and bestowed upon him John, and We made his wife fit (to bear a child).[86] Verily they hastened in doing good works and called upon Us with longing and fear, and humbled themselves to Us.[87]

فَٱسْتَجَبْنَا لَهُۥ وَنَجَّيْنَٰهُ مِنَ ٱلْغَمِّ
وَكَذَٰلِكَ نُـۨجِى ٱلْمُؤْمِنِينَ ﴿٨٨﴾
وَزَكَرِيَّآ إِذْ نَادَىٰ رَبَّهُۥ رَبِّ
لَا تَذَرْنِى فَرْدًا وَأَنتَ خَيْرُ
ٱلْوَٰرِثِينَ ﴿٨٩﴾ فَٱسْتَجَبْنَا لَهُۥ
وَوَهَبْنَا لَهُۥ يَحْيَىٰ وَأَصْلَحْنَا
لَهُۥ زَوْجَهُۥٓ ۚ إِنَّهُمْ كَانُوا۟
يُسَٰرِعُونَ فِى ٱلْخَيْرَٰتِ
وَيَدْعُونَنَا رَغَبًا وَرَهَبًا ۖ
وَكَانُوا۟ لَنَا خَٰشِعِينَ ﴿٩٠﴾

86. For a detailed discussion see *Towards Understanding the Qur'ān*, vol. I, *Āl 'Imrān* 3: 37–41 and nn. 35–42, pp. 249–52 and *Maryam* 19: 2–15 above. The Qur'ānic statement that God made Zechariah's wife fit for him refers to the fact that God cured her of her infertility thus enabling her to conceive in spite of her old age. The remaining part of the verse: 'You are the best Inheritor', means that he would have no regrets even if he was not blessed with any offspring for God suffices to inherit.

87. It is pertinent here to recall the purpose for which the Prophets were raised. Zechariah's (peace be on him) story is repeated in order to emphasize that all the Prophets were no more than human beings and servants of God, who were devoid of even a shred of divinity. Nor did the Prophets have the power to grant offspring to others, for they themselves had to pray to God whenever they were in need of their own.

Jonah's case is also mentioned for a purpose. For even though he was a Prophet of great stature, he was nevertheless taken to task by God when he suffered a lapse. Later, when he turned to God in sincere penitence and humility, he received the exceptional favour of being brought out alive from the belly of the fish which had devoured him.

(91) And also recall the woman who guarded her chastity.[88] We breathed into her of Our spirit,[89] and made her and her son a sign to the whole world.[90]

وَٱلَّتِيٓ أَحۡصَنَتۡ فَرۡجَهَا فَنَفَخۡنَا فِيهَا مِن رُّوحِنَا وَجَعَلۡنَٰهَا وَٱبۡنَهَآ ءَايَةٗ لِّلۡعَٰلَمِينَ ﴿٩١﴾

The Prophet Job's story was also narrated to illustrate that it was not unusual for Prophets, like other human beings, to be subjected to suffering. When a Prophet is thus afflicted he turns to God, in prayer, in the hope that He will remove that affliction from him, as did Job.

Another important point which is underscored here is that all Prophets believed in God's Oneness and addressed all their needs to Him alone. Furthermore, God has always come to a Prophet's rescue in exceptional ways. Although they may initially face a variety of afflictions, their prayers are eventually granted in a rather miraculous fashion.

88. The reference made here is to Mary.

89. The Qur'ān also makes the following statement about the Prophet Adam: 'I am about to create man from clay. When I have fashioned him in due proportion and breathed into him of My spirit, prostrate yourselves before him' (*Ṣād* 38: 71–2). The same statement is made in several places about the Prophet Jesus (peace be on him): 'The Messiah, Jesus, son of Mary, was only a Messenger of Allah, and His command that He conveyed unto Mary, and a spirit from Him' (*al-Nisā'* 4: 171). The Qur'ān also states elsewhere that Mary was the daughter of 'Imrān, who guarded her chastity that: '. . . We breathed [into her body] of Our Spirit' (*al-Taḥrīm* 66: 12).

It is noteworthy that God describes the birth of Jesus and of Adam in identical terms. For example, it has been said: 'Surely the similitude of the creation of Jesus in the sight of Allah is as the creation of Adam whom He created out of dust, then said to him "Be" and he was' (*Āl 'Imrān* 3: 59). (See *Towards Understanding the Qur'ān,* vol. I, *Āl 'Imrān,* 3: 59, p. 260 – Ed.)

It would appear from these verses that when God brings someone into being directly by His command, rather than by the ordinary process of procreation, the expression used for it is: 'breathing of God's spirit'. The spirit is ascribed to God since its breathing is something miraculous. (For further details see *Towards Understanding the Qur'ān,* vol. II, *al-Nisā'* 4, nn. 212–13, p. 116 – Ed.)

(92) Verily this community of yours is a single community, and I am your Lord; so worship Me. (93) But they tore asunder their faith into many parts.[91] But to Us they are bound to return. (94) Then whosoever does righteous works, while believing, his striving will not go unappreciated. We record them all for him. (95) It has been ordained against every town that We ever destroyed that they shall not return (to enjoy a new lease of life)[92] ▶

إِنَّ هَٰذِهِۦٓ أُمَّتُكُمۡ أُمَّةٗ وَٰحِدَةٗ
وَأَنَا۠ رَبُّكُمۡ فَٱعۡبُدُونِ
﴿٩٢﴾ وَتَقَطَّعُوٓاْ أَمۡرَهُم بَيۡنَهُمۡۖ
كُلٌّ إِلَيۡنَا رَٰجِعُونَ ﴿٩٣﴾
فَمَن يَعۡمَلۡ مِنَ ٱلصَّٰلِحَٰتِ
وَهُوَ مُؤۡمِنٞ فَلَا كُفۡرَانَ
لِسَعۡيِهِۦ وَإِنَّا لَهُۥ كَٰتِبُونَ
﴿٩٤﴾ وَحَرَٰمٌ عَلَىٰ قَرۡيَةٍ
أَهۡلَكۡنَٰهَآ أَنَّهُمۡ لَا
يَرۡجِعُونَ ﴿٩٥﴾

90. Neither Jesus nor Mary had any share whatsoever in godhead. They were merely those among many signs from God. For a full discussion on the meaning of 'sign', see *Maryam* 19, n. 21 above; and *al-Mu'minūn* 23, n. 43.

91. The imperative to serve God is addressed to all mankind. All human beings were originally part of one community, followers of the same faith. All the Prophets who were raised to guide mankind, called people to that same religion. The core of this religion being that the One True God alone is Lord of all mankind, and He alone should be served and worshipped. Those religions which emerged later in history are all distortions of this one true, original religion. Some elements of this original religion were taken over by a particular creed while other elements were taken over by yet different creeds with a great many innovations added later.

These deviations from and distortions of, the original religion have given rise to a multiplicity of religions. It would, however, be altogether wrong to consider the Prophets as being the founders of these different religions or even to blame them for giving rise to religious disagreements among mankind. True, followers of different religions today claim their allegiance to Prophets of different ages, but such claims do not establish that the Prophets were responsible for the founding of these. God's Prophets called people to embrace only the one true religion, and to serve only the One True God.

(96) until Gog and Magog are
let loose, and begin swooping
from every mound, (97)
and the time for the fulfilment
of the true promise of Allah
draws near,[93] whereupon the
eyes of those who disbelieved
will stare in fear, and they will
say: 'Woe to us, we were
indeed heedless of this; nay,
we were wrong-doers.'[94] ▶

حَتَّىٰٓ إِذَا فُتِحَتۡ يَأۡجُوجُ وَمَأۡجُوجُ
وَهُم مِّن كُلِّ حَدَبٖ يَنسِلُونَ
﴿٩٦﴾ وَٱقۡتَرَبَ ٱلۡوَعۡدُ ٱلۡحَقُّ فَإِذَا
هِيَ شَٰخِصَةٌ أَبۡصَٰرُ ٱلَّذِينَ
كَفَرُواْ يَٰوَيۡلَنَا قَدۡ كُنَّا فِي
غَفۡلَةٖ مِّنۡ هَٰذَا بَلۡ كُنَّا
ظَٰلِمِينَ ﴿٩٧﴾

---

92. This verse may be interpreted in three ways. First, it can mean that once a community has been subjected to God's scourge, it can never have a fresh lease of life, a rejuvenation. Second, that once a community is destroyed, it never has the chance to be tested by God again. The only occasion when it will undergo any such test is on the Day of Judgement. Third, when a community goes too far with its inequity and transgression, and when its deviation from the true path reaches a high watermark, God will destroy it. Such a community will be denied the opportunity to repent and return to God for it is unable to relinquish its error and so embrace true guidance.

93. We have already attempted to explain Gog and Magog (see *al-Kahf* 18, nn. 62 and 69 above). For the purposes of these notes, however, it is worth repeating that Gog and Magog will be let loose to pounce upon mankind in the manner that animals pounce upon their prey.

The statement that 'the time of the fulfilment of the true promise of Allah draws near' clearly indicates that the incursions of Gog and Magog will take place on a world-wide scale during the last days of human life on earth. This will shortly be followed by the Day of Judgement. One of the Prophet Muḥammad's (peace be on him) statements further elaborates this point. This saying of the Prophet (peace be on him) was reported by Ḥudhayfah ibn Asīd al-Ghifārī, and is recorded in the *Saḥīḥ* of Muslim: 'The Resurrection will not take place until you have witnessed the following ten signs: the smoke; the Dajjāl; the beast; the rising of the sun from the west; the descent of Jesus, son of Mary; the (incursions of) Gog and Magog; three major landslides: one in the east, the other in the west and the third one in the Arabian peninsula. Lastly, a fierce fire will break out in and spread from Yemen driving mankind to the Plain of Judgement.' (Muslim, *K. al-Fitan wa Ashrāṭ al-Sā'ah, 'Bāb fī al-Āyāt al-Latī takūn qabl al-Sā'ah'* – Ed.)

(98) (They will be told): 'Verily you and the gods you worshipped beside Allah are the fuel of Hell. All of you are bound to arrive there.[95] (99) Had these indeed been gods, they would not have gone there. But (as it is), all of you shall ever abide in it.' ▶

إِنَّكُمْ وَمَا تَعْبُدُونَ مِن
دُونِ ٱللَّهِ حَصَبُ جَهَنَّمَ أَنتُمْ
لَهَا وَٰرِدُونَ ﴿٩٨﴾ لَوْ كَانَ
هَٰٓؤُلَآءِ ءَالِهَةً مَّا وَرَدُوهَا
وَكُلٌّ فِيهَا خَٰلِدُونَ ﴿٩٩﴾

In another *ḥadīth* referring to the incursions of Gog and Magog, it is said that these would take place when the Last Day was extremely close, so close that predicting its actual advent would be as difficult as predicting the precise moment of a child's birth. The information about Gog and Magog from the Qur'ān and the *Ḥadīth* does not suggest that the two – Gog and Magog – will jointly swoop on the world. It is even possible that before the Day of Judgement the two will enter into internecine conflicts leading to world-wide strife.

94. The word *ghaflah* (carelessness, neglect) carries a nuance of apology and regret. Thus, after mentioning peoples' heedlessness, it is also said that these same will openly admit that the Prophets warned them that the Day of Judgement was at hand. Thus, they will acknowledge not only that they were careless and ignorant, but that they were among the evil-doers.

95. According to some reports, 'Abd Allāh ibn al-Ziba'rá objected to the import of this verse, saying that it implied that not only their deities but also Jesus, Ezra and the angels would be cast into Hell as they too had been worshipped by people. The Prophet Muḥammad (peace be on him) thereupon affirmed: 'Yes, everyone who preferred that he be worshipped beside God, will be in the company of his worshippers [in Hell].' (See Ibn Kathīr, *Tafsīr,* comments on verses 98–9; and Ibn Hishām, *Sīrah,* vol. 1, p. 359 – Ed.)

We thus learn that those who taught people to worship the One True God will certainly not be thrown into Hell. And this is regardless of whether some ignorant people took them to be gods, or whether others were totally unaware of them. In other words, those who taught of the One True God were not responsible for the polytheism which was falsely practised in their name. The same, however, cannot be said of those who claim to be co-sharers in godhead, and who are a party to the polytheism of their followers; they will be hurled into Hell along with their votaries. Likewise, all those who, in pursuit of their

(100) There they shall groan
with anguish[96] and the din and
noise in Hell will not let them
hear anything. (101) But for
those whom We had decided
to favour with good reward,
they shall be kept far removed
from Hell.[97] (102) They
shall not hear even a whisper
of it, and they shall live for
ever in the delights which they
had desired. (103) The Hour
of the Great Terror shall not
grieve them,[98] and the angels
shall receive them, saying:
'This is your Day which you
had been promised.'

لَهُمْ فِيهَا زَفِيرٌ وَهُمْ فِيهَا لَا
يَسْمَعُونَ ﴿١٠٠﴾ إِنَّ الَّذِينَ
سَبَقَتْ لَهُم مِّنَّا الْحُسْنَىٰ
أُولَٰئِكَ عَنْهَا مُبْعَدُونَ ﴿١٠١﴾
لَا يَسْمَعُونَ حَسِيسَهَا وَهُمْ
فِي مَا اشْتَهَتْ أَنفُسُهُمْ
خَالِدُونَ ﴿١٠٢﴾ لَا يَحْزُنُهُمُ
الْفَزَعُ الْأَكْبَرُ وَتَتَلَقَّاهُمُ
الْمَلَائِكَةُ هَٰذَا يَوْمُكُمُ الَّذِي
كُنتُمْ تُوعَدُونَ ﴿١٠٣﴾

---

selfish interests, cause other than God to become deities, will be hurled into Hell. In this case they will be regarded as the real objects of worship in the same way as those who wilfully set themselves up as deities.

This category of beings is headed by Satan for it is at his instigation that some human beings are taken as god. It would be appropriate to say then that the deity that is actually worshipped is Satan and not the deities whom he sponsors. Moreover, objects of worship – whether stones, pieces of wood or whatever – will also be thrown into Hell along with their polytheist subscribers so that they may aggravate its fire. The sight of these deities burning in Hell will add to the polytheists' sufferings, for they will now discover that those upon whose intercession they had pinned all their hopes will be of no avail to them. What is more, they will prove to be instrumental in causing them greater pain.

96. The Qur'ān here mentions the word *zafīr*. In particular, this is used to convey loud sounds of exhalation followed by deep inhalation, especially during fierce heat or under extreme toil and fatigue.

97. Here reference is made to those who followed the path of righteousness and virtue. God has promised them safety from punishment and has assured their salvation.

(104) On that Day We shall
roll up the heavens like a scroll
for writing. Even as We
originated the creation first so
We shall repeat it. This is a
promise binding on Us; and
so We shall do. (105) And
surely We wrote in the
Psalms, after the exhortation,
'that the earth shall be
inherited by My righteous
servants.' (106) Herein,
surely, is a message for those
devoted to worship.[99]

يَوْمَ نَطْوِي ٱلسَّمَآءَ كَطَيِّ ٱلسِّجِلِّ
لِلْكُتُبِ كَمَا بَدَأْنَآ أَوَّلَ
خَلْقٍ نُّعِيدُهُۥ وَعْدًا عَلَيْنَآ إِنَّا
كُنَّا فَـٰعِلِينَ ﴿١٠٤﴾ وَلَقَدْ
كَتَبْنَا فِى ٱلزَّبُورِ مِنۢ بَعْدِ
ٱلذِّكْرِ أَنَّ ٱلْأَرْضَ يَرِثُهَا عِبَادِىَ
ٱلصَّـٰلِحُونَ ﴿١٠٥﴾ إِنَّ فِى هَـٰذَا
لَبَلَـٰغًا لِّقَوْمٍ عَـٰبِدِينَ ﴿١٠٦﴾

98. When mankind appears before God for its reckoning, ordinary people will be seized by panic. As for the righteous, they will be relaxed and contented for things will proceed according to their expectations. That treasure of faith and righteous deeds which accompanied their departure from this world will stand them in good stead; it will serve as a means of solace, will remove fear and grief from their hearts and give rise to the hope that they will soon be able to see the good results of their striving.

99. This verse has been seriously misinterpreted by some people; this has led to a view that strikes at the very root of Qur'ānic teachings and negates the whole world-view of Islam. At the heart of this miscomprehension is the belief that it guarantees inheritance of the earth (i.e. governance of and control over the resources of the earth) only to the righteous; that God will bestow this bounty on them alone. This generalization is then used to derive further conclusions. Some, for example, inferring that the enjoyment of political power is the criterion of righteousness; that those who enjoy it are righteous; whilst those who do not have it are unrighteous. Such people, even go a step further. They look around at those nations which have been 'inheritors of the earth' either in the past or currently so, and they note that unbelievers, polytheists, transgressors and sinners have all at one time or another enjoyed 'inheritance of the earth'. Communities abounding in traits which the Qur'ān unequivocally brands as sin and evil have enjoyed political power in the past as well as the present. From the likes of Pharaoh and Nimrod to the oppressive rulers of our own day, there have been many who have openly rejected and defied God; yet they have continued to enjoy political power. Because of this,

such interpreters of the Qur'ān contend that since the principle – that only the righteous will inherit the earth – cannot be wrong, the meaning so far associated with 'righteousness' is fallacious. They, therefore, seek a new meaning of righteousness which may indiscriminately be applied to all those who have ruled over the earth, whether they be Abū Bakr and 'Umar (may Allah be pleased with them) or Chengis Khan and Halaku. In this pursuit, they are helped by the Darwinian concept of evolution. They try to adapt the Qur'ānic concept of *ṣalāḥ* (rectitude; righteousness) to the Darwinian concept of 'fitness' (survival of the fittest).

According to this new interpretation, whoever is capable of conquering land efficiently, ruling over others and successfully exploiting the earth's material resources is a 'righteous servant of God', and his conduct is a model for other worshippers of God for true worship consists of worldly success. Failure to offer this special type of worship and, as a result, inability to rule over the earth will exclude whoever from the category of God's righteous servants.

Those responsible for interpreting this verse in such a way must, however, face the question: if righteousness and worship are so signified, what, then, is meant by faith? Faith in God, in the Last Day, in the Messengers and in the Books – a faith without which, according to the Qur'ān, no good deed is acceptable to God. (See, for instance, *al-Kahf* 18: 104–6; and in many other places in the Qur'ān – Ed.) Additionally, what is meant by the Qur'ānic call that one must follow the moral system and the way of life communicated to mankind on God's behalf by His Messengers? Such interpreters also fail to answer as to why the Qur'ān repeatedly states that those who do not believe in the Messenger or do not obey God's command, are unbelievers, transgressors worthy of God's punishment and wrath. Had these people, seriously and honestly, reflected over such questions they would have realized the error of their interpretation.

Far from admitting their mistake, however, they have had the audacity to distort the very meaning of their faith: monotheism, the Hereafter and Messengership; in short, of every basic Islamic concept. So as to make these conform to their own peculiar interpretation of this verse, they have had no qualms about tampering with the entire body of Qur'ānic teachings. Ironically enough, they have even had the temerity to fling at those who disagree with their distortions of the Qur'ān, the following sentence from one of Muḥammad Iqbal's well-known couplets: 'Rather than change themselves, they change the Qur'ān.'

All this is because of some Muslims' obsession with material progress, a progress which has caused them to lose their poise and allowed them to brazenly, and without hesitation, distort the teachings of the Qur'ān.

The basic error of this approach is that people take a single verse of the Qur'ān and then subject it to an interpretation which conflicts with the totality of Qur'ānic teachings. As a matter of principle, only that interpretation which is in consonance with the totality of Qur'ānic statements and with the overall Qur'ānic world-view, can be considered as sound. Anyone who is conversant with what the Qur'ān calls righteousness, virtue and piety, cannot then go on to equate these with material prosperity and the capacity to rule. If *ṣalāḥ* (righteousness) is simply taken here to mean competence and effectiveness, this would run counter to the thrust of Qur'ānic teachings when taken as a whole.

Another factor which accounts for their error is the way in which they interpret this verse in isolation from its context and subject it to a meaning which has no other basis except their arbitrary whims. Any interpretation of a Qur'ānic verse can only be correct if it is considered in its context. Had this principle been followed, they would have seen that the context of the verse is the question itself, i.e. what is the ultimate end of unbelievers and polytheists? Furthermore, why should we imagine that they would suddenly jump from this question to consider a totally different one? The latter being: what is the principle which governs the entrusting of political power to some and not others?

If we employ the correct principles of Qur'ānic exegesis, the meaning of this verse is instantly evident. All it means is that in the World to Come, the inheritors of the earth will be the righteous; the transient arrangement found on the earth today will not endure in the Next, Everlasting Life. The evil-doers and unjust who have had the opportunity to dominate this earthly world will find that the principles operating in the Hereafter are very different.

It is precisely this very point which was clearly stated in the concluding verses to *Sūrah al-Zumar*. These verses refer to the Next Life, to the blowing of the two Trumpets, to God's Final Judgement, to the ultimate end of those who disbelieve, and finally, to the believers' own end:

> And those who feared their Lord will be led to the Garden in crowds; until behold, they arrive there; its gates will be opened and its keepers will say: 'Peace be upon you! You have done well. Enter you herein to abide for ever.' They will say: 'Praise be to Allah, Who has truly fulfilled His promise to us, and has given us this land in heritage. We can dwell in the Garden as we will: how excellent a reward for those who work righteousness!' (*al-Zumar* 39: 73–4).

It is clear that the verses – verse 105 of the present *sūrah* and verses 73 to 74 of *al-Zumar* – are concerned with the same subject, the inheritance of the earth in the Life to Come.

Let us now turn to the Psalms to which the same verse also refers. It is difficult for us to say whether or not what is known as the Psalms today exists in a pure, unadulterated form. For in the present Psalms there are several exhortations to goodness, honesty and contentment:

> For the wicked shall be cut off; but those who wait for the Lord shall possess the land. Yet a little while, and the wicked will be no more; though you look well at his place, he will not be there. But the meek shall possess the land, and delight themselves in abundant prosperity (*Psalms* 37: 9–11).

(107) We have sent you forth as a mercy to all men of the world.[100] (108) Say: 'It is revealed to me that your god is only One God. Will you, then, submit to Him?' ▶

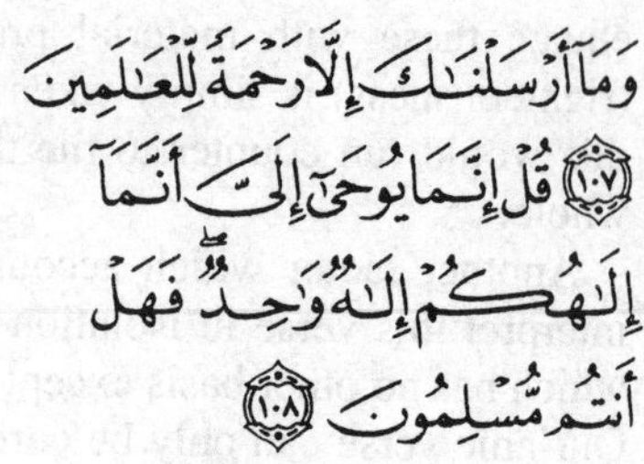

. . . and their heritage will abide for ever . . . The righteous shall possess the land, and dwell upon it for ever (*ibid.*, 37: 18, 29).

As for the temporary inheritance of the land in this world, Qur'ānic law is set forth in *Sūrah al-A'rāf*: 'The earth is Allah's. He bestows it on those of His servants He chooses.' (See *Towards Understanding the Qur'ān,* vol. III, *al-A'rāf,* 7: 128, p. 70.) In accordance with God's will this inheritance is conferred on unbelievers as well as believers, and both the sinners and the righteous share it. It is not granted, however, as a recompense for one's deeds, rather the bestowal of political power, as stated in the Qur'ān: 'Your Lord will soon destroy your enemy and make you rulers in the land. Then He will see how you act.' (See *Towards Understanding the Qur'ān,* vol. III, *al-A'rāf* 7: 129, p. 70.) As it is, this inheritance is not everlasting. It does not represent a permanent arrangement. Being a trial, conducted in accordance with God's Law, it is served on different communities in turn. By contrast, the arrangement will be a permanent one in the Hereafter and will be in accordance with the law, as stated earlier, that the earth being God's will be inherited only by His believing and righteous servants. Unlike this world, inheritance of the earth in the Hereafter will not be a test to those who 'inherit' the earth; rather it will be an everlasting recompense for the good conduct of such people in their worldly life. (For further details see *al-Nūr* 24, n. 83.)

100. This may alternatively be rendered as the following: 'We have sent you only as a mercy for mankind.' Be that as it may, the verse clearly means the Prophet Muḥammad's (peace be on him) advent was a result of God's mercy towards mankind. It was Muḥammad (peace be on him) who warned and cautioned man and enabled him to gain that knowledge which might help him distinguish truth from falsehood, who explained in clear terms, the way which leads towards man's advantage and the way which leads to his perdition. The Makkan unbelievers viewed the Prophet's advent as a curse, holding that he caused dissension among them. They are once again told that what they consider a curse is in fact God's Blessing and Mercy.

(109) If they turn away, say to
them: 'I have warned you all
alike; and I cannot say
whether what you have been
promised[101] is near or distant.
(110) Indeed He knows what
you say loudly and what you
hide.[102] (111) I think that
this [reprieve] is possibly a
trial for you,[103] an opportunity
to enjoy yourselves until an
appointed time.'

(112) The Messenger said:
'My Lord! Judge with truth.
Our Compassionate Lord
alone is our support against
your (blasphemous) statements.'

فَإِن تَوَلَّوْا فَقُلْ ءَاذَنتُكُمْ عَلَىٰ
سَوَآءٍ وَإِنْ أَدْرِيٓ أَقَرِيبٌ أَم
بَعِيدٌ مَّا تُوعَدُونَ ﴿١٠٩﴾ إِنَّهُۥ
يَعْلَمُ ٱلْجَهْرَ مِنَ ٱلْقَوْلِ
وَيَعْلَمُ مَا تَكْتُمُونَ ﴿١١٠﴾
وَإِنْ أَدْرِي لَعَلَّهُۥ فِتْنَةٌ لَّكُمْ
وَمَتَٰعٌ إِلَىٰ حِينٍ ﴿١١١﴾ قَٰلَ رَبِّ
ٱحْكُم بِٱلْحَقِّ وَرَبُّنَا ٱلرَّحْمَٰنُ
ٱلْمُسْتَعَانُ عَلَىٰ مَا تَصِفُونَ ﴿١١٢﴾

101. The reference here is to God's promise to punish the unbelievers for their rejection of the Prophet's call – a punishment which might be meted out in a wide variety of forms.

102. This alludes to the hostile criticisms, the conspiracies and the whisper campaigns made against Islam at the outset of this *sūrah* (see verse 3 ff.). The Prophet (peace be on him) was directed to tell the Makkans that God hears and is well aware of all that they say. The unbelievers should not remain under any illusion that their utterances had evaporated into thin air and that they will not be questioned about them.

103. The respite granted to the unbelievers had deluded them; it was intended that it would enable them to mend their ways, so that they would not be hastily brought to book. Because they had not been punished, however, the unbelievers continued to entertain illusions. Rather than appreciate God for His forbearing, they fell prey to the notion that the teachings of the Prophet (peace be on him) were false. Were this not the case, they foolishly thought, they would have been taken to task long ago.

Appendix I

The Seven Sleepers

Additional to n. 9 of *Sūrah al-Kahf*

Ephesus, the locale of the event of the Seven Sleepers, was built around the eleventh century B.C. It subsequently grew into a major centre of idol-worship with Diana, the moon goddess, as the chief deity. In ancient times the temple of Diana was considered one of the wonders of the world. The people of Asia Minor were also among the worshippers of Diana. The range of influence of Diana increased over the course of time and the Romans also included it in their pantheon.

As the message of the Prophet Jesus (peace be on him) spread to different parts of the Roman Empire, some youths of Ephesus gave up idol-worship and accepted God as their Only True Lord. A detailed account of the story of these youths, drawn from Christian sources, is found in the *Miraculorum Libri* of Gregory of Tours.* The following is the gist of the account in that book:

> They were seven youths. When the Emperor Decius came to know of their change of faith, he sent for them and enquired of them about their new faith. Although they knew about the emperor's hostility to the followers of Christ they fearlessly declared that the Lord of the heavens and the earth was their One and Only True Lord, and that they invoked no other deity beside Him for they considered it a mortal sin to do so. The enraged emperor ordered them to simply shut up or else he would have them instantly put to death. After a while he cooled down a bit and declared that since they were young he had granted them three days' respite to mend their ways and revert to their old faith. He warned them, however, that they would be beheaded if they did not oblige.

*Unfortunately this book was not available to us and hence what follows is a translation of the Urdu version of the Gregory of Tours' writing – Ed.

Taking advantage of this respite, the seven youths fled the town and headed to the mountains to seek refuge in a cave. On the way a dog followed them and despite their best efforts to dissuade it, it did not forsake them. Eventually they took shelter in a deep cave while the dog sat at its mouth and soon they fell into a deep sleep. This event took place around 250 C.E. After about one hundred and ninety seven years, in 447 C.E., in the time of the emperor Theodosius the Second, they rose from their sleep. But by then the Roman empire had accepted Christianity as the state religion and the Ephesians had abandoned idol-worship.

This was the time when the Romans were fiercely divided on the question of Life-after-Death. The emperor, however, was keen to find some means whereby he could persuade the people to give up their denial of the Hereafter. He was so concerned about the matter that on one occasion he earnestly prayed to God to show a miraculous sign that would make people believe in the After-Life. It was in such circumstances that the astonishing incident of the Seven Sleepers took place – their waking up after a very long spell of sleep.

When they woke up they asked one another how long they had slept. Some thought that they might have slept just a day; others thought only part of a day. Unable to resolve the matter they stopped wrangling about it after a while and said that the matter was best known to God. Then they sent Jean, one of their companions, to the town for shopping, giving him some of the silver coins that they had and instructing him to take care lest they were found out for in that case they would be seized and compelled to worship the goddess Diana.

When Jean reached the market he was baffled to find that everything had completely changed. The whole population had embraced Christianity and there were none who worshipped Diana. He went to a shop to buy bread and handed over a silver coin to the shopkeeper. The shopkeeper was simply astounded to find that the coin bore the image of emperor Decius. He asked the stranger how he had got hold of the coin. The question upset Jean who simply said that it belonged to him; and to no one else. There ensued an altercation between the two which attracted a crowd. The matter was reported to the city chief who took it for granted that Jean had laid his hands on some treasure, whereas Jean continued to plead his innocence. The officer was not prepared to accept Jean's story since the coins were centuries-old which even the older people of the town had not seen, let alone that they should be in the possession of a young man such as Jean.

When Jean became fully convinced that Decius had indeed passed away long ago he was baffled and remained dumbfounded for a

> while. Then he began to narrate his story in a subdued voice, telling the audience that he and his six companions had fled the town only the other day and had taken refuge in a cave to escape persecution at the hands of Decius. Amazed, the officer followed Jean to the cave with a large crowd behind them. When they reached the cave it was established beyond all doubt that the youths had indeed lived in the time of Decius. The emperor Theodosius was apprised of the matter and he visited these youths and received grace from them. Then the seven youths retired again to the cave and soon breathed their last. When people witnessed this unmistakable sign they felt fully convinced and began to have faith in Life-after-Death. A monument was erected over the cave under orders from the Caesar which later became an object of pilgrimage.

The above account, even though it is based on Christian sources, is so close to the Qur'ānic version that it would be appropriate to regard the Seven Sleepers in the above story as none other than the People of the Cave mentioned in the Qur'ān. Some people, however, disagree with this view on the ground that the incident is related to the inhabitants of Asia Minor whereas the Qur'ān does not concern itself with events that take place outside Arabia. This view is not quite correct. What is correct is that the Qur'ān concerns itself only with the nations with which its primary addressees were familiar regardless of whether they lie within Arabia or outside. The Qur'ān gives consideration to this in order that the instruction that it seeks to impart should be meaningful to its primary addressees. It is for this reason that the Qur'ān concerns itself with the ancient history of Egypt, even though it does not lie in the Arabian peninsula. Now, if the Qur'ān concerns itself with ancient Egypt, why should it surprise anyone if it alludes to an incident which took place in an area under Roman dominance? For the Arabs were as familiar with the Romans as they were with the Egyptians. The borders of the Roman empire lay adjacent to northern Ḥijāz and the Arab trade caravans regularly passed through the areas which formed part of the Roman empire. Many Arab tribes also lived under Roman influence. Thus the Romans were no strangers to the Arabs, a fact which is amply borne out by *Sūrah al-Rūm.*

It is also worth noting that God gave the story of the Seven Sleepers in the Qur'ān in response to the query of the Makkan unbelievers. The Jews and the Christians had goaded them to ask the Prophet (peace be on him) about this particular incident with a view to testing the Prophet's knowledge about matters of which the Arabs were absolutely ignorant.

Appendix II

Dhū al-Qarnayn

Additional to n. 71 of *Sūrah al-Kahf*

Some persons misapprehend the wall erected by Dhū al-Qarnayn to be the same as the wall of China. This is altogether incorrect. For the former wall was constructed between Darband and Daryal, two towns in Daghestan in the Caucasus region in the area lying between the Black Sea and the Caspian Sea. There is a range of high mountains between the Black Sea and Daryal, with passes too narrow for any large army to pass through. However, there are no high mountains dotting the area between Darband and Daryal. Also the mountain range in that region has wide tracks. In ancient times, when the savage nations of the north used to swoop on the south, they had recourse to this route with the result that the Persian rulers usually faced the threat of military attack from this direction. With a view to repulsing these attacks an impenetrable wall was constructed: one that was 50 miles long, 29 feet high and 10 feet wide.

At the present stage of historical research it is not conclusively established as to who initially erected this wall. Muslim historians and geographers, however, consider the wall to have been erected by Dhū al-Qarnayn. The remnants of the wall seem to correspond to the Qur'ānic account of its construction.

Ibn Jarīr al-Ṭabarī and Ibn Kathīr have recorded in their histories, and Yāqūt has also referred to it in his *Mu'jam al-Buldān,* that after the conquest of Azerbaijan, 'Umar dispatched Surāqah ibn 'Amr in 22 A.H. on an expedition to Bāb al-Abwāb, i.e. Darband. Surāqah placed 'Abd al-Raḥmān ibn Rabī'ah at the head of the vanguard. When the latter entered Armenia, its ruler Shahrbarāz capitulated without fighting. The Muslims then decided to proceed to Darband. Shahrbarāz sent one of his men along with the Muslim army to help them carry out a reconnaissance of the wall of Dhū al-Qarnayn and of the region as a whole. (See al-Ṭabarī, *Ta'rīkh,* vol. III, p. 253; Ibn Kathīr, *al-Bidāyah wa al-Nihāyah,* vol. VII, pp. 122–5; Yāqūt, *Mu'jam al-Buldān,* q.v. 'Bāb al-Abwāb'.)

Two hundred years later, the Abbasid Caliph al-Wāthiq (227–33 A.H.) dispatched a team of fifty persons under the command of Sallām al-Tarjumān to study the wall erected by Dhū al-Qarnayn. A detailed account of this expedition features in Yāqūt, *Mu'jam al-Buldān* and Ibn Kathīr, *al-Bidāyah wa al-Nihāyah.* According to them, the expedition proceeded via Sāmarrā', Tiflis, al-Sarīr, and al-Lān and then arrived at Fīlānshāh. It then proceeded to the Caspian region, and finally arrived at Darband where it observed the wall. (See *al-Bidāyah wa al-Nihāyah,* vol. II, p. 111 and vol. VII, pp. 122–5, and *Mu'jam al-Buldān,* art. 'Bāb al-Abwāb'.) What this clearly indicates is that until the third century *Hijrah* Muslims generally believed this wall in the Caucasus to be the one built by Dhū al-Qarnayn.

Yāqūt makes the same point at several places in his *Mu'jam.* For example, he describes the Caspian as the 'territory belonging to the Turks, which adjoins the wall constructed by Dhū al-Qarnayn and lies behind Bāb al-Abwāb, which is also known as Darband'. He cites a report by Aḥmad ibn Faḍlān, the emissary of the Caliph al-Muqtadar bi Allāh, which described in detail the Caspian region. It mentions the Caspian as a kingdom which had Itil as its capital, a city through which the river of the same name flows, whence it goes across Russia and Bulgaria to the Caspian Sea.

About Darband, the *Mu'jam* states that it is a town situated by the Caspian Sea which is almost impassable for those journeying from the north to the south. Darband was once part of the Persian kingdom of Nawshīrwān. The fortification of its border always had a high priority with the Persian rulers.

Glossary of Terms

Al-Ākhirah (After-life, Hereafter, Next World). The term embraces the following ideas:

1. that man is answerable to God;
2. that the present order of existence will some day come to an end;
3. that after the disruption of the present order, when God will bring another order into being in which He will resurrect all human beings, gather them together and examine their conduct, and requite them with justice and mercy;
4. that those who are reckoned good will be rewarded whereas the evil-doers will be punished; and
5. that, as a natural corollary of the above, the real measure of success or failure of a person is not the extent of his prosperity in the present life, but his success in the Next.

'Aṣr, taken literally, signifies 'time, age, and epoch'; it also signifies 'afternoon'. The *'Aṣr* Prayer is one of the five obligatory Prayers and is performed after the time for the *Ẓuhr* Prayer ends, and before the time for the *Maghrib* Prayer begins. The time for the *'Aṣr* Prayer is reckoned to start when the shadow of a thing exceeds its size (and according to the Ḥanafī school, when the shadow of an object becomes double its size), and ends with sunset.

Burāq was the name of the heavenly steed on which the Prophet (peace be on him) rode on his nocturnal journey from Makka to Jerusalem, and then to the heavens. (For this nocturnal journey q.v. *Mi'rāj.*)

Dhikr means remembrance. In the Islamic context, it is used in the sense of 'remembrance of God'. In *al-Baqarah* 2: 198, *dhikr* refers to remembering God on a specific occasion, namely during the Pilgrimage at Minā.

Falak, plural *aflāk,* means celestial sphere, celestial body and the orbit of a celestial body.

Fiqh, which literally means 'understanding of a speaker's purpose from his speech', technically refers to the branch of learning concerned with the injunctions of the *Sharī'ah* relating to human actions, derived from the detailed evidence pertaining to them.

Ḥadīth taken literally, means communication or narration. In the Islamic context it has come to denote the record of whatever the Prophet (peace be on him) said, did, or tacitly approved. According to some scholars, the word *ḥadīth* also covers reports about the sayings and deeds, etc., of the Companions of the Prophet in addition to those of the Prophet himself. The whole body of traditions is termed *Ḥadīth* and the science which deals with it is called *'Ilm al-Ḥadīth.*

Ḥijrah signifies migration from a land where a Muslim is unable to live according to the precepts of his faith to a land where it is possible to do so. The *ḥijrah par excellence* for Muslims is the *ḥijrah* of the Prophet (peace be on him) which not only provided him and his followers refuge from persecution, but also an opportunity to build a society and state according to the ideals of Islam.

Ilhām, literally means 'to suggest, to indicate'. In Islamic parlance it signifies communicating something directly to a person's heart as a special favour from God rather than as a result of the effort of the person concerned, or as a result of his recourse to the rational faculty. Certain ideas are put into the heart of a person in this extraordinary manner to enable him to get rid of the state of uncertainty and reluctance. Hence, it is a form of revelation but, in technical usage, it is a degree below the revelation made to the Prophets (see also *Waḥy*).

'Ishā' (Night) Prayer signifies one of the five obligatory Prayers which is performed after the night has set in and the red glow of sunset has disappeared. It may be performed until the beginning of the time of *Fajr* Prayer.

Jāhilīyah denotes all those world-views and ways of life which are based on rejection or disregard of heavenly guidance communicated to mankind through the Prophets and Messengers of God; the attitude of behaving in life – either wholly or partly – independently of the directives of God.

Jinn are an independent species of creation about which little is known except that unlike men, who were created out of earth, they were created out of fire. But like men, God's Message has also been addressed to them and they too have been endowed with the capacity to choose between good and evil, between obedience and disobedience.

Kufr means 'to conceal'. This word has been variously used in the Qur'ān to denote: (1) the state of absolute lack of faith; (2) the rejection or denial of any of the essentials of Islam; (3) the attitude of ingratitude and thanklessness to God; and (4) the non-fulfilment of certain basic requirements of faith. In the accepted technical sense, *kufr* consists of rejection of the Divine Guidance communicated through the Prophets and Messengers of God. More specifically, ever since the advent of the last of the Prophets and Messengers, Muḥammad (peace be on him), the rejection of his teaching constitutes *kufr*.

Maghrib Prayer is one of the five obligatory Prayers. The time for its performance begins with sunset and ends when the red glow of sunset disappears.

Mi'rāj, literally meaning 'ladder', refers to the miraculous nocturnal journey of the Prophet (peace be on him) from Jerusalem, where he was taken during the night by God (*Banī Isrā'īl* 17: 1), to the heavens. The details of this nocturnal journey are mentioned in *Ḥadīth*.

Nafl Prayer is a voluntary prayer, an act of supererogatory devotion.

Qiṣās literally means doing with another person what he himself has done. Technically, it means carrying out retaliatory action against anyone guilty of homicide or injury.

Rasūl, plural *rusul,* literally meaning 'message-bearer', has been used in the Qur'ān with reference both to the angels who bear God's Message to the Prophets, and to the Prophets entrusted with the communication of God's Message. Technically, it is used in Islamic parlance in the latter sense. There is some disagreement among Muslim scholars as to whether the terms *nabī* (Prophet) and *rasūl* (Messenger) are equivalent, and which of the two – *nabī* or *rasūl* – has a higher status. The majority of scholars are of the opinion that while every *rasūl* (Messenger) is a *nabī* (Prophet), every *nabī* is not a *rasūl*; and that the Messengers (*rusul*), therefore, have a higher status and are entrusted with a greater mission than the Prophets.

Ṣalāh literally means prayer. In Islamic parlance *ṣalāh* refers to the ritual which is so called because it includes praying. *Ṣalāh* is an obligatory act of devotion which all adult Muslims are required to perform five times a day and consists of certain specific acts such as *takbīr* which signals the commencement of *ṣalāh,* and includes such other acts as *qiyām* (standing), *rukū'* (bowing), and *sujūd* (prostration). Apart from obligatory *ṣalāh,* there are other categories of *ṣalāh* as well. (For one such *ṣalāh* q.v. *Tahajjud.*)

Sharī'ah signifies the entire Islamic way of life, especially the Law of Islam.

Ṣuḥuf, sing. *ṣaḥīfah,* signifies the materials on which something is written; by extension, the word denotes the writing itself. The word *ṣuḥuf* has generally been used in the Qur'ān in the sense of revealed scriptures. (See, for instance, 'the earlier scriptures', *Ṭā Hā* 20: 133 and *al-A'lā* 87: 19; 'the scriptures of Moses', *al-Najm* 53: 36; 'in the scriptures held in great honour', *'Abasa* 80: 13; 'the scriptures of Abraham and Moses', *al-A'lā* 87: 19; 'the scriptures kept pure', *al-Bayyinah* 98: 2.) The word *ṣuḥuf* has also been used in the Qur'ān with reference to the written words of the deeds of people which will be handed over to them on the Day of Judgement. (See *al-Muddath-thir* 74: 52; *al-Takwīr* 81: 10.)

Tahajjud is the Prayer offered in the last quarter of the night, at any time before the commencement of the time of *Fajr* Prayer. It is a recommended rather than an obligatory Prayer, but one which has been emphasized in the Qur'ān and in the *Ḥadīth* as meriting great reward from God.

Tawbah basically means 'to come back; to turn towards someone'. *Tawbah* on the part of man signifies that he has given up his disobedience and has returned to submission and obedience to God. The same word used in respect of God means that He has mercifully turned to His repentant servant and that the latter has once again become an object of His compassionate attention.

Waḥy refers to Revelation which consists of communicating God's Message to a Prophet or Messenger of God. The highest form of revelation is the Qur'ān of which even the words are from God.

Waqf, as a technical term, signifies the appropriation or dedication of property to charitable uses and to the service of God. It is an endowment the object of which must be of a perpetual nature so that the property so endowed may not be sold or transferred. Thus, while the substance of the property is retained, its usufruct is devoted to the good purposes laid down by its owner who, however, forfeits his power of its disposal, out of his intent to please God, by willing that his property be perpetually devoted to purposes that are pleasing to God.

Zakāh literally means purification, whence it is used to express a portion of property bestowed in alms, as a means of purifying the person concerned and the remainder of his property. *Zakāh* is among the five pillars of Islam and refers to the mandatory amount that a Muslim must pay out of his property to please God. The detailed rules of *zakāh* have been laid down in the books of *Fiqh*.

Ẓuhr Prayer is one of the five obligatory Prayers which is performed after the sun has passed the meridian. It may be performed until the time for the beginning of *'Aṣr* Prayer (q.v.).

Biographical Notes

'Abd Allāh ibn 'Abbās see Biographical Notes, vols. I and II.

'Abd Allāh ibn Abī Rabī'ah 36 A.H./656 C.E. was a Companion of the Prophet (peace be on him). Originally his name was Bujayr, but when he accepted Islam the Prophet (peace be on him) changed it to 'Abd Allāh.

'Abd Allāh ibn Mas'ūd see Biographical Notes, vols. I and II.

'Abd Allāh ibn 'Umar see Biographical Notes, vols. I and II.

'Abd Allāh ibn al-Ziba'rá ibn Qays al-Qurashī, d. *circa* 15 A.H./*circa* 636 C.E., accepted Islam after the conquest of Makka. He apologized to the Prophet (peace be on him) for what he might have said and done in the past against Islam and Muslims for he was the poet of the Quraysh and in that capacity had composed poetry lampooning Islam and Muslims.

Abū Bakr al-Ṣiddīq see Biographical Notes, vols. I and II.

Abū Barzah al-Aslamī, Naḍlah ibn 'Ubayd ibn al-Ḥārith, d. 65 A.H./685 C.E., was a Companion of the Prophet (peace be on him).

Abū Dā'ūd see Biographical Notes, vols. I and II.

Abū Dharr al-Ghifārī, Jundub ibn Junādah, d. 32 A.H./652 C.E., was a prominent Companion and among the earliest converts to Islam. He was known for his piety, austerity and straightforwardness.

Abū Ḥanīfah see Biographical Notes, vol. II.

Abū Ḥudhayfah ibn 'Utbah ibn Rabī'ah, d. 12 A.H./633 C.E., was a Companion of the Prophet (peace be on him). He was among those who migrated twice: first to Abyssinia and then to Madina. He also participated in all the military expeditions led by the Prophet (peace be on him).

Abū Hurayrah see Biographical Notes, vol. II.

Abū Jahl see Biographical Notes, vol. I.

Abū Mūsá al-Ash'arī see Biographical Notes, vols. I and II.

Abū Qatādah al-Ḥārith ibn Rabī' al-Anṣārī, d. 54 A.H./674 C.E., was a famous Companion of the Prophet (peace be on him). He was called 'the cavalier of the Prophet' in recognition of his chivalry and his devotion to the Prophet (peace be on him).

Abū Sufyān ibn Ḥarb see Biographical Notes, vol. I.

Abū Ṭālib see Biographical Notes, vol. II.

Abū Umāmah As'ad ibn Zurārah ibn 'Adas al-Najjārī, d. 1 A.H./622 C.E., was a Companion of the Prophet (peace be on him). He came to Makka from Madina (then known as Yathrib) before *Hijrah* and accepted Islam. He is considered the first person to have entered Madina as a Muslim.

Abū al-Walīd see 'Utbah ibn Rabī'ah.

Abū Yūsuf see Biographical Notes, vol. II.

Aḥmad ibn Ḥanbal see Biographical Notes, vols. I and II.

'Ā'ishah see Biographical Notes, vols. I and II.

'Alī see Biographical Notes, vols. I and II.

Al-Ālūsī see Biographical Notes, vols. I and II.

'Āmir ibn Fuhayrah, d. 4 A.H./625 C.E., was a Companion of the Prophet (peace be on him). Originally a slave, he was bought and set free by Abū Bakr, the first Caliph of Islam. He died as a martyr.

'Āmir ibn Rabī'ah ibn Ka'b al-'Anzī, d. 33 A.H./653 C.E., was a Companion of the Prophet (peace be on him) and one of the early converts to Islam who took part in all the military encounters that took place during the life of the Prophet (peace be on him).

'Ammār ibn Yāsir see Biographical Notes, vol. II.

'Amr ibn 'Anbasah see Biographical Notes, vol. III.

'Amr ibn al-'Āṣ ibn Wā'il, d. 43 A.H./664 C.E., was a noted Companion of the Prophet (peace be on him) who conquered Egypt. He was the Muslim commander in many battles during the life of the Prophet (peace be on him) and the caliphates of Abū Bakr and 'Umar ibn al-Khaṭṭāb.

Anas ibn Mālik see Biographical Notes, vols. I and II.

Al-'Āṣ ibn Wā'il, d. *circa* 3 B.H./620 C.E., was a staunch enemy of Islam who never tired of ridiculing Islam and Muslims.

'Aṭā' see Biographical Notes, vols. I and II.

Al-'Awfī, 'Aṭīyah ibn Sa'd ibn Junādah, d. 111 A.H./729 C.E., was a specialist in *Ḥadīth*.

Al-Awzā'ī see Biographical Notes, vol. II.

'Ayyāsh ibn Abī Rabī'ah, d. 15 A.H./636 C.E., was a Companion of the Prophet (peace be on him) and one of the early converts to Islam. He first made *Hijrah* to Abyssinia and subsequently from there to Madina.

Azād, Abū al-Kalām Aḥmad ibn Khayr al-Dīn, d. 1377 A.H./1958 C.E., was one of the leaders of the independence movement in the subcontinent. He wrote several books including a *tafsīr* of the Qur'ān. The founder and editor of *al-Hilāl* magazine in Urdu, he became the first Minister of Education in post-independence India.

Al-Azharī, Abū Manṣūr Muḥammad ibn Aḥmad ibn al-Azhar al-Hirawī, d. 370 A.H./981 C.E., was known as a linguist and wrote the famous book *Tahdhīb al-Lughah*.

Al-Baghdādī, al-Junayd ibn Muḥammad, d. 297 A.H./910 C.E., was a religious scholar and Sufi. He is reckoned among those Sufis who emphasize very strict adherence to the *Sharī'ah*.

Al-Bayhaqī, Abū Bakr Aḥmad ibn al-Ḥusayn ibn 'Alī, d. 458 A.H./1066 C.E., was an erudite scholar of *Ḥadīth* and a prominent scholar of the Shāfi'ī school of jurisprudence. He contributed richly to *Ḥadīth* and was the author of some well-known books, especially *al-Sunan al-Kubrá* and *Dalā'il al-Nubūwah*.

Bilāl see Biographical Notes, vols. I and II.

Al-Bukhārī, Abū 'Abd Allāh see Biographical Notes, vol. II.

Buraydah ibn al-Ḥusayb ibn 'Abd Allāh ibn al-Ḥārith al-Aslamī, d. 63 A.H./683 C.E., was a prominent Companion of the Prophet (peace be on him). He accepted Islam before the battle of Badr and took part in the battle of Khaybar and the conquest of Makka. He was assigned the collection of alms by the Prophet (peace be on him).

Fāṭimah bint al-Khaṭṭāb was the sister of 'Umar ibn al-Khaṭṭāb (q.v.) and wife of Sa'īd ibn Zayd (q.v.). She accepted Islam along with her husband in the early days of Islam.

Al-Ghazālī, Abū Ḥāmid Muḥammad ibn Muḥammad, d. 505 A.H./1111 C.E., was one of the greatest Muslim thinkers of all times. He was primarily a theologian and a Sufi, though his works cover virtually the whole spectrum of Islamic thought and learning. His main role in the history of Islamic thought consists in his sustained attack on Greek philosophy, which greatly undermined its position.

Al-Ḥākim al-Nayshābūrī, Muhammad ibn 'Abd Allāh ibn Ḥamdawayh, d. 405 A.H./1014 C.E., was known both for having memorized a very large number of traditions and for enriching the field of *Ḥadīth* by his works, especially by *al-Mustadrak 'alá al-Ṣaḥīḥayn*.

Al-Ḥasan al-Baṣrī see Biographical Notes, vols. I and II.

Hāshim ibn Abī Ḥudhayfah was a Companion of the Prophet (peace be on him) and one of the early converts to Islam.

Hind bint 'Utbah ibn Rabī'ah, d. 14 A.H./635 C.E., was the wife of Abū Sufyān and the mother of Mu'āwiyah. She accepted Islam after the conquest of Makka.

Ḥudhayfah ibn Asīd al-Ghifārī, d. 42 A.H./662 C.E., was a Companion of the Prophet (peace be on him), who took part in the expeditions which led to the Truce of Ḥudaybiyah.

Ḥudhayfah ibn al-Yamān see Biographical Notes, vol. II.

Ibn 'Abbās see 'Abd Allāh ibn 'Abbās.

Ibn 'Arabī, Muḥī al-Dīn Muḥammad ibn 'Alī ibn Muḥammad al-Andalusī, d. 638 A.H./1240 C.E., was a great Sufi-cum-philosopher of Islam, who wrote many well-known books from a Sufi perspective. He is especially famous as the most outstanding exponent of the monist philosophy known as *waḥdat al-wujūd* (unity of existence).

Ibn Isḥāq, Muḥammad see Biographical Notes, vol. IV.

Ibn Jarīr al-Ṭabarī see al-Ṭabarī.

Ibn Kathīr see Biographical Notes, vols. I and II.

Ibn Mas'ūd see 'Abd Allāh ibn Mas'ūd.

Isfandiyār, son of Gushtasp, was a legendary Persian conqueror of many territories in and around Persia.

Isḥāq ibn Rāhwayh ibn Ibrāhīm ibn Makhlad al-Marwazī, d. 238 A.H./853 C.E., was an erudite scholar of *Ḥadīth* who had memorized a vast body of traditions. Some of the most outstanding traditionists – al-Bukhārī, Muslim, al-Tirmidhī, al-Nasā'ī and Aḥmad ibn Ḥanbal – benefited from his knowledge of *Ḥadīth*.

Ja'far al-Ṣādiq ibn Muḥammad al-Bāqir ibn 'Alī Zayn al-'Ābidīn ibn Ḥusayn ibn 'Alī, d. 148 A.H./765 C.E. is considered by the Twelver-Shī'ites to be their sixth *imām*. He was a great scholar and a pious man. Great scholars such as Abū Ḥanīfah and Mālik ibn Anas benefited from his knowledge.

Ja'far al-Ṭayyār see Biographical Notes, vol. IV.

Al-Jaylānī, 'Abd al-Qādir ibn Mūsá al-Ḥasanī, d. 561 A.H./1166 C.E., was a pious scholar and Sufi. His sermons were famous for their great impact on the lives of the audience. He was the founder of the Qādirīyah, a well-known Sufi order.

Khabbāb ibn al-Aratt see Biographical Notes, vols. II and IV.

Khadījah see Biographical Notes, vol. II.

Al-Kharrāz, Abū Sa'īd Aḥmad ibn 'Īsá, d. *circa* 279 A.H., C.E. 892, a great Sufi and scholar of mysticism of his time.

Al-Khudrī, Abū Sa'īd Sa'd ibn Mālik ibn Sinān al-Anṣārī, d. 74 A.H./693 C.E., was a Companion of the Prophet (peace be on him) who tried to keep the Prophet's company to the maximum. He narrated a very large number of traditions; as many as 1170 traditions narrated by him are extant in the *Ḥadīth*-collections.

Al-Kisā'ī, 'Alī ibn Ḥamzah ibn 'Abd Allāh, d. 189 A.H./805 C.E., was a great linguist and grammarian of Arabic and a prominent scholar of the science of *Qirā'ah.* He was the tutor of the Caliphs al-Hārūn al-Rashīd and his son, al-Amīn.

Laylá bint Abī Ḥathmah was the wife of 'Āmir ibn Rabī'ah al-'Anzī, who accepted Islam and migrated to Abyssinia with her husband, and then migrated from Abyssinia to Madina.

Mālik ibn Ṣa'ṣa'ah al-Anṣārī was a Companion of the Prophet (peace be on him). The traditions pertaining to the Prophet's nocturnal journey from Makka to Jerusalem and from there to the heavens narrated by him are considered to be the most authentic.

Al-Māwardī, Abū al-Ḥasan 'Alī ibn Muḥammad ibn Ḥabīb, d. 450 A.H./1058 C.E., was a noted jurist of his time whose *al-Aḥkām al-Sulṭānīyah* is among the most important works in the field of Muslim political thought and constitutional theory.

Al-Mughīrah ibn Shu'bah, d. 50 A.H./670 C.E., was a Companion of the Prophet (peace be on him) who was famous for his intelligence, wisdom and tactfulness.

Muḥammad al-Bāqir ibn 'Alī Zayn al-'Ābidīn ibn al-Ḥusayn, d. 114 A.H./732 C.E., was the father of Ja'far al-Ṣādiq. He is considered the fifth *imām* by the Twelver-Shī'ites.

Mujaddid-i Alf-i Thānī q.v. al-Sarhindī.

Mujāhid see Biographical Notes, vol. II.

Muslim ibn Ḥajjāj see Biographical Notes, vols. I and II.

Naḍr ibn al-Ḥārith see Biographical Notes, vol. I.

Al-Nasā'ī see Biographical Notes, vols. I and II.

Al-Nūrī, Abū al-Ḥusayn Aḥmad ibn Muḥammad, d. 295 A.H., 907 or 908 C.E., was a great Sufi and scholar of his time and a friend of Sarī al-Saqaṭī.

Qatādah see Biographical Notes, vol. II.

Al-Rāzī, Fakhr al-Dīn see Biographical Notes, vol. III.

Rustam is a legendary figure of Persia known for his valour and chivalry and is credited as a legendary Persian warrior who was the champion of Zaroaster. He is credited, in Persian legend, with the conquest of many territories in and around Persia and with playing a great role in extricating the Persian Kayānī monarchs from their difficulties.

Sahlah bint Suhayl ibn 'Amr was a Companion who migrated with her husband to Abyssinia, and subsequently to Madina. Thus she had the credit of having made *Hijrah* twice.

Sa'īd ibn al-Jubayr see Biographical Notes, vol. II.

Sa'īd ibn Zayd ibn 'Amr ibn Nufayl al-Qurashī, d. 51 A.H./671 C.E., was a Companion of the Prophet (peace be on him). He was one of the ten Companions who, according to the Prophet (peace be on him), are destined to enter Paradise.

Salamah ibn Hishām ibn al-Mughīrah al-Makhzūmī, d. 14 A.H./635 C.E., was a Companion of the Prophet (peace be on him) and an early convert to Islam. He was a brother of Abū Jahl.

Al-Sarhindī, Aḥmad ibn 'Abd al-Aḥmad ibn Zayn al-Dīn, reverentially called Mujaddid-i-Alf-i Thānī, d. 1034 A.H./1625 C.E., was a great Sufi reformer of the subcontinent. He vehemently opposed the un-Islamic religious practices prevalent among the Muslims in his time. Emperor Jahāngīr imprisoned him for his refusal to prostrate himself before him as a mark of respect, but released him after about three years. His ideas are mainly embodied in the collections of the letters he wrote to his contemporaries.

Sarī al-Saqaṭī, Sarī ibn al-Mughallas, d. 253 A.H./867 C.E., ranks among the great Sufīs. He was Junayd's uncle and his mentor.

Al-Sha'bī see Biographical Notes, vol. II.

Al-Sha'rānī, 'Abd al-Wahhāb ibn Aḥmad ibn 'Alī, d. 973 A.H./1565 C.E., was one of the great Sufi scholars of his time.

Ṣuhayb see Biographical Notes, vol. II.

Suhayl ibn 'Amr see Biographical Notes, vol. III.

Al-Ṭabarī see Biographical Notes, vols. I and II.

Al-Tirmidhī see Biographical Notes, vols. I and II.

Ṭufayl ibn ʻAmr al-Dawsī, d. 11 A.H./633 C.E., was a Companion of the Prophet (peace be on him) who belonged to a noble family. He was a poet and an affluent person who was greatly respected by his fellow-tribesmen and was generally known for his hospitality. He was martyred in the battle of al-Yamāmah.

Ubayy ibn Kaʻb see Biographical Notes, vols. I and II.

ʻUmar ibn al-Khaṭṭāb see Biographical Notes, vols. I and II.

Umm Ḥabībah Ramlah bint Abī Sufyān, d. 44 A.H/664 C.E., was a wife of the Prophet (peace be on him) and sister of Muʻāwiyah, the founder of the Umayyad dynasty. She was known for her wisdom and intelligence. Sixty-five traditions from the Prophet (peace be on him) which she narrated are extant in the *Ḥadīth*-collections.

Umm Salamah see Biographical Notes, vols. I and II.

Umm ʻUbays was a slave woman of Makka who embraced Islam, and like other converts to Islam, was subjected to cruel persecution by her master. Abū Bakr bought her and set her free as he had done in respect of many others.

ʻUtbah ibn Rabīʻah ibn ʻAbd Shams, Abū al-Walīd, d. 2 A.H./624 C.E., was one of the notables of the Quraysh. He was killed in the battle of Badr fighting against the Muslims.

Wahb ibn Munabbih, d. 114 A.H./732 C.E., was a scholar interested in historical information pertaining to ancient lore, especially the Israeli traditions. He narrated stories derived from the ancient books and was considered an authority on *Israʼīlīyāt*.

Zinnīrah was one of those slaves of Makka who accepted Islam and, like other converts, was tortured by her master. Abū Bakr bought her as well as other slaves who were being persecuted and set them free.

Tufayl ibn 'Amr al-Dawsi, d. 11 A.H./633 C.E. was a Companion of the Prophet (peace be on him) who belonged to a noble family. He was a poet and an affluent person who was greatly respected by his fellow-tribesmen and was generally known for his hospitality. He was martyred in the battle of al-Yamamah.

Ubayy ibn Ka'b see Biographical Notes, vols. I and II.

'Umar ibn al-Khattab see Biographical Notes, vols. I and II.

Umm Habibah Ramlah bint Abi Sufyan, d. 44 A.H./664 C.E. was a wife of the Prophet (peace be on him) and sister of Mu'awiyah, the founder of the Umayyad dynasty. She was known for her wisdom and intelligence. Sixty-five traditions from the Prophet (peace be on him) which she narrated are extant in the *Hadith* collections.

Umm Salamah see Biographical Notes, vols. I and II.

Umm 'Ubays was a slave woman of Makkah who embraced Islam and like other converts to Islam, was subjected to cruel persecution by her master. Abu Bakr bought her and set her free as he had done in respect of many others.

'Utbah ibn Rabi'ah ibn 'Abd Shams, Abu al-Walid, d. 2 A.H./624 C.E., was one of the notables of the Quraysh. He was killed in the battle of Badr fighting against the Muslims.

Wahb ibn Munabbih, d. 114 A.H./732 C.E., was a scholar interested in historical information pertaining to ancient lore, especially the Israelite traditions. He narrated stories derived from the ancient books and was considered an authority on *Isra'iliyat*.

Zinnirah was one of those slaves of Makkah who accepted Islam and like other converts, was tortured by her master. Abu Bakr bought her as well as other slaves who were being persecuted and set them free.

Bibliography

Abū Dā'ūd, Sulaymān ibn al-Ash'ath al-Sijistānī, *al-Sunan.*

Arundell, T., *Discoveries in Asia Minor,* London, 1834.

Azād, Abū al-Kalām, *Tarjumān al-Qur'ān,* New Delhi, 1970.

Al-Azharī, *Tahdhīb al-Lughah,* Cairo, 1967.

Al-Bukhārī, Abū 'Abd Allāh Muḥammad ibn Ismā'īl, *al-Jāmi' al-Ṣaḥīḥ.*

Al-Dāraquṭnī, 'Alī ibn 'Umar, *al-Sunan,* 4 vols., Beirut, 'Ālam al-Kutub, n.d.

Al-Dārimī, Abū Muḥammad 'Abd Allāh ibn 'Abd al-Raḥmān, *al-Sunan,* 2 vols., Cairo, Dār al-Fikr, 1978.

Encyclopaedia Britannica, XIVth edition.

Al-Fīrūzābādī, *al-Qāmūs al-Muḥīṭ,* Cairo, al-Ḥalabī, 1952. Second Edition.

Gibbon, Edward, *The History of the Decline and Fall of the Roman Empire,* 6 vols., London, 1846.

Hershon, Paul Isaac, *Talmudic Miscellany,* London, 1880.

The Holy Bible, Revised Standard Edition, New York, 1952.

Ibn al-'Arabī, Abū Bakr, *Aḥkām al-Qur'ān.*

Ibn Baṭṭuṭah, *Muhadhdhab Riḥlat Ibn Baṭṭuṭah,* ed. Aḥmad al-'Awāmir Muḥammad Jād al-Mawlá', Cairo, al-Amiriyah, 1934.

Ibn Hishām, Abū Muḥammad 'Abd al-Malik, *Sīrah,* eds. Muṣṭafá al-Saqqā et al., II edition, Cairo, 1955.

Ibn Isḥāq, *The Life of Muḥammad,* tr. and notes by A. Guillaume, Oxford University Press, 1955.

Ibn Kathīr, *Mukhtaṣar Tafsīr Ibn Kathīr,* ed. Muḥammad 'Alị al-Ṣābūnī, 7th edition, 3 vols., Beirut, 1402/1981.

Ibn Mājah, Abū 'Abd Allāh Muḥammad ibn Yazīd al-Qazwīnī, *al-Sunan.*

Ibn Manẓūr, *Lisān al-'Arab,* Beirut, Dār Ṣādīr, n.d.

Ibn Rushd, *Bidāyat al-Mujtahid,* 2 vols., Cairo, n.d.

Ibn Sa'd, Abū 'Abd Allāh Muḥammad, *Al-Ṭabaqāt al-Kubrá,* 8 vols., Beirut, 1957–60.

Ibn Taymīyah, Taqī al-Dīn, *Majmū' al-Fatāwá Ibn Tymīyah,* ed. Muḥammad ibn 'Abd al-Raḥmān ibn Qāsim, 37 vols., Riyadh, 1398.

Al-Jaṣṣāṣ, Abū Bakr, *Aḥkām al-Qur'ān,* 3 vols., Cairo, 1347 A.H.

Al-Jazīrī, 'Abd al-Raḥmān, *al-Fiqh 'alá al-Madhāhib al-Arba'ah,* 5 vols., Beirut, Dār Iḥyā' al-Turāth, 1980.

Mālik ibn Anas, *al-Muwaṭṭa',* ed. Muḥammad Fu'ād 'Abd al-Bāqī, 2 vols., Cairo, 1951.

Mawdūdī, Abul A'lā, *Rasā'īl wa Masā'il* (Urdu), Lahore, 1957.

Muslim, ibn al-Ḥajjāj, *al-Ṣaḥīḥ.*

Al-Nasā'ī, Abū 'Abd al-Raḥmān Aḥmad ibn Shu'ayb, *al-Sunan.*

Al-Nawawī, Yaḥyá ibn Sharaf, *Al-Arba'īn.*

Al-Nayshābūrī, al-Ḥākim, *al-Mustadrak,* Riyadh.

Polano, H., *The Talmud Selections,* London, Frederick Warne & Co.

Al-Qurṭubī, *al-Jāmi' li Aḥkām al-Qur'ān,* 8 vols., Cairo, Dār al-Sha'b, n.d.

Al-Ṣābūnī, Muḥammad 'Alī, *Ṣafwat al-Tafāsīr,* 3 vols., 4th edition, Beirut, 1402/1981.

Al-Ṣāliḥ, Ṣubḥī, *Mabāḥith fī 'Ulūm al-Qur'ān,* Beirut, 1977.

Al-Ṭabarī, Muḥammad b. Jarīr, *Tafsīr.*

Thānawi, Muhammad ibn A'la, *Kashshāf Iṣtilaḥat al-Funūn,* Calcutta, 1863.

Al-Tirmidhī, Abū 'Īsá Muḥammad ibn 'Īsá, *al-Jāmi' al-Ṣaḥīḥ.*

Toynbee, Arnold, *A Study of History,* London, 1962.

Al-Wāqidī, Muḥammad ibn 'Umar, *al-Maghāzī,* ed. M. Jones, 3 vols., Cairo, 1966.

Wensinck, A.J., *Concordance et indices de la tradition musulmane,* 7 vols., Leiden, 1939–69.

Zaghloul, R. El-Naggar, *The Geological Concept of Mountains in the Holy Qur'ān,* Herndon, Virginia, 1991.

Subject Index

General Index